# FUNCTIONAL BEHAVIORAL ASSESSMENT, DIAGNOSIS, AND TREATMENT

## A COMPLETE SYSTEM FOR EDUCATION AND MENTAL HEALTH SETTINGS, SECOND EDITION

# About the Authors

**Ennio Cipani, PhD,** a graduate of Florida State University, is a licensed psychologist and a full professor in the Department of Special Education at National University—Fresno. He has published numerous articles, chapters, books, and instructional material (including software) in the areas of child behavior management in homes and schools. His latest books are *Classroom Management for All Teachers: Evidence-Based Practice* (3rd edition, 2008), *Triumphs in Early Autism Treatment* (2008), and *Punishment on Trial* (free at www. ecipani.com/PoT.pdf, 2004). He has given many workshops at state and national conventions, as well as continuing education courses for psychologists, social workers, marriage and family therapists, and others, focusing on the effective management of problem child behavior. Dr. Cipani has been doing in-home behavioral consultation for families with problem behaviors since 1982. He has dealt with many families and a variety of behavior problems, conducting assessment and intervention activities in homes and classrooms.

**Keven M. Schock, MA, BCBA,** a graduate of California State University, Stanislaus, is a Board-certified behavior analyst and an independent consultant. He has worked with a wide variety of child and adult populations, including people diagnosed with mental illness, people with developmental disabilities, people with brain injuries, and runaway and foster children, as well as in the field of forensics. He has served as an administrator, applied program developer, and direct service provider. He has presented applied programs and research findings at numerous conferences, and he has designed and implemented pragmatic staff trainings. His specialty is in developing pragmatic solutions for people with extremely challenging behaviors who have been resistive to previous treatment.

# FUNCTIONAL BEHAVIORAL ASSESSMENT, DIAGNOSIS, AND TREATMENT

## A COMPLETE SYSTEM FOR EDUCATION AND MENTAL HEALTH SETTINGS, SECOND EDITION

ENNIO CIPANI, PhD
and
KEVEN M. SCHOCK, MA, BCBA

SPRINGER PUBLISHING COMPANY

New York

Springer Publishing Company, LLC
11 West 42nd Street
New York, NY 10036
www.springerpub.com

*Acquisitions Editor: Nancy S. Hale*
*Senior Production Editor: Diane Davis*
*Cover Design: Mimi Flow*
*Composition: Apex CoVantage*

ISBN: 978-0-8261-0604-9
E-book ISBN: 978-0-8261-0605-6

13/   8

The author and the publisher of this Work have made every effort to use sources believed to be reliable to provide information that is accurate and compatible with the standards generally accepted at the time of publication. Because medical science is continually advancing, our knowledge base continues to expand. Therefore, as new information becomes available, changes in procedures become necessary. We recommend that the reader always consult current research and specific institutional policies before performing any clinical procedure. The author and publisher shall not be liable for any special, consequential, or exemplary damages resulting, in whole or in part, from the readers' use of, or reliance on, the information contained in this book. The publisher has no responsibility for the persistence or accuracy of URLs for external or third-party Internet Web sites referred to in this publication and does not guarantee that any content on such Web sites is, or will remain, accurate or appropriate.

**Library of Congress Cataloging-in-Publication Data**

Cipani, Ennio.
    Functional behavioral assessment, diagnosis, and treatment : a complete system for education and mental health settings / Ennio Cipani and Keven M. Schock. — 2nd ed.
        p. ; cm.
    Includes bibliographical references and index.
    ISBN 978-0-8261-0604-9 (alk. paper)
    1. Behavior modification—Handbooks, manuals, etc.   2. People with mental disabilities—Behavior modification—Handbooks, manuals, etc.   3. Behavioral assessment—Handbooks, manuals, etc.
I. Schock, Keven M.  II. Title.
    [DNLM: 1. Behavior Therapy—methods. 2. Personality Assessment.  3. Clinical Protocols.
4. Mental Disorders—diagnosis. 5. Mental Disorders—therapy.   WM 425]
    LB1060.2.C568  2010
    370.15'28—dc22          2010032179

Special discounts on bulk quantities of our books are available to corporations, professional associations, pharmaceutical companies, health care organizations and other qualifying groups.
If you are interested in a custom book, including chapters from more than one of our titles, we can provide that service as well.

For details, please contact:
Special Sales Department, Springer Publishing Company, LLC
11 West 42nd Street, 15th Floor, New York, NY 10036-8002
Phone: 877-687-7476 or 212-431-4370; Fax: 212-941-7842
E-mail: sales@springerpub.com

Printed in the United States by Bradford and Bigelow.

# Contents

# Preface

## PURPOSE OF THIS BOOK

This book provides a comprehensive approach to designing behavioral treatments for children in homes and residential facilities, students in special and general education settings, and adults residing in inpatient units and facilities. Providing effective behavioral treatment strategies in these settings requires a greater knowledge of behavioral assessment and intervention than simply identifying the target behavior. An understanding of the problem behavior's environmental function is essential in designing behavioral interventions. This book provides a comprehensive approach to functional behavioral assessment, function-based diagnostic classification of the target problem, and functional behavioral treatment.

How is a functional approach different from merely prescribing treatment based on the form of behavior? Let's say we have identified the following target behaviors for a student in a special education class for behavior disorders: aggressive behavior, noncompliance, and tantrum behaviors. Suppose behavioral assessment data reveal that all these behaviors occur when the student is asked to read a passage aloud. The child may initially refuse to read when called upon. If this is unsuccessful, as the teacher moves closer to the child to "coax" him, he then throws a tantrum. If the tantrum doesn't work, the teacher becomes more coercive. Finally, the student gets out of his seat and issues profanities about the assignment. By understanding that all these behaviors have the same environmental function, a functional treatment can address them as a response class. Further, one may be able to determine why such a task generates escape behavior with this child.

In the 21st century, selecting effective treatment for specific individual problem behaviors requires a greater understanding of the environmental function of problem behavior. This book addresses that need for a variety of potential users of behavioral technology. At the heart of this approach are three phases: (1) Functional Behavior Assessment (FBA), (2) function-based diagnostic classification of problem behavior, and (3) functional behavior-analytic treatment.

This functional approach is suited for cases in which the problem behaviors are primarily operant in nature. The rate of operant behaviors is determined by their consequences. In some cases, referred problems may be respondent in nature (e.g., crying due to extreme physical pain; see Bailey & Pyles, 1989, for greater delineation of these factors). In these cases, this system is not applicable because the behavior may not be a function of any desired consequence (on the part of the client). Under these circumstances, it might be advisable to consult with a professional who may have experience with such problems.

## AUDIENCE

This book can serve as a primary text for university graduate training programs in applied behavior analysis (ABA). This book is also intended for applied personnel who design behavior programs for persons with challenging behaviors in a variety of settings, such as individual or group residences; public or private facilities; schools; hospital, community, or clinic settings; and inpatient settings. This book should be helpful to people who are trained in ABA and are looking for an additional resource to guide them in their assessment and treatment design activities. It also is written to serve personnel who have some familiarity with behavioral programs but have not discerned how to provide a functional behavioral treatment for specific functions of target problem behavior. The following areas are particularly pertinent for personnel with knowledge in functional behavior analytic treatments.

### Personnel Who Work in Inpatient Units and Residential Facilities

The use of behavior analytic treatments is finding its way into inpatient units, residential facilities, and community settings for persons with severe mental illness, developmental disabilities, and sustained brain injury. Although there is no federal or state imperative requiring an FBA or functional behavioral intervention plan in these settings, simply designing arbitrary contingency interventions can lead to ineffective treatment or worse, disastrous treatment. Mental health providers in these settings who determine what the function of presenting problem behaviors serve will be more capable in ameliorating behavior problems. The client's possible reintegration into mainstream settings will hinge on such progress.

### Personnel Who Provide Parent Training/Consultation

Parent training and consultation, from a behavioral framework, has been verified as an efficacious treatment for child problems in home settings. Psychologists, psychiatrists, nurses, and other mental health providers should be providing technical behavioral assistance to parents who need specific help for problem behaviors. This book provides such professionals with a resource for designing individualized functional behavioral treatment programs.

## OVERVIEW OF NEW MATERIAL IN SECOND EDITION

This book is divided into the same five chapters as appeared in the first edition. However, there is significant additional material to this second edition, including a greater number of illustrative clinical real-life cases from both authors (delineated by initials E.C. or K.S. in each case example). In Chapter 1, material will be presented that will allow the reader to acquire the basics of an ABA approach to understanding human behavior. This second edition provides a greater analysis of the role of establishing operations (EO) and abolishing operations (AO) in the section of the first chapter titled "What Makes a Reinforcer a Reinforcer?" This aligns the current edition with material on motivative variables from Michael's chapter in the Cooper, Heron, and Heward (2007) text. Also, a section discussing the nature of contrived contingencies and their relation to behavioral function was added at the end of Chapter 1. Understanding why contrived contingencies may work is important for behavior analysts who intervene at a group level, not just at an individual case level.

Chapter 2 allows the user to develop skills in collecting the requisite behavioral data needed for an FBA. Each step of data collection is detailed with multiple examples of hypothetical data provided for the reader. In a departure from the first edition, the behavioral contingency is defined in this edition as the A-B-C analysis, but the consequent events are divided into socially mediated effects and direct effects. Also, the analysis of EO variables in descriptive analyses is given greater consideration than in our first edition. An additional section on problems with descriptive analyses is included, followed by a procedure to utilize a trigger analysis with behavioral descriptions as a new innovation in descriptive assessment methods.

While this book provides content on functional behavioral assessment, not all applied problems in clinical settings require only an individual analysis of behavioral function. It can often be the case that problem behaviors are generated by the systemic contingencies that are misdirected. The last part of Chapter 2 involves a presentation of an ecosystemic assessment within classrooms to determine if classroom contingencies might be at the heart of a referred student's problem behavior. By conducting such an assessment, the behavior analyst might uncover systemic contingencies that do not facilitate student or client performance, which allow other contingencies that detract from such to flourish. For example, in a classroom, one might find that a system that provides powerful reinforcers for academic performance is lacking. The installation of such a class-wide reinforcement system across the group would significantly alter performance problems in the target student and others.

Chapter 3 covers the four major categories of our unique function-based, diagnostic classification system for problem behavior. This function-based classification system provides a distinctive numbering system for delineating major diagnostic categories as well as subcategories within each major category. The current edition is very similar to the first edition, but we have included more real-life case examples.

Chapter 4 covers the identification of the replacement behavior and the delineation of a number of replacement behavior options for each major function. The second edition provides some additional methods for assessing the feasibility of reinforcing the replacement behavior instead of the current functional problem behavior. Chapter 4 in the current edition presents a method for evaluating potential extinction bursts and their severity and length via a trigger analysis. The unique, three-category classification system for determining the current strength of the replacement behavior(s) is still presented in Appendix A. This second edition has added analogue experimental tests to the end of Appendix A. This methodology provides a test to determine whether a misdirected contingency diagnosis or inept repertoire diagnosis best explains why the replacement behavior is at low or non-existent levels. With permission, Appendix B is taken from the book *Triumphs in Early Autism Treatment* (Cipani, 2008b). It provides an analysis of persistent error patterns through the findings of basic research in stimulus overselectivity.

Chapter 5 provides the same compendium of behavioral treatment protocols as the earlier edition. A hypothetical example taken from the previous chapters is used to illustrate how all the phases are linked in designing a functional treatment. Each functional treatment program follows a uniform format in Chapter 5. First, we present a brief description of the procedures involved, as well as definitions of terms. Next, we delineate the procedures for collecting baseline data, and we present the procedural components of the treatment. Lastly, we present a hypothetical example illustrating the application.

## A Note to Instructors

This new edition has also been enhanced with several features that will expand students' learning experiences as well as provide instructors with resources for teaching. Dr. Cipani has worked with the publisher to prepare several multimedia presentations that students can directly access online. More information on these multimedia features, along with additional resources that can be assigned to students—including directions for accessing them—is found on the inside front cover of the book.

In addition, an online Instructor's Manual is available for qualified faculty who use this book as a text for their course. Instructors can send an e-mail to textbook@springerpub.com to request access to these useful materials.

# Acknowledgments

The functional behavioral diagnostic systems delineated in this text are an outgrowth of both authors' collective experience in clinical and teaching positions over several decades. An earlier version of this system, called the Cipani Behavioral Assessment and Diagnostic (C-BAD) System, had many behavior analysts who provided feedback and input into that system. Such feedback improved the basic concepts and instructional content presented in the first edition. In particular, the authors would like to recognize Dr. Heidi Toro of the Florida Department of Children and Families, Dr. Merrill Winston of Professional Crisis Management, Dr. Steve Eversol of Behavior Development Solutions, and Mr. Chris Clay of the Community Re-Entry Program for their valuable suggestions over the years. Our association with them has allowed us to improve our analysis and presentation of the C-BAD system into its current form. Finally, I wish to thank Dr. Jose Martinez-Diaz of the Florida Institute of Technology for making the distinction between motivative variables and discriminative stimuli more clear to me (E.C.).

# Basic Concepts and Principles

## WHY DOES HE DO THAT?

Why does he do that? This is the age-old question that people ask when they see a child throw a fit in public. Why does he behave like that? To date, an often-cited explanation of such undesirable behavior involves a hypothesis about the brain's development in the child who is "afflicted" with such behavior. The underpinning of the undesirable tantrum behavior is hypothesized to be the result of some abnormality or underdevelopment of some part or parts of the brain. As further evidence of brain involvement, in some cases, such behavior along with other behaviors form the basis of a mental disorder. Following is an excerpt from a hypothetical lecture in a child psychology class.

*Student:* Dr. Trait, I have a question. Why do some children have tantrums that are clearly inappropriate for their age?

*Dr. Trait:* The child throws the tantrum because he is immature for his age; his brain has not fully developed. Once his brain matures—particularly the frontal lobe, which is responsible for executive functioning—he will not respond to social situations in that manner. Until that point, we can expect this child to continue behaving in such a fashion because of his inability to process events adequately. Teenagers have a similar problem with brain immaturity when they behave impulsively. Their brain is not like the adult brain; hence, they too cannot be fully responsible for their impulsivity.

Variations and extensions of this immature brain explanation exist. The following is a continuation of this conversation in a class in developmental psychology, with a slightly different explanation.

*Student:* In Dr. Trait's class, we were told that children who have severe tantrums that are clearly inappropriate for their age do so because their brain is not fully developed. Is there any experimental cause-and-effect evidence for such an assertion?

*Dr. Stager:* Well, I believe there is more to it than just the brain's development, although I would concur that neurological issues are part of the problem. Children behave in a certain manner because they have not proceeded through certain invariant developmental stages. I would say that these children have not progressed past the egocentric stage. Of course, once the brain has developed, it is more likely that these children will interpret the actions of others as reasonable and not view everything from a "me first" perspective. When this happens, he will not react in such a manner, but will respond to conflict in a more age-appropriate way.

Suppose we believe that the child throws a tantrum because his brain is not yet fully developed. What are the ramifications of dealing with such behavior when the supposed cause is brain malfunction? Do we wait until his brain becomes more fully developed? For clients who have continued such "immature" behaviors throughout their adolescence and into adulthood, do we still continue to wait? What can be done in the interim to reduce the child's tantrums and develop a more acceptable manner of dealing with his social environment?

What is wrong with these interpretations about tantrum behavior? The role of the environmental response to such behavior is trivialized. If the brain has not developed, apparently what people do in response to the child's behavior, whatever the form, is insignificant

Welcome!
*Video*

and, therefore, irrelevant. One can only hope that the child's brain becomes more fully developed. We believe there is a better conceptualization of why tantrum behavior occurs.

Instead of saying that the child throws a tantrum because he is immature, we would possibly ascribe such an incident to the purpose or function such tantrum behavior serves in that child's environment. That conceptualization would generate an examination of observable events in the social environment. In the case of a child's tantrum behavior, one would examine what the social environment does when the child has a fit in public. What is the antecedent context for such tantrum behavior? How does the social environment react to these tantrums in the short and long term? This examination of temporally ordered environmental events can reveal the purpose of this behavior in this context.

This approach is termed a functional behavior-analytic approach to understanding human behavior (Bailey & Pyles, 1989; Cipani, 1990; Cipani & Trotter, 1990; Iwata, Vollmer, & Zarcone, 1990; LaVigna, Willis, & Donnellan, 1989; Lennox & Miltenberger, 1989). In a functional behavior-analytic approach, all behavior is viewed as serving an environmental function, either to access something or to terminate/avoid something (not withstanding genetic influences for some behaviors). Although other psychological explanations invoke hypothesized traits or developmental stages to explain behavior, a functional behavior-analytic viewpoint examines the roles of both the social and physical context—it deals with events that are both observable and measurable.

For example, to say that a hypothetical 7-year-old child named Oskar who is diagnosed with oppositional defiant disorder (see the *Diagnostic and Statistical Manual of Mental Disorders,* 4th edition, text revision [*DSM-IV-TR*]) is aggressive, is sufficient for many mental health professionals. When asked why this child is aggressive, their response would be: "It is a symptom of his underlying disorder—oppositional defiant disorder. He acts aggressively because he has this disorder." As you can see, this is a trial lawyer's dream. People do things because they have a disorder. If they have this disorder, they cannot help it.

Whenever the behavior occurs, it is the disorder that made him do it. One should expect that he will engage in this behavior from time to time. It further presumes that such a behavior will occur irrespective of context and consequences. The child engaged in the aggressive behavior because of his malfunctioning brain. Such brain malfunctions are not predicated on the presence of any environmental context. One never knows when the neurons misfire; when they misfire, aggressive behavior results.

In contrast, a functional behavior-analytic view would explain such behavior more from the social context of the behavior. One would examine Oskar's history of aggressive behavior and how, when exhibited, it alters his existing social environment. An understanding of why the behavior occurs is accomplished through an analysis of the behavior's ability to either produce desired events or terminate undesirable events.

For example, we may discover that Oskar often engages in aggressive behavior when he comes home from school. Oskar's mother wants him to stay in the house for a while and either do his homework or finish cleaning his room. Oskar, of course, wants to go outside and play with his friends. He sometimes will complain and whine. His mother will respond to such complaining with the following retort: "You need to finish your homework. How do you expect to pass third grade? Once you are done with your homework, then you can go outside." This parental response to his behavior incurs more arguing from him, with retractions for each assertion by his mother. When Oskar sees that his arguing with his mother is not helping his cause (i.e., getting to go outside) he tries another tact. He states, "I'm going to leave and you can't stop me." When he begins to exit the house, she grabs him. At this point, he yells at her, calls her names, and hits her. After a struggle, Oskar pulls away and heads out the door. His mother, tired of fighting with her son, lets him go, complaining he is just like his father.

With this information, what is a more plausible explanation for Oskar's behavior during these circumstances? Does he act out because he is disordered? Or does the explanation lie in an understanding of how such a behavior impacts his environment? Does arguing with his mother result in him going outside? Or does he get to go outside when he becomes assertive (walking to the door) and combative (when he hits his mother as she tries to get him to stay inside)? What is the best explanation for Oskar's aggressive behavior in the afternoon? He does it because it "works" for him when he wants to go outside, and other behaviors such as complaining are less effective.

## WHY IS TRADITIONAL COUNSELING OFTEN NOT EFFECTIVE WITH MANY CHILDREN WITH SEVERE PROBLEM BEHAVIORS?

In 2010 many people believe that sending children with severe problem behaviors to counseling is the best method for changing these behaviors. Can anyone (through counseling) convince Oskar that aggressive behavior is not in his best interest? What is in a child's best short-term interest when he is placed in time out? It is getting out of time out. As a reader of these materials, do you believe that any adult, no matter how many advanced degrees she or he may possess, can talk to Oskar once or twice a week and convince him not to behave aggressively toward his mother when he is told he cannot go outside?

How will Oskar's behavior change? Ultimately, it is up to the care providers and parents to change their own behavior in order to change the child's behavior. If Oskar's mother continues to handle this situation in the same manner, I cannot see where anyone can convince him to respect his mother's wishes and do his homework before going outside. In a functional behavioral-analytic approach, the presenting problem is not just with the child. It is also with the way the child's environment responds to his behavior.

You change child behavior by changing the behavior of the adults who deal with that child. Pure and simple!

## THE CORNERSTONE FOR UNDERSTANDING WHY

In a functional behavior-analytic approach, behavior is viewed as functional (i.e., purposeful) for certain antecedent contexts because of the contingency or contingencies involved. A contingency is the temporal relationship between behavior and a consequence. It is often stated as an "if, then" rule. *If* you get an A on your quiz, *then* I will take you out for ice cream. *If* you stick your hand in the door and it closes on your hand, *then* you will experience pain and yell loudly. Such social and environmental consequences influence whether the behavior that produces them will become more or less probable in the same or similar context.

For example, the manner in which Oskar's mother responds to his complaining behavior makes that behavior ineffective. If Oskar wants to go out, and he complains, it seems that such behavior is not instrumental in getting him outside in the immediate future. Therefore, complaining behavior becomes less likely in subsequent afternoons when Oskar wants to go outside. The current arrangement between complaining and not getting to go outside makes complaining a less viable alternative in these circumstances.

However, the story for verbal and physical aggression is quite the opposite. These behaviors, including defying her wish to stay inside by physically leaving, are functional in accessing the desired event. The next day, when Oskar's request to go outside is denied, what would he likely to do? You guessed it. If Oskar's mother continues to respond to her son's defiance and aggression in the same manner, such behaviors become functional in that context. If this relationship between aggressive behavior and going outside becomes strengthened, under certain motivative and antecedent conditions, then such a relationship defines *a maintaining contingency.* There are two types of maintaining contingencies for problem (or other) behavior: positive reinforcement and negative reinforcement.

**DISCUSSION QUESTION**

What argument(s) can be advanced for understanding a client's behavior from the perspective of maintaining contingencies?

## MAINTAINING CONTINGENCIES INVOLVING POSITIVE REINFORCEMENT

Positive-reinforcement contingencies involve behaviors that produce an environmental event that subsequently increases the level of occurrence of that behavior under the same or similar conditions. In other words, the operation of positive reinforcement involves a behavior that produces an event (activity, object) that subsequently strengthens the occurrence of that behavior in the future (under certain motivational contexts). The two requirements for identifying a contingency as one involving positive reinforcement are: (1) the level of the behavior is at higher or increased levels than the level without the contingent relation, and (2) the contingency is one of a behavior producing an environmental event. For purposes of the function-based diagnostic system delineated in Chapter 3, behaviors that are maintained because of positive reinforcement are termed *access behaviors,* that is, these behaviors access positive reinforcers.

What are some hypothetical illustrations of behaviors maintained by positive reinforcement? Milton, an inpatient client with schizophrenia, is reported to frequently pinch other clients. Is this pinching behavior the result of his schizophrenia? Is it the result of his inability to control his impulses? I believe neither explanation would serve a useful or parsimonious purpose. When Milton pinches others, after some duration and frequency (to be explained in Chapter 2) we find that staff take him for a walk. Their rationale for such a response to his pinching is that they want to get him away from other clients. They report that Milton seems to be less anxious when he is on his walk and that the walk calms him down. Facility staff thereby interpret their use of a walk as an anxiety-reductive procedure and believe that this practice is clinically sound. However, what escapes them is the long-term result of this reliable contingency between what Milton does and what they do. The behavior of pinching others subsequently increases to a level that constitutes a major problem, which now jeopardizes Milton's ability to remain in the current inpatient unit. Note that the result of the staff providing a walk to Milton, contingent on the pinching behavior, is an increase in the level of the behavior across time. Milton has learned how to get a walk with staff—pinch someone! We would say that pinching other people is a functional behavior when Milton desires a walk. Unfortunately, other more appropriate behaviors do not appear to be more functional in getting a walk.

Bea, a residential adult female client, throws a tantrum (consisting of screaming and slapping herself) at certain times during the day. Bea's tantrum behaviors are reported to consist of yelling, hitting or slapping herself, calling staff profane names, claiming she was placed in this facility by the Mafia, and making verbal threatening statements to staff and other residents. When she engages in such behavior for a period of time, one can observe staff members give her something to eat. These staff members interpret her behavior, after some duration, as a sign that she is hungry. Of course, feeding her certainly stops the threats made to them and others. Although feeding Bea may produce the desired result, it creates long-term disaster. Such tantrum behaviors then become more probable for Bea when she is relatively hungry (or at least when she wants certain food items). You might conclude that Bea's tantrum behavior is maintained because it is capable of acquiring food when she is hungry. Bea may also learn to engage in the same type of tantrum behavior when she wants her CD player and is told she has to wait until after dinner for it. If such behavior reliably results in Bea getting the CD player before dinner, then such tantrum behavior also becomes functional under those conditions. When that transpires, tantrum behavior is also positively reinforced under the context conditions of Bea desiring the CD player. We would expect an increase in the frequency of tantrum behavior across the next few weeks as it becomes strengthened as a functional behavior when she desires the CD player.

A 4-year-old child named Elvira, diagnosed with autism, will engage in screaming and hitting herself multiple times during the day. Many people will explain such behavior by referring to her developmental disorder. They will proclaim, "Elvira throws a tantrum because she is autistic. Her autism is the cause of this behavior." But is this really a good explanation? Can one predict that all autistic children will engage in such behaviors independent of social context? Does such behavior differentiate children with autism from children with other developmental and/or mental disorders (i.e., only autistic children hit themselves)? If such behavior is caused by autism, what options remain for the successful treatment of such behaviors, ameliorating or eliminating autism? Although eliminating or curing autism is certainly a laudable goal, is it reasonable to suspect that this will occur in time to help Elvira before she enters school? Before she becomes an adult?

A more functional approach focuses on the current maintaining variables. For Elvira, screaming might reliably access parental attention, or hugging, under conditions in which she desires such activities or events. When Elvira desires parental attention because it has been some time, tantrum behavior becomes more probable. The production of attention for some level and duration of tantrum behavior then maintains Elvira's behavior as functional in accessing positive reinforcement.

## DISCUSSION QUESTIONS

Can you describe a maintaining contingency involving positive reinforcement for self-injury? Can you describe a maintaining contingency involving positive reinforcement for refusal to comply with a task demand?

## MAINTAINING CONTINGENCIES INVOLVING NEGATIVE REINFORCEMENT

Although many people are familiar with positive reinforcement, negative reinforcement is often misunderstood (Cipani, 1995; Cipani & Spooner, 1997; Iwata, 1987). An understanding of negative reinforcement operations is critical to the design of effective treatments, particularly if you serve individuals who more often engage in behavior problems during task demands, compliance situations, instructional conditions, or chores and work.

In negative reinforcement, the effect of the behavior is to terminate the existence of, or postpone (for some time) the presentation of, an aversive event. Such an event is commonly referred to as aversive or unpleasant (relative to the individual), and it is fine to refer to such stimuli or events as aversive if you realize that the term is relative. What is aversive to one person may not be to another; what is aversive today may be less aversive next week. The subsequent effect of a negative reinforcement contingency on behavior is one of increasing its probability under the same or similar conditions in the future. All behaviors that are maintained as a result of negative reinforcement are called *escape behaviors,* that is, escape (or avoid) negative reinforcers.

Examples of negative reinforcement of problem behavior can be used with the previous hypothetical cases by altering the behavioral effect of the problem behavior. The form or topography of the behavior does not usually dictate what environmental function exists. Bea's tantrum behavior was illustrated previously as a functional behavior in accessing food, thereby demonstrating a positive reinforcement function. However, tantrum behavior can also be maintained by its ability to terminate an already existing antecedent condition (e.g., noise, task demands, instructional requests, presence of an individual, or other conditions deemed aversive to the individual). For example, Bea is asked to clean up her room. She will often refuse such an initial request. When staff persons at the facility warn her that she will not get to watch television that night, she screams and yells at them. After an intense episode, Bea sometimes gets put in time out and loses her television privileges. However, with certain staff persons, if she promises not to raise a commotion, the staff person will clean up Bea's room for her so she can watch television. Such a behavioral effect subsequently increases the probability of Bea screaming in those conditions (or similar conditions) in the future.

Can pinching people occur for a different reason than wanting a walk? Let us say that Milton also pinches people when he is asked to go to group therapy (which he finds aversive). Why would he now do this? Suppose the following events play out when Milton pinches a staff person when it is time to go to group therapy. When he pinches a staff person, someone decides that he should be taught that this is wrong. Milton should be put in time out to teach him that pinching is inappropriate. The staff keep him in time out until he is quiet and is able to say he is sorry for pinching the staff person. This does not occur readily and the minutes go by. By the time Milton is allowed to leave time out, his group's therapy hour is almost over. He therefore is able to shorten his participation in group therapy by going to time out and being adamant about his right to pinch people. Unfortunately, Milton does not learn the lesson that the time out was intended to teach, and he exacerbates his rate of pinching people before group therapy. One staff person remarks that it almost seems as if Milton pinches to avoid going to therapy, but others quickly dismiss such a contention. After all, he is schizophrenic so he lacks rational thought when he engages in bizarre and unacceptable behavior.

As a result of this imposed time out for pinching, Milton is pinching more often when it is time to go to group therapy. Consequently, he misses most therapy sessions in a given week. Can you see why he is pinching when it is time to go to therapy? Pinching avoids an activity Milton dreads—going to group therapy. As a side note, it might be interesting in this case to find out why Milton does not like to go to group therapy (i.e., what does he wish to avoid) in order to solve this behavior problem in the long term. Beyond that, one might question why he should go to group therapy. If it was to help him uncover the reasons for his pinching mode of interaction, we could now dispense with such a requirement (given its obvious lack of effectiveness).

Another example illustrating a negative reinforcement function is the self-abusive behavior of a child with pervasive developmental disorder (PDD). As a general note, very often in classroom situations, problem behaviors such as self-abuse can often function to avoid or terminate instruction. Hence, under such conditions certain behaviors become very "adaptive." This child hits his head with his open hand or closed fist, and such behavior often seems to occur during group instruction. Self-abuse is a difficult behavior to work through. Hence, a teacher will often stop instruction or remove the child to deal with his self-abuse. Self-abuse becomes functional in lessening or avoiding such a context.

Unfortunately, self-abuse is often unintentionally exacerbated. The severity of the head hitting may intensify as a result of staff trying to ignore minor forms of self-abuse. If staff feel that he hits himself for their attention, they think that ignoring such a behavior will make it decrease and eventually disappear. When the function of self-abuse is misdiagnosed (or undiagnosed), ignoring minor forms can lead to more disastrous results. Perhaps, at the beginning of the year, the teaching personnel reported to the individual education plan

(IEP) team that this child does engage in self-abuse, but they can handle it. Of course, this was under the presumption that their ignoring strategy would work. Now, at mid-year, this child may no longer be suitable for this classroom because his self-injury has resulted in a broken nose and gashes on his forehead. He may now require a placement where a more intensive behavioral approach is available.

---

### DISCUSSION QUESTIONS

Describe a maintaining contingency involving negative reinforcement for self-injury.
    Describe a maintaining contingency involving negative reinforcement for tantrum behavior when presented with a task demand.

---

## CONTRASTING THE TWO TYPES OF MAINTAINING CONTINGENCIES

Table 1.1 provides more examples of behaviors that illustrate positive reinforcement contingencies. Note that in all instances the effect of the reinforcement contingency is one that strengthens the behavior that produces the desired event.

Now examine how the same topographical behaviors in each of the four circumstances in Table 1.1 can have a different behavioral function, which maintains their likelihood in given circumstances. In Table 1.2 the middle column illustrates how behaviors that previously produced desired events now function to terminate aversive events. We conclude that the form of the client's problem behavior does not usually give a clue as to behavioral function. Hence, a diagnostic system that focuses exclusively on symptoms to differentiate clients misses the mark.

Tables 1.1 and 1.2 illustrate how the same behavior can produce different environmental effects, that is, consequences that maintain such behaviors. Note that the motivation of the individual is different in each circumstance, and the behavior (although the same form of response) produces two different outcomes. In Table 1.1, the behavior of Bobby hitting his brother resulted in his mother intervening and giving him the toy that his brother had. If hitting reliably results in mom's mediation of the conflict via giving in

---

*TABLE 1.1* ■ **EXAMPLES OF MAINTAINING CONTINGENCIES INVOLVING POSITIVE REINFORCEMENT OPERATIONS**

| Behavior | Contingency Produced | Effect of Contingency on Behavior |
|---|---|---|
| Child cries | Gets cookie | Increases likelihood of crying when child wants cookie in the future |
| Man on inpatient unit stomps foot on floor, kicks wall | Gets nurse to come over and give social attention, engage him in pleasant conversation | Increases likelihood of such behaviors when man wants to socially interact with that nurse in the future |
| Child hits brother | Mom tells brother, "Give Bobby the toy; he is not as mature as you are" and gets toy | Increases likelihood of aggression when child wants some toy or item his brother has |
| Student says, "This is not fair, I never get a turn" | Teacher gives child a turn on tetherball | Increases likelihood of such demand/tantrum behaviors when child wants to get tetherball or other activity and does not want to wait for peers to give him access |

*TABLE 1.2* ■ **EXAMPLES OF MAINTAINING CONTINGENCIES INVOLVING NEGATIVE REINFORCEMENT OPERATIONS**

| Behavior | Contingency Produced | Effect of Contingency on Behavior |
| --- | --- | --- |
| Child cries | Released from "room time" | Crying is more likely when child is placed in room for discipline |
| Man on inpatient unit stomps foot on floor kicks wall | Gets nurse to leave him alone for awhile instead of taking his medication | Such aggressive behaviors are more probable when nurses are trying to get this man to do something he does not desire |
| Child hits brother | Brother leaves room | Aggressive behavior becomes more probable when this child wants to be left alone |
| Student screams, "This is not fair, I always get more work" | Teacher talks to student, agrees to reduce assignment by half | Increases likelihood of such demand/ tantrum behaviors when child wants to do less (or no) work |

to Bobby's desire for some object or item, hitting becomes more probable when Bobby wants something his brother has.

In contrast, in Table 1.2 note how hitting serves to remove an aversive stimulus for the same topography (form) of behavior. Bobby hitting his brother makes his brother leave the room. Hence, whenever, Bobby wants to be alone without his brother in the room, what behavior will he now resort to? Hitting! To summarize, hitting that occurs under the context of his brother playing with a toy that he wants functions to get the toy via mediation of such behavior by his mother. Hitting that occurs when Bobby wants to be alone results in the removal of the unwanted party via the brother leaving the room. This is the same behavior with two different functions.

Compliance situations involve a parent issuing a request or directive toward a child to engage in some requested behavior (called a "do" command), or in some cases to desist a behavior (called a "don't" command). Examples of compliance situations involving a do command are: (1) "pick up your trash and place it in the trash can," (2) "open the door to the laundry room," (3) "put your sneakers on." Examples of don't commands are: (1) "stop running through the hallway," (2) "stop yelling," (3) "do not throw the ball against the house again." When oppositional behavior occurs in compliance situations (i.e., the child refuses to follow through with the request), it can be analyzed in terms of function (Cipani, 1998).

In some cases, noncompliance takes an innocuous form, such as the individual simply not attending to the person issuing the command. Such a lack of response is maintained by negative reinforcement. A command is issued and the child or client does not respond but rather continues engaging in the ongoing activity. The form of noncompliance at this moment is simply nonresponding. If the adult making these requests often forgets about what task was requested as a result of inactivity on the part of the client, one can see that such behavior (nonattending) is negatively reinforced.

Compliance situations can be examined from the perspective of what the client is currently doing and what she is asked to do. What the client is currently doing is more preferred than what she is asked to do. Therefore, the client must stop a higher probability behavior to engage in a lower probability behavior. This sets up the conditions for negative reinforcement of escape or avoidance behaviors.

With some children or clients, their opposition to the request or command is comprised of more than just ignoring the request. For example, the child is "forced" to engage in other forms of protest when the adult fails to leave them alone when they simply opt out of compliance peacefully. The response of the adult to the child's deaf ear approach (i.e., to request again) does not provide escape from the compliance situation. When the adult responds with another request the child now retorts, "I'm not doing it!" Because simply ignoring the request did not work, maybe becoming insolent at the person making the request will force him to leave. The form of noncompliance can then become exacerbated as mild forms of opposition do not have the effect desired (i.e., termination of the request). To illustrate this point, following is a hypothetical scenario with an adult client in a group home.

*Staff member:* Mr. Smith, please pick up your dirty clothes from the floor and place them in the hamper.

*Mr. Smith:* Leave me alone. I'm watching *American Idol.*

*Staff member:* Mr. Smith, I need you to pick up your clothes. Someone may trip over them when they are in the middle of the day room.

*Mr. Smith:* Then that would be their own stupid fault!

*Staff member:* (Moves closer to Mr. Smith) Mr. Smith, would you like me to help you?

*Mr. Smith:* I would like you to leave me alone! If you are so interested in my dirty clothes, you pick them up.

*Staff member:* Please address me with respect.

*Mr. Smith:* Quit ragging on me, you———.

*Staff member:* Okay, Mr. Smith. I will get Raul and Robert to help me assist you.

*Mr. Smith:* (Gets up and runs out of the day room with staff in tow. He hides in the bathroom and does not come out. After 25 minutes, he finally opens the door and is allowed to go back and watch television with the clothes now having been picked up by someone else.)

Note that in this scenario, simply protesting was not an effective method of being left alone. Such behavior only resulted in continued verbal requests on the part of the staff member. However, with continued requests and the threat of having several staff members help him get his clothes off the floor, Mr. Smith engages in more than just noncompliance. He runs out of the room and locks himself in the bathroom, which of course makes picking up his clothes very unlikely. Do you think Mr. Smith will conclude that the bathroom is a good place to escape from staff?

## DIRECT VERSUS SOCIALLY MEDIATED CONTINGENCIES

There are two ways to access positive reinforcers: direct and socially mediated. Escape behaviors can function to produce termination of an aversive event (i.e., negative reinforcement operations) in the same two ways: direct and through social mediation. This leaves four ways reinforcement can be produced.

| *Positive Reinforcement* | *Negative Reinforcement* |
| --- | --- |
| Direct access | Direct escape |
| Socially mediated access | Socially mediated escape |

### Direct Access

With a direct access behavior, the client's behavior immediately produces access to positive reinforcement (Cipani, 1990, 1994; Michael, 1982; Vargas, 1988). In other words, the behavior produces the positive reinforcer. An individual is hungry and therefore goes to the refrigerator, opens the door, selects an apple, and eats it. This chain of behaviors involved in getting the apple directly produced the reinforcer—the ingestion of the apple. We would not say that the individual exhibits those behaviors because of the attention someone gives to him, regardless of whether such attention is positive, negative, or neutral. Attention is a tangential consequent event. Getting the apple is the desired reinforcer. This is an example of a direct access behavior.

What are some other examples of direct access behaviors? Putting the key in the car and turning it produces the desired result (car starting). Lying down on the bed when one is tired is a chain of behaviors that produces the reinforcer (rest). It is important to note that these behaviors produce the reinforcer immediately and directly.

How many people do you know that sing in the car while driving to work? Or sing in the shower? What motivates this behavior? Does someone reinforce this behavior? Probably not! Their behavior is maintained as a result of the direct environmental effect produced, that is, the sound (hopefully of a somewhat melodious nature). Particularly in the shower, the sound reverberation can be sensorial reinforcing. Such singing behavior in the absence of an audience is reinforced because it produces an inherent pleasurable event. The behavior produces its own reinforcer.

Too often, personnel assume that the problem behavior is maintained because it is mediated, for example, it receives attention, results in physical contact, and so on. However, there are behaviors that occur under specific conditions, not as a result of anything staff or teachers do after the behavior. Rather, some problem behaviors are maintained because of the immediate result they produce. Let's look at an example.

A client in a residential facility for persons with developmental disabilities jumps out of a wheelchair with some frequency (J. S. Bailey, personal communication, 1989). On one of these jumps, he falls to the ground, and his head begins to bleed. Obviously, the behavioral treatment program needs some adjustment. The facility calls in a nationally recognized expert in applied behavior analysis (Dr. Jon Bailey). Staff claim to. Dr. Bailey that the client jumps out of his wheelchair because he loves the medical attention he receives upon getting hurt.

What is the natural result of jumping out of the wheelchair? On some occasions, it does seem to be contusions and abrasions to this person's body. However, the one result that always occurs is being on the floor (or, conversely, being out of the wheelchair).

Every time this person pushes himself out of the wheelchair, he gets the freedom to roam around on the floor. Could sitting in a wheelchair for sometimes 12 to 16 hours a day, every day, be a motivational context for desiring "out of wheelchair" time? Any person who has driven a long time in a car or flown on a transcontinental nonstop flight may be able to relate. The problem with this behavior is not what the client wants but the manner in which he seems to have to access it. If this client was unable to verbally communicate his desire to staff, it would seem plausible that he would take matters into his own hands.

## Socially Mediated Access

Other behaviors achieve their effect through the behavior being mediated by someone else (Cipani, 1990, 1994; Michael, 1982; Sundberg, 1983). These behaviors produce the desired positive reinforcer through the efforts of someone else.

The following scenario utilizing the previous example can provide the contrast between direct access behaviors and socially mediated access behaviors. Previously, the individual wanting to eat an apple (the person is hungry) performed a chain of behaviors that directly produced the apple. The same behavioral effect can occur when the individual requests someone standing next to the refrigerator to hand him an apple. Note the different manner in which the reinforcer (ingesting apple) is gained. In the current example, the requesting behavior is mediated by another person, and subsequently, the reinforcing event is produced.

Socially mediated access often occurs through some form of vocal request, but it need not be so. A celebrity gestures to his driver, who subsequently opens the door to the limousine for him. The gesture functioned in the same manner as a verbal request, "Henri, the door please." A child at a residential facility comes to the dinner table, and staff provide him with his snack for the afternoon. Coming to the dinner table is interpreted as "he is hungry." In some cases, the vocal request may not even appear to be a request. A client with schizophrenia mutters about people stealing her money. Subsequently, after meeting with the facility administrator, she gets a few dollars to spend on candy and soda in the vending machines.

In the previous case involving a client jumping out of a wheelchair, other behaviors might also produce the same function through mediation of the behavior from staff. This client may also have learned how to have toileting accidents if these accidents reliably result in getting pulled out of the wheelchair in order for staff to clean him up. If he is then placed on the floor for some period of time, one can begin to see that urinating in one's pants is a less dangerous manner of getting the desired event. However, if staff clean him up and then place him back in the wheelchair, such a response is not as effective as jumping out of the wheelchair. Note the role staff, care providers, and adults play in the maintenance of this type of problem behavior.

## Direct Escape

Behavior can also produce direct termination of existing environmental events, serving a direct escape function (Cipani, 1990, 1994). For example, an individual walks into a noisy room, finds the level of noise aversive, and subsequently walks out. Note that the removal of the aversive stimulus (i.e., the heightened noise level in the room) was terminated through a chain of behaviors ending in leaving the room. Walking out of the room is a direct escape behavior because it directly produced the removal of the negative reinforcer. Closing the blinds when the sun is too bright (for you) directly terminates the aversive stimulus (i.e., bright sun light). Taking a shower involves a chain of behaviors that is highly probable for many of us under conditions of being hot and sweaty (after physical exertion) because it directly terminates that condition (being hot and sweaty). These are all examples of chains of behaviors that produce escape (or avoidance) of aversive stimulation in a direct manner.

## Socially Mediated Escape Behaviors

Escape behaviors can often achieve their effect of removing or postponing an aversive condition through the behavior of someone else (Cipani, 1995; Iwata, 1987; Iwata, Dorsey, Slifer, Bauman, & Richman, 1982). In the case of the noisy movie theater, an individual verbally protests to the manager of the facility, who then gets the crowd to quiet down. The verbal protest behavior exerted its desired effect through the behavior of another person—the manager. If the individual yells loudly, "let's have some quiet in here," and the room quiets down, the desired result was produced through a verbal request. The result (cessation of noise) was produced through other people becoming more quiet as a result of this behavior. Both of these examples involve a behavior that achieves its effect indirectly, through the behavior of someone else. However, if this annoyed person simply leaves the theater, thus terminating the noise, such a behavior produced its effect when the chain of behaviors ended in leaving the theater.

Negative reinforcement effects can also explain why care providers, parents, and staff respond to their child or client's behavior in the manner they do. In conducting workshops,

I (E.C.) have seen participants begin to realize how much of a role the client's social environment plays in the rate of problem behavior. Invariably, someone will make the following comment: "Why doesn't the parent [care provider/staff members, teachers, aides, etc.] see that they are enabling [now you would say maintaining] the child's misbehaviors?"

Before ascribing a dim view of such people, realize that maintaining contingencies also explain the behavior of parents, care providers, and teachers as well! Analysis of behavioral function is not just for explaining why clients do what they do. Recall the case of the child who cries when he is put in the time out room. As delineated previously, crying in this circumstance is probable because it affects the length of time the child stays in the time out area. When the child cries, he is more likely to get out early. When he does not cry, he is less likely to get out early. That is an analysis of the child's crying behavior in time out. But what analysis fits the parent who reinforces (mistakenly) that crying behavior by letting the child out?

When the parent removes the child from the time out, what environmental effect do you think that produces? Does the child exacerbate his crying upon being let out? No, in fact the opposite. The child stops (at some point) his crying and whining. As you can see, the child's behavior also affects the parent's behavior. If you put the child in time out, then you fill the room or house with crying. If you take the child out of time out, the crying stops. What operation explains the contingency that results in increasing a behavior that terminates an aversive event? Negative reinforcement! The parent's response to the child's crying is under control of the presence of the aversive event (crying). When the parent's response results in the child stopping his tantrum in time out, such a response becomes more likely in the future. The parent learns to terminate (escape) the aversive state of her child crying by terminating the time out prematurely.

In fact, the parent can avoid the crying in the first place by not putting the child in time out when he misbehaves. Instead of placing the child in time out, mild warnings are issued, but not often followed by time out. Therefore, time out becomes less frequent even though the parent "knows" that the child should go for the target behavior. The parent learns to avoid the aversive stimulus by not producing time out as frequently as needed. Unfortunately, this does not help the long-term effectiveness of time out in reducing the rate of the child's target behaviors. This phenomenon explains why follow through on consequences by some personnel and parents is weak and inconsistent. It would be nice if children and clients made it easy for us to administer consequences for behavior, but unfortunately, they do not.

## DISCUSSION QUESTIONS

Contrast the difference between a behavior that produces direct access versus one that produces socially mediated access. Contrast the difference between a behavior that produces direct access versus one that produces direct escape.

## WHAT MAKES A REINFORCER A REINFORCER?

What can function as a reinforcer for one person may not function as a reinforcer for another person. For the hypothetical client Milton, who pinches to get staff to take him for a walk, the walk would be termed the reinforcer. Is getting a walk a reinforcer for all inpatient clients with schizophrenia? Obviously not. Different strokes for different folks. But is a walk always a desired event for this hypothetical client? Again, obviously not. A walk becomes a desired event for Milton (i.e., reinforcer) when he has not had one for awhile.

Milton may want a walk around 9 A.M., but after having a walk, he does not want one for another 5 or 6 hours. Hence, pinching will cease for a period of time until getting a walk becomes more of a desire on the part of this client. Pinching as a means to get a walk only becomes functional under the conditions where Milton desires a walk. Realize that the longer the time since Milton's last walk, the greater the value of a walk. In layman's terms, he wants to take a walk. In day-to-day communication this explanation is not a problem. However, when we attempt to engage in a scientific examination and explanation of how Milton comes to "want" a walk, we need a more precise terminology that allows us to analyze the environmental factors that lead a person to "want" a particular item or event.

Keller and Schoenfeld (1950) first used the term *establishing operations* (EO) to refer to the operations (deprivation or stimulation) that establish drives. Many years later the concept was refined by Dr. Jack Michael at Western Michigan University who proposed a precise terminology that designated the role of motivative variables as (a) an antecedent variable and (b) separate from the role of a discriminative stimulus (Michael, 1988, 1993). *Motivating operations* (MO) are environmental events that affect an organisms behavior by altering the reinforcing or punishing *effectiveness* of some environmental change (consequence) and the *frequency* of occurrence of the behaviors that have in the past been associated with the occurrence of those consequences. They differ from the layman's terms *motivation, desire, drive,* or *want* in that they are quantifiable and verifiable changes in the person's environment that affect the value of a particular outcome for that person. The first articles regarding these variables referred to motivative variables as establishing operations (Michael, 1983, 1988); however, more recent articles and text have labeled these variables *motivating operations* (Laraway, Snycerski, Michael, & Poling, 2003; Michael, 2007).

Motivating operations can be divided into two distinct operations (see Table 1.3): (1) *establishing* operations (EO) refer to the process by which the value of a particular outcome is *increased;* and (2) *abolishing* operations (AO) refer to the process by which the value of a particular outcome is *decreased.* Motivating operations affect the current rate of behavior by increasing (EO) or decreasing (AO) the *value* of the outcome associated with that behavior. For example, behavior that is associated with obtaining food is more likely when you have not eaten for several hours (EO: value of food is increased) than it is right after a five-course meal (AO: value of food is decreased).

The other antecedent variables that affect the current rate of behavior are the discriminative stimulus ($S^D$) and the delta stimulus ($S^{Delta}$). The $S^D$ is a stimulus associated with the *availability* of an outcome. The $S^{Delta}$ is a stimulus associated with the outcome *not* being *available.* Although there is little direct research in this area it appears that MOs also have the effect of altering the value of an $S^D$ as a conditioned reinforcer/punisher (Michael, 1983, 1988; Cooper, Heron, & Heward, 2007; Laraway et al., 2003). The simplest abol-

---

*TABLE 1.3* ■ **COMPONENTS OF THE MOTIVATING OPERATION (MO)**

(A) Establishing operations (EO)
    a. Environmental changes that increase the *value* of some outcome (*value altering effect*) and
    b. Increase the likelihood of occurrence of behaviors that in the past have been correlated with that particular environmental change (*behavior altering effect*—Evocative)
    c. Increase the *value* of an $S^D$ as a conditioned reinforcer and an $S^{DPunishment}$ as a conditioned punisher
(B) Abolishing operations (AO)
    a. Environmental changes that decrease the *value* of some outcome (*value altering effect*) and
    b. Decrease the likelihood of occurrence of behavior that in the past has been correlated with that particular environmental change (*behavior altering effect*—Abative)
    c. Decrease the *value* of an $S^D$ as a conditioned reinforcer and an $S^{DPunishment}$ as a conditioned punisher

---

*Note:* Environmental change here refers to the environment both outside *and* inside the person's skin.
*Source:* Cooper, Heron, & Heward, 2007; Laraway, Snycerski, Michael, & Poling, 2003; Michael, 1983, 1988.

ishing operations are a resolution of the conditions that established the value of a particular environmental change. For example, food deprivation operates as an EO for food, and eating food operates as an AO for food; sleep deprivation operates as an EO for sleep, and sleeping operates as an AO for sleep; deprivation of social interaction operates as an EO for social interaction, and interacting with friends operates as an AO for social interaction. It is not only resolving the environmental change that establishes the value of the reinforcer that acts as an abolishing operation. Consider the graduate student who has been sleep deprived: sleep deprivation operates as an EO for sleep, and consumption of caffeine or other stimulants operates as an AO for sleep.

Additionally, one can look at the behavior of an animal that has been food deprived for 48 hours such that food has been established as a reinforcer (EO). If there is an $S^D$ for food availability present, the animal will engage in behavior that produces food. This will hold true unless we establish the value of another reinforcer, such as escape from tissue damage, by introducing a predator to the area in which the food is located. Under these conditions the value of food is temporarily abolished, and the behaviors associated with food are abated until such time as the predator leaves the area.

## TYPES OF MOTIVATING OPERATIONS

There are two general types of motivating operations: *conditioned* and *unconditioned* (Michael, 2007). Unconditioned motivating operations (UMOs) do not require any learning history to establish the reinforcing value of a particular outcome. These are the genetically selected items or events that are needed for basic survival of the individual and the species. Consider that from birth, for all organisms, after some period of time without food, food or calorie intake is established as a reinforcing event. No learning has to take place for the food to be valuable to the organism.

Unconditioned motivating operations have also been identified for sleep, thirst, sexual stimulation, breathing, activity, temperature regulation, and pain or tissue damage (Michael, 2007). Any environmental change that alters the organism's physiology such that it is outside the optimal level for continued survival will operate as an unconditioned establishing operation (UEO), increasing the value of an environmental change that restores physiological homeostasis. Conditioned motivating operations (CMOs) acquire their reinforcing value as a result of the individual's unique conditioning history. CMOs acquire their properties to make some events reinforcing to some people and not others via stimulus pairing with UMOs or with other CMOs.

Consider how the value of an umbrella might be established. If rain falls on your head, it will reduce your body temperature. A reduction in body temperature establishes the value unconditioned establishing operation) of increased body temperature (warmth). By being paired with a reduction in body temperature, rain on the head becomes a conditioned establishing operation. Rain on the head is now sufficient to establish the value of *terminating* rain on the head (CEO).

Let's say you have never experienced an umbrella before, and rain is falling on you (CEO). Another person joins you, deploys their umbrella, and places it so that you are no longer being rained on. The umbrella has now been paired with the termination of an aversive event (conditioned abolishing operation). Because it has been associated directly with terminating rain on your head, the value of an umbrella will now also be established (CEO) when rain is falling on your head.

Three subtypes of CMOs have been identified as of this writing: surrogate, transitive, and reflexive (Michael, 2007).

**Surrogate** *conditioned motivating operation* (CMO-S)—A stimulus that acquires its affect as an MO by being reliably paired with the occurrence of another UMO or CMO and has the same value-altering and behavior-altering affects as the MO with which it was paired.

Examples: A weather forecast for rain can act as a surrogate CMO establishing the value of umbrellas by being reliably paired with rain on the head.

Reading an outdoor thermometer that indicates the temperature is minus 20 degrees can act as a surrogate CMO establishing the value of warm clothes by being associated with the UMO of being cold.

**Transitive** *conditioned motivating operation* (CMO-T)—A stimulus that acquires its reinforcing value by being paired with an item or event that is needed to access another CMO or UMO.

Examples: If the value of food has been established and you only have access to food in a can, this condition will also establish the value of a can opener.

If the value of food has been established and the only food you have access to is in a locked cabinet, this condition will increase the value of the key and also increase the value of interaction with any person that has the key.

**Reflexive** *conditioned motivating operation* (CMO-R)—A stimulus that acquires its reinforcing value by systematically preceding avoidable worsening and establishes the value of its own termination as effective reinforcement.

Examples: Some students find lengthy tasks aversive. The delivery of a task demand for a lengthy task may establish its removal as a reinforcer. If task demands reliably precede or warn of any type of worsening situation, then any behavior that removes the warning signal (task demand) will be strengthened.

## Motivating Operations Are Idiosyncratic

Based on current research, all motivating operations (UMO and CMO) appear to be unique to the individual person. Each person will differ regarding the specific conditions that establish the value of a particular outcome. In the case of UMOs this is primarily determined by biological variables. In the case of CMOs this is primarily determined by the person's conditioning history.

Consider the question "What is the point at which food will operate as an effective reinforcer [i.e., food deprivation, increased calorie expenditure]?" For some people it is four hours after they finished eating lunch. For other people, the point at which food will operate as an effective reinforcer does not occur until the end of the day. One cannot say food will operate as an effective reinforcer when we deny access to food for a 10-hour period (absolute value), nor can one say that it will be a static time period for that individual without considering the level of calorie expenditure for that person. Food deprivation is relative to the individual under consideration and dependent on level of activity.

Therefore, the point in time when a given individual will engage in behaviors that make access to food highly likely is different for each individual and each situation. However, each of the variables that determine when food will be effective as a reinforcer for a particular person are quantifiable and can be determined with a high degree of accuracy using one of the various analog assessment procedures (see Chapter 2).

## Establishing Operations for Access Diagnosis

Establishing operations relative to positive reinforcement (access diagnosis) typically involve some period of deprivation of that item or event. However, many people will mistakenly consider that only deprivation increases the value of some outcome. The value of a positive reinforcer can also be established when an item or event is added to the person's environment.

You are all familiar with the saying "You can lead a horse to water but you can't make him drink." Restated behaviorally, when you present the $S^D$ for a particular behavior the organism does not always engage in the previously learned behavior. If we include the MO (in this case the establishing operation), it is clear that there are at least three conditions that will increase the value of fluids: (1) deprive the organism of fluids for some period of time, (2) increase the amount of salt the organism consumes, and (3) increase the level of fluid loss (sweating, blood loss). Therefore, reformulating the old saying slightly, "You can lead a horse to water, but you cannot induce drinking behavior unless you have increased the value of water to the maximal level for this horse."

Table 1.4 presents several motivating operations and the more informal, layman's term used to describe these events in general conversation. Note that in some cases the layman's explanation is consistent with the actual abolishing operation, but in other cases it is not. The more precise analysis made possible by the use of the MO in many cases allows for the design of more effective interventions. In the first example, a person may have eaten breakfast but missed lunch, so by the time dinner is being prepared the value of food is very high. Therefore, any behavior or set of behaviors that result in obtaining food will be strengthened. The value of food will be abolished when some volume of food has been ingested causing the stomach to expand. In the second example, a person may have eaten the same number of calories as she usually intakes, however, on this day she engages in strenuous exercise for several hours. This unusual level of calorie expenditure will increase the value of calories (food), and the loss of fluids secondary to sweating will increase the value of fluids. Here again, any behavior or set of behaviors that results in obtaining food or fluids will be strengthened. In the third example, if a person has not had any fluids for several hours the value of fluids will be established. Any behaviors that result in obtaining fluids will be strengthened. In this case, ingesting fluids will operate as an abolishing operation.

**TABLE 1.4 ■ RELATIONSHIP BETWEEN MOTIVATING OPERATION AND REINFORCER FOR DIRECT AND SOCIALLY MEDIATED ACCESS DIAGNOSIS (POSITIVE REINFORCEMENT)**

| | Establishing Operation | Lay Term | Reinforcer for Some Behavior | Abolishing Operation |
|---|---|---|---|---|
| 1. | Deprived of food | Hungry | Food | Intake of some volume of food (Expansion of stomach) |
| 2. | Strenuous exercise for several hours | Hungry and thirsty | Drink and food | Intake of some volume of food and fluids |
| 3. | Deprived of drink | Thirsty | Drink, liquids | Intake of some volume of fluids |
| 4. | Ingested salt | Thirsty | Drink, liquids | Intake of some volume of fluids |
| 5. | Deprived of physical contact | Wants hugs | Physical contact (specific type) | Some duration of physical contact |
| 6. | Deprived of attention | Annoying, wants attention | Attention (specific person/type) | Some duration of attention |
| 7. | Deprived of TV | Wants TV | TV | Some duration of TV |
| 8. | Deprived of stimulation, all varieties | Wants stimulation | Stimulation (specific kind) | Some duration of stimulation |
| 9. | Smoker deprived of cigarettes | Wants to smoke | Inhalation of cigarette smoke | Some level of nicotine in system |
| 10. | Smoker deprived of nicotine with cigarette but no way to light it | Wants to smoke | A light and inhalation of cigarette smoke | Lit cigarette |

In the fourth example, consider that bartenders have long understood how to effectively establish the value of fluid intake. Have you ever been to a bar at happy hour? There are typically many food items available for free. Have you also noticed that when you eat the free food you seem to get thirsty much more quickly than usual? Most of the food items served at happy hour are either high in salt content or very spicy. This, of course, tends to establish the value of fluids, and the $S^D$ for availability of fluids is typically the bartender. The fifth example considers that for most people not having physical contact (or a specific type of physical contact) for an extended period of time will establish the value of physical interaction. Under this condition any behavior that results in some level of physical interaction will be strengthened. It appears that there is a UEO for some level of physical contact. It also appears that most people develop multiple CEOs for specific types and durations of physical contact.

The sixth example demonstrates that for most people access to tangible reinforcers has been paired with social interaction; this results in a CEO for attention. Having no social interactions for a specific period of time will increase the value of any interaction. Acquiring attention will act as an abolishing operation. In regards to attention, the EO may be for a specific person, which means the abolishing operation would be attention from the specific person. All of the socially mediated access and escape diagnoses involve a CEO for attention. In the seventh example we consider the case of a child with a history of watching TV every day after school. The television stops working, so the child does not have access to TV after school for a period of about 1 week. The value of TV watching will increase such that, given the opportunity, he will engage in high levels of behavior to get access to viewing TV.

Example eight presents that some level of stimulation appears to be a UMO as demonstrated by various sensory deprivation experiments. Deprivation of all types of stimulation for some period of time will increase the value of any type of stimulation. Consider the case of an individual with restricted mobility living in an environment that is deprived of stimulation. Under this condition individuals will frequently engage in "mouthing" of clothing, hands, or any item they can manipulate. These behaviors produce some level of stimulation, and therefore, under this condition the mouthing behaviors will be strengthened.

The ninth example demonstrates that people who smoke certainly value cigarettes, and we can clearly establish the value of a cigarette by ensuring the person does not smoke for some period of time (CEO). Under this condition any behavior that produces access to cigarette smoke will be strengthened. The abolishing operation in this case appears to be levels of nicotine in the persons body. In example ten, considering that same person who smokes, we can also increase the value of matches or a lighter (CEO) by giving the person a cigarette with no means to light it. If we set up a situation such that the only way to access a lighter is by talking to another person, we will also increase the value of social interaction that results in obtaining a means to light a cigarette (CEO). The abolishing operation in this case would be obtaining a means to light the cigarette. Note that the social mediation here is only important as a way to get a light. Under the same conditions, if a vending machine were available that dispensed lighters the value of the social interaction would not be established. This CEO would be consistent with a socially mediated access to tangible items diagnosis (2.3 SMA—Tangible reinforcer).

It is important to remember that we tend to talk in general terms regarding the events that operate as an establishing operation. We generally would refer to food deprivation as the EO, however, in some cases it is valuable to talk about deprivation of specific nutrients as establishing the value of particular foods. A person who has low levels of potassium will be particularly reinforced for consuming food high in potassium, such as bananas.

The same is true for deprivation of attention as an EO. In many cases it is deprivation of attention from a particular person that acts as an EO. If I (K.S.) am at a conference I will interact with many people so the EO for attention in general is very low; however, the EO relative to attention from my wife is still at strength. It is important to note that the person does not need to be able to verbalize this relation for it to affect their behavior.

### Establishing Operations for Escape Diagnosis

Thus far we have only considered MO for behaviors maintained by positive reinforcement (access diagnosis). MO for behaviors maintained by negative reinforcement (escape diagnosis) have the same characteristics (see Table 1.4), however, the environmental event in this case is related to an outcome that the organism is acting to avoid or terminate (see Table 1.5).

In the first example, a teacher may present a relatively difficult task to the child. Because the child is not capable of performing such a task or demand, he finds the presence of such a task demand aversive (CEO). Therefore, a behavior, or set of behaviors, in the repertoire of this child that results in its removal (CAO) will be strengthened. Realize that what is difficult for one child may be easy for another, hence, *difficult task* is a relative term.

In example two, a behavior that terminates the presence of a person's obnoxious behavior will be strengthened under conditions involving the presence of the noxious conditions

**TABLE 1.5 ■ RELATIONSHIP BETWEEN MOTIVATING OPERATION AND REINFORCER FOR DIRECT AND SOCIALLY MEDIATED ESCAPE DIAGNOSIS (NEGATIVE REINFORCEMENT)**

| | Establishing Operation | Lay Term | Reinforcer for Some Behavior | Abolishing Operation |
|---|---|---|---|---|
| 1. | Presence of difficult task | Lazy | Removal of task | Removal or delay of task or removal of that portion of the task that is difficult |
| 2. | Person acting in an obnoxious manner | Annoyed | Terminating engagement in social situation | Removal or avoidance of specific person or type of interaction |
| 3. | Presence of pain | In pain | Termination of painful stimulus | Reduction or avoidance of pain stimulus |
| 4. | Rain on the head | Does not want to get wet | Termination of rain on head | Removal or avoidance of rain on head |
| 5. | Request to complete a long task | Unmotivated | Shortening or termination of the long task | Removal or avoidance of the request or reduction in the length of the task |
| 6. | Occurrence of extra pyramidal symptoms (EPS) | Wants symptoms to stop | Termination of the EPS | Removal, reduction, or avoidance of the symptoms |
| 7. | Allergic rhinitis | Want relief from allergies | Termination or reduction in allergy symptoms | Removal, reduction, or avoidance of the symptoms |
| 8. | Drug withdrawal symptoms | Wants more drugs | Termination or reduction of withdrawal symptoms | Removal, reduction, or avoidance of the symptoms |
| 9. | Alcohol withdrawal symptoms | Wants more alcohol | Termination or reduction of withdrawal symptoms | Removal, reduction, or avoidance of the symptoms |
| 10. | Presence of auditory hallucinations | Hearing voices, crazy, mentally ill | Termination of auditory hallucinations | Removal, reduction, or avoidance of the symptoms |

(CEO). Let us say this person's obnoxious behavior is using foul language. If a person does something that affects this person whereby he lessens or eliminates such language (CAO), such behavior will be strengthened in the future when faced with this person's foul language. But let us say that nothing seems to perturb this individual, and he goes right on with his rude language. Leaving the area then becomes probable. Why? Because it terminates the person having to listen and put up with such language (CAO). In example three, painful stimulation establishes the value of termination of the discomfort (UEO) Any behaviors that produce escape or avoidance of such painful stimulation (UAO) will be strengthened. Again, *painful* is a relative phenomenon, varying according to the individual.

In example four we consider that for many people rain on the head establishes the value of terminating rain on the head (CEO). This group of people will therefore engage in behavior that results in rain no longer falling on their head (CAO). This may include using an umbrella, holding something else over their head, or simply going under cover. Any of these behaviors have the same effect of stopping rain on the head (CAO) and will therefore be strengthened. Example five is similar to example one, however, in this case, the teacher may present a relatively long task to the child. Because the child is not capable of performing such a task or demand for that long period of time, the task demand is aversive (CEO). Therefore, a behavior, or set of behaviors, in the repertoire of this child that results in its removal (CAO) will be strengthened.

Example six considers the behavioral effects of extra pyramidal symptoms (EPS), which are side effects associated with many antipsychotic medications. These EPS can be quite aversive. The occurrence of EPS will establish the value of (UEO) terminating the EPS. The most direct means to terminate the EPS (UAO) is to stop taking the medications that cause the EPS. This MO is frequently the major factor in medication noncompliance for people diagnosed with major mental illness. In example seven we consider that for people who have allergies and experience the private event of a sinus headache, the value of terminating that stimulus is established (UEO) when they are in the midst of a sinus headache. Most have found multiple means to do this: (1) take sinus medication; (2) take a hot, steamy shower; and (3) apply ice packs to the affected area. Consider, however, if you are living in an institution, and you are not verbal and unable to communicate that you have a sinus headache. The most direct way to terminate the sinus pain (UAO), albeit briefly, is to press on or hit the sinus area that is producing the pain, thus these behaviors would be strengthened.

Examples eight and nine review how the occurrence of drug or alcohol withdrawal symptoms will establish the value of terminating the withdrawal symptoms (UEO). The most direct means to terminate the withdrawal symptoms (UAO) is to take the drug associated with the withdrawal symptoms, thus strengthening this behavior. This UEO can be a major factor in the initial termination of drug use. The first use of drugs and long-term abstinence is associated with several other CEOs. The particular CEOs involved are typically idiosyncratic but can and should be delineated when approaching the treatment of substance abuse.

In example ten we review the MOs involved in auditory hallucinations. Many people report private events that could be classified as *auditory hallucinations*. For some people these events are aversive either due to content or duration. For this group of people the onset of auditory hallucinations establishes the value of terminating that private event (UEO). Any behavior that results in a reduction or elimination of the event will be strengthened. Many people report that increasing doses of alcohol and other substances will temporarily act to suppress (UAO) the private event. This process may help to explain the high rate of substance use in people who are later treated for a mental illness. Identifying the motivating operation that is at strength is a fairly straightforward process in people with relatively normal physiology. However, in clinical populations it is often the case that physiological processes are in some way disrupted. There is clear evidence that people with brain injuries and most major mental illnesses differ significantly from the norm in the way that their brains function. These differences appear to affect the MO both in establishing and abolishing the value of particular outcomes as reinforces.

Consider some people with the genetic syndrome called Prader-Willi. They never seem to ingest enough food or calories to abolish food as a reinforcer. For these individuals the value of food is established anytime they are not ingesting food. For people diagnosed with borderline personality disorder the value of adult or peer attention is difficult to abolish, and the value of attention is established very quickly after the last social interaction. Both of these examples are probably best analyzed as difficulties associated with ineffective abolishing operations. In both cases you could reduce the value of the reinforcer (food, attention) by continuous, noncontingent reinforcement, but in both cases this presents pragmatic and ethical concerns.

### How Do Other Antecedent Stimuli Interact With the MO?

You should now understand the role of motivation in the current and future rate of any behavior. However, you may be asking the question "Why would a person exhibit a particular behavior [e.g., pinching] that has in the past been paired with the occurrence of a specific reinforcer [e.g., going for a walk] at a specific time and not engage in that behavior at other times? Especially if the criterion to establish the value of the outcome has clearly been met [e.g., it has been 5 days since Milton's last walk, but he has not pinched anyone]?"

The answer lays in the other antecedent variables that affect the current rate of behavior: (a) the discriminative stimulus ($S^D$), and (b) the delta stimulus ($S^{Delta}$). The $S^D$ is a stimulus associated with the *availability* of an outcome. The $S^{Delta}$ is a stimulus associated with the outcome *not* being *available*. In order for the behavior to occur the person has to be motivated to get the item or event (the *value* of the outcome has to be established), and there needs to be some stimulus indicating that the outcome is *available*. If it has been several hours since you have eaten (value of food is high), and you are close to a favorite restaurant, will you go in to get food? It depends! If the sign on the door says OPEN ($S^D$: food is available), you are likely to go in and order food; if the sign says CLOSED ($S^{Delta}$: food is not available), you are not likely to go in and obtain food (Table 1.6).

Note that the Open/Closed sign on the restaurant is a neutral stimulus if the value of food has not been established. One could argue that seeing the Open sign acts as conditioned reinforcement for looking at the sign, but only if the value of food has been established. Once you have consumed some quantity of food, the intake of that food will abolish the value of food as a reinforcer (Cooper et al., 2007; Hesse, 1993; Laraway et al., 2003; Michael, 2005).

In some cases there may be a considerable delay between the EO and the actual occurrence of any behavior related to that specific EO. Some clients in treatment facilities will retaliate against a peer that has assaulted them. This is easily explained when the retaliation

*TABLE 1.6* ■ **MO-AO RELATIONSHIP**

| MO–EO | Stimulus | Behavior | Consequence | MO–AO |
| --- | --- | --- | --- | --- |
| Deprived of food for several hours (food is more valuable) | "Open" sign (SD), indicates food is available | Enter and order food | Obtain food | Consuming food (food is now less valuable) |
| Deprived of food for several hours (food is more valuable) | "Closed" sign (SDelta), indicates food is not available | Test door, unable to enter | NO Food | Food is still valuable |

is immediate, but how do you explain retaliation that occurs several days later? Clearly the EO establishing the value of damage to the other person is already at maximal value immediately after the person is assaulted. What would account of the delay? The most likely explanation is related to the availability of retaliation (damage to the other person) as a reinforcing event. Specifically, after an assault event, staff are more likely to be vigilant in order to avoid the retaliation. They are more likely to be present when the two clients are in the same area. Staff presence is an $S^{Delta}$ for retaliation because the staff would prevent the occurrence of damage to the other client. Over time the staff are less vigilant, and eventually the two clients are left alone. Under this condition assault is highly likely to produce damage to the other client because the staff are unlikely to be close enough to intervene, so the retaliation then occurs. Because this may occur several weeks after the initial assault event, staff my report that it happened for no reason or "out of the blue."

## Is It an MO or an S<sup>D</sup>?

As Michael (2007) points out, it can be difficult at times to distinguish an MO from an $S^D$. There are two simple questions to answer in making this determination:

1. In the presence of this stimulus is a particular environmental change more or less *valuable*? If the answer is yes, you are dealing with an MO.
2. In the presence of this stimulus is a particular environmental change more or less *available*? If the answer is yes, you are dealing with an $S^D$.

Consider the following example. A squirrel is engaged in eating when a predator approaches. The squirrel stops eating and runs up a tree to avoid the predator. Escape is *equally available* if the predator is there or not there; the squirrel could run up the tree at any time. Escape is much *more valuable* when the predator is present than when it is absent. The presence of the predator is an EO; specifically, it establishes the value of escape or avoidance of physical damage.

A more pragmatic example would be the smell of good food cooking. The smell of the food does *not* make food more *valuable* as a reinforcer. The smell of food does, however, indicate that food is more *available,* so it is therefore an $S^D$. In applied settings the pragmatic questions to consider regarding motivating operations and discriminative stimuli relative to a particular behavior-consequence relation are

1. What conditions would make that particular outcome valuable?
2. What conditions would reduce the value of that particular outcome?
3. Are there known biological conditions that would increase or decrease the value of that particular outcome?
4. What level (amount or duration) of the conditions that make a particular outcome valuable must occur before the targeted behavior is highly likely to occur?
5. What level (amount or duration) of the particular outcome must occur before the targeted behavior will stop?
6. After the behavior stops, how long is it before it reoccurs?
7. When the reinforcer is valuable, what are the stimulus conditions that indicate the outcome is available ($S^D$)?
8. When the reinforcer is valuable, what are the stimulus conditions that indicate the outcome is not available ($S^{Delta}$)?

## CHANGING BEHAVIOR BY ALTERING THE MOTIVATING OPERATION

When considering behavior change at the MO level it is important to be aware that the greater the value of the EO the greater the strength of the behavior. A person deprived of food for 24 hours will be much more likely to engage in behavior that is associated with food than a person who has just finished eating a full meal. As the value of the EO increases, the frequency (both absolute and relative), duration, and intensity of behaviors associated with abolishing that EO will also increase. As the value of the EO increases, the response latency following onset of the $S^D$ will decrease. In short, the higher the value of the EO the more rapid, frequent, and intense the behavior associated with that EO.

## Decreasing Targeted Behaviors by Altering Motivating Operations

In most cases we can decrease, if not eliminate, the behavior associated with a particular EO by ensuring that it never becomes valuable. In the case of access diagnosis (1.0 Direct Access, 2.0 Socially Mediated Access) this involves providing the reinforcer frequently and at high enough levels such that the value is never established. While this antecedent manipulation does not alter the function of the target behavior directly, it will reduce the behavior in frequency, duration, and intensity as well as increasing response latency. Table 1.7 provides some examples of this methodology.

For example, if a child engages in a behavior to get a certain preferred activity, such as computer time, then increasing the child's time on the computer two- or three-fold over the current access level will do two things. First, such a manipulation will reduce the value of this particular event. Second, it will alter the frequency of the target behavior as a result of the alteration of the EO for this target behavior. In regards to target behaviors maintained by escape diagnosis (3.0 direct escape, 4.0 socially mediated escape), the method of changing the motivational condition for such behaviors is to eliminate the presence of the aversive event, make it less aversive, or terminate the aversive condition noncontingently (see Table 1.8).

In regards to behaviors maintained by negative reinforcement, another methodology has been developed that impacts the motivational condition. It may also be possible to

---

**TABLE 1.7 ■ ANTECEDENT MANIPULATIONS AFFECTING MOTIVATING OPERATIONS FOR BEHAVIOR MAINTAINED BY POSITIVE REINFORCEMENT (ACCESS DIAGNOSIS)**

| Maintaining Reinforcer | Antecedent Manipulation |
| --- | --- |
| Adult attention | Increase frequency/duration of attention |
| Tangible reinforcer (food) | Increase availability of food throughout the day/time period |
| Tangible reinforcer (free time) | Increase availability of free time throughout the day/time period |
| Tangible reinforcer (preferred activity) | Increase availability of preferred activity throughout the day/time period |

---

**TABLE 1.8 ■ ANTECEDENT MANIPULATIONS AFFECTING MOTIVATING OPERATIONS FOR BEHAVIOR MAINTAINED BY NEGATIVE REINFORCEMENT (ESCAPE DIAGNOSIS)**

| Maintaining Negative Reinforcer | Antecedent Manipulation |
| --- | --- |
| Presence of unpleasant social situation | Avoid presenting such events, or reduce the level of aversion by altering some aspect of the situation |
| Presence of relatively lengthy task, chore, or assignment | Avoid presenting such tasks, chores, or assignments, or reduce the level of aversion by altering the length of the task |
| Presence of relatively difficult task, chore, or assignment | Avoid presenting such tasks, chores, or assignments, or reduce the level of aversion by altering the difficulty of the task |
| Presence of physically aversive stimulus | Avoid presenting such aversive stimuli, or reduce the level of aversion by altering some critical aspect of the stimulus |

alter slightly the conditions, removing just the factor or factors that establish the value of the escape behavior. In the previous example, making the instructional task less difficult by teaching the student how to perform such tasks would reduce the problem behavior. By teaching the child directly how to perform the task to mastery, two effects are created. First, the aversiveness of the event is altered, thus reducing the value of escaping such a task. Concurrently, it will alter the frequency and intensity of the target behavior and increase the response latency of the target behavior. For example, if a student engages in oppositional behavior when given a difficult task, then not providing that task will do two things. First, such a manipulation will ensure that the value of escape or avoidance of that task is never established; as a result, the frequency and intensity of the oppositional behavior will be reduced or eliminated.

## Increasing Behavior by Altering Motivating Operations

As should be clear to you by now, any behavior is unlikely to occur if the value of a particular outcome has not been established. When attempting to teach a new behavior it is important to understand that there are two ways to ensure that a reinforcer is at its maximal value. First, you could wait for naturally occurring environmental changes that establish the value of a particular outcome. For example, if you are trying to work on establishing behaviors related to accessing food, you could wait until right before meal times to use food as a reinforcer. Second, you could contrive a situation that increases the value of some outcome as a reinforcer. For example, if you are trying to work on establishing behaviors related to accessing fluids, you could provide very salty food to a person prior to and during training, thereby ensuring that the value of fluids remains at a relatively high level.

A more frequent use of contrived establishing operations is seen in the teaching of social skills and verbal behavior. We can manipulate the value of social/verbal interactions by establishing the value of a tangible reinforcer and then making access to that reinforcer dependent on a social interaction. This arrangement will establish the value of social interaction. Once the value of social or verbal interaction is established, we can effectively invoke the social behavior (Table 1.9).

Consider the following example. If we want to teach a person to request an item using verbal behavior, we could establish the value of a food item by simply waiting until a half hour prior to a usual mealtime. Assuming that the person has a history of socially mediated access to food, we could establish the value of social interaction by ensuring that no food item was directly available. We have now contrived a situation in which the only way to access a food item is by interacting with the staff person. Under this condition the person we are teaching to request an item is very likely to engage in some social interaction. We need only to ensure that the person engages in some approximation of the verbal behavior we are teaching prior to the staff providing the food item.

In regards to behaviors maintained by negative reinforcement, another methodology has been developed that impacts the motivating condition. It may also be possible to alter slightly the conditions, removing the factor that establishes the value of the escape

*TABLE 1.9* ■ **CONTRIVED ESTABLISHING OPERATIONS**

| UEO—Food | | CEO—Staff Attention | Behavior | Reinforcer | AO |
|---|---|---|---|---|---|
| Food deprived for short period of time | No direct access to food | Staff person with access to food | Client approaches staff and requests food | Staff provides food | Value of staff attention reduced |
| | | | | Client eats food | Value of food reduced |

behavior. In the previous example, making the instructional task less difficult by teaching the student how to perform such tasks would reduce the problem behavior. By teaching the child directly how to perform the task to mastery, two effects are created. First, the aversiveness of the event is altered, thus affecting the value of escape from such a task. Concurrently, it will alter the frequency of the target behavior as a result of the alteration of motivating conditions for this target behavior.

For example, if a student engages in oppositional behavior when given a difficult task, then not providing that task will do two things. First, such a manipulation will remove the controlling stimulus for the behavior, thus affecting the motivational condition for escape or avoidance. Concurrently, it will alter the frequency of the oppositional behavior as a result of the alteration of relatively aversive motivating conditions that occasion reinforcement for this target behavior.

## WHY DO SOME CLIENTS ENGAGE IN SEVERE DESTRUCTIVE BEHAVIORS?

In some settings, clients engage in severe forms of self-injury, aggression to others, and property destruction. Many people take this as an example that these people have uncontrollable rages as a result of their disorder. "Obviously these people have no control over what they do. They are *driven to destruction!*"

Take the case of the previously discussed child who gets sent to the time out room and cries to get "a more lenient sentence" once there. He might be judged to be less "disordered" than another child who engages in property destruction when placed in time out. Why does he cry and not become destructive? Although this child currently does not engage in property destruction, he may not be far from learning how to do such. This is a scenario of how more severe tantrum behaviors can be shaped by the social environment.

Suppose the parent decides to ignore the tantrum behavior in the time out area. He will "stick to his guns" and not allow the child to get out early. The child goes to time out and begins his crying episode but to no avail. He cries louder, but that does not result in removal either. He then throws something at the wall. The parent then comes into the room to find out what has happened. Note the effect of the throwing behavior in the sequence of events. If crying does not work, throw something. That will bring in Dad.

With time, the parent ignores some of the throwing episodes until a shoe goes through the dry wall near the door. As you can see, with each new exacerbation of behavior, the parent "has to" attend to the child to stop any further escalation. Hence, months later the child is now destroying the room, as opposed to just crying when placed in time out.

## CONTRIVED CONTINGENCIES PRODUCE A FUNCTION

Reinforcement systems that are designed to simply target appropriate behavior for increase have been referred to as contrived contingencies. The derivation of the specific contingency is contrived in that the functional relationship between problem behavior and its enabling contingency was not deduced. In using contrived contingencies to solve problems, one simply selects a powerful reinforcer, of unknown relationship to the current problem behavior, and delineates a temporal relationship between it and some desirable behavior.

Nevertheless, contrived contingencies produce function, and there are many reasons why they may be preferred as a first stage of an ecological intervention in many settings. A contrived classroom contingency arranges a functional relationship between some target criterion behavior (e.g., a designated percentage of time on-task, designated score on quiz grades, etc.) and production of effective reinforcers (Barrish, Saunders, & Wolf, 1969; Greenwood, Hops, Delquadri, & Guild, 1974). Point or token systems entail conditioned reinforcers (points) that are traded in for back-up reinforcers. The designation of potent back-up reinforcers provides the system with the requisite mechanism to influence behavior (Inkster & McLaughlin, 1993). Therefore, such contrived contingencies make student performance on the assignment or material of consequence. Many people refer to contrived contingencies as nonfunctional contingencies. You should now realize that functional is determined by the environment, given the presence of certain MOs. Designating a contrived contingency makes some behaviors functional with respect to the delivery of certain stimuli that are hopefully invaluable at that moment in time. Contrived contingencies introduce competing consequent stimuli to some functions that may exist for problem behaviors. Let us examine how contrived contingencies produce functions.

Ms. Tally designs a point system that provides points for on-task behavior during intermittent observations of such behavior. She has learned in her behavior analysis courses that contrived reinforcement contingencies have been demonstrated to be effective with many students, including those labeled as unmotivated and not intrinsically motivated. She feels that the term *intrinsically motivated* describes a certain percentage of students in her classroom, and she wants them to perform to a higher level. She implements a beeper system to increase student on-task behavior (see Cipani, 2008a, for details). *On-task behavior* is often defined as looking at the materials during seat assignments or at the teacher during lesson presentations or instructions. A beep is produced at random intervals. With these random beeps, she intermittently observes the students in her class and records whether they are engaged with their class assignment. When students are demonstrating on-task at the time of the sampling, they earn points. If they are not on-task at that point in time, they do not earn points. Points are traded in later for a variety of back-up reinforcers, such as tangible items and preferred activities.

Ms. Tally implements this program for four weeks subsequent to a baseline. As a result of implementing the beeper system, the mean rate of on-task behavior goes from 46% during baseline to 77% for the first 4 weeks of treatment. Further evidence of the efficacy of the beeper system is the substantial improvement on the students' quiz grades. Why does this procedural arrangement between student engagement and contrived reinforcement contingencies work? In using the beeper system, it was not necessary for Ms. Tally to determine the function of the existing off-task behaviors in order to reduce the level. Why does such a contingent relationship alter student performance in the desirable direction?

The environment often creates, through the class routine involving instructional periods, deprivation with respect to some item or activity. As a result, the ability of some behavior or chains of behavior to abolish the deprivation is determined by the teaching staff. The extent to which the contrived contingencies involving points will increase the rate or level of on-task behavior (or other targeted behavior) depends on the relative deprivation of the back-up items and also the aversive nature of the current tasks or activities. When the back-up items and events are relatively deprived, behaviors that produce such become more probable. In using the beeper system, on-task behavior becomes functional in producing points. The points accumulated are then traded in for back-up reinforcers. Therefore, appropriate on-task and engagement behaviors become functional in producing the deprived events and items. Like any other functional analysis, classroom behaviors that produce desired events (under relevant MOs) become more probable under the discriminative stimuli involving the presence of the teacher and some rule-specifying contingency.

An important point about contrived contingent reinforcers is their ability to possibly override existing weak functions of problem behaviors that are incompatible with on-task behavior. Contrived contingencies may address MOs that are far more powerful in terms of their value-altering effects than the MO for the current problem behavior. For example, a student engages in gazing out the window for minutes at a time to take in the view. We could say that such behavior may either be a function of direct access to visual sensory reinforcement or direct escape of engagement with instructional materials. Under the absence of contrived reinforcers for performance, such behavior occurs several times (of variable duration) in a given instructional period. The teacher may even report that this student gets easily distracted. However, when contrived contingencies for on-task behavior are deployed, via the beeper system, gazing out the window goes down to a markedly lower frequency and also of very short duration. Note that the MO addressed by the contrived contingency overrides (momentarily operates as an AO for) the weaker MO for viewing the scenery or directly escaping the task.

What about the students who do not need teacher-designed contrived contingencies for selected appropriate task engagement behaviors? Some students (often labeled as "good") continue to perform despite getting more work after they complete their initial assignment. Is this an instance of intrinsic reinforcement? While many nonbehavioral educators point to this as an example of intrinsic motivation, they fail to understand the powerful role of other superimposed contingencies on classroom performance. Performing well in class can bring teacher, parent, or other adult attention and, in some cases, peer approval and attention. Grades also provide a source of social contingencies, and some additional benefits from rule-specifying contingencies ("If I get good grades, I'll go to college."). Therefore, in these students, because other MOs are present (e.g., attention from teacher, parents, peers), and there are discriminative stimuli for such behavior, their behavior is well understood within a contingency analysis. These students' performances are sustained because of these inherent superimposed contingencies in a given student's life.

While such superimposed additional contingencies can explain why some competent students do not need contrived contingencies to maintain classroom performance, what about those who do not perform under such conditions? These students cannot perform at the academic levels that recruit such reinforcers. What happens to learners who do not have the competence to be affected by such superimposed contingencies? Very often, the failure to use contrived contingencies with these students results in a decrement in everyday performance. Their performance in the classroom becomes highly variable. On some days, they perform at admirable levels, and other days they do not complete their assignments. Unfortunately, when their performance over time fails to recruit superimposed additional reinforcement contingencies, such as good grades and adult approval, they become even more unproductive. When these learners fail to consistently recruit those contingencies, their daily work does not come under control of such consequences.

As a result of this failure to recruit superimposed contingencies, classroom instruction and tasks become an aversive condition. Instruction, task assignments, and other learning activities develop aversive stimulus properties, which become EOs for escape and avoidance behaviors. With the reluctance of the teacher to designate some alternate (performance-based) criterion for terminating tasks (see the case of the wacky contingency, Chapter 3, page 110), undesirable behaviors become strengthened through the selective reinforcement of such.

## SUMMARY

Behavior (operant) that occurs with high probability in certain contexts is functional. This is true for both desirable and undesirable behaviors. Functional translates to the behavior producing a stimulus change that maintains such a behavior. Behavior achieves a desired environmental effect through one of two operations: (1) producing a desired event or item or (2) removing or avoiding an undesired event. Further, the manner in which such results are produced can be one of two methods: (1) direct or (2) socially mediated. The following chapters will expound on this concept of specific operant behavior becoming functional under certain motivational contexts as a result of its environmental effect.

# THE CHILD WITHOUT A CONSCIENCE: THE FUNCTION OF BEHAVIOR IN A COMPLEX CASE

When mental health personnel view behavior as a result of an internal condition, behavior is often explained as the result of such a condition. Hence, such behavior is to be expected from time to time, and environmental contexts are relegated to an immaterial role. The following case is instructive for several reasons. First, the type of behaviors occurring at such a young age was rather unusual and of a form that intimidated the adults caring for the child. Second, an analysis of the probable function of such behaviors revealed "super-ordinate" contingencies that existed in foster care placement. Such contingencies are invoked when foster children of a young age engage in behaviors that make the current placement caretakers no longer willing to care for them.

## Description of Case

Polly was a 5-year-old child who had been referred to me (E.C.) for in-home behavior management. She was currently residing at her second foster home, having been detained from her biological mother's home previously by Child Protective Services (CPS). Polly's biological mother was reported to have perpetrated several incidents involving physically abusive behavior toward Polly and her other siblings. Her first foster placement ended rather quickly (prior to my involvement) as she reportedly exhibited uncontrollable outbursts and tantrums. Subsequently, the foster parent requested a termination of this placement, and the county department of social service turned her case over to a foster family agency (FFA) for placement. The family whom Polly was residing with at the time of my involvement belonged to this FFA. I did not receive much information besides this brief placement history prior to my first home appointment to meet this family. An initial phone contact with the foster mother provided some basic information regarding Polly's current problems in her home. Polly was described as an out of control child who did not respect adult authority. Further, she could become verbally aggressive and sometimes physically destructive when upset.

Background information obtained from the case manager revealed that Polly was initially raised by her biological mother along with four other siblings. Two of the siblings were children of Polly's mother and father (although Dad had long since disappeared). Her other half-siblings were each fathered by a different man. The mother at the time of detainment was raising all the children on her own.

When Polly attended preschool and childcare, while still in her mother's custody, she was expelled as a result of severe behavior problems that the school could not tolerate. She was reported by the preschool staff to hit, pinch, bite, and attack other children without provocation. She would not respond to directions from the teachers, particularly directions to go to time out for misbehaviors. It was during these times that she would become verbally abusive. While staff noted that she could be pleasant and happy on many days, it was her bad days that made the situation intolerable, thus requiring her expulsion.

When Polly was 5 years old, CPS was notified by Polly's elementary school of possible child endangerment. A CPS social worker came out to investigate that referral and found an abrasion on Polly's chin. Her brother was found to have a similar mark on his back. The school also reported to CPS that Polly was often 30 minutes early to school without supervision, often dirty and with no snack. Polly told CPS that there was no food in the house. As a result of all this information, Polly and her younger siblings were detained and placed in foster homes.

On my first appointment I pulled up to the curb of the foster parent's house and covertly noted that the foster family lived in a nice neighborhood. I was greeted at the door by the foster mother and shown into the living room. Polly was sitting in a chair at the dining room table engaged in some innocuous activity (*I thought to myself—"looks good so far"*). Present in the room were the foster father, a social worker from the county, and a social worker from the FFA, who would coordinate the behavioral treatment. I began interviewing the foster parents as to the nature of Polly's behaviors, that is, under what conditions did she seem to exhibit such behaviors and what was their method of attempting to manage her. The parents painted a picture of a child with a dual personality (*I am not implying the diagnosis here, their implication, not mine*). Sometimes, she was the most well-behaved child, played with peers in an appropriate manner, and was so angelic. But on the other hand, when she was upset, watch out. Her demeanor changed, she was no longer pleasant, and profane language and hurtful words poured out of her mouth. However, during the entire time I was interviewing the foster parents and the social workers, I noted no incidence of such behavior. She continued to entertain herself at the table as per the direction of the foster parents.

As I obtained enough information from the foster parents at that time I then decided to test the waters. If at all possible, I like to see how children handle commands and instructions from me to give me an indication about their compliance to adult instructions. I gave Polly a few brief requests, which were all responded to with a smile. When I praised her and told her she did an excellent job in following my instruction, her smile went from coast to coast. I then attempted to correct her on a math task I assigned. This is often a good test of a child's ability to handle criticism appropriately. This "simulated criticism" can usually evoke some level of agitation with children who are disrespectful of adult instructions. She made no objection or dispute of my correction! Over the course of the 15–20 minutes of individual work with her, in the dining room, while all the adults watched on, she appeared to be the antithesis of the child that was described to me. At that point, I just could not picture what someone would have to do in order for Polly to become a child who was out of control. I could not even envision her being in the vicinity of a screaming tantrum, replete with profanity, let alone being the source of such verbiage.

If first impressions are a valid measure of a child's behavior in their social environment, one might surmise that Polly's demonic nature was a figment of the foster parent's imagination. Could the parents possibly be over-controlling and require perfectionism? How could this innocent child do anything but good! With such great compliance from Polly the thought of these foster parents being so inept that they could "bungle" parenting such a sweet child ran through my mind but was quickly dismissed. The evidence to the contrary was substantial. In addition to the report from these foster parents, severe behavioral episodes and reactions were also reported by Polly's previous teachers and foster parents.

With no incident of behavior that remotely resembled a troubled child, the foster parents wanted to assure me that this is what they expected for my visit. They indicated that it was Polly's nature to be angelic with other people. They informed me that she had a mental disorder, which made her act this way in front of strangers, but then she would quickly turn on the parent figure. Could this be the granddaughter of Norman Bates? They handed me some material on reactive attachment disorder (RAD). They implied that the description of children with this disorder fit Polly to a tee. In the article given to me (Hindle, 1995, *Adoptive Families,* Sept/Oct, pp. 20 & 21), the author reports that such children can appear normal and personable to outside observers. However, the adoptive or foster parent (who is the target of their rage) experiences all the problems.

Why do these children behave like this? According to attachment theorists (who predominate this field), these children fail to develop attachments because of an early trauma (such as abuse, neglect, or separation). As a result they fail to "bond" with a significant caretaking adult. Because there was no initial bond between the child and mother, they feel no remorse for hurtful incidents regarding other people. According to attachment theorists, a "moral conscience" is only developed as a result of a baby's attachment to an adult early in life. People who argue this view trivialize the role of social consequences of behavior in teaching children to learn to refrain from saying spiteful things to people. The foster mother reiterated that Polly feels no remorse for persons she hurts or offends. Further, I should not be fooled by the display of good behavior, as these children are the masters at this behavioral deception. She again reassured me that Polly is really disruptive to their family situation, and I should not be fooled by her deceptive appearance on this visit.

## Intervention

Fortunately, that sermon about RAD did not sway me from my objective: to bring problem behaviors under control of more systematic contingencies. In some cases, treatment merely requires a manipulation of contingencies; in others, skill training is added to that component. The child's caretakers, whether they be biological parents, foster parents, or group home staff, are then trained on-the-job to perform the requisite behaviors in response to the child's behavior.

I like to target just one problem area at time, bringing desired change in that area before tackling another. I chose to target a daily context that was generating problems in child management: bedtime. Polly was reported to have difficulty going to bed and staying there. She would get up constantly and have to be put back to bed. To get Polly to accept bedtime more readily, the foster parents had tried enforcing bedtime at a predictable time and incorporating low-key activities prior to bedtime. With that regimen, Polly was having less of a problem at bedtime than in the prior placement. However, on nights when she had difficulty, she had severe tantrums and would get out of the bed constantly.

While these were good first steps on the part of the current caretakers to address bedtime problems, I suggested some additional procedures. There should be an incentive for good bedtime behaviors to compete with the desirability of creating havoc in the family household. My plan was to allow Polly to earn a half-hour of later bedtime the following night for good bedtime behavior (the current night). Good bedtime behavior was defined as (1) the lack of tantrum behavior and (2) not getting out of bed once she was placed in bed. She could also lose an hour off of regular bedtime the following night if she got up or had tantrums.

The first two nights of this regimen were not good. The parents estimated that Polly got up about 25 times that first night and a little less the second night. It was fortuitous that the foster parents did not bail out at that point. I had prepared them for this possibility. On the third night, the plan resulted in her complete cooperation and access to the privilege of staying up late the following night. For the entire next week she responded well to the plan, always getting her extra half hour each subsequent night. Parental persistence paid off.

However, these parents gave notice to have her moved prior to my third visit. She was moved to another home about 25 miles away. I was notified initially to discontinue the case because the new foster parent reported that Polly was not a management problem at the time. I noted to myself that a prevention approach was not high on anyone's list. I was eventually contacted about a month after she was moved, with the presenting problem as arguing behavior (also termed mouthy behavior, although the foul language had not yet set in). There were also two reports of major screaming bouts, but the overall impression of the new foster mother was that Polly was manageable and not unlike other foster children she has had.

However, shortly thereafter, and before my first scheduled visit, Polly's level of tantrums had increased. Of even more significance, her inappropriate language was back in full force. Its form took on a new and ugly twist, one that frightened this foster mother tremendously. She was now threatening to do bodily harm to the foster mother and her toddler grandson, who would come to play at her house (e.g., "I'm going to hurt you" or "I'm going to hit him"). She had not acted on these threats, but I obviously wanted to address this before it reached that stage.

Let's say that the foster mother just told Polly, after a request, that she could not go outside and play (for whatever reason). Polly may not cry like other children. Perhaps her conditioning history taught her that such was not a fruitful approach to getting what you wanted. However, saying, "I hate you, you are a ____ and I am going to ____ you or ____ your baby " was quite the opposite. What would you imagine would happen next? A probable reaction from an adult upon hearing such a threat from a young child is to ask the child why she would want to do that. For example, a parent might say to the child, "Why would you be so mean?" Or, "You don't mean that, do you?" This would be followed by Polly saying, "Because I hate you," or, "Oh yes I do." This subsequently escalates the fear (increases the value of terminating such statements) on the part of the parent, as the child shows that she can be vindictive and spiteful (apply contingencies aversive to the foster parents). Their reaction to this type of behavior promotes the continued verbal assertion on the part of the child that she does mean it, or will do it, or is not sorry for saying that, and so forth. Again, in Polly's case, this dynamic between child and adult only increased everyone's belief that she has no conscience and may never develop one and, therefore, is someone to be feared. Of course, such a behavior probably will cut down on any future tendencies on the part of the parent to deny a desired activity or event to Polly.

I perceived my first job in this circumstance as one of teaching the foster mother to place these threats in context. This is not to say that I do not take these threats seriously. It was my contention that attempting to reason with her at that point in time only fuels the fire! What is needed from the parent is a refutation of such behavior as unacceptable, with a consequence for saying such spiteful things. I immediately set up a behavioral program, targeting threats with an early bedtime contingency. Each time she threatened, she was told that such statements were unacceptable in a firm manner (not inquiring as to why she would say something like that). The incident will be marked on the board in the living room. If she had more than three marks at the end of that day, then it was early bedtime that night (hey, it worked before, let's keep using it).

How did this plan work? The data on the frequency of threats was the following (plan began on 6/7). Please note, that without baseline data being taken, data in Table 1.10 probably represent an immediate overall decrease in this behavior over the previous week.

As one can notice, Polly developed amazing self-control in her ability not to go over three threats in a day (*maybe she developed a conscience each day as the day proceeded*). Subsequently,

*TABLE 1.10* ■ **TARGET BEHAVIOR DATA**

| Date | Frequency of Threats |
| --- | --- |
| 6/7 | 3 |
| 6/8 | 3 |
| 6/9 | 0 |
| 6/10 | 0 |
| 6/11 | 2 |
| 6/12 | 2 |
| 6/13 | 2 |
| 6/14 | 2 |
| 6/15 | 1 |

the program was then changed to allow only one incident of threatening behavior before the early bedtime contingency was enacted. This produced the desired change in the behavior as weeks went by with no threats to family members at a month's follow-up. The board had actually been put away, but the foster mother was instructed to initiate the planned contingencies again should threats develop again.

## Fix One Problem, Get Another!

However, as is often the case, as one problem gets solved a new problem develops "critical mass." It began innocuously as Polly was asked by the FFA social worker if she wanted to see her brother and sister. Polly replied in the affirmative. Following that meeting her behavior slowly escalated to refusal of all requests during the day, in the home. The reason offered (by the social worker) for this acting out contagion was that during the same meeting, Polly had dealt with sensitive abuse issues. Therefore, her behavior was a reaction to this "bringing up" of traumatic issues. In my experience, traditionally trained therapists often attribute the existence of problem behaviors to prior traumatic events, even after many years.

I inquired further, not feeling that this explained why Polly was being defiant. I would rather look for environmental factors that make such a behavioral pattern more functional in the current environment. I was more intrigued by the fact that this escalation coincided with her having a proposed visit with her siblings. Upon receiving this information, I first conjectured that maybe Polly did not want to see her siblings. Certainly acting out would be a functional way to get such a visit postponed (due to her bad behavior). However, I discarded that hypothesis when the foster mother relayed some information about what transpired after the talk with the social worker. She did not think this information was important at the time but now thought that it might help me in my quest to figure this out. The foster mother told me that Polly, subsequent to that meeting, inquired over a several day period about the visit and wanted to know when it would happen. My hypothesis regarding her attempting to get out of the visit did not seem plausible. Rather she seemed eager to go. Then it hit me!

With the mention that she might get to see her siblings, Polly, being the 5 year old that she was, translated that in the following 5-year-old English—"You absolutely positively will get to see your brother and sister, we have them en-route right now and they will be arriving in 5 minutes!" If you believed that your visit with your brother and sister was imminent, would you be upset if 15 minutes goes by and nobody arrives? How upset would you be when one whole day passes, two days, and so forth? Polly knows one powerful way to influence adult decisions. If you do not get your way, then utter profane words at someone in authority.

Another incident seemed to confirm this hypothesis. One day, Polly asked her foster mother if she could go to her friend's house after school. The answer she got was not a "yes," and not a "no," but a "we will check it out" (i.e., "we will get back to you on that"). Well, once again that got translated into 5-year-old English, which probably went this way—"Oh what the heck, Just take the bus home with him tomorrow and I'm sure his parents will not mind." The next day the foster mother gets a call from the parent of Polly's friend, saying that Polly showed up with her son on his bus after school. Subsequent to the foster mother picking her up, Polly engaged in tantrum behavior that day and the following day (*remember my hypothesis—when I don't get my way, I'll make it so miserable for you that you will have to give in*).

In order to teach Polly not to react inappropriately when she wants something, she was taught that making a request for some item or activity will usually be honored at some point, provided she complies with some request or instruction from the foster mother. This procedure allowed me to build in a time delay from request to delivery of reinforcer. The type and number of tasks to be done depend on Polly's request. For example, for a food item such as a piece of chocolate cake, Polly would have to possibly do several small compliant behaviors, such as picking up a few toys, washing her hands, and so forth. For a more extensive request, she may have to do something over a 2-day period. The foster mother was asked to keep track of the number of requests per day that Polly made, with a target goal of five to eight per day. The data for the first week showed that requests ranged from a low of two occurrences per day to a high of five.

The foster mother reported that the strategy was going well. I'm not quite sure she understood the necessity for this approach, and I therefore speculated that it was not being used as often as it should have been. Shortly after reporting that "things" were going well, this foster mother gave social service a 30-day notice on Polly for change of placement. As I suspected, "things" were not going well. The utility of teaching this skill is that if it is reinforced in the social environment (home), then inappropriate ways of getting items and activities will be replaced by this more acceptable and effective method. However, to utilize this, one must implement it at the time that demands are being made. One should not give into demands immediately, that is, without the "work" component, or deny them completely (except for untenable requests).

## Case Analysis: What Does Polly Teach Us?

In this case, I was struck by the forecasting of many people in the system. They attributed everything that Polly did, in terms of severe problem incidents, to Polly's mental disorder. These professionals further prognosticated that such incidents would be repeated over and over again due to her reactive attachment disorder. I observed that this armchair philosophizing had resulted in not getting past theorizing and into the needs of solving the problem behavior. The parents and I were successful on several fronts in the short term when I looked past the predictions of what one could expect from a child with such a disorder. In contrast, I focused on what we would do when she engaged in such inappropriate behaviors. Apparently, children who are diagnosed with RAD can benefit from a contextual analysis of their problem behaviors.

One of the consequences of severe behavioral incidents is the child being moved from one placement to another. Foster children with severe disruptive and challenging behaviors have frequent changes in their residential placements. This occurs from a policy standpoint because the current care provider is not required to house the child. If her behavior is deemed too difficult for the provider to handle, she is moved to another placement. Often this is sanctified in the name of "finding the perfect fit." But could behavioral contingencies be at work in some of these cases where a child has six placements in 3 years, mostly as a function of the provider giving notice to terminate placement as a result of behavior?

It seemed to me that Polly would continually misbehave until she either got what she wanted (caregiver gives in to appease her) or she moved to a new home (*where maybe she would get a better deal this time around*). The possibility that the change in placements might be a functional reinforcer did not strike me until I began reviewing the records of her prior placements. The pattern revealed that Polly would behave for a short honeymoon, where the new foster parents probably wondered why the previous parents had so much trouble managing this poor innocent child. However, they soon began gasping for air, as this short honeymoon was followed by a downhill spiral of bad behavior and mean remarks.

Why would circumstances start off well and then turn south? Let's speculate that during the honeymoon period, her new foster parents are probably more lenient and likely to provide her with many of the items and activities she wants (hence, no need to act out). However, after awhile, the parents begin to tighten the reins, and Polly starts to have problems. Over the long haul, when Polly did not get what she wanted, her misbehavior and hateful comments toward the caregivers would escalate and thereby force her case manager to find a new home for her because the current parents would no longer tolerate her behavior. I remember saying to the clinical supervisor of the FFA that we need to draw a line in the sand. The next placement needs to deal with this cycle of behavior without throwing in the towel at the end and moving her. The only way we are going to solve her problems in the long run is to not allow her misbehavior to alter her placement. What the system has taught Polly (at a very young age) is that extreme disruptive behavior, over long periods, makes you move to another house. From a behavior analysis perspective, the system needs to redirect such contingencies to not support severe misbehavior.

# Functional Behavioral Assessment of Problem Behavior

## 2

This chapter will delineate procedures, activities, and instruments that can be used for collecting functional assessment data on target problem behaviors. In addition to determining the baseline rate of occurrence for the target problem behavior or behaviors, one must also collect data that provides evidence for the environmental function of the target behavior. A functional behavior assessment (FBA) can involve multiple methods of assessing the problem behavior's current function under specific antecedent conditions. An FBA can provide various forms of evidence regarding the current purpose or function of the problem behavior under a specific antecedent condition or multiple conditions. This information then leads to the generation of a function-based behavioral diagnosis for the problem behavior (Chapter 3).

## DETERMINING THE NEED FOR INTERVENTION

As will be evident, conducting a functional behavioral assessment is a time-consuming effort (as well as a monetary expense). Given this substantial effort, you should make an initial tentative determination as to the possible need for a comprehensive functional behavioral assessment. In emergency medicine, triage is the stage at which the professional makes a determination as to which patients are in need of immediate consideration and the relative needs of the remaining patients. Prior to extensive data collection activities, you should make a brief screening of the individual case. The following questions in Table 2.1 should help guide you in this phase of the assessment process (Barlow & Hersen, 1984; Kazdin, 1982).

Dangerous behaviors, such as aggression, self-injury, and property destruction, certainly warrant immediate clinical consideration because of their potential to impact the client's (and others') welfare and safety. Here is a case in point. I (E.C.) was a behavioral consultant to an adult day treatment program for persons with severe developmental disabilities. One of the clients came in one day with her neck raw from scratching. She had engaged in severe, intense, and lengthy self-abuse to her neck the prior afternoon and evening. I called up the residential facility and inquired what was being done to treat her. The response I received was, "We are taking baseline data." I replied, "Your baseline has just ended and you better be intervening with her tonight!" The seriousness of this client's behavior problem warranted immediate clinical attention. I suggested that whatever antecedent condition was producing this intense self-abuse should be halted until an effective plan could be designed. In this case, some effort at controlling the behavior must be considered prior to, or concurrent with, behavioral assessment activities.

Aggressive behavior poses the same immediate concern. If a student with moderate disabilities occasionally bites his fellow classmates, such behavior obviously jeopardizes the welfare of other students in the class. Although it may require some time and effort to develop a comprehensive plan to effectively address this client's behavior, steps should be taken immediately to ensure the safety of others. Closer vigilance of this student is most important; another temporary solution is reducing his time around the other students. Although these strategies may not constitute the definitive manner in dealing with this situation, they do provide a short-term safety net.

The social significance of changing severe self-injury and aggression is obvious. A client receiving employment training who is not physically or verbally aggressive to his co-workers will be more likely to maintain his job placement. Absence of these behaviors will likely also affect his future employability and his satisfaction at the work site (particularly

---

*TABLE 2.1* ■ **SCREENING QUESTIONS**

■ Does the individual's behavior pose a danger to himself or others?

■ Does the behavior pose a health or safety hazard to the individual client or others?

■ Does the behavior affect the client's welfare in the current environment?

■ Does the behavior prevent the individual from accessing less restrictive environments in either the school, home, or community settings?

---

if the intervention developed alternate behaviors that produced reinforcement). Similarly, altering the intensity and rate of scratching in the client mentioned previously would be desirable for her health and her state of emotion.

Some presenting problem behaviors are important to address because they prohibit a child or client from accessing a less restrictive educational, residential, or community environment or setting. For example, a young child's ability to use the toilet independently, although certainly not a life-threatening behavior, may impact that child's ability to attend a regular preschool program. The inability to use the toilet limits this opportunity. Many would agree that attending preschool is an important step in developing requisite skills for success in early elementary grade levels. In many cases, young children with disabilities are precluded from entering private preschool programs if they have frequent toileting accidents or are not toilet trained at all. This is not to make a value judgment on such criteria, only to realize that many private preschools have such entrance criteria for all children being considered. As is the case with toileting, the presence of aggressive behavior can have the same impeding impact on a child's ability to be educated in a more mainstream environment.

There are other behaviors that, when present, often result in some form of segregation of the child or client from environments with same-aged peers. A child who constantly gets out of his seat while riding the school bus, in spite of verbal admonishments from the bus driver to sit down, may eventually present a situation that calls for expulsion from the regular school bus. Although many children do occasionally get out of their seat, a child who repeatedly fails to heed the driver's warning to stay in his seat creates a significant management problem. The school transportation personnel may press for alternate transportation arrangements to be made for this child, thus removing him from this experience with his same-aged peers.

Adult clients can also exhibit behaviors that result in their removal and segregation from the mainstream. An adult client with a diagnosed mental illness may be more than adequate at performing the requisite tasks in an employment situation with sufficient support from a job coach. However, his behavior during lunch, breaks, or other social activities often can result in termination of employment. For example, if the client bothers people while on break and such behavior reaches the level of what one person considers sexual harassment, then the client's job is in jeopardy. The following real-life case scenario is evidence of seemingly innocent behaviors producing disastrous results (taken from Cipani, 2004, with permission).

## THE CASE OF THE INTIMATE DISCLOSURE

In the early 1990s, we (E.C. and a behavioral specialist) received a referral for a 21-year-old female, Clarine, with a very unique but problematic behavior. Clarine had mild mental retardation and lived with foster parents subsequent to her being taken out of her father's home (the reason will be apparent in a minute). She was a fairly capable and pleasant individual and could engage in a variety of tasks that would allow her to gain paid employment with some help. At the time of the referral, she was working at a convalescent hospital and was being trained by an agency to gain and maintain that place of employment.

Her work at the hospital seemed to meet everyone's expectations, but she was to be fired from her job for a reason other than her ability to make a bed. Clarine made friends easily, perhaps too easily. She would initiate a conversation with the patients at the hospital in an appropriate manner (this attention is often a welcome event in these patients' lives). However, without a moment's notice, she would begin talking with them as if they had been hired as her psychiatrist or social worker. For example, in midconversation, Clarine would provide explicit details about her biological father sexually abusing her (in graphic details) as well as a rape that occurred to her when she was in school. The conversation might start with, "Hi, my name is Clarine. What is your name? How are you doing? Do you like it here? Do you want to hear how my father undressed me and ———?"

The staff person who worked with her had tried many strategies to get her to stop disclosing all the intricacies of her unfortunate past, but to no avail. This staff person must have felt like she was swimming upstream in her attempt to get Clarine to desist. Imagine the reaction you would have if you were a patient in this hospital. Here comes a pleasant individual who wants to converse with you. Your agenda is not entirely filled up on this particular day, so you greet her with a smile. The conversation is pleasant and seems to be going along fine, and then you do a double take, discounting the possibility that you heard ———. Nope, there is nothing wrong with your ears. Your smile turns to a look of apprehension and, finally, distaste. As you might guess, Clarine did not pick up on some subtle cues that your interest had turned to aversion to her story. The patient's attention was all that mattered, and this was being given in abundance because of Clarine's remarks about her unfortunate past life.

To complicate matters, this probable attention from patients would make it more difficult to eliminate such a behavior. One could not count on this attention to stop in the near future. It would be improbable to get everyone at her work site, as well as visitors, to agree to ignore this one worker when she revealed her shocking story. I don't believe the Americans with Disabilities Act would extend that far in terms of a reasonable accommodation. This situation required that we come up with a strategy that would make it more uncomfortable for her to engage in this behavior and override the social attention it receives.

The administrators at the hospital were adamant about her leaving, and they fired her. Luckily, another job at a day care center was procured by her social worker. My behavioral specialist and I felt that it was essential to have a plan in place that would be so powerful that it would make Clarine think twice before launching into her sermon. Prior to Clarine showing up at her new position, my behavioral specialist worked with the foster parents to teach them how to use evening privileges as a consequent event. If Clarine had an incident at work that day, all evening privileges were revoked. She would basically become bored until she went to sleep that night. Tomorrow was another day when she could keep or lose that evening's privileges.

What would she have to do to lose evening privileges? You guessed it. Each day, the supervisor would meet with Clarine's staff aide to determine if there had been any incidents of inappropriate conversation. If any incident occurred, this was conveyed to her parents, and privileges were revoked that evening. Conversely, if she kept her conversation appropriate, then she did not lose evening privileges. Additionally, any chores at work that were assigned and not completed due to lack of motivation on her part would also result in her evening privileges being revoked.

Apparently, this consequence struck fear into Clarine. Not one single major incident of inappropriate disclosure occurred at the day care center within the first 2 months. This plan was effective because it provided a powerful consequence for inappropriate disclosure as well as a reinforcing condition if she did not disclose such facts while at work.

This case is instructive for another reason as well. Sometimes, a punishing consequence has to be used to override the effects of a powerful social reinforcer that the behavior automatically produces because people are people! When some people do or say wacky things, other people stand up and take notice, and laugh and attend. Overriding this built-in reinforcement for intimate disclosures required the foster parents to remove preferred events when such occurred. Although other people may have felt that Clarine needed to talk about this earlier trauma in her life, my position was that its indiscriminate occurrence was not healthy for anyone. Subsequent to the success of this program, I do not see that Clarine's emotional health suffered because we punished such a disclosure. In fact, Clarine was better for it, and I'm sure the day care center was also happy with the result.

Taken with permission from *Punishment on Trial,* by E. Cipani, pp. 115–117, Context Press.

Table 2.2 includes some questions to consider when determining if the problem behaviors are jeopardizing current or future mainstream environments in students and clients. In assessing the impact of the problem behaviors of students in educational settings, consider how such behaviors ameliorate or eliminate the potential to be educated in a less restrictive educational placement. In assessing the impact of the problem behavior in

---

*TABLE 2.2* ■ **INTERVIEW QUESTIONS ON RELEVANCE OF PROBLEM BEHAVIOR FOR MAINSTREAM ENVIRONMENTS**

---

1. What specific behaviors are comprised in the problem? On the surface, would such behaviors pose a problem for current (or future) educational work or residential mainstream environments? Is the problem behavior inappropriate in mainstream environments of people or children of similar age to the client?

2. What ramifications does the problem behavior incur for the client? Do they restrict the client's access to activities, events, and people that are of some reinforcing value in the current environment? For example, is the client often prevented from accessing community events because of her behavior when in the community?

3. What are the standards of social behavior that the current (or future) environment has in place? Are they in writing or are they implied?

4. Is there some variation on these standards or are they strictly enforced?

---

*TABLE 2.3* ■ **FIVE STEPS TO COLLECTING FUNCTIONAL BEHAVIORAL ASSESSMENT DATA**

---

1. Obtain a baseline measurement of observable problem behaviors.

2. Conduct a functional behavior assessment (FBA).

3. Perform a discrepancy analysis.

4. Review previous treatments.

5. Review health and medical records.

---

clients living in residential settings, examine how the problem behavior affects their ability to live in more mainstream environments.

Once the need for an assessment has been established, a number of activities and data collection efforts should be conducted. The steps in Table 2.3 certainly are not presented as an invariant sequence. Very often, several assessment activities may be undertaken concurrently. Reviewing health and medical records and possibly involving a medical consultation can be done concurrently with pinpointing a problem behavior. Use the steps shown in Table 2.3 to ensure that each step is covered during your behavioral assessment.

## BASELINE MEASUREMENT OF OBSERVABLE PROBLEM BEHAVIORS

In a functional behavioral assessment, the critical first step is to define the presenting problem in discrete observable behaviors. Very often in clinical and educational settings, client problems are phrased in ambiguous terminology. As an example, consider the following referral for behavior problems in a hypothetical school classroom: "John Smith, a 3rd grade mainstreamed student with anger issues, is reported by his teacher to be uncontrollable and incorrigible!" This lack of specifics on what constitutes uncontrollable or incorrigible is all too frequent from persons making referrals for a behavioral assessment.

What is wrong with this type of information? It requires that you get to the bottom of the child's problem by obtaining specifics of the problem behaviors. Unobservable behaviors, personality characteristics, or traits do not constitute the primary criterion for measurement of behaviors in a functional behavioral assessment, even though they make us sound more clinical in our conversation. Your first task is to take the unobservable entities often provided by the referral agent and define them into discrete, observable, and measurable behaviors. This is called *pinpointing a target behavior.* The pinpointing of observable target behaviors can be obtained by one of two methods: (1) behavioral interviewing and (2) direct observation (by you).

Very often, initial data gathering is gained through a behavioral interview of significant others who are directly involved with the client in everyday life. These relevant individuals can be parents, care providers, teachers, facility staff, siblings, and friends or peers (in some cases), depending on the setting or settings in which the problem behavior is occurring. For the present concern, the purpose of behavioral interviewing is to identify observable behaviors that appear to constitute the reason for the referral. Following is a list of behaviors you would have to pinpoint further in observable, measurable terms:

- Hyperactive
- Oppositional
- Lazy
- Uncaring
- Unappreciative
- Disturbed
- Undersocialized
- Emotionally labile

- Forgetful
- Impulsive
- Spiteful
- Aggressive
- Angry
- Schizophrenic
- Borderline personality

Why is it important to pinpoint such terms? Can one conduct an FBA on a child's hyperactivity? Absolutely not. Ambiguous terms lead to unreliability in recording the frequency of behavior. If the rate of the target behavior cannot be counted on to be accurate (reliable) from one day to the next, how can any other information that is tied to such data be accurate? It cannot! What happens if you attempt to conduct an FBA of an unobservable vague entity instead of a pinpointed target problem behavior? You get a bumper sticker slogan: Garbage in, garbage out!

One useful technique to utilize in a behavioral interview to pinpoint specific observable behaviors is called the Incident Method. Using the Incident Method, you try to get the interviewee to specify incidents that represent the referred problem or trait being presented. For example, if the referral source indicated that a child was incorrigible, you would ask the referral source to identify previous events or incidents that were representative of the child's incorrigibility. This often leads to specific observable behaviors and usually identifies the antecedent conditions for the behavior.

As an example, Table 2.4 shows some questions you might pose to help uncover the observable behaviors that constitute the reason for the referral of the child who was uncontrollable and incorrigible.

The questions in Table 2.4 attempt to get the interviewee to pinpoint specific observable behaviors. If they still use unobservable terms when describing the child or client, stop them at that point in the conversation and ask them to describe specifically what the child did or did not do. I often use the phrase "Tell me what I would have seen the child

### *TABLE 2.4* ■ QUESTIONS USED TO "PINPOINT" WITH THE INCIDENT METHOD

1. Can you remember a time when(the child) was incorrigible? For example, was the child incorrigible anytime today? If so, what happened?

2. Describe to me the circumstances that occurred at this time.

3. What did you consider in this incident to be representative of his incorrigibility?

4. Are there any other circumstances that really describe that same attitude or behavior? Describe exactly what happened.

5. Are there any other incidents of behavior that you feel I should be aware of and that possibly shed more light on his demeanor? If so, paint me a picture of that (those) incident(s).

do if I was there." Eventually, one can get down to specific observable behaviors using this method.

The Incident Method is very useful from the standpoint of time and efficiency. However, in some cases, the Incident Method may not yield the specific observable behaviors that are deemed problematic. A second effective method to help pinpoint observable behaviors is to schedule time to observe the client when it is highly likely that she will exhibit the behavior of interest. With the aid of the referral sources indicating times when the behavior problem is most likely, you can directly observe the problem behavior in the setting of interest. Subsequently, you can formulate a definition of the problem behavior in observable terms that matches what you observed. If the behavior problem is highly frequent, so that one can view a number of occurrences in a short (30–60 minute) session, this second method may be preferable to the Incident Method. However, some circumstances may preclude direct observation of the client in natural environments for a long enough period. In these circumstances, an initial definition of the problem behavior may need to be obtained through the Incident Method.

### DISCUSSION QUESTIONS

1. Hyperactivity is not a pinpointed behavior. Yet, you may receive a referral for a child with *hyperactivity* listed as the problem. Detail how you would decide what observable behaviors define a particular child's problem of hyperactivity.
2. *Auditory hallucinations* is not a pinpointed behavior, although it is a frequent referral problem. How would you define an observable event that could be measured objectively and would capture the behavior that led to the person being identified as having auditory hallucinations?

## MEASURING OBSERVABLE BEHAVIOR

Once a behavior has been pinpointed, you need to identify and select a method of quantifying the level of the behavior. Methods of measuring and quantifying the level of behavior are presented elsewhere in greater detail (Alberto & Troutman, 2006; Martin & Pear, 2007; Miltenberger, 2004) but basically include the following: frequency of occurrence, duration (or length of time), and percentage of occurrence (interval recording methods). Collecting such data has been termed *baseline assessment*.

Frequency is the most common measure of behavior because it is the least complex. Frequency counts merely require that someone count (and record) the number of times a behavior occurs.

Table 2.5 presents hypothetical data for three target behaviors across a 3-day period for a 5-year-old girl living with her adoptive parents. Note on 9/21, the girl had three instances of tantrums (defined as yelling, screaming, threats to parent, kicking walls and furniture), five instances of verbal refusal (defined as verbally refusing to follow a parental instruction to complete a task, chore, or assignment), and no instances of hitting either of her two siblings. Data similarly was collected on the same target behaviors for 9/22 and 9/23.

*TABLE 2.5* ■ **FREQUENCY OF THREE TARGET BEHAVIORS FOR A 5-YEAR-OLD GIRL IN THE HOME**

| Date | Frequency of Tantrums | Frequency of Verbal Refusal | Frequency of Hitting Siblings |
|------|----------------------|----------------------------|-------------------------------|
| 9/21 | XXX | XXXXX | 0 |
| 9/22 | 0 | X | 0 |
| 9/23 | XXXX | XXXXXX | X |

*TABLE 2.6* ■ **DURATION OF TWO TARGET BEHAVIORS FOR A 25-YEAR-OLD CLIENT IN AN INPATIENT TREATMENT FACILITY**

| Date | Duration of Verbal Outburst/Tantrum | Duration of Leaving Area Unauthorized |
|---|---|---|
| 9/1 | (25″) (16″) | (21′) (7′) (17′) |
| 9/22 | (50″) (85″) | (3′) (33′) (65′) |

Duration measurement requires that one measure the length of time a behavior occurs. Therefore, such a measurement system requires a timepiece of some kind (e.g., stopwatch, second hand on a watch). For that reason, duration measures are not frequently used in classrooms, residential settings, or community and work environments.

Table 2.6 shows the duration of each episode of target behavior. On 9/2, the client had two verbal outbursts: one of 50 seconds and one of 1 minute and 25 seconds in length. The client also left the area unauthorized three times on 9/2, one time for 3 minutes, one time for 33 minutes, and the last instance for 65 minutes.

Duration measures are preferred when the target behavior occurs across varying time frames. For example, in Table 2.6, the range of leaving area unauthorized on 9/2 is from 3 minutes to 65 minutes. To depict such a phenomenon as only occurring three times is to miss the fact that two of those episodes were quite lengthy. Although three tantrums on a given day for this client may seem reasonable, when they last for long periods, a significant problem exists. To not portray the duration data with a client and target problem such as this would probably misrepresent the nature and extent of the problem. In these cases, frequency data alone is insufficient as an accurate method of portraying the extent of the target behavior.

Percentage of occurrence is very popular with test items or situations where a client is given a certain number of opportunities to do something, and one can therefore measure the number of times a behavior occurs over the total number of opportunities. Percentage of occurrence is also utilized in interval recording systems, but such systems are too labor intensive to be considered in most applied settings. In most applied settings, frequency data is the most often collected data due to the impracticality of the other methods and will be primarily addressed in this section. The following hypothetical example provides another data sheet illustrating the frequency of two problem behaviors for an adolescent male in a residential treatment center.

The staff at the facility records the number of incidents of the two behaviors in Table 2.7: (1) verbal abuse to peers and (2) threatening gestures to peers. The data sheet is kept on a desk or a clipboard. Whenever Lorenzo exhibits either or both behaviors, the staff put one mark in the appropriate column and row (behavior and date of occurrence). The data sheet in Table 2.7 indicates that Lorenzo had seven instances of verbal abuse on 3/16 and one incident of threatening gestures toward a peer. For school personnel, a number of problem behaviors with definitions from research studies is provided in Table 2.8.

*TABLE 2.7* ■ **FREQUENCY DATA SHEET FOR TWO PROBLEM BEHAVIORS**

Child's Name: Lorenzo Vittorio
Baseline Condition

| Date | Problem Behaviors | |
|---|---|---|
| | Verbal abuse to peers | Threatening gestures to peers |
| 3/16 | XXXXX XX | X |
| 3/17 | XX | XXX |
| 3/20 | XXXXX XXXX | XXXX |

*TABLE 2.8* ■ **DEFINITIONS OF COMMON CLASSROOM PROBLEM BEHAVIORS**

| Reference | Behavior/Definition |
|---|---|
| Hall, Lund, & Jackson (1968) | *study behavior*<br>orientation toward appropriate person or object |
| Thomas, Becker, & Armstrong (1968) | disruptive behavior<br>*gross motor*<br>getting out of seat, running, hopping, rocking, moving chair<br>*noise making*<br>tapping feet, clapping, rattling, slamming or tapping objects on desk<br>*orienting*<br>turning head or body away from teacher<br>*verbalization*<br>conversation with other students, calling out the teacher's name, coughing loudly<br>*aggression*<br>hitting any part of self or another person |
| Zeilberger, Sampen, & Sloane (1968) | *bossing*<br>directing another child or adult to do (or not do) something |
| Hart, Reynolds, Baer, Brawley, & Harris (1968) | *cooperative play*<br>examples listed in article |
| Madsen, Becker, & Thomas (1968) | inappropriate classroom behavior<br>examples listed in article<br>*appropriate behavior*<br>time on task |
| Phillips (1968) | *Aggressive statements*<br>examples listed in article<br>punctuality<br>examples listed in article<br>*poor grammar*<br>"ain't" |
| Sailor, Guess, Rutherford, & Baer (1968) | tantrum behaviors<br>see article |
| Walker & Buckley (1968) | *attending behavior (on-task)*<br>looking at assignment pages, working problems, recording *responses*<br>*nonattending behavior*<br>those incompatible with above |
| Ward & Baker (1968) | *disruptive behaviors*<br>see article<br>*motor behavior (at seat)*<br>gross motor behavior (not at seat)<br>*aggression*<br>deviant talking<br>*nonattending disobedience*<br>*thumb sucking*<br>*hand raising* |
| O'Leary, Becker, Evans, & Saudargas (1969) | *disturbing another's property*<br>tearing up others paper, grabbing their book(s)<br>*inappropriate tasks:*<br>working on spelling during math, doodling |
| Zimmerman, Zimmerman, & Russell (1969) | *instruction-following behaviors*<br>30 instructions, see article |
| Barrish, Saunders, & Wolf (1969) | *talking out, out of seat* |
| Wahler (1969) | *oppositional behavior:*<br>failure to follow request of parent |
| Schmidt & Ulrich (1969) | *classroom noise*<br>sound-level meter 42 dB or higher |
| Cantrell, Cantrell, Huddleston, & Woolridge (1969) | *assignment completion* |
| Schutte & Hopkins (1970) | *instruction following (kindergarten)*<br>10 common instructions |
| Bailey, Phillips, & Wolf (1970) | *rule violations*<br>6 rules in article |

It is helpful to provide the person(s) at the sites with the tools to collect the baseline observation data of the client. The following is a list of tools that facilitate the collection of baseline data:

1. Wrist counters (for frequency measures)
2. Data sheets
3. Stopwatches (for duration measures)
4. Tape recorders (for frequency measures)
5. Laptop computer or PDA
6. iPhone or Blackberry

Is behavioral data collection just as important in psychiatric and mental health facilities? Of course. Such data collection is just as crucial to the understanding of the client's problems. Examine the following scenario of a hypothetical client in an inpatient unit whose social worker reports that she is "decompensating." If the professional staff do not get more explicit, intervention will be difficult. There is no effective behavioral intervention for the phenomenon of "decompensating." Unless specific observable measures of actual behaviors are being measured, one does not have the slightest idea of what problems need to be addressed.

## CASE EXAMPLE

Maria, an adult female diagnosed with schizophrenia who resides in an inpatient unit at a mental health facility, is described by Ms. Johnson as decompensating. After several months of case conferences and different milieu treatments, Maria's condition does not improve. A behavioral consultant, Dr. Kellog, is contacted to consult with staff. The staff report to Dr. Kellog that Maria used to be more responsive to her social environment. Her GAF score on Axis V of the *DSM IV-R* manual was 65, now it is 30. She has continued to "decompensate." Staff provide the behavioral consultant nursing progress notes from the last 3 months. These records have various remarks about her eating habits and interactions with staff and other residents. Although there are hints of some problem behaviors in these notes, they are inadequate for Dr. Kellog's need for specific target behaviors. Further, such notes do not provide a baseline measurement of such behaviors. Social withdrawal appears in several entries. Unfortunately, there are no definable behaviors that delineate what Maria does (or does not do) when she exhibits social withdrawal. Was she curled up in a corner? Was she not getting out of bed? Did she not respond to someone's verbal initiation to her? The nursing notes do not clearly specify the behavior problems.

After interviewing staff and utilizing the incident method, Dr. Kellog surmises that three behaviors may be at the heart of Maria's problem, which was described by staff as decompensating. The target behaviors that were gleaned to be problematic are the following: (1) physical aggression, (2) making hallucinatory statements, and (3) failure to engage in and sustain social conversations with staff or peers. Physical aggression was defined as striking or pushing another person. Hallucinatory statements were defined as verbal statements referencing auditory events that were not observed by others who were in the area. Sustaining conversations was defined as any time that the client initiated and sustained an appropriate conversation with a staff person or other client on the unit. With this information, the following data was collected across the period of 4/13 through 4/21 (see Table 2.9).

### TABLE 2.9 ■ DATA FOR MARIA

| Date Sustained | Physical Aggression | Hallucinatory Statements | Conversations |
|---|---|---|---|
| 4/13 | 10 | 6 | 2 |
| 4/14 | 5 | 3 | 3 |
| 4/15 | 5 | 3 | 1 |
| 4/16 | 2 | 9 | 0 |
| 4/17 | 3 | 12 | 0 |
| 4/18 | 9 | 16 | 2 |
| 4/19 | 1 | 0 | 0 |
| 4/20 | 0 | 1 | 3 |
| 4/21 | 2 | 11 | 0 |

In viewing the data, one can see that there are days when physical aggression is high, as is the frequency of hallucinatory statements. It is quite possible that the increase in these two behaviors combined with a low frequency of initiating and sustaining appropriate conversations is leading to the judgment by professional staff that Maria is decompensating. However, now it is clearer what target behaviors need to be addressed with a behavioral intervention plan.

## DISCUSSION QUESTION

Why is it important to define a client's problem in observable terms, as in the case of Dr. Kellogg's evaluation?

It is important to collect the rate of occurrence of a problem behavior in the baseline assessment period. However, schools and agencies have found that it often is not perceived as important by personnel who are asked to collect such data in addition to their other duties (whether this perception is valid or not). As a result, data collection may not be conducted in a timely fashion, if at all. To make everyone's life simpler in these circumstances, let us look at some possible solutions to this dilemma.

Rather than having the teacher, staff person, or parent collect continuous data (observing for the behavior all the time), you might consider a time sampling data collection method. In some cases, the behavior being targeted is so infrequent and distinct that one can easily measure its occurrence whenever it happens, for example, loud tantrums in the classroom. In these situations, asking for each occurrence may not be perceived as a difficult or unreasonable request. However, in some cases where the behavior occurs more than several times an hour (an estimate can be provided by the interviewee), asking personnel to collect data for each occurrence may give them the impression that you are demanding and unaware of their other responsibilities. In these circumstances, you can have the person collect data on a limited sample of the total length of time.

For example, if you were interested in collecting data on a child's rate of disruptive behaviors during class time, you would sample possibly three to five, 15- to 20-minute time periods across a 1- or 2-week period. Note that you can be flexible here. It doesn't have to be exactly three or five sampling periods, nor does it have to be 20 minutes each time, and you can extend the length of time needed to collect the data from 1 to 2 weeks (for that matter, if need be, 3 weeks). Flexibility is appreciated in applied settings, and inflexibility is often punished by personnel failing to follow through on your requests and avoiding you in future circumstances.

A second possibility to collect baseline data when a continuous measure may not be feasible is to conduct a trigger analysis (Rolider, 2003; Rolider & Axelrod, 2000). In this method, you present the antecedent condition that you suspect triggers the problem behavior. If you present this trigger 10 times over a 1-week period, you can determine what percentage of time the problem behavior occurs to the trigger. Of course, you have to have a reasonable suspicion that such an antecedent condition is a trigger.

Let's say you are referred an adult with developmental disabilities in a community-based program. The case manager reports that the client does not cooperate with coworkers when asked. You spend several hours over two afternoons watching him. Disappointingly, these direct observations do not provide sufficient opportunities to view his cooperative behavior in the natural context. As a result of the client's lack of cooperation, such opportunities are rarely presented by staff (because they predict the outcome of such encounters).

You determine that contriving a situation may provide the needed information on this client's problem in a more timely fashion. To assess the client's ability to cooperate, as well as the presence of possible unacceptable behaviors, you set up the following situation with help from the client's coworkers. They will present the client with the opportunity to cooperate with them in a task, such as helping them pick up the tools at their workstation. You would make sure that tools were left out to set up the condition for social interaction. Further, you coach the other workers to make a request of the client to help them pick up the tools. It then becomes easier to determine if cooperation occurs (or not) in these contrived conditions. These tests can be designed over several different situations (helping at the lunch table, helping with other work tasks, etc.) until you feel you have a handle on this client's rate of cooperative behavior.

A trigger analysis is particularly suited in examining the rate of relatively infrequent problem behaviors. With low rate behaviors, it may take weeks (or months) to observe a single instance of target behavior. However, if you are reasonably certain that such a low-rate behavior is triggered by a relatively infrequent event in the environment, then a trigger analysis is a great method to study such a behavior. In order to conduct the trigger analysis of low-rate problem behaviors, you may have to expose the client or child to the motivating condition (present aversive stimulus or deprive access to reinforcer) prior to the presentation of the trigger. This is termed *presession exposure* to the establishing or abolishing operation (Rolider, Iwata, & Camp, 2006) and allows for more probable conditions for target behavior to occur.

Table 2.10 presents a chart illustrating how one would conduct a trigger analysis for three suspected triggers for three different children across a 1-week period (Rolider, 2003). You will note that in the first two hypothetical examples, the data indicates that the behavior analyst has identified the trigger. In the third example, it would seem something else is triggering (another MO or discriminative stimulus) the behavior.

## DISCUSSION QUESTION

How would you use trigger analysis to collect data for a client who engages in property destructive behavior when asked to end his break and get back to work? Apparently, such behavior does not occur each time he is asked to get back to work. However, the severity of the incident makes effective intervention a high priority. The staff persons have reported the client rarely gets disruptive, but when he does the area "gets leveled." They say they have figured out how to handle this circumstance, and therefore, the reported rate of occurrence is low (hence the need for a trigger analysis). Why would the rate of such behavior be low in "real-life" when compared to the proportion or rate a trigger analysis may generate?

*TABLE 2.10* ■ **PRESENTING SUSPECTED "TRIGGERS" FOR TARGET PROBLEM BEHAVIOR**

| Child | Suspected Trigger | Presented Stimulus Condition | Across Different Settings and/or Persons | Ratio or Percentage of Occurrence of Target Behavior[a] |
|---|---|---|---|---|
| 8-year-old child who infrequently screams violently at adults (form makes it a problem) | Interrupting child during preferred event | When child is engaged in favored activity, interrupt him with a question or request | School, home, park, mom, dad, teacher | 6/8 times with mom, 3/4 times with teacher[a] |
| 5-year-old child who bangs her head on floor once every few months | Withholding desired item, child required to wait | Ask child to wait contingent upon a request for a favored item | Mom, dad, older sibling | 5/5 with older sibling, 1/3 times with dad[a] |
| 11-year-old student with developmental disabilities who throws personal property three times a year, but damages property and hurts nearby clients with this tirade | Giving child nonpreferred event | When child asks for an item, give him a less preferred item instead | At school across different teachers and aides | 1/5 with aide, 2/7 times with teacher, 4/4 times with substitute teacher[a] |

[a]Number of times problem behavior occurs to the trigger / total number of times the trigger was presented.

### What Is Baseline Data?

The result of this first step in the behavioral assessment is the production of the baseline rate of occurrence for the problem behavior. Baseline data is the measurement of the target behavior in its current natural state prior to the proposed intervention (Alberto & Troutman, 2006; Martin & Pear, 2007; Miltenberger, 2004). Baseline data presents the level of the target behavior prior to the intervention and reflects the level of behavior under the current conditions, whereby such a level of behavior would be predicted in the future should the baseline conditions remain in effect.

How long should one collect baseline data? There is no set definitive answer. Rather, baseline data should be collected for as long as necessary for a reliable pattern to emerge. If the data is trending up or down, it is essential to continue collecting baseline data until some stability is achieved.

A sample summary data sheet for a hypothetical 6-year-old child across 8 days of baseline data collection for three different behaviors is presented in Table 2.11. This data sheet indicates the rate of tantrum behavior on 4/13 was 10 occurrences. The rate of leaving the house on the same day was 6 times, whereas the rate of noncompliance was 9 times.

Baseline data has several purposes. First, baseline data gives you a quantitative view of the level of the target behavior at the current level. In contrast to someone saying "it happens a lot," when questioned how much a behavior occurs, one can quantitatively represent the level of the behavior. Second, it provides you with a basis for comparison when deploying a treatment. If the rate of the target behavior of toileting accidents is between 1 and 4 per day (mean of 2), a comparison between the problem behavior before treatment and after is possible. One can see that a treatment to address toileting accidents that results in 1 to 2 per week produced substantial improvement. Such a treatment is well worth maintaining until the behavior can be under control over naturally occurring contingencies. Finally, it often is used in designing the initial behavioral criterion for reinforcement for both the target problem behavior as well as the replacement behavior.

## CONDUCTING A FUNCTIONAL BEHAVIOR ASSESSMENT (FBA)

With the first step, you have now identified how frequent the problem behavior is occurring. You have collected the baseline level of target problem behavior. However, so much more needs to be understood before you are ready to develop a hypothesis about the reason for the client's behavior and, further, what functional behavior analytic treatments are best suited for these circumstances. For example, knowing that a child is noncompliant to

*TABLE 2.11* ■ **SAMPLE FREQUENCY DATA SHEET FOR PROBLEM BEHAVIORS IN HOME**

| Date | Tantrum Behavior | Leaving the House | Noncompliance |
|------|------------------|-------------------|---------------|
| 4/13 | 10 | 6 | 9 |
| 4/14 | 5 | 3 | 5 |
| 4/17 | 3 | 0 | 2 |
| 4/18 | 9 | 1 | 3 |
| 4/20 | 6 | 4 | 4 |
| 4/21 | 5 | 5 | 7 |
| 4/22 | 6 | 4 | 5 |
| 4/25 | 7 | 5 | 7 |

parental requests between 30% to 60% of the time across five baseline sessions does not provide any information on why he is noncompliant. It merely tells us that his level may be unacceptable (depending on his age). What is also needed is information that reveals the purpose or function this behavior serves in the client's current environment. Determining the environmental purpose a problem behavior serves cannot be gleaned from data presenting its rate of occurrence only. One needs to collect additional information that provides clues as to the environmental events responsible for the maintenance of the problem behavior. The process of determining the function or purpose of a problem behavior is a requisite for functional treatment. We have termed this process a Functional Behavior Assessment (FBA).

You generate a hypothesis about the reason for the maintenance of problem behavior prior to prescribing a treatment. This hypothesis is generated when certain questions are answered (tentatively, of course) through one or several behavioral assessment methods that are designed to uncover a problem behavior's current maintaining contingency. Based on your hypothesis about the function (purpose) of the behavior, you then can select a treatment strategy for the problem behavior that addresses the functional characteristics of the problem situation.

Table 2.12 illustrates the role of hypothesis generation in a case of noncompliance. The selected hypothesis leads in selecting a designated treatment that will be unique to that hypothesis regarding the *current environmental function or purpose* of the target behavior.

## DISCUSSION QUESTIONS

Explain how the aggressive behavior of a hypothetical 12-year-old child can require two different behavioral treatments. Why would different treatments be needed for the same target behavior?

One caveat needs to be made in determining the function or functions of the problem behavior. Selecting a hypothesis regarding the maintenance of the behavior does not mean that you have identified the original factor in the genesis of the behavior. The reason for the current maintenance of a behavior could be quite different from its original cause. Your focus is on the current maintaining contingencies. You examine the existing conditions of the problem behavior and determine that the recorded level of the problem behavior is being maintained as a result of its current purpose or function.

There are at least five common methods, varying in form and reliability, in collecting evidence via an FBA: (1) behavioral interviewing, (2) scatter plot data, (3) A-B-C descriptive analysis method, (4) analogue assessment, and (5) in-situ hypothesis test.

### Behavioral Interviewing

Directly observing the referred child or client in the natural setting is always the most preferable approach to collecting data. The latter four techniques do require direct observation

*TABLE 2.12* ■ **HYPOTHESIS GENERATION**

| Hypothesis | | Functional Treatment |
| --- | --- | --- |
| noncompliance maintained by function A | $\rightarrow$ | specific treatment for problems maintained by A |
| noncompliance maintained by function B | $\rightarrow$ | specific treatment for problems maintained by B (different from above) |

of the client and, therefore, are inherently more preferable. However, very often you may find yourself relying, to some extent, on a behavioral interview in an attempt to analyze a problem behavior's function. Behavioral interviews can be useful in uncovering the maintaining contingencies, given the right questions. Additionally, they can provide information that allows you to be more exacting in what to measure with the other assessment methods.

In conducting a behavioral interview, the people primarily involved with the child or client in the specific setting or settings (e.g., parents, teachers, therapists, staff, etc.) are interviewed. In collecting interview information on why a problem behavior is occurring, you examine the relationship between the behavior and some consequent event. Your use of specific questions can help you discern possible functional relationships between the problem behavior and the current maintaining contingencies. Table 2.13 presents general questions aimed at discerning if the problem behavior serves a positive reinforcement function, whereas Table 2.14 presents questions for a negative reinforcement function.

The first question assesses the possibility that the behavior is maintained by access to a specific item or event, either directly or indirectly. In reviewing the information obtained, ask the following questions: What environmental changes occur as a result of the person's behavior? Does the behavior serve to get something that was not available before the behavior occurred? Is it possible that the problem behavior has to occur for some duration, or at some level of occurrence, before it accesses the desired event or item?

The second question asks, "Why does the client resort to this behavior over other behaviors to get the desired item/activity?" Suppose the answer to Question 1 reveals that a child's tantrum behavior of several minutes duration is effective in getting Dad to let the child go outside after dinner. If tantrum behavior is adaptive, other behaviors are apparently less functional in that regard. Perhaps asking nicely to go outside is ignored or responded to in the following manner: "Not until you finish all your chores and homework." Hence, the utility of an appropriate verbal request in getting outside in a short time frame is "zero." Given that scenario, tantrum behavior may be a faster manner of getting outside to play with friends than finishing all one's homework.

You should consider that some problem behaviors may produce different reinforcers under different conditions. Question 3 makes such inquiries during the interview process. For example, a baby cries when it wants to be picked up, get fed, get clothes changed, be coddled, and a host of other events. To assume that crying always means a food request from the baby would be a gross mistake and would result in many vain attempts to feed the infant when she is not hungry.

### TABLE 2.13 ■ QUESTIONS FOR ASCERTAINING A POSITIVE REINFORCEMENT FUNCTION

1.  Is the problem behavior maintained by accessing some event, or set of events, directly or through social mediation? Does such behavior serve to access that event every time or intermittently? Is there a reliable relation between the problem behavior and the presentation of this event? What is the specific object, activity, or event that the client is attempting to access through this behavior?

2.  Are there other behaviors in the client's repertoire that also can produce this desired event or set of events? Are they as efficient at producing the specific positive reinforcer as the problem behavior (see Horner & Day, 1991)? Is the problem behavior more likely to produce the desired event than these other behaviors? Which behavior produces the greatest density of specific reinforcement in terms of the event?

3.  Does the problem behavior produce more than one positive reinforcer? What are the conditions under which it produces one reinforcer in contrast to another reinforcer? In other words, what are the different antecedent conditions in which the behavior may serve different purposes?

*TABLE 2.14* ■ **QUESTIONS FOR ASCERTAINING A NEGATIVE REINFORCEMENT FUNCTION**

1.  Is the problem behavior maintained by escaping (or in some cases completely avoiding) some event, directly or through social mediation? Does such behavior serve to escape that event every time, or on some intermittent schedule? Is there a reliable relation between the problem behavior and the termination or postponement of the aversive event(s)? What is the specific object, activity, or event that the client is attempting to escape through this behavior?

2.  Are there other behaviors in the client's repertoire that also can escape (or avoid) such aversive conditions and events? Are they as efficient at escaping the aversive conditions as the problem behavior (see Horner & Day, 1991)? Which behavior produces the greatest density of reinforcement upon its occurrence, given the presence of the aversive event (or its impending presentation)?

3.  Does the problem behavior successfully escape most aversive conditions? Is the behavior successful at escaping many instructional conditions or requests? What are the presenting aversive conditions when such a behavior serves an escape function or purpose? Is there more than one event or activity in which the client uses these behaviors to escape?

The three questions in Table 2.14 aim to uncover possible escape functions of problem behaviors. The questions are similar to the questions in Table 2.13, except the focus here is determining if the function of the problem behavior is primarily escape (or avoidance) of an aversive event. Negative reinforcement is probably inherent when the problem behavior reliably results in withdrawal or termination of the undesired event or activity. The target behavior should also be more successful in achieving that end of activity than other behaviors. Lastly, the target behavior occurs in the presence of an aversive event (or one that is about to be presented).

The questions from Tables 2.13 and 2.14 are aimed at uncovering the event or events responsible for the maintenance of the problem behavior. Please do not always assume that the behavior is maintained by the first event or "thing" one sees after the behavior occurs. Very often, it is not. You have to examine all the events that reliably occur after the behavior as well as all the events that are abruptly stopped or withdrawn. It is a lot like playing detective, and your hypothesis is a hunch about the factors responsible for the problem behavior.

A hypothetical example can aid in your understanding of the importance of good leading questions during a behavioral interview. Let's take the case of the 4-year-old child who throws toys (previous example) as an illustration of examining possible scenarios in which he throws his toys and how that allows for a hypothesis about the function of the behavior (see Table 2.15).

Note that the questions are aimed at uncovering the reason for the problem behavior, either as behavior that is positively reinforced, or one that serves its purpose by removing an aversive command or request or impending activity (i.e., negative reinforcement). Note that only at the end do you ask the interviewee why he or she thinks the client does the behavior. Presenting this question at the end allows the interviewee to see that you are interested in a current environmental reason for the behavior. Asking the staff or parents that question first often leads to some explanation of factors that are far removed from the current social context, for example, "He does it because he is autistic, comes from a broken home, is conduct-disordered, hates me." Such inferences and explanations do not help in conducting an FBA and should only be examined once the data from the client's current social context is available. At the University of Florida, work is under way to develop and validate a rating scale questionnaire that produces information about a problem behavior's possible function from parents or care providers and children. It is called the Questionnaire About Behavioral Function, or QABF (Van Camp, Witherup, Vollmer, & Prestemon, 2006).

### TABLE 2.15 ■ POSSIBLE PARENT INTERVIEW QUESTIONS FOR TOY THROWING BEHAVIOR

1.  When he throws his toys, does he reliably get attention or physical contact from his parents? Is throwing toys better than other behaviors are at getting his parents' attention? Do other people also give him attention in that manner when he throws his toys? If not, is the rate of toy throwing higher with his parents than when he is with other caregivers?

2.  When he throws his toys, does somebody get him another toy or object? Is it conceivable that he throws the toy he is currently in possession of to play with another toy at that time?

3.  Is there anything tangible (food, drink, etc.) that he gets when he throws his toys from his parents or someone else? Will he continue throwing the toys until someone brings him the desired food or drink item?

4.  Does someone get hit with the toy when he throws it? Is it possible that he is aiming at someone in particular? If he does hit, for example, a child with the toy, what is that child's reaction upon being hit? Does the child cry and become upset? What does he do when they cry?

5.  Where does the toy usually land? Does it usually hit a wall? Does it usually break? Does he like the sound it produces when it hits the wall? Does he appear to enjoy that result?

6.  Does he throw toys when it is time to change from a play activity to another activity that he may deem as not fun? Does he throw toys when he is asked to put them *away*? Does he throw his toys when he is asked to do something? When he throws the toys under one of these conditions, does it usually postpone the impending activity or transition to another activity for some time?

7.  Why do you think this child throws his toys?

Understanding the result of the behavior as a socially mediated environmental effect or the direct consequence of the behavior (under certain antecedent conditions) can allow you to determine the maintaining contingency. Your task is to discern the desired result of the behavior from the individual's standpoint. The questions in Table 2.16 can help you "zero in" on the maintaining contingency from the host of answers you receive to these interview questions:

The four questions in Table 2.16 will be used once all the information has been collected to determine which of four major diagnostic categories is most relevant for understanding the function of the problem behavior. Question 1 attempts to determine if a reliable contingency exists between the problem behavior and the hypothesized maintaining contingency. In ascertaining this, one needs to address whether such a behavior is more efficient and effective at getting the desired event than other behaviors (see Question 2). If a client is allowed to get food from the refrigerator when he wants, then other problem behaviors become less probable when food access is the motivational condition. Therefore, diagnosing the problem behavior in terms of such a contingency would not make sense. In contrast, when other behaviors, such as getting your own food or asking nicely, are impeded and therefore not reinforced, then the conditions are ripe for problem behavior to become instrumental in getting food when relatively hungry.

### TABLE 2.16 ■ QUESTIONS TO ZERO IN ON MAINTAINING CONTINGENCY

1.  Does the problem behavior appear to reliably produce the hypothesized contingency?

2.  Is the problem behavior more efficient and effective at producing such a contingency, in contrast to other behaviors that may (or may not) produce the same contingency?

3.  In the case of a positive reinforcement contingency, does the behavior usually occur in the absence of the desired event or object?

4.  In the case of a negative reinforcement contingency, does the behavior usually occur in the presence (or advent) of the aversive, undesired event or object?

Question 3 addresses the operative motivating condition, given the hypothesized maintaining contingency. If a behavior is functional in getting food, then its occurrence would be in the absence of having food, or possibly as the individual has finished all her food (and wants more). In other words, in order for a behavior to be maintained because it produces a specific reinforcer, such an event must be in a relative deprivation at the time of the response occurrence. Concurrently, once food is accessed, does the problem behavior desist once access to the supposed reinforcer took place? Let's say that being picked up by a child's parents is hypothesized as the factor maintaining her crying. If the child is picked up and continues to cry, does it make sense that she cried to get picked up? It would appear that being picked up was not the motivational variable in this case of crying. One would venture to state that crying had a different function at that time.

Question 4 addresses the same issue as Question 3 except that in negative reinforcement, the motivating condition is present—the undesired event. Possibly, with purely avoidance functions, the aversive event is not currently present but is impending (making such avoidance behavior difficult to diagnose). Once the event is removed or terminated does the behavior stop, given that escape has resulted?

## DISCUSSION QUESTIONS

What are some interview questions you would ask if you suspect that a child's self-injury is maintained by positive reinforcement? What questions would you pose if negative reinforcement seems to be the maintaining contingency?

The following is a hypothetical scenario of a behavioral interview with a parent (Mrs. M) who has presented the problem of her 4-year-old child throwing his toys. The hypothetical responses are provided along with the analysis of the answer, contained in parentheses, by the behavioral psychologist.

*Dr. Cipani:* Mrs. M. I would like to find out more about the circumstances when John throws his toys, so I will better understand this behavior problem. When John throws his toys, what do you do? What do you say to him?

*Mom:* I tell him he won't get any more toys if he mistreats them. I sometimes put him in time out, but that does not seem to work.

*Dr. Cipani:* (*I am not sure if either of those consequences, that is, warning him and time out, are followed through reliably enough for me to consider their possible role in toy throwing.*) Mrs. M, do you pick him up when he throws his toys, possibly in an effort to redirect him?

*Mom:* Well, sometimes I do, but very often I have his almost 2-year-old sister in my arms. When I go to pick him up, and put her down, then she starts crying. It seems like I do not have enough arms.

*Dr. Cipani:* (*Aha! Maybe we are getting somewhere now. Possibly this child becomes jealous when his sister is getting attention and physical contact from his mother, thus setting up the motivational context for him to engage in behavior that results in mom picking him up. Let me follow that up with an analysis of the strength of more appropriate behaviors in getting mom's arms.*) Yes, Mrs. M., you do seem to have your hands full. Does John ever ask to be picked up when he is playing with his toys? Especially at times that it would be difficult because you have his sister in your arms?

*Mom:* Well sometimes he does, but you know I cannot oblige him when I have his sister in my arms. I am just not strong enough to hold both of them. He also whines sometimes when I do not pick him up. But I was told by experts on TV to ignore "whiney-type" behavior.

*Dr. Cipani: (OK, it appears that John does resort to other behaviors to get picked up, but such are not as successful as toy throwing in getting his mom to pick him up. Let me test out the possibility of toy throwing serving a socially mediated escape function from a demand to put away his toys.)* Does John throw his toys when he is asked to put them away?

*Mom:* Not usually. In some cases, I don't even ask him to pick up his toys, if we need to go somewhere, I will do it with him later. However, he is often pretty good about putting away his toys, especially when I help him and we make it a fun activity, with his sister getting in the act, too.

*Dr. Cipani: (It does not appear that such a demand is driving the toy throwing. In her answer, I keep seeing John's desire for her attention when his sister is around, and the sister competing for it as well. Let me make sure that leaving the play time period is not a condition that sets off toy throwing.)* Does John object to leaving the play area to go to another activity?

*Mom:* Sometimes, like when it is time to take a bath in the evening. He will cry and scream and throw a tantrum on the floor, particularly if the play period was kind of short. I think he hates to take a bath.

*Dr. Cipani:* Any toy throwing occurring before bath time, say over the last 2 weeks?

*Mom:* No, just tantrum behavior usually.

*Dr. Cipani: (Well, it looks like toy throwing serves to get mom to pick him up on some intermittent basis. Other behaviors are not as reliable in getting mom to pick him up when his sibling is competing for the same thing. However, tantrum behaviors appear to be the optimal selection when John wants to avoid taking a bath. Perhaps the A-B-C chart should be set up for recording behavior when he is playing with toys and to determine whether toy throwing is correlated with his sister being held and receiving attention from his mom at the time.)* Thank you. You have been most helpful. I would like to suggest that we start examining John's toy throwing behavior by collecting what we call "baseline data" [explanation of such is offered].

A series of interview questions are presented in Tables 2.17 and 2.18 that address different socially mediated functions relevant for school settings.

---

### DISCUSSION QUESTION

Explain how a client's spitting behavior can be maintained by two different reinforcement contingencies. (Hint: think of people who chew tobacco.)

---

### A-B-C Descriptive Analysis

Professionals are at a loss when treating children or clients with problem behavior. Professional involvement in the child's daily life is minimal, if at all. Rather, teachers, parents, staff persons in facilities, and care providers are people who can be intimately familiar with the circumstances involving the client and target behavior. In a perfect world, such direct line personnel would be sufficiently trained in applied behavior analysis to be able to analyze behavioral function and the antecedent conditions. They would simply come to the professional in the end and say,

*TABLE 2.17* ■ **INTERVIEW QUESTIONS FOR SOCIALLY MEDIATED ACCESS FUNCTIONS FOR SCHOOL SETTINGS**

1. *Adult attention hypothesis:*

   a. When he engages in the target behavior, what do you do?
   b. What do you say after he does the target behavior?
   c. Are there other adults who might give him attention when he does the target behavior?
   d. Does he do this when you are with someone else?
   e. When he throws his books, what do you always say or do?
   f. Does he do anything else that will get you to respond in this manner?

2. *Peer attention hypothesis:*

   a. When he does the target behavior, what do his fellow students do?
   b. Do some or all laugh?
   c. Does he seem to have friends who think he is "cool" because he engages in the target behavior in class or during a group activity?
   d. Does anyone (or many) egg him on?

3. *Tangible reinforcer hypothesis:*

   a. When he engages in the target behavior, does he get something else? What is he given (even if it is several minutes after)?
   b. Does he stop the behavior once he is given this alternate activity/item?
   c. Does he get to choose an alternate activity (e.g., drawing or computer) when he is mad so that he will not do something worse?

Bobby's spitting behavior on the playground is significantly more likely when he is asked to share the tetherball or it is time for another child to have the tetherball. Further, it appears that such behavior seems to be negatively reinforced by the playground aide. This aide will make the other children wait longer for their turn when he spits on them. She tells them they must be patient because Bobby is emotionally immature. We believe this is a mistake and that such a contingency is actually exacerbating the probability of Bobby spitting on other children when it is time for him to give up the tetherball. As a result, we think the following treatment program addresses this function by removing tetherball for at least a 4-minute period when he spits. In addition, if he waits at least two minutes, without spitting, he will then be allowed to play. This DRO interval will then be progressively altered until it reaches the average wait time for tetherball. If you write up that plan we feel it could probably work.

*TABLE 2.18* ■ **INTERVIEW QUESTIONS FOR SOCIALLY MEDIATED ESCAPE FUNCTIONS FOR SCHOOL SETTINGS**

1. *Escape of instruction: lengthy task, assignment, or chore hypothesis:*

   a. Does this behavior occur subsequent to the initiation of the task or chore?
   b. Is the behavior more likely 10, 20, or 30 minutes into the task?
   c. When the behavior occurs, what happens?
   d. Is the task or assignment changed in favor of something else?
   e. Is the task postponed?
   f. How many times must the child do this behavior before the task is changed or postponed?

2. *Escape of instruction-difficult task, assignment, or chore hypothesis:*

   a. Does this behavior occur when the child is given a difficult task?
   b. Are there corollary behaviors that might indicate that the child is having difficulty with the material or assignment?
   c. Is the behavior less likely (or unlikely) when the child is given easy assignments?

3. *Escape of unpleasant social situation hypothesis:*

   a. Does this behavior allow the child to avoid a potential interaction that he may find unpleasant?
   b. What event or interaction would that be?

Sound nice? Yes! However, in the real world you are more likely to get the following analysis of Bobby's behavior: "Bobby does it because he is ADHD."

Having direct line personnel describe the conditions surrounding the behavior has been termed the A-B-C descriptive analysis method (Bijou, Peterson & Ault, 1968; Lalli, Browder, Mace, & Brown, 1993). In an A-B-C descriptive analysis system, direct line personnel observe the client. There are usually three columns for the data collection: the first column is reserved for a description of the *antecedent* conditions, the client's *behavior* is delineated in the middle column, and the final column provides a description of the *consequences* of the behavior.

In the first edition of this book, we offered a slight variation that we felt was worthwhile in your efforts to uncover the reason or reasons for the problem behavior. The slight variation examined both socially mediated consequences as well as natural (physical environment) consequences. The charting system had one column, C, for socially mediated events. The physical environmental effects were recorded in column D. Therefore, column C was reserved solely for socially mediated consequent events. We have decided that such a variation may be misunderstood, so we are reverting back to the use of the C column for both. However, the C column will be split into social mediated consequences, C-1, and direct consequences produced on the physical environment, C-2. For the future, the user should record the social consequences produced by the behavior in one area of the C column and the direct consequences in another area. An example of an A-B-C chart for a child's aggressive behavior is provided in Table 2.19.

In the example shown in Table 2.19, the targeted behavior is a particular child's aggression (i.e., hitting another child in the elementary kindergarten class). The teacher identifies the antecedent context as story time. After this behavior occurred, the teacher noted that she removed the child from the story group (*consequences*). The teacher also surmised that the natural result of the child hitting another child was that his hand probably hurt, and a sound was produced when the hitting occurred. Note that the termination of some group activity seems to be the commonality between these two descriptive analyses of the incidents. If this result "holds-up" with other incidents, then a socially mediated escape function might be entertained for the diagnosis of this behavior, given certain group activities.

The information derived from this technique is similar to that which can be obtained via behavioral interview. The A-B-C method differs from behavioral interviewing in that it requires teachers, facility staff, or parents to collect data in real time rather than recollecting past events. It may be more indicative (reliable) of actual events in that it is being collected right at the time when the behavior occurs. The A-B-C descriptive analysis method can serve as a good complement to behavioral interview data.

How does one utilize such data? You will want to review all the incidents of the target problem behavior and look for reliable relations between behavior and its consequences. Commonalties may show patterns across time between the problem behavior and certain consequences. For example, with the child in Table 2.19, his removal almost always

### TABLE 2.19 ■ EXAMPLE OF A-B-C CHART

| Antecedent Conditions | Target Behavior | Consequences of Behavior | |
| --- | --- | --- | --- |
| | | C-1 | C-2 |
| 9:20 during story time, 15 minutes into the story, | Hit peer | Removed him from story time, peer flinched, cried | Hand probably hurt, possible throbbing sensation |
| 10:30 during group music time | Hit another peer | Told to stop, peer hit back, removed both of them, sound of hit | Hand probably hurt more than prior hit |

occurs when he hits another child. Further, this behavior is more common during story time (when the child gets bored with the story and wants to escape), or during group time (probably when he wishes to terminate his participation). If other behaviors are not successful in producing escape or avoidance of the undesired activity, then hitting another child to escape or avoid these activities becomes a more plausible function. It is also possible to identify contingent relations from descriptive data using a contingency space analysis (Martens, DiGennaro, Reed, Ezczech, & Rosenthal, 2008). In a contingency space analysis, the probability of the contingency is specified for two sets of behavior classes: (1) the target problem behavior and (2) other behaviors. Therefore, in addition to viewing whether there is a reliable relation between problem behavior and the consequence deemed to be the maintaining reinforcer, the analysis also views the probability of such an consequent event in the absence of the target behavior.

## Problems With Descriptive Data

Information gleaned from A-B-C descriptive analyses often generates problems in the interpretation of a behavior's function. Perhaps two of the biggest problems in determining function are: (1) the insufficient description of the antecedent (A) condition by the user and (2) the tendency to view almost all behaviors as the result of social attention (D. Wilder, personal communication, September 1, 2009). An analysis of each of these problems follows.

The antecedent condition contains two variables, MOs and discriminative stimuli. Unfortunately, behavioral descriptions of the antecedent condition often lack a depiction of the MO. Here is why. When a behavior is maintained by negative reinforcement, the presence (or presentation) of the aversive condition (i.e., the MO) is somewhat easy to spot. Hopefully, the person who is filling out the A-B-C chart describes what someone is doing or saying to the client in column A preceding the behavior. By specifying this observable phenomenon, the behavioral description of the antecedent conditions can encumber the MO variable. Hence, the analysis of this antecedent event's value-altering effect on the reinforcer can be gleaned from the written record. Also if the user specified the person (or persons) involved in the presentation of these events, discriminative stimuli can be identified.

However, with problem behaviors maintained by positive reinforcement, deprivation will produce a value-altering effect on the potential reinforcer. Unlike the presentation of a task or social situation, one cannot usually see deprivation (MO). In cases of behavior maintained by direct or socially mediated access, the MO is not seen but has to be inferred. Therefore, to record what is happening at the time of the behavior may be tangential to the operating MO. At best, such events may be discriminative for the behavior but do not identify the MO. Hence, a naïve user does not usually delineate the deprivation condition in an A-B-C chart because this would require an adequate knowledge of the role of motivative variables.

This information can lead to a false interpretation regarding the role of the setting event as having stimulus control over the problem behavior. Actually, the setting event may be irrelevant. The particular setting event may have coincided with the deprivation state simply by chance. For example, a child skips lunch and later that day attends his brother's baseball game. He starts whining about wanting a hot dog and engages in a number of undesirable behaviors. Of course the presence of his parents is discriminative for such behaviors, but neither them nor the baseball context serve as the motivating operation. The MO condition was dictated by what happened earlier, that is, he skipped lunch. It was the food deprivation that produced the value-altering effect of the potential reinforcer and the functional relationship between behavior and a specific reinforcer. (The value of food was established by being deprived of food (EO); the availability of food (S$^D$) was indicated by his parents being present and food being present.)

All too often, written FBAs present interpretations about a problems behavior's function that designate the antecedent to be some aspect of the context when the behavior occurs. You may see reports that indicate that the behavior is highly likely under a variety of context conditions, for example, when there are bright lights in the classroom, when there are too many chairs, not enough chairs, and so forth. These interpretations are an artifact of the data system missing the analysis of the MO as one of deprivation. The next assessment method, trigger analysis, corrects that omission.

Another problem with descriptive analysis is the over-selection of social attention as the maintaining contingency. Very often you hear personnel indicate that the behavior is maintained by attention, and they point to the record to show that attention (in some form) always follows the behavior. This interpretation regarding behavioral function is an artifact in the manner in which descriptive analyses collect information. While attention, either in the form of a verbal statement, physical proximity, or physical contact, will often follow the problem behavior, it may be tangential to the reinforcer addressing the MO.

When would some adult's attention not be an event subsequent to the behavior? Only with behaviors that produce their effects directly, that is, direct access and direct escape problems. Therefore, someone's attention may be coincidental to the actual function, which may be access to a tangible reinforcer, escape from an unpleasant social situation, escape from task demands, and so forth. However, because the adult mediates such access or escape from the aversive stimuli, his or her attention is involved but often construed as having a primary role. In many cases, the role of an adult's presence in socially mediated behavior is one of the delivery of the desired event, and one's attention is a necessary condition but not the maintaining reinforcer. Again, an understanding of the MO and its influence in establishing the value of a particular reinforcer is missing in these analyses.

### Trigger Analysis With Behavioral Description

The utility of a trigger analysis (Rolider, 2003; Rolider & Axelrod, 2000) as a behavioral assessment method is the ability to collect data on infrequent target problem behaviors. It requires the presentation of the hypothesized motivating operation and S$^D$ in the real life context, with the persons who normally are involved with the client. The occurrence (or absence) of the target problem behavior is then noted. You can then compute the percentage of times the target behavior occurs by determining the ratio of occurrences over the total number of times the MO/S$^D$ condition was presented. But a trigger analysis can also provide the clinician with more information about behavioral function. It can be used to note which behavior (target problem or nonproblem) abolishes the value of an outcome in the real-life context for each presentation of the MO. The user can provide a running description of behaviors that occur prior to the targeted behavior that results in the desired reinforcer. Unlike a descriptive analysis, this measurement instrument would focus the analysis of behavior and consequent events given a particular MO condition.

This is how the data will be collected. The antecedent condition would be a delineation of both the MO condition (EO) and the discriminative stimuli (people) for the behaviors. This would remain the same for the descriptive record until the MO condition is abolished (AO). All behavioral entries in column B would be described. For example, descriptions of what the client does are listed vertically in chronological order. Information that indicates whether the MO condition was abolished (or not) is entered in column C, which covers the functional reinforcer. Therefore, the only consequence being considered is the one that is related to the deprivation or aversive condition inherent in the hypothesized MO. Therefore, the B column could describe various behaviors that occur under the delineated MO and their effect on the MO, that is, whether they establish or abolish it. For socially mediated access behaviors, the MO is one of deprivation. A behavior exhibited by the person changes the MO in one of two ways: (a) the deprivation is maintained or increased, (b) or the deprivation is reduced or abolished to a sufficient degree that it no longer serves as an existing MO. This information, the effect on the MO, is written in the C column (instead of just delineating what the person observes).

The trigger analysis presents the MO condition in one of two ways. The clinician can induce the MO condition in the real-life context with the existent personnel. In the prior material on trigger analysis within this chapter, several examples were given. With MOs involving deprivation required for the value-altering effect to exist on a specific reinforcer, the client's access to the reinforcer at certain times is interrupted by taking the item away or stopping the activity. In the case of aversive conditions such as MOs, the stimulus condition is presented by the staff person at the request of the clinician.

When the MO is predictable in the real-life context, the behavior analyst would just study and describe the behaviors under these natural routine conditions. Then it is simply a matter of using the chart, again until the positive reinforcer is presented or negative reinforcer is removed. Let us say we have a student in a mainstream class who does not like to read aloud when it is her turn. Therefore, the value of terminating the oral reading task is established whenever her oral reading group comes up to the teacher's desk, and the value is increased when it gets closer to being her turn to read. In the case of a trigger analysis, the teacher would present this instructional format when it usually occurs and at a few unscheduled times to determine if the behavior can be "provoked" by the antecedent condition. A simple analysis of whether the behavior occurred or not would reveal the number of times the problem behavior occurred over the number of opportunities. For example, over a 2-week period, the number of times she engages in the identified target behavior (some form of nonresponsiveness when called upon) was 8/9.

However, what is not identified by a mere determination of the percentage of times the problem behavior occurs is the inefficiency of other behaviors to recruit escape. Table 2.20 illustrates what a behavioral description would provide.

The first column (A) remains the same throughout all the frames because the MO hypothesized to establish the value of a potential reinforcer stays until it is abolished in favor of some other MO. Note in column B, there are several behavioral descriptions. What is fruitful is each behavioral episode (description) is now evaluated against its ability to alter the individual's motivating operation. Upon examination of the chart, one can see that this student exhibited two behaviors that had little or no effect on terminating the aversive event. The user of this chart simply delineates whether the MO condition was removed at that point in time. However, with the entry of the third behavioral description, one can see that the aversive condition is avoided effectively. If other descriptions of this context over

---

*TABLE 2.20* ■ **BEHAVIORAL DESCRIPTION**

| Antecedent (A) | Behavior (B) | Contingency (C) |
|---|---|---|
| Presence of a relatively aversive social condition, oral reading group with 3rd-grade teacher | Gets to group and opens book | Not effective in avoiding advent of task demand |
| | Sits in seat in group for 3 minutes while others read | Not effective in avoiding advent of task demand |
| | When called on to read, stammers, then puts head under the table | Effective, teacher moved to next person to read aloud |

future opportunities show that such similar nonresponsive and inappropriate behaviors are effective in terminating or avoiding reading aloud, one has better evidence about the function of these types of behaviors.

The argument regarding the hypothesized function is strengthened by the description of other behavioral episodes. One can see the differential effectiveness of varied behaviors on the relevant function. When determining function it is important to view not only the reliable relation between the problem behavior and a maintaining contingency (in the presence of some MO), but also the inefficiency of other behaviors relative to the target behavior. Following is a real-life case that illustrates the analysis of behavioral function of aggression with respect to the initial MO involving the value of play on tricycles.

### Head Start and the Tricycles

I (E.C.) was a behavioral consultant to Head Start in the early 1990s.[1] I provided specific strategies to deal with problem behaviors of the children attending the particular site. Often the referral was for a child who was aggressive (overwhelmingly boys). One of the referrals for aggression was a boy who exhibited such behavior during outside play time. The catalyst for such behavior revolved around the desire of many children to ride one of the three tricycles. If six children want three tricycles, all at once, a conflict arises. The children argued and pushed each other away from the bikes in order to establish themselves as the bike riders. Once a child landed in the seat, she or he usually went unchallenged (kind of like *King of the Mountain*). As you could guess, my client was quite good at getting the bike and keeping it.

As is evident, aggression in this context is a behavior that produces access to the tricycle and maintains such engagement with the tricycle. In comparison to other behaviors, aggression, when performed adeptly, is far more effective and efficient than other behaviors, such as pleading, whining, or crying. But how the teachers reacted explained why aggression was functional. They did not resolve such disputes when some children complained to them. Instead, the child was told to go back and work things out for themselves. I asked one of the teachers why none of the staff mediated the disputes with the bike (until someone was hit). She remarked, "Our philosophy here is that we want the children to learn to work out their problems on their own. If we solve their interpersonal squabbles and problems, they will never learn to develop self-control and personal responsibility to themselves and their fellow human beings."

Let's examine what the contextual conditions are for this case by answering three questions (see Table 2.21).

What would a trigger analysis with descriptive assessment chart look like? While this was not done, the hypothetical illustration in Table 2.22 would be plausible given the information from Table 2.21.

In this case, the failure of the social environment to mediate other behaviors to facilitate getting the tricycles was a major factor in the continued utility of aggressive behavior. Intervention would have to significantly alter the manner in which the teachers intervened in this context. Aggression had to be made less functional, while more appropriate behavior had to become functional in getting the tricycle. This was accomplished by designating a contingency for aggression of removal from the play area for a brief time and loss of any tricycle time that recess period. But an additional component would have to strengthen the alternate more acceptable form for getting the tricycle. I decided to reward complaining to the teacher by making children accept a "plea deal from the teacher." The plea deal meant the parties involved in the complaint would all get a shorter allotment of time on the tricycle. The teacher would announce the following: "You get the tricycle for 3 minutes, then she gets it for 3 minutes," and so forth.

*TABLE 2.21* ■ **QUESTIONS TO CONSIDER**

1.  Is the existing motivational condition for that child one of relative deprivation of that item or activity?
    *Answer:* Yes. Three tricycles and many children desiring such sets up the MO for such an activity. In point of fact, if there were 10 tricycles, with no need to wait for a tricycle to become available, the MO would be low because the desired event would be freely available.

2.  Is there a reliable, somewhat frequent relation, between the child's problem behavior and accessing certain items or activities? What is the form of the behavior and what items or activities are produced?
    *Answer:* Yes. Aggression against other children in a profound manner resulted in this child getting the tricycle on a regular basis (or any other item/toy he wanted).

3.  Is the problem behavior more likely to produce the tangible reinforcer than acceptable appropriate behaviors?
    *Answer:* Yes. Particularly in light of the failure of the social environment to selectively reinforce a more appropriate behavior by controlling who initially gets the tricycles and for how long they have access to the tricycles.

*TABLE 2.22* ■ **TRIGGER ANALYSIS WITH DESCRIPTIVE ASSESSMENT**

| Antecedent (A) | Behavior (B) | Contingency (C) | Future Probability of Behavior under MO |
|---|---|---|---|
| Relative deprivation state with respect to riding the tricycles, children let outside for play time activity | Asks if he can get on tricycle | Not told anything, Not effective in getting tricycle, | Less likely |
| | Says he is going to tell the teacher | Verbal statement ignored. Not effective, MO still present | Less likely |
| | Pushes kid off tricycle, she cries and goes to another area of the play area | Effective immediately, kid rides tricycle and is not challenged by another, deprivation state abolished | More likely |

   With this approach, aggressive behavior dropped dramatically, including the aggressive behavior of the child referred to me. The removal of the opportunity to ride the tricycle whenever a child aggressed made such a behavior unproductive in this context. The teachers remarked that the children were now bringing their complaints surrounding toys and bikes to them frequently. These functional treatment contingencies produced a more acceptable way for children to work out their impulsive behavior. What was also an interesting finding in this program was that many of the children who needed the tricycle right away learned one of two things: how to wait, or how to find something else interesting to play with that was not in as great a demand as the bikes. Can children actually learn to refrain from aggression? This finding does not settle with the old adage, "boys will be boys." Perhaps we adults have a lot more to do with aggression than scholars portend.

### Trigger Analysis During Language Tasks

For socially mediated escape behaviors, the recordings would entail the delineation of the suspect aversive event in the column for the MO and the people involved with that presentation as possible discriminative stimuli. The C column would just indicate whether the aversive task was removed or not following the behavioral description. The following hypothetical example illustrates this trigger analysis, and the resulting descriptions of be-

**TABLE 2.23 ■ ANALYSIS OF LANGUAGE TASK**

| Antecedent (A) | Behavior (B) | Contingency (C) |
| --- | --- | --- |
| Presentation of language task with speech pathologist, requiring full sentences (MO is hypothesized to be the presence of difficult language tasks) | "I, not" and turning her head away from person | Not effective (speech path chides her to try, re-presents task) |
| | Cries | Not effective, continues with task |
| | Said a full sentence, "I see a dog." to picture card | Not effective, praised for full sentence and next item presented (requiring full sentence) |
| | Slaps self | Effective immediately, therapist says "let's try something else" and goes outside to play with the girl |

havior and effective consequences are recorded, with the self-injurious behavior of a hypothetical child with disabilities. In this assessment, it was not necessary to contrive the MO, all that was necessary was to study the behavior under this naturally occurring context. If the behavior analyst wanted to induce the MO several times in a single session, the speech therapist would have to agree to alter the request for full sentences with tasks that are less difficult, for example, receptive labeling.

In Table 2.23, the presentation of a language task that requires speaking in sentences creates the aversive condition for this hypothetical child with severe developmental disabilities. The therapist becomes a discriminative stimulus for certain behaviors that are more efficient than others, at least temporarily removing or postponing this activity. Note that the first behavior, one of saying "I, not," did not produce escape. Neither did exhibiting the target appropriate language skill (see third row) result in the termination of the task. As a result of not allowing such to terminate this instructional activity, shortly thereafter, she slaps herself. Contingent upon this the therapist changes the instructional format, terminating the aversive condition and changing to a more preferred activity (where speaking in full sentences is not demanded).

Let us take the same instructional context and present a trigger analysis for another student whose self-injury is hypothesized to function as access to a tangible reinforcer. A hypothetical 6-year old student with autism goes to speech two times a week and at varying times is given a favored toy. Sometimes it occurs right at the outset of the session, sometimes only after the session has ensued. Because the clinician is not sure when the self-injury occurs, she will ask the speech therapist to delay giving the toy. Rather, the clinician will hide the toy for a period of time. The hypothesized MO could be presented several times in the therapy session by taking the favored toy away after short periods of access. The running description of this hypothesized function is given in Table 2.24.

**TABLE 2.24 ■ TRIGGER ANALYSIS**

| Antecedent (A) | Behavior (B) | Contingency (C) |
| --- | --- | --- |
| In speech therapy room with therapist, deprivation of favored toy, access blocked temporarily | "I want" | Therapist says "good asking" but not effective in getting the toy |
| | Cries | Not effective, continues with task and is told to wait for the toy until she does some work |
| | Said a full sentence, "I see a dog" to picture card | Not effective, praised for full sentence and next item (requiring full sentence) presented |
| | Slaps self four times | Effective after fourth slap, OK, you can have the toy to hold if you will work as well |

In summary, a trigger analysis with a descriptive assessment requires an analysis of the effect of many child behaviors displayed on the abatement of the motivating operation that give rise to the enhanced value of the reinforcer. In the case of access behaviors, a behavioral description of various incidents when deprivation is in place identifies its efficiency and effectiveness (or lack thereof) to abate the MO. In the case of escape behaviors, each behavior's ability to terminate the aversive event is evaluated.

## Scatter Plot

You receive a referral for a client who runs out of the residential unit once a day, pretty much every day. You ask the staff (mistakenly), "Why do you think he does that?" The reply provides little information (and verifies why you should never ask that question first): "He's just being Bobby. You know he is autistic!"

Like me, you are probably still wondering why Bobby does this only one time each day. Is there a particular time this daily event happens? If the recording of this behavior also specified the time it occurred, such information might be available. Suppose you see that this behavior occurs around 2:30 P.M. every day. Now your interest is really peaked! What happens at 2:30 that sets the occasion for Bobby to run out of the unit? The answer: shift change. With shift change comes new people coming in from the parking lot. But why does Bobby run out of the parking lot during shift change? The answer: to see one car in particular. You now know the function of this behavior.

Not all referrals will be as simple as this illustration. Often the behavior occurs several times across the day, and it is not easy to pick out what "trigger event" seems to occasion the exhibition of the problem behavior. The scatter plot (Touchette, MacDonald, & Langer, 1985) is an important tool to determine if certain times and events seem to occasion higher levels of problem behavior across time. It is a variation of the descriptive analysis (Lerman & Iwata, 1993) and provides general information on possible time periods across the day that seem to promote higher rates of behavior than other time periods.

In the study by Touchette and colleagues (1985), a scatter plot was used to gain information on the antecedent conditions for the assaultive behavior of a 14-year-old female. She had a history of such behavior from the age of 4. In her current placement, she would assault both peers and staff at the residential school for students with autism. Staff plotted assaults as a function of 30-minute intervals. This data was transformed to a new grid, which made it easier to view patterns of target behavior. If a given 30-minute block of time had only one assault, an open circle was placed on the new grid for that time period. More than one assault during a 30-minute block of time required a filled-in circle to be placed on the new grid. Blocks of time during which no assaults occurred had no circle. This new grid would reveal longitudinal patterns of behavior.

By examining this grid for filled-in circles, these researchers identified specific time periods between 1 and 4 P.M. during which multiple assaults were occurring. From Monday through Thursday during this time period, the student was in group prevocational and community living classes. In contrast, Fridays, Saturdays, and Sundays rarely contained assaults, and she did not attend these classes on those days. With this information, they redesigned her schedule. Her new schedule removed the afternoon classes that occasioned high rates of assaultive behavior. In their place, the activities she engaged in on Friday through Sunday (such activities that inhibited assaultive behavior) were substituted. With this programmatic change, assaults immediately dropped to zero levels on multiple days. This was maintained over the next phase where the prevocational classes were progressively introduced back into her schedule. This progressive alteration of the amount of time she would spend in these classes occurred over a 1-year period, at the end of which she was participating in three of the four class hours with only one assault occurring during a 14-day period.

To use the scatter plot as a mechanism for revealing patterns of behavior across the week, staff record occurrence of target behavior as a function of time of day. This is accomplished in time blocks, for example, 9–10 A.M., 10–11 A.M., and so on. You then examine the data across multiple days, looking for patterns of high rates and low rates of target behavior across the same time of the day. Table 2.25 is a hypothetical illustration of a scatter plot to identify patterns of "refusal to comply" behavior of an 8-year-old child with attention-deficit hyperactivity disorder (ADHD) in a third-grade elementary school classroom.

Table 2.25 plots the frequency of the target behavior, that is, refusal to comply, across five days of the week in terms of half-hour time segments for each day. One can then examine the data for patterns of behavior across certain time patterns or activities. For example, between 10:00 and 10:30 on Monday, the child refused to comply with a teacher request five times. Refusal behavior is highly likely during this period as evident by the data for the remainder of the week. In examining the scatter plot, two time periods account for the overwhelming majority of instances of refusal behavior (i.e., 8:30–9:00 and 10:00–10:30) during this 1-week period. One can then begin to examine more closely the antecedent conditions that are present in those time periods where higher rates of problem behavior exist. Once identified, these risk conditions for target behavior can then be used in designing an effective treatment. It is also important to note from the scatter plot data that there are certain time periods when refusal behavior was unlikely. This information is also valuable in ascertaining what contexts are "safe" conditions for target problem behavior. Collecting scatter plot data can aid in identifying risk and safe conditions for the target problem behavior.

If you are attempting to monitor multiple behaviors with a scatter plot format, you might want to code each target behavior at the top of each data sheet. For example, physical aggressiveness could be coded "PA," and a "T" could represent tantrums incidents. Try to limit yourself to collecting scatter plot data on only two or three target behaviors at a time. The day should be divided into time periods that reflect natural divisions in regularly scheduled activities. For example, a scatter plot for a client attending a work site might be designed to reflect the natural activities and breaks during the workday (see Table 2.26).

*TABLE 2.25* ■ **SCATTER PLOT ILLUSTRATION: OCCURRENCE OF REFUSAL TO COMPLY WITH TEACHER/STAFF INSTRUCTION**

| Time of Day A.M. | M | T | W | Th | F |
|---|---|---|---|---|---|
| 8:00–8:30 | | X | | X | |
| 8:30–9:00 | XXX | XX | XXX XX | XX | XXX |
| 9:00–9:30 | X | | | X | |
| 9:30–10:00 | X | | | | |
| 10:00–10:30 | XXX XX | XXX X | XXX X | XXX XX | XX |
| 10:30–11:00 | X | | | X | |
| 11:00–11:30 | X | X | | | |

**TABLE 2.26 ■ SAMPLE TIME PERIODS FOR SCATTER PLOT DATA**

| 8:00–8:15 | → | ® arrived at work site |
|---|---|---|
| 8:15–8:30 | → | ® morning staff meetings |
| 8:30–10:00 | → | ® clean bathrooms in building |
| 10:00–10:10 | → | ® break |
| 10:10–11:30 | → | ® sweeps out and cleans cafeteria, mops up floor |
| 11:30–12:00 | → | ® lunch |

Table 2.27 is a scatter plot of this client's tantrum behaviors according to the general activity and time period delineated in Table 2.26. The scatter plot might be able to pin down what work tasks or situations seem to trigger such tantrums.

A new grid to reflect time periods when the target behavior occurred at all (open circle) versus when the target behavior did not occur (left blank) is depicted in Table 2.28.

The time period of 8:15–8:30 indicates a high rate of tantrums. Apparently, cleaning bathrooms does not generate many tantrums (see 8:30–10:00 time period). However, cleaning the cafeteria is another condition that results in high rates of tantrums (see 10:10–11:30).

In this hypothetical example, why would the client have minimal problems with cleaning the bathroom, but then have problems cleaning the cafeteria? Should we conclude that it is the nature of the specific tasks that generates tantrums? Although this is certainly possible, it may not be the primary factor. Perhaps it is the requirement to work with other coworkers when cleaning the cafeteria. If cleaning the bathrooms is done in solitude, while cleaning the cafeteria is done as a group, perhaps that is the problem. This client may not like to work with other people. If this client had several people with him during bathroom custodial duties, he may exhibit some of the same problem behaviors. We don't know which of these two possibilities is the controlling variable. However, the scatter plot data gives you a place to start looking. It requires additional investigation in order to pin down possible behavioral functions. Once you identify the events or stimuli that occasion such behavior it becomes possible to alter these events to get an immediate change in the target behavior (Touchette et al., 1985).

**TABLE 2.27 ■ SCATTER PLOT ILLUSTRATION**

Date: 3/9/05
Target Behavior: Tantrum behavior at work site

| Time of work day | M | T | W | Th | F |
|---|---|---|---|---|---|
| 8:00–8:15 | | | | | |
| 8:15–8:30 | XXX | XX | XX | XX | XXX |
| | | | XX | | |
| 8:30–10:00 | | | | X | |
| 10:00–10:10 | X | | | | |
| 10:10–11:30 | XXX | XXX | XXX | XXX | XX |
| | XX | X | X | X | |
| 11:30–12:00 | X | | | | |

*TABLE 2.28* ■ **SCATTER PLOT ILLUSTRATION**

Date: 3/9/05
Target Behavior: Tantrum behavior at work site

| Time of work day | M | T | W | Th | F |
|---|---|---|---|---|---|
| 8:00–8:15 | | | | | |
| 8:15–8:30 | O | O | O | O | O |
| 8:30–10:00 | | | | O | |
| 10:00–10:10 | O | | | | |
| 10:10–11:30 | O | O | O | O | O |
| 11:30–12:00 | O | | | | |

If you are going to collect scatter plot data in residential or inpatient facilities, consider tracking the client's problem behavior as a function of activities. This is particularly ideal for clients who have an established routine during the weekdays. For example, the client may get back to the residence from the day program at 3 P.M. He has a snack that lasts for 10 to 15 minutes. This could be the first category under which frequencies of the target behaviors are recorded. Following his snack, he changes clothes, and again, frequency of behavior should be recorded under that context.

Scatter plot data can be very useful in educational settings. You would set up blocks of time involving specific instructional tasks or content areas. To further delineate what might be a risk condition for target behavior, you can use a coding system to indicate specific activities. For example, seat work would be "SW," and reading groups would be represented by "RG." You could also note if the task was a seat work task or a task requiring the child to pay attention to the teacher. Table 2.29 provides some questions you might consider when examining scatter plot data.

## DISCUSSION QUESTIONS

Suppose you have collected scatter plot information on a student's rate of leaving the classroom unauthorized. What information would the scatter plot data provide? What do you look for? What would the absence of the target behavior tell you?

## Analogue Assessment

With the prior three assessment methods, an actual test of the maintaining contingencies is not conducted. Rather, all three methods are descriptive in nature. Analogue assessment (also known as functional analysis of behavior) involves an experimental analysis of the function of the behavior under contrived test conditions (Iwata, Vollmer, & Zarcone, 1990).

*TABLE 2.29* ■ **QUESTIONS TO CONSIDER IN EXAMINING SCATTER PLOT DATA**

1. Are there time periods when the behavior is highly likely?
2. What activities or events are typically associated with these time periods?
3. Are there time periods when the behavior is highly unlikely?
4. What activities or events are typically associated with these time periods?

These contrived test conditions attempt to simulate or mimic the variables hypothesized to be operating in the child's classroom or school environment (Iwata, Dorsey, Slifer, Bauman, & Richman, 1982; Steege, Wacker, Berg, Cigrand, & Cooper, 1989). Analogue assessment utilizes a quick switching of hypothesized variables to determine the effect on the child's behavior, similar to conducting a scientific experiment. If the rate of behavior increased in one condition over another reliably, then a hypothesis about a behavior's function has more solid empirical evidence.

Analogue assessment is a more labor-intensive method that allows you to "test" potential hypotheses regarding why the behavior is occurring, in terms of controlling variables (Iwata et al., 1982, 1990; Lerman & Iwata, 1993). It has received extensive validation (Day, Rea, Schussler, Larsen, & Johnson, 1988) and is superior to other assessment methods described previously (Lerman & Iwata, 1993).

Analogue assessment methods were developed and empirically validated in a clinic for self-injurious behavior and other problem behaviors at the Johns Hopkins School of Medicine (Iwata et al., 1982). The children referred to Dr. Iwata at the clinic came from various distances and locations, which probably precluded an analysis of their behavior in real-life (in-situ) environments. These researchers ingeniously developed an assessment protocol that allowed them to experimentally analyze the potential function of self-injury in a short period of time. In order to verify hypotheses about the problem behaviors' functions, Iwata and colleagues (1982) attempted to mimic possible controlling environmental variables in the clinic setting. They developed four test conditions under which self-injury rates would be evaluated: (1) attention, (2) demand, (3) alone, and (4) play (enriched environment).

In the attention condition, the therapist's attention was contingent on self-injurious behavior, in the form of a disapproval statement such as "don't do that" and touching the child lightly on the arm or shoulder. What would such a simulation demonstrate? If behavior rates increase during this condition, relative to the other conditions, one has strong evidence that attention is the maintaining variable. In the demand condition, escape-motivated functions were tested. The therapist would present task demands to the subject in the form of self-care or educational tasks every 30 seconds. The task or trial would be removed for a 30-second period contingent on self-injurious behavior. If the rate of problem behavior is heightened relative to the other conditions, then evidence of escape-motivated behavior exists. In the alone condition, the client was placed alone in the therapy room, with no toys or other materials. This condition tested the possibility of sensory reinforcement for behavior. If the self-injury occurred frequently in this condition, one could most probably rule out socially mediated functions. Finally, a control condition (play or enriched environment) involving access to toys and materials served to allow a contrast between the other conditions and one where pleasurable activities were provided noncontingently.

Simulation of plausible natural contingencies under these test conditions allowed the researchers to determine possible controlling variables of the self-injurious behavior. The ability to discern a pattern of target behaviors by quick switching of these four conditions across time gave these researchers experimental proof of the problem behavior's function. The Iwata and colleagues (1982) protocol can be used when such information is needed in a short period of time. The research data involving the efficacy of this methodology in developing effective functional treatments is overwhelming.

Analogue assessment can also focus on testing a specific hypothesis about a problem behavior's function. This assessment methodology is a slight departure from the study by Iwata and colleagues (1982) in that the baseline condition consists of the absence of the antecedent variable, and only one hypothesis is tested at a time. The following two hypothetical case scenarios illustrate this application.

## CASE EXAMPLE 1

After reviewing information obtained via scatter plot and A-B-C descriptive analysis, you hypothesize that the referred child with ADHD has more frequent behavior problems when the seat work is relatively difficult for him. This second grade student's problem behavior consists of not finishing assignments coupled with frequent verbal complaints about the assignments. You suspect that such behavior is being negatively reinforced and appears to be more likely with difficult seat work. Negative reinforcement of complaining behavior would involve the teacher temporarily halting the task when the student begins or continues to complain.

To test this, it is essential to set up a test condition that has two requirements. One requirement is to alternate different instructional conditions across brief sessions. For example, in some sessions you present easy assignments, in some sessions you present difficult assignments, and in some sessions you do not give an assignment. Therefore, in brief sessions, difficult tasks are going to be presented and interspersed with easier tasks and no task at all. You will record the frequency or rate of problem behaviors under each of these three conditions. As the consultant, you will implement the analogue assessment in a separate room.

Further, to mimic the hypothesized classroom conditions, the occurrence of verbal complaining will be reinforced by your temporary removal of the task (either difficult or easy). For example, if this student proclaims, "This is stupid, I don't need to know who Captain Cook is!" you would comment, "OK, why don't you take a break for a while. I will call you back when you are rested." After 30 seconds of allowing him to get out of his seat, you call him back again. However, contingent upon any verbal complaining, you allow him another 30-second break. Therefore, in this analogue test, the occurrence of the problem behavior in either of the task conditions (easy vs. hard) is negatively reinforced with the brief removal of the task.

What is evidence of escape behavior during difficult tasks in this analogue test? If there is differential responding in problem behavior, in favor of higher rates during difficult tasks, one can surmise the conditions under which such escape problem behaviors become more probable. Therefore, the hypothesis of escape from instruction-task difficulty seems to be more plausible.

## CASE EXAMPLE 2

You have been referred a client who lives in an institutional setting. She engages in severe property destruction. After reviewing information obtained via behavioral interviewing and A-B-C descriptive focused analysis, you hypothesize that her property destruction seems to occur in the context of requests or demands made of her by staff. You will test this out by alternating 10-minute sessions of task demands with sessions having no task demands. In one condition, you present the types of task demands made by staff (e.g., "Come here and put on your sweater. Pick up this towel."). In the other condition, no demands are made of her. Therefore, in short alternating 10-minute sessions, imposing demands of this client are interspersed with no task demands (alone condition), while the frequency of tantrums and property destruction is recorded under each of these conditions.

Further, to mimic the hypothesized classroom conditions, the occurrence of problem behaviors (tantrum or property destruction) results in you (the behavioral specialist) leaving her alone for a while (e.g., 30 seconds). In other words, the demand situation is removed contingent upon the target behavior, thus simulating what the in-situ environment would do if such a behavior is truly serving an escape function. If there is differential responding in problem behavior between the demand condition and the alone condition, in favor of higher rates during demands, you can surmise the conditions under which such escape behaviors become more probable. Therefore, the hypothesis of escape from task demands and chores seems to be more plausible.

In school settings, analogue assessments can provide additional useful information in determining the function of problem behavior during seat work. The test condition could be the presence of the hypothesized contingency. The control condition could be the absence of such a contingency. For example, suppose you hypothesize that the child's disruptive behavior is serving an escape from instruction function due to lengthy seat work assignments. The analogue test would involve the following characteristics:

- Quick switching between two conditions: (1) sessions involving a short assignment and (2) sessions involving a lengthy assignment(s)
- Hypothesized negative reinforcer is contingent on the problem behavior in both conditions (i.e., brief removal of task, e.g., "why don't you take a short break?")
- On-task behavior should be measured across both conditions
- Comparison of rates of problem behavior and on-task behavior between these two conditions is used to verify the hypothesis

Table 2.30 presents the procedures and test conditions of the analogue test for an escape from instruction hypothesis for lengthy task assignments.

A possible hypothetical sample of an analogue assessment, with resulting data for several 50-minute sessions (F) versus several short sessions (S), is presented in Table 2.31 (frequency of behaviors and on-task rate in rows two and three).

In examining these data, the rates of problem behavior are higher in the 50-minute sessions (frequencies of 8, 7, 12, and 6) than in the short sessions (frequencies of 1, 4, 1, and 0). There also exists a significant discrepancy in the on-task rate between full instructional sessions versus short sessions. It is obvious that the child has more frequent problem behaviors during longer assignments. Longer assignments pr sessions create the motivational condition for escape and are relatively aversive for this child.

In a similar vein, a test of the problem behavior serving an escape function due to task difficulty could be done with another student. The basic instructions for conducting an analogue assessment for this hypothesis are given in Table 2.32. Again, with the occurrence of a target problem behavior, the assignment or task is stopped for a 1–2 minute break, then reintroduced. A possible hypothetical sample of data across eight brief sessions is presented in Table 2.33 for the two sets of conditions: difficult tasks (D) versus easy tasks (E). One can see by the data collected that the presentation of difficult tasks generates high frequencies of problem behavior and low rates of on-task behavior. Conversely, easy tasks generate a low frequency of problem behavior and high rates of on-task behavior.

*TABLE 2.30* ■ **ANALOGUE ASSESSMENT TESTING FOR ESCAPE/AVOIDANCE OF INSTRUCTION-TASK DURATION DIAGNOSIS**

1. Conduct 8 mini-sessions up to 50 minutes in length.

2. Get the same (or similar) materials that are used in class.

3. For four sessions, present assignments that last an entire 50 minutes (full = F), that is, student keeps working continuously for 50 minutes, with one instructor in one test area.

4. For four sessions, present short assignments that last only 10–15 minutes (short = S). Once the assignment is finished, end the session, and go to an entertaining activity. Provide a cue that the condition involves a short amount of work, for example, "Let's do just this one task before we take a break." Use a different instructor and place to maximize the differences between full and short sessions.

5. Each time the problem target behavior occurs in either the short or full sessions, give the student a 1–2 minute break from the assignment.

6. Compare rates of problem behavior and on-task behavior.

*TABLE 2.31* ■ **DATA FOR ANALOGUE ASSESSMENT**

| Session Type | 1 | 2 | 3 | 4 | 5 | 6 | 7 | 8 |
|---|---|---|---|---|---|---|---|---|
| (F or S) | F | F | S | F | S | S | F | S |
| No. of behaviors | 8 | 7 | 1 | 12 | 4 | 1 | 6 | 0 |
| On-task % | 40 | 30 | 70 | 25 | 60 | 75 | 45 | 65 |

### TABLE 2.32 ■ ANALOGUE ASSESSMENT TESTING FOR ESCAPE/AVOIDANCE OF INSTRUCTION-TASK DIFFICULTY DIAGNOSTIC

1. Conduct eight brief, 20-minute sessions of equal length.
2. For four sessions—present difficult (D) tasks with the same instructor and test room as the easy tasks.
3. For four sessions—present easy (E) tasks with the same instructor and test room as the hard tasks.
4. Each time the target problem behavior occurs, give the student a 1–2 minute break.
5. Compare rates of problem behavior and on-task behavior.

### TABLE 2.33 ■ DATA ON EASY VS DIFFICULT TASKS

| Session Type | 1 | 2 | 3 | 4 | 5 | 6 | 7 | 8 |
|---|---|---|---|---|---|---|---|---|
| (F or S) | D | E | E | D | D | E | E | D |
| No. of behaviors | 12 | 0 | 3 | 7 | 14 | 2 | 1 | 18 |
| On-task % | 20 | 80 | 85 | 30 | 30 | 65 | 80 | 15 |

## DISCUSSION QUESTIONS

In an analogue assessment, why does the therapist/teacher/staff person provide specific reinforcement when the client engages in the target behavior? Why would you want to reinforce the target behavior? Why is an analogue assessment an experimental demonstration of function whereas the A-B-C analysis is not?

In many educational and mental health settings, extensive use of analogue assessment will probably be prohibitive due to time and fiscal constraints. So when would its use be most appropriate? There are three compelling reasons for utilizing this strategy: (1) when several prior behavior programs have not succeeded in reducing the problem behavior, (2) before a student loses his or her current educational or residential placement, and (3) when there is a huge time and resource investment in training a large number of staff to implement a plan.

Analogue tests can also be conducted with other socially mediated access and escape problem behaviors (see Table 2.34). For example, some clients have difficulty when presented with a novel task or routine. This can be tested in a contrived condition by alternating the presentation of novel tasks with familiar tasks (see Example 1 in Table 2.34). The same requirement for allowing the problem behavior to terminate the condition would be in effect for both conditions. In Example 2, a test of the antecedent for socially mediated problem behavior involving an inability to wait for a reinforcer is tested. In one condition a wait of some interval is imposed, with the target behavior being given after some criterion level of problem behavior has been demonstrated. A differential result between the wait condition and the no-wait condition would provide evidence regarding a hypothesis of tangible reinforcer. The real-life example in Table 2.34 illustrates this elegant use of an in-vivo analogue assessment with an extremely unhealthy behavior for the client and staff.

### When I Say "NO"

Fred was an individual who was referred to me (K.S.) for evaluation of severe self-injurious behavior (SIB). In its most severe form, his SIB involved tearing pieces of flesh from his legs and throwing them at staff members. This resulted in significant levels of blood loss

*TABLE 2.34* ■ **ANALOGUE TESTS**

| Hypothesized Antecedent | Condition A: Presence of Antecedent | Condition B: Absence of Antecedent | Other Considerations |
|---|---|---|---|
| Example 1: Novel tasks | Novel tasks presented consecutively | Familiar tasks | Equate length of time between both conditions |
| Example 2: Inability to wait for desired item/event | Wait time required from request (e.g., 1–5 minutes) | No wait time from request | Require some criterion level of problem behaviors to produce reinforcer |

and significant risk to his life. Given the severity of this behavior the facility had responded with progressively more restrictive procedures. These procedures included 1:1 staffing, psychotropic medications, and locked, hard plastic boots to prevent access to his legs.

My first observation of Fred's SIB revealed a sequence of behaviors that he engaged in prior to the severe form of self-injury. While I was observing him a staff person came into his room and asked him to go wash his hands before breakfast. He said "no." The staff then insisted that he must get ready for breakfast and told him again to go wash his hands. He then began screaming "no." The staff person again told him that he must wash his hands; he continued to yell "NO" and began to spit at the staff. The staff again directed him to go wash his hands. Fred then stopped spitting and attempted to hit the staff person. The staff stepped out of the way and again repeated the direction to wash his hands. He stopped trying to hit the staff and began pinching his own arms. The staff now prompted him to stop pinching himself and go wash his hands. Fred then began grabbing the flesh on his legs causing a wound and bleeding. The staff blocked Fred from grabbing his legs and called emergency staff. The emergency staff attended to his wounds, but no more requests were made to wash his hands.

I then talked with staff who had worked with Fred for several years who indicated that the most likely conditions to evoke the self-injury were repeated and persistent demands to complete any task. Staff who had reported success in avoiding self-injury told me that they simply stopped task demands when he said "no" and would re-present those demands in 15 minutes, at which time Fred would typically comply with the request.

I presented the findings from the descriptive assessment to the treatment team. Despite the data depicting clearly the function of escape from a social demand, the team disagreed with my findings. They were insistent that Fred was engaging in SIB for attention. Their logic was the following: when Fred engaged in the severe form of SIB, that is, throwing his pieces of skin at them, multiple staff came to interact. When multiple staff arrived, he would then stop tearing flesh from his legs. Subsequently, he received one-on-one attention from the nurse. Rather than engaging in a protracted argument, I offered to provide empirical support that this behavior was maintained by escape. To provide such data, I tested three different conditions. In this case, due to the form of Fred's severe SIB, I selected a precursor form of self-injury (pinching and pulling on the skin of his forearm) as the response measure during one of the three test conditions. In all conditions simple demands to complete tasks, such as get out of bed, go to the day room, hand me the towel, and so forth, were delivered. To test the escape function, the ability to escape the task demand was evaluated as a function of continued demands. Therefore, in one condition the task demands were stopped for an alternate behavior, and in another condition they were terminated contingent upon the less severe form of SIB. A third condition evaluated a temporary delay in the advent of the next compliance request. The three test conditions were the following:

*TABLE 2.35* ■ **DATA ON SELF-INJURY FOR CONDITIONS AND DAYS**

Number of Occurrences of Self-injurious Behavior

|  | Condition 1 | Condition 2 | Condition 3 | Compliance with demand on second request (condition 3) |
|---|---|---|---|---|
| Day 1 | 0 | 3 | 0 | Y |
| Day 2 | 0 | 5 | 0 | Y |
| Day 3 | 0 | 1 | 0 | N |
| Day 4 | 0 | 2 | 0 | Y |

■ Condition 1—The task demands were stopped any time Fred said "No."
■ Condition 2—The task demands continued after Fred said "No" and were terminated when he completed the task or when he engaged in the less severe form of SIB.
■ Condition 3—The task demands were terminated when Fred said "No" and then re-presented after a 15-minute delay.

A session consisted of presenting each of the three conditions per day, with a 1-hour interval between each test condition. This type of data was collected for 4 consecutive days. Data was recorded for occurrences of self-injury in all conditions. Compliance with demand was recorded only for condition 3. The last column indicates whether compliance occurred in condition 3 after the command was presented the second time, that is, after he said "no." I included this condition and additional data on compliance because some staff reported that he would comply if you re-presented a demand after a brief delay (see Table 2.35).

When tasks demands were stopped when he said "no," the rate of SIB was zero. The function of escape is further elucidated when one compares this with what happened in condition 2, where SIB produces escape (rather than saying "no"). Also, staff perceptions about his SIB behavior being less likely when you wait a short time to re-present the demand after the initial refusal seemed correct. Self-injury was absent during this condition, while compliance to the second request occurred 3 times.

Based on this data, I was able to demonstrate that attention was an incidental variable involved in the severe form. Consider that when attention is given to Fred when he picked flesh from his legs, he also experienced a removal of the task demand. It was the latter stimulus change that was driving his behavior, not the attention that also resulted. I designed a simple intervention that resulted in 0 occurrences of severe SIB immediately upon implementation. The plan was successful over a long period subsequent to the initial contingency change. Over the next 2 years there were no occurrences of the severe SIB. There were two occurrences of the less severe SIB. Both occurred when Fred was at medical appointments and the medical staff at the facility was insistent that he comply with their demands even after he had refused.

## DISCUSSION QUESTIONS

1. How would you empirically demonstrate that one behavior really was a precursor behavior relative to another more problematic behavior?
2. Why would you do an analysis of a precursor behavior as opposed to the targeted behavior?
3. How would you design an analysis of a client's hitting behavior that typically resulted in a broken nose for the victim?

## In-Situ Hypothesis Testing

An in-situ hypothesis test uses a design similar to that described in analogue assessments, that is, a quick switching of conditions. However, an in-situ hypothesis test contrasts with an analogue assessment in two dimensions: (1) it is conducted in the setting of interest and (2) a functional treatment (based on the entertained hypothesis) is alternated with a baseline condition (Repp, Felce, & Barton, 1988). In this manner a comparison is made between the rates of problem behavior during the functional treatment and the rates of behavior during the baseline (i.e., treatment not implemented).

The personnel in the in-situ setting (school, home residence, treatment facility) implement the data collection for the two conditions for only a brief period of the day, rather than across the entire day. The test is not conducted across the entire target time period. Rather, it is abbreviated in length, as its purpose is merely to test and not treat (at this point). At select time periods, across a week to several weeks, the teacher alternates two conditions—baseline and treatment conditions. For example, on one day, during math period, the baseline condition is implemented. The following day, the treatment condition is implemented. Therefore, you would select only one hypothesis to test. The following is a case example of this assessment method.

*I Hear Voices.* In-situ hypothesis tests are well suited to assessing the symptoms of mental illness. Consider the case of Joann, a 41-year-old female who had been diagnosed as having schizophrenia. She frequently would report that she heard voices telling her to harm herself. She often reported that she felt worthless and that she had let her family down by "getting mental illness." I (K.S.) developed an initial hypothesis involving this class of verbal behaviors as maintained by staff (adult) attention. I observed that her talking about hearing voices resulted in staff talking with her for extended periods of time. Such behavior appeared to be functional in accessing protracted conversations, with staff becoming an interested audience. Here is a great example of this function. A staff person might ask her how the meds were working. At that point, she began to talk about "hearing voices." This led to multiple questions from the staff about the content of the "voices," with a conversation that could last 15 minutes. Unfortunately, the times when she tried to start a friendly, but nonsymptomatic conversation, the opposite result occurred. The staff person would be polite, but the conversation lasted less than 1 minute. It seemed like lengthy attention from staff was the differential consequence that explained her verbal behavior. I set up two test conditions to see if two rates of symptomatic behavior would result.

The usual contingencies were kept in place at the mental health center. This required no manipulation of what had previously happened when Joanne reported hearing voices. The staff person would talk with Joann and ask her about the content of her hallucinations. The length of social interaction was typically dependent on Joann reporting higher levels of hallucinations and describing the content of the hallucinations in some detail. This is termed condition one. Every report about hallucinations and hearing voices was tallied in this setting.

I implemented the test condition in her home (condition two). The same behavior (reporting to staff that she was hearing voices) was the dependent measure. The staff members in the home were instructed to provide differential levels of social attention dependent on the content of her conversation. The staff responded to any reports of auditory hallucinations by simply saying, "What coping skills are you using for that?" and then a prompt to Joanne to "Go practice them and let me know how it worked." However, if Joann initiated a conversation that did not involve references to auditory hallucinations the staff would simply talk with her about the topic she presented during the appointment. In other words, a treatment based on attention was deployed in this setting only. If the symptomatic behavior went down in the home while still remaining at heightened levels at the center, the data confirms the attention hypothesis. Each test condition was in place on alternating weeks (for a total of 8 weeks). Results are presented in Figure 2.1. This data clearly demonstrates that for this individual, the reports of auditory hallucinations functioned to access staff attention.

*It's Attention I Desire!* I (K.S.) was referred the case of Marta, a 28-year-old female who was diagnosed with borderline personality disorder. She engaged in several difficult behaviors, including threats to harm herself as well as an incident involving a self-administered overdose of medications. I had the opportunity to observe Marta both at a drop-in socialization center and when she initially moved into my facility. I noted that when she made a threat to harm herself there was a dramatic increase in the level of social interaction from her peers and the professional staff at the center. All she needed to do was to say "I don't feel like living anymore, no one would care if I disappeared," and staff came to her immediately. Standard operating policies in the mental health system required that professional staff assess her risk of suicide immediately. Therefore, all verbal threats were taken as a potential prelude to the actual act of hurting oneself and attempting suicide. Of course, the process of assessing this risk necessarily involved a great deal of one-on-one interaction with staff. The incident of her overdose on medication also resulted in both immediate increases in social interaction, starting with the emergency transport to the hospital and continuing with the medical staff once admitted to the hospital.

Based on these direct observations, I hypothesized that her threats and attempts to harm herself were maintained by staff attention. I decided to empirically determine if attention was the maintaining contingency by conducting two test conditions. In the first condition, noncontingent continuous attention from staff was provided for the entire day. In the second condition, the usual level of staff interaction was provided. These two conditions were presented in an alternating fashion on 6 consecutive days. The results were rather dramatic. There were no threats to harm herself and no attempts to harm herself on the days when attention was provided noncontingently.

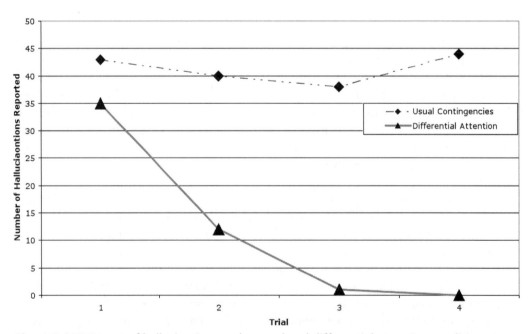

*Figure 2.1* ■ Report of hallucinations under usual and differential attention conditions.

*TABLE 2.36* ■ **DATA UNDER EACH CONDITION**

| Day | NCR Attention | Usual Attention |
| --- | --- | --- |
| 1 | | 6 threats to harm herself |
| 2 | 0 threats | |
| 3 | | 8 threats to harm herself |
| 4 | 0 threats | |
| 5 | | 4 threats and 1 attempt to harm herself |
| 6 | 0 threats | |

There were multiple threats to harm herself on the days that attention was at usual levels (see Table 2.36).

Based on this in-situ assessment, we were able to determine that the problematic behaviors that had led to a diagnosis of borderline personality disorder were maintained by staff attention. We were then able to design an effective treatment that involved an initial habituation phase of continuous noncontingent attention and then thinning the schedule of staff attention. The intervention also included the development of a network of peers to provide sufficient levels of social interaction.

## DISCUSSION QUESTIONS

1. How would you design an empirical test for the function of behavior associated with other mental illnesses? Auditory hallucinations? Delusional statements? Fixed delusions? Paranoid statements? Suicidal threats?
2. How would you ensure the safety of the client and at the same time ensure the fidelity of your assessment protocol?

*In Classrooms.* How would you use in-situ hypothesis tests in educational settings? You believe a child's problem behavior in an elementary special day class serves to access teacher attention on some intermittent basis. The in-situ hypothesis test for teacher attention as the maintaining variable would involve 6–10 short sessions (30 to 45 minutes in length) over a 2-week period. For half the sessions, the teacher would not alter his usual manner of managing the student (baseline condition). For the other half of the sessions, if the child was engaged in work, the teacher would provide attention in the form of social approval and points for on-task behavior during the randomly occurring beep (see the beeper system in Cipani, 2008a). Therefore, in the functional treatment condition, a treatment addressing an attention hypothesis is implemented for a short period of time during the day. If problem behaviors are dramatically more frequent during baseline sessions, the maintaining contingency would seem to be teacher attention.

An in-situ hypothesis test provides the following advantages:

■ It is a direct assessment of the target behavior in the setting of interest, with all relevant contextual variables present.
■ If treatment fidelity is obtained, an effective treatment is discovered, leaving only the requirement to develop staff monitoring for extended periods of application.
■ The staff, parents, and teachers who implemented the test probably need less convincing that an effective treatment will be worth the time because they "had a hand" in the test.

## WHY DID YOU DO THAT?

Some naive people ask the children or clients, "Why did you do that?" The individual being asked supposedly examines her thought process and purposes behind such behavior and then provides an answer. In other words, the purpose of behavior is often assumed to be available by simply asking the client to engage in self-introspection. The following is a hypothetical scenario of such an interaction.

*Teacher:*  Jose, why did you hit Bobby?

*Jose:*  Well, Ms. Farrier, I believe that I am more likely to hit other students when we both want the same thing. I have noticed that when I hit most of the children on the playground, they pretty much back away from whatever it is I want. I then get access to the item, toy, or activity, unencumbered by anyone else. I guess my hitting capability is pretty effective in accessing tangible reinforcers and is maintained because of this effect it has on the other children. I guess being "feared" on the playground has its advantages.

*Teacher:*  Well thank you, Jose, for your fabulous insight.

Now there is an insightful analysis by this student of his aggressive behavior's function. If that does not sound like anything you have heard, that is because it never happens like that in real life! Here is a more typical scenario.

*Teacher:*  Jose, why did you hit Bobby?

*Jose:*  I don't know.

*Teacher:*  What kind of answer is that?

*Jose:*  I don't know. He makes me mad.

*Teacher:*  He makes you mad? How do you think he feels when he gets hit?

*Jose:*  I don't know.

If asking the individual why he exhibited a particular behavior would lead to an FBA, we would only be writing the chapter on functional treatment. Think how much easier it would be for everyone! Some promising work is under way in the area of developing questions about function (Van Camp et al., 2006). However, it is still necessary for a person with training in behavior analysis to collect several sources of objective and subjective data when determining why somebody does something.

### What Is Not an FBA?

Functional behavior assessment has grown in popularity since it was specified as a federal requirement for special education students with disabilities who engage in certain problem behaviors. A common approach to this requirement from personnel who have not received training in applied behavior analysis is to simply list all the activities and events that occur prior to the behavior in one column (called antecedents). Concurrently, these untrained personnel then observe and record all the staff responses that occur subsequent to the behavior. These are listed in a column to the right of the behavior. Their analysis then concludes that antecedents for the target behavior can be any of a number of events and stimuli. Concurrently, the consequences of the behavior can also be any of a number of events that follow the response. Table 2.37 illustrates this (technically incorrect) format for analyzing problem behavior (often found in many reports called FBA).

*TABLE 2.37* ■ **NONEXAMPLE OF FBA**

| Antecedents | Target Behavior(s) | Consequent Events |
|---|---|---|
| During instruction | Verbal abuse and oppositional behavior | Negative teacher attention |
| When bored | | Peer attention |
| Too much light | | Controls environment |
| Not enough light | | Gets his way |
| Too much noise | | |
| When playing games with others | | |

It should now be clear that this type of analysis ignores basic tenets of an FBA in this text. Note in Table 2.37 that one of the antecedents for verbal abuse and oppositional behavior (which would need a more pinpointed definition) is during instruction. If such behavior is more likely under this condition, which of the consequent events listed in the third column is the maintaining contingency? The answer is: We don't know because the author of this type of report is probably oblivious to a true understanding of behavioral function!

An FBA does not simply entail a listing of observed phenomena. One must examine data and information and make sense of it. One should conclude that the target behavior is maintained because of what it produces or removes reliably in the social or physical environment. Now that you have read this material, be an advocate for the correct deployment of an FBA in school and other settings. Point out that the analysis in Table 2.37 does not reflect sufficient knowledge for the author to claim an FBA has been conducted!

## ECO-SYSTEMIC ASSESSMENT

Is it necessary to conduct an FBA for every significant behavior problem? It might very well be that simply correcting "wacky contingencies" in the classroom (or other settings where task demands are made) would produce the desired effect (see Chapter 3). In classroom settings, contingencies for desired classroom behavior should be considered first, whether such are produced for on-task behavior, assignment accuracy and completion, or the absence or low rates of problem behavior. An eco-systemic assessment of the existent classroom contingencies may reveal inequities in differential reinforcement (see Table 2.38).

If the rate of on-task behavior does not matter, in terms of access to preferred events, than on-task behavior is of no consequence. Whether a student is on-task 20% or 80% of the time does not affect his length of time with preferred activities. Similarly, if completing assignments results in the same access to preferred events as failing to start the assignment, then there does not exist a powerful contingency for assignment completion. Finishing the assignment does not produce a different result for the student than not finishing the assignment in the short term. The only probable contingency of repeatedly failing to finish class work is lower grades, which may not be an effective contingency.

Depending on your findings, you may conclude that designing an individualized or class-wide contingency management plan that either differentially reinforces acceptable levels of on-task behavior, differentially reinforces assignment completion, or targets disruptive behavior is indicated before resorting to a functional behavioral assessment and treatment. There are many plans that address each of these areas (see Cipani, 2008). For on-task behavior an efficient management strategy is the beeper system (Cipani, 2008).

---

**TABLE 2.38 ■ ECO-SYSTEMIC ASSESSMENT OF CLASSROOM CONTINGENCIES**

---

1. Is student on-task behavior systematically producing a powerful reinforcer?

   a. Is on-task behavior or attending behavior systematically and frequently monitored (and not via a daily rating scale)?

   b. When the student engages in higher rates of on-task behavior, is either a conditional reinforcer (points) or a tangible reinforcer provided?

   c. When a student engages in high rates of on-task behavior, is the result more work (i.e., additional nonpreferred assignments) until the end of the time period?

   d. When a student has a lower rate of on-task behavior during a period, does he lose access to a designated reinforcer?

   e. Is the reinforcer potent enough to motivate the student day in and day out?

2. Is student assignment completion systematically producing a powerful reinforcer?

   a. Is completing assignments systematically and frequently monitored (does teacher immediately receive material when student completes assignment)?

   b. When the student completes an assignment, is either a conditional reinforcer (points) or a tangible reinforcer provided at that point?

   c. Is a Premack contingency in effect for completing work? Does the student get access to a high-probability behavior contingent on successful (accuracy) completion of a prespecified amount of class assignment?

   d. When the student completes an assignment, is the result another assignment (without earning points) for them to complete until the end of the time period?

   e. When the student fails to complete an assignment on a given day, does the student immediately lose access to a designated reinforcer?

   f. Is the reinforcer potent enough to motivate the student day in and day out?

3. Is there either a DRL, DRO, or DRA program in effect targeting specifically problem disruptive behavior by the student?

   a. Is disruptive behavior defined in discrete terms and recorded with each occurrence?

   b. Is there a behavioral standard, across a period(s), half day, or full school day that delineates the number of disruptive incidents that will involve removal of a specific contingent reinforcing item or event?

   c. Over the last 2–3 weeks, how often has the student earned such a reinforcer, and how often has the student lost access to this reinforcer?

---

Beeps at unpredictable intervals require the teacher or student (if self-management is utilized) to determine if on-task behavior is occurring at that point in time (i.e., momentary time sampling). The teacher initially designates a level of on-task behavior that accesses a powerful reinforcer (e.g., 60% on-task rate accesses the designated reinforcer). If 20 unpredictable beeps occurred in a 1-hour period and the student rated herself on-task for 12 of them, her rate of on-task behavior is 60%, and she would earn the reinforcer.

If you determine that assignment completion is not being systematically reinforced in the classroom, then a *beat the clock* contingency system would be a good strategy to effect (Cipani, 2004). In "beat the clock," a designated period of time is given to complete the assignment. If the student completes the assignment within the time period (to some designated accuracy level), points are given. Points are then exchanged at a later date or time for the reinforcer. A point system across the day is established so that multiple "beat the clock" plans can be implemented across multiple assignments in different content areas. A behavioral plan called the *Disruptive Incident Barometer* could be implemented to target a reduction in disruptive behaviors (Cipani, 2008). This plan basically involves a differential reinforcement of low-rate behavior (DRL) program for specified target problem behaviors.

## CONDUCT A PERFORMANCE DISCREPANCY ANALYSIS

A performance discrepancy analysis is the final step in determining whether the referred problem behavior is indeed at problematic levels. As indicated before, behaviors that impair the health and welfare of the client or others are apparent and require immediate intervention. However, with other behaviors, such as noncompliance, off-task behavior, failure to follow directions, or tantrum behaviors, there does not exist a readily available standard to determine whether the client's level of behavior falls within age-appropriate norms. One would likely assume that the acceptable level of behavior can be a function of several variables, such as age of the child or client and context. The basic question for these problem behavior referrals is "How much of this behavior is too much (or often)?"

Let's examine the hypothetical case of a 4-year-old child referred to you because he doesn't follow directions at home. Your data-gathering efforts may find that there are certainly occasions when he doesn't follow directions. However, there are also occasions when he does follow directions. Is this child in need of intervention? Without entering any personal bias, the question becomes, "What is an acceptable level of noncompliance in a 4-year-old child under certain events or activities?" Surely, we do not expect the child to be compliant to all presented instructions and requests every day (please separate delusions from reality here). On the other extreme, never following instructions is certainly unacceptable. What is the happy acceptable medium? A performance discrepancy analysis allows you to determine, in an objective manner, the behavioral standard for acceptability. You can then judge where the current child's behavior falls in relation to that standard.

A performance discrepancy analysis involves a comparison of the rates of a client's problem behavior with the acceptable level (or rate) of that behavior. How does one determine what is an acceptable level of any behavior? A method for objectively determining what is an acceptable level of a behavior is the normative comparison method (Kazdin, 1977; Matson, Esveldt-Dawson, & Kazdin, 1983). The method allows one to identify, in measurable terms, the norm for one behavior under specific antecedent conditions.

In utilizing a normative comparison method, one first identifies same-aged peers or persons who are judged to be nonproblematic with respect to the behavior. For example, if you were trying to determine what is an acceptable level of noncompliance for a referred 4-year-old child (noncompliance as a percentage of noncompliance to total first requests), you would want to identify a number of 4 year olds whose parents or teachers report that they do not have a serious problem with noncompliance. This process is called the criterion group selection (Kazdin & Matson, 1981).

Once the criterion group is selected, you want to measure the occurrence of noncompliance with the criterion group under the same situations as those identified as generating noncompliance in the target child. To simplify potential logistical problems, you can select children that are readily available at your particular site. Once this data is available, you would not need to go out again and repeat this part of the process for other referrals. The observation of these children in the criterion group as well as observation of the target child should occur over multiple observation sessions so that a stable rate of the behavior for each child can be obtained. You have now established a norm with respect to the level of the behavior that is deemed acceptable.

If this aspect of the performance discrepancy is difficult to gather, that is, observing same-aged peers, you may be able to substitute interview data from other teachers or parents for the norms of acceptable behavior. However, realize that such data may not be as reliable as direct observation of a criterion group. Often people verbally state one standard, for example, "All children must raise their hands whenever they want to be recognized," whereas direct observation may reveal that it is not an exacting standard. Although children may often raise their hand to be recognized, there is a small percentage of times when other behaviors result in recognition by the teacher. If interview data will be the method by which you collect data on the criterion group, try to identify the percentage of occurrence by increments of 10% (0%–10%, 10%–20%, 20%–30%, 30%–40%, etc.).

With the data collected, you can then determine the ranges at which the noncompliant behavior is acceptable and the ranges of noncompliant behavior that appear to be

*TABLE 2.39* ■ **NONCOMPLIANCE DATA ACROSS 10 CHILDREN**

| Child | % Noncompliance |
|-------|-----------------|
| 1 | 24 |
| 2 | 33 |
| 3 | 42 |
| 4 | 41 |
| 5 | 37 |
| 6 | 69 |
| 7 | 28 |
| 8 | 81 |
| 9 | 44 |
| 10 | 33 |

socially unacceptable. As an example, let's say that you identified 10 4-year-old children for the criterion group. You directly measured their rate of noncompliance in target situations. The mean percentage of noncompliance computed across several observation sessions for each child in the criterion group was reported as follows (see Table 2.39).

In examining the data in Table 2.39, with the exception of two children, the mean percentage of noncompliance is between 24% and 44%. This range of noncompliance can then be used as a basis for identifying an acceptable level of noncompliance and used as the standard when assessing and subsequently examining the target child's level of noncompliance. Table 2.40 presents seven steps to follow in conducting a discrepancy analysis.

*TABLE 2.40* ■ **STEPS TO PERFORMING A DISCREPANCY ANALYSIS**

1. Identify the problem behavior in observable terms.
2. Select a criterion group of same-aged peers in the same or similar locale.
3. Measure the occurrence of the target behavior of persons in the criterion group across several days under the same situations in which the referred client has problems.
4. Identify the range and average (mean) level of occurrence of the problem behavior.
5. Measure the target referred client's problem behavior.
6. Compare the client's rates of problem behavior with the criterion group's range and the average rate of occurrence.
7. Identify any discrepancy between the client's data and the criterion group data.

## DISCUSSION QUESTIONS

How is a performance discrepancy analysis used in determining the target objective? What is its function in a functional behavioral assessment?

## REVIEW PREVIOUS TREATMENTS IMPLEMENTED

A review of previous treatments implemented should be conducted prior to the design of the intervention strategy. In some cases, the problem behavior may have been previously treated successfully. This review may provide an easy solution to the present concern. In other cases, one might be able to identify ineffective techniques. In reviewing previous treatments, the professional should still take into account the possibility that the maintaining variables might be different from the previous circumstances.

What are some issues to examine when reviewing documentation on previous programs implemented for a client's problem behaviors? Previous treatments that were not written up in detail are hard to evaluate, in that the specifics of the treatment deployed are not delineated for your current examination. In addition, in reviewing previous effective or ineffective treatments, the professional must determine whether the treatment strategy was implemented with integrity. Sometimes, previously conducted treatments that were judged ineffective might have been proven effective if carried out reliably over a reasonable period of time. Judging the integrity of previous treatments may be hard to evaluate unless recorded data is available in anecdotal or objective form that demonstrates the integrity of the treatment implementation. Table 2.41 provides some questions to consider when reviewing previous treatments implemented.

If consent is obtained, it can really be helpful to interview staff at agencies that previously served the client. What may not be available in written documentation upon review are factors that may have led to the success or failure of the previous treatment. Talking to someone that was previously involved with the client's treatment may allow you to discern if the previous treatment failed due to poor design, inadequate functional analysis, or poor implementation of the program procedures. When possible, with the client's consent for disclosure of information, make the call!

## REVIEW OF HEALTH AND MEDICAL RECORDS

A review of medical records and the files of the client may indicate contraindications to certain treatments. In other cases, it may reveal important factors that suggest a pattern of behavior. Does the behavior occur during certain seasons of the year or certain times of the month (Bailey & Pyles, 1989)? The records may also reveal that the problem behavior may be a side effect of medication the client is currently on (Bailey & Pyles, 1989). If any of these possibilities exist, a medical consultation and evaluation are recommended. The questions in Table 2.42 can be considered in light of a medical consultation as possible referral questions for the medical professional (adapted from Bailey & Pyles, 1989). When making the referral, minimally provide the medical professional with the problem behaviors and any information currently gathered through the current or previous behavioral assessments. Also, indicate to the medical professional that your request for a consult would be to evaluate the possibility of medical causes or interventions along with the concurrent use of a behavioral intervention program.

*TABLE 2.41* ■ **QUESTIONS TO CONSIDER IN REVIEWING PREVIOUS TREATMENTS IMPLEMENTED**

1. What was the focus of the treatment?
2. Is the current problem behavior the same or similar to that targeted in earlier interventions?
3. What was the treatment procedure? Was it effective in remediating the problem?
4. If a functional analysis was conducted, what was the conclusion drawn regarding the function(s) of the problem behavior at that time? Does the current problem look similar in function(s) to its previous function?
5. How extensive was the staff training program? How were staff trained on the procedures of the program?
6. Has consent for release of information from the individual or legal guardian and agency administration been obtained, or can it be obtained to interview personnel from previous settings? Are the person(s) who were involved with the previous treatment available for contact?

**TABLE 2.42 ■ QUESTIONS TO CONSIDER IN REVIEWING MEDICAL/HEALTH RECORDS**

1. Could the problem behavior be the result of a medical condition of the client?
2. Is it possibly an allergic reaction?
3. If the client is or has been on medication, could the problem behavior be a side effect of the medication or a behavioral effect of the medication?
4. Are there any potential treatment procedures contraindicated, given the client's physical and metabolic condition?
5. Could the problem behavior be an allergic or seasonal reaction?
6. Is this type of problem commonly treated effectively with medical interventions? If so, what are those procedures, and what is the role of the agency in their implementation?

In some circumstances, behavioral data can guide you to the proper decision involving a medical consult. Nolan was a 28-year-old male who had been referred to my (K.S.) facility to deal with self-induced vomiting. He had been treated for many years by the local mental health provider for various symptoms of depression and psychosis. He had been living in board and care homes for several years prior to his most recent admission to the inpatient psychiatric unit. The vomiting and concomitant weight loss had started about 3 months prior to his admission and had resulted in his losing placement in his group home as well as being admitted to an inpatient psychiatric facility because no obvious medical cause could be determined. Interviews with the inpatient staff and a review of inpatient records did not contain a notation of medical issues. The inpatient staff indicated that Nolan would simply go to the bathroom after a meal and vomit. When efforts were introduced to prevent this (a staff person accompanied him into the bathroom) he began to vomit in other areas of the psychiatric facility and deny that the vomitus the staff found was his.

Upon entry to our facility we began the process of observing him and attempting to determine what contingencies might be maintaining this behavior. We observed that the vomiting occurred after meals, however, it did not occur after eating a small food item such as a snack or candy bar. Quantity of food seemed to be a factor. Socially mediated contingencies were evaluated by examining the conditions present in our facility as well as reports from the prior psychiatric facility. Staff attention seemed unlikely because he made active attempts to avoid detection both while vomiting and to hide the vomitus seemingly to avoid detection. Tangible reinforcement seemed unlikely because no additional items were brought to him after vomiting. Escape as a hypothesis for the vomiting seemed unlikely because no demands were terminated after vomiting. There was no increase or decrease in social interaction following the vomiting behavior. It appeared to be a behavior that produced an immediate effect, that is, a direct contingency.

I made a full review of Nolan's medical records and found that several years prior to his present admission, he had been hospitalized and treated for ingesting lye while living in another county. The record indicated that he had received several procedures to treat scar tissue that had accumulated in his esophagus. My assistant contacted the physician who had originally treated Nolan and asked if the procedures to treat the scar tissue could have any effect on his current problem with vomiting. The physician indicated that it was highly likely. Further, he had been scheduled to have a procedure to reopen his esophagus 2 years prior, but when he moved they had lost touch with him. We quickly scheduled Nolan for the necessary procedure. Following the procedure, vomiting events dropped to 0 for the next 3 weeks. Nolan was discharged from our facility, and 1-year follow-up data indicated that the vomiting behavior did not recur in the community group home he was discharged to.

## DISCUSSION QUESTIONS

1. How would you set up conditions to determine the targeted behavior is directly related to a medical condition?
2. Under what conditions might a medical condition act as an MO for targeted behaviors?
3. How could you set up an analgesic trial to determine the contribution of pain as an MO related to a targeted behavior?
4. How would you present your findings to a medical doctor so that they provided actionable information for the doctor?

## SUMMARY

This chapter presented five steps in conducting a functional behavioral assessment. First, the problem behavior has to be pinpointed into observable terms, thereby laying the groundwork for a reliable method of measuring the problem behavior. In addition to collecting baseline data on the rate of occurrence of the behavior, an FBA is conducted for the behavior problem, through one or several methods for collecting such data. Once all the data is collected, a performance discrepancy analysis is conducted to determine if the problem behavior is at excessive levels (relative to same-aged peers), and discrepancies are prioritized for intervention. Finally, previous treatments implemented as well as the client's medical and health records are reviewed. With all this data, you are now prepared to analyze and interpret this information. In identifying the function of the problem behavior, you will now identify which of four diagnostic categories is most likely.

## *Note*

1. Taken from Cipani (2004), with permission.

# A Function-Based, Diagnostic Classification System for Problem Behaviors

## 3

This chapter presents a function-based diagnostic classification system for target problem behaviors. There are four major categories in this system, previously delineated (Cipani, 1990, 1994). Each major diagnostic category delineates a specific maintaining contingency with respect to two parameters: (a) the type of reinforcement contingency (positive or negative) and (b) the method by which the contingency is produced by the behavior (direct versus socially mediated). Problem behaviors producing positive reinforcement are termed *access behaviors* (two diagnostic categories) and behaviors producing negative reinforcement (two diagnostic categories) are termed *escape behaviors* (to also incorporate avoidance functions as well). Within each major category, several subcategories are delineated.

## CHARACTERISTICS OF FUNCTION-BASED CLASSIFICATION SYSTEMS

The characteristics of a function-based diagnostic classification system are the following (Cipani, 1994):

- Diagnosis of behavior problem characteristics, not child characteristics
- Prescriptive differential treatment derived from a differential diagnosis
- Assessment data collected to provide information on context variables, not just rate of behavior
- Assessment phase concludes with diagnosis phase, in which a function-based category is selected

### Diagnose Behavior, Not Client

A function-based diagnostic classification system examines the contextual nature of the problem behavior. It does not presume that the exhibition of behavior is driven by characteristics inherent in the client or child. This sharply contrasts with the current psychiatric approach to diagnosing client behavior (e.g., *DSM-IV-R*).

Let's say you have three different children you are involved with as a behavioral consultant. Each child engages in a topographically (form) different set of target behaviors. In the traditional psychiatric diagnostic system, each child may receive a different diagnosis because the form of the problem behaviors is different. Because the behaviors or symptoms are different, their presumed cause must be different. In contrast, a function-based classification of the problem behaviors may reveal that the problem behaviors exhibited by these three children are similar in function, even though topographically dissimilar. Therefore, the diagnostic classification of these behaviors could be the same.

In a function-based diagnostic classification system, the form of the behavior (in most cases) does not dictate a particular function. In contrast to symptoms or target behaviors being the key to diagnosing the child, a function-based diagnostic approach will assess the environmental function of the client's behaviors to make a differential diagnosis. In this example, functional behavioral assessment data may indicate that all three children's behavior represents the same function. Hence, the function-based diagnosis for all three sets of problems might be subsumed in the same major category—socially mediated escape

(SME) function. Therefore, despite the obvious individual differences between these children, the prescription for behavior-analytic treatment will be similar in composition.

## Prescriptive Differential Treatment

A function-based diagnostic classification system also has implications for differential prescriptive treatment. A child diagnosed with a *DSM-IV-R* criteria of oppositional defiant disorder is referred for a number of behavior problems. Such problems are assumed to be a result of his mental disorder. These problem behaviors include aggressive behavior toward residential staff, noncompliance, and running away from the facility. Aggression, noncompliance, and running away are topographically dissimilar behaviors. Does that mean that different behavioral contingencies should be invoked, depending on which behavior is exhibited at a particular time? Not in the least! If all three behaviors are found to serve the same environmental function, the treatment program would specify the same contingency across the occurrence of any of these behaviors. In other words, irrespective of which behavior occurs, the contingency it would produce (according to the treatment plan) would be the same. However, if noncompliance and running away serve a different function than the child's aggressive behavior, there would be one treatment contingency for aggression that would vary from that deployed when the child is either noncompliant or runs from the facility. Treatment is driven by function of behavior.

Here is another example contrasting the difference between a traditional versus function-based classification system. A child named Susanna, diagnosed with conduct disorder, hits the teacher. A different child named Billy, diagnosed with oppositional defiant disorder, throws a tantrum during class and refuses to follow even simple directions. A third child, Raul, who is diagnosed with ADHD, cries and throws a tantrum when he is prevented from running out of the classroom. With the traditional psychiatric approach, one assumes that each of these three children exhibit such behaviors because of their disorder. Susanna hits her teacher (and others) because of her affliction with conduct disorders. Billy throws a tantrum because he has oppositional defiant disorder. Raul cries and throws a tantrum because he is impulsive and is incapable of delaying gratification because of his ADHD. Research studies in applied behavior analysis have failed to demonstrate that certain behavioral procedures only work for children with conduct disorder, and not for those with ADHD. As an example, time out, under certain conditions, functions as a punisher for target behavior, irrespective of the traditional diagnosis. Yet in the function-based system, treatments do vary as a function of the diagnosis. Time out can not only function as a punisher for socially mediated access problems, but also, alternatively, function as a reinforcer for behavior problems under escape contingencies.

Classifying problem behaviors according to environmental function does make a difference in the design of a functional behavioral treatment. In contrast, differential diagnosis using the traditional psychiatric *Diagnostic and Statistical Manual of Mental Disorders* does not prove fruitful in determining functional behavioral treatments based on syndromes of behaviors.

## Assess Context Variables

It should now be clear that behavioral assessment is concerned with more than determining the rate of the target behavior. Rather, you need to examine the environmental events that precede the behavior as well as the consequent events. Further, an understanding of the client's motivational condition at the time makes for a clearer picture of why certain consequent events function as reinforcers at those times. Assessment is driven by the need to determine the environmental factors that are present when the problem behavior occurs, that is, the social and physical environmental context.

## GOT CONTEXT DATA?

I (E.C.) was involved in a case consultation years ago where a student who was attending a nonpublic school for emotionally disturbed children was being discussed at an interdisciplinary team meeting. Both school and mental health professionals were in attendance at this meeting. Although no actual behavioral assessment data were reported on specific target behaviors, the school and residential staff indicated that his behavior had worsened. They ascribed it to a litany of possible reasons. The reasons ranged from wrong diagnosis (e.g., "I don't believe he is schizophrenic. I think he is manic-depressive!") to blaming his dysfunctional family and his home visits. About 45 minutes went by without any discussion about specific target behaviors in the classroom. As the meeting was winding down one of the teachers asked, "OK, what do we do when he acts up?" Somebody volunteered what appeared to be a solution, "Let's use time out." Why was time out being recommended? Was it important to comprehend that he was from a dysfunctional family, according to some experts? Are students who come from dysfunctional families best treated with time out? Was it because time out works best with manic-depressive children (but not, apparently, schizophrenia)? Nothing in the prior discussion had any relation to discussing the behavioral reasons for this proposed treatment. Nor was the rate of target behaviors presented. What was also missing was an analysis of the context under which these target behaviors occur. Further assessment of the contextual nature of the behavioral problems was required.

### Assessment Phase Concludes With a Differential Diagnosis Phase

In the early development of the field of applied behavior analysis, the design of behavioral treatments often did not include a diagnostic phase. The collection of behavioral data often would lead directly to the formulation of a behavioral treatment regimen. In part, this occurred because the word *diagnosis* was associated with the mental health diagnostic system, which proved useless in the design of behavioral treatments. Given the lack of utility of a traditional diagnosis in prescribing functional behavioral treatments, many behavior therapists have often worked with only two stages of service.

We believe that a function-based diagnostic classification system serves an important intermediate step. Such an intermediate phase between assessment and intervention would provide for a more guided and deliberate approach to behavioral treatment selection. Jumping to treatment from assessment may exacerbate the problem.

### WHAT IS THE UTILITY OF A FUNCTION-BASED DIAGNOSTIC CLASSIFICATION SYSTEM?

For people naive to behavioral-analytic formulations, it may appear that one simply identifies a consequence for a selected target behavior. The selected consequence should be capable of ameliorating the level of the target behavior problem when applied as a contingency. Therefore, the only technical skill needed is to pinpoint the referred problem in observable terms and follow it with an effective consequence. For example, if a referred client is disruptive in an enclave-work environment, first one defines the disruptive behavior in observable terms. Then the professional identifies a consequence to follow the target behavior and specifies the treatment contingency. If this contingency does not work, the professional would select another consequence and design another behavioral treatment contingency.

Functional behavior-analytic treatment stems from hypotheses about the function or purpose of the target behavior. These hypotheses (diagnoses) are generated from the collection and examination of functional behavioral assessment data. The function-based diagnostic classification of the problem behavior results from the clinician reviewing the information gathered during the functional behavioral assessment process. Such a process is analogous to procedures used in other science-based fields.

For example, in medicine, during an office visit, the physician gathers information about your current medical condition by asking you a series of questions, called a diagnostic interview. She or he then obtains other information, possibly from a physical examination as well as individual tests run on medical equipment. The physician then analyzes all the data obtained relevant to your condition and hypothesizes about your current medical problem. The physician then makes a differential diagnosis. This diagnosis subsequently allows the physician to prescribe a treatment based on that diagnosis. This treatment prescription makes "good sense" given this diagnosis. The treatment for a diagnosis of flu is different from a treatment prescription for a diagnosis of whooping cough. We believe it is just as important to determine the function of the problem behavior to ensure that the behavioral treatment being prescribed is functionally related to the problem behavior.

## THE FUNCTION-BASED DIAGNOSTIC CLASSIFICATION SYSTEM

Cipani (1990, 1994) previously delineated four major diagnostic categories for classifying the environmental function of problem behaviors. The current chapter continues the use of these four major categories. Problem behaviors will be classified with regard to the reinforcement operation currently maintaining the problem behavior (positive or negative) as well as the method of access to such reinforcement (direct or socially mediated). Problem behaviors that serve a positive reinforcement function are termed *access behaviors* (i.e., access positive reinforcers). Problem behaviors that serve a negative reinforcement function are termed *escape behaviors* (i.e., escape or avoid negative reinforcers). Access can be either socially mediated or direct. Escape can also be either socially mediated or direct.

The following major categories constitute this classification system:

(1.0)  Direct access (DA)
(2.0)  Socially mediated access (SMA)
(3.0)  Direct escape (DE)
(4.0)  Socially mediated escape (SME)

Within each category, subcategories are offered. Each subcategory contains the basic reinforcement properties inherent in the major category. For each major category, a subcategory of "other" is offered to cover any functions not specified explicitly in the differential diagnostic system. The subcategories within each major category are:

(1.0)  Direct access (DA)
    1.1  DA: immediate sensory stimuli (specify type and location of stimulation)
    1.2  DA: direct chain to tangible reinforcers (specify tangible or class of tangible accessed)
(2.0)  Socially mediated access (SMA)
    2.1  SMA: adult/staff attention (specify which adults/staff)
    2.2  SMA: peer attention (specify which peers)
    2.3  SMA: tangible reinforcers (specify tangible or class of tangible accessed)
(3.0)  Direct escape (DE)
    3.1  DE: Unpleasant social situations (specify situation(s))
    3.2  DE: relatively lengthy tasks/chores (specify length of task)
    3.3  DE: relatively difficult tasks/chores (specify task or component of task that is difficult)
    3.4  DE: aversive physical stimuli/events (specify aversive physical stimulus)
(4.0)  Socially mediated escape (SME)
    4.1  SME: unpleasant social situations (specify situation(s))
    4.2  SME: relatively lengthy tasks/chores (specify length of task)

4.3 SME: relatively difficult tasks/chores (specify task or component of task that is difficult)

4.4 SME: aversive physical stimuli/event (specify aversive physical stimulus)

## Category 1.0: Direct Access (DA)

Access to positive reinforcement is produced directly through the problem behavior or a chain of behaviors. In much of the professional literature, this category of behaviors has been referred to as *automatic reinforcement* (Vaughn & Michael, 1982; Vollmer, 2006). Vollmer provides four factors as evidence for problem behaviors being considered in this category (Table 3.1).

Our approach is slightly different from the currently in vogue use of the term *automatic reinforcement*. The use of the term *direct access* (and the latter term, *direct escape*) removes some of the possible misinterpretation of the term *automatic*. It borrows such terminology from Skinner's verbal behavior writings in describing verbal and nonverbal behavior (Skinner, 1957; Vargas, 1988).

We believe there is an advantage to the use of the term *direct*, in contrast to *automatic reinforcement*. Using the term *direct* is defined as behavior that contacts the nonsocial contingency directly, within a .5-second time interval. In other words, the reinforcing event occurs within .5 seconds of the terminal response occurring. If a behavior is maintained by an event that occurs subsequent to this time frame, it is probably not in this category. Further, not all direct access behaviors involve stereotypic behaviors that produce sensory reinforcement as the maintaining contingency (see subcategory 1.2).

There are two subcategories, in addition to "other," serving direct access functions: (1.1) immediate sensory stimuli and (1.2) tangible reinforcers.

### (1.1) DA: Immediate Sensory Stimuli

Probably one of the greatest advancements in treating difficult problem behaviors exhibited by persons with severe disabilities, such as stereotypic behavior, is the understanding and demonstration that such behaviors may not be socially mediated (Caudrey, Iwata, & Pace, 1990; Iwata, Dorsey, Slifer, Bauman, & Richman, 1982; Mason & Iwata, 1990). Problem behaviors in this category produce immediately (often within .5 seconds of terminal response) the sensory event that maintains such behavior. For example, persons who engage in frequent repetitive movements such as hand flapping often do so because of the sensory result such repetitive behaviors produce. Flapping their hands in a certain fashion produces a kinesthetic result that automatically creates its own *built in* reinforcer.

Here is another example. Try rocking back and forth in a chair, and note the rhythm produced. Such a chain of behaviors produces a *built in* sensory event. This built in event can function as a reinforcer for the "rocking in the chair" behavior. Such an automatically produced result becomes frequently more desired by persons who cannot create many forms of sensory stimulation due to their cognitive impairments. In contrast, nonhandicapped people who are able to watch TV, read a book, listen to music, go on swings, and so on only occasionally engage in such a behavior. Therefore, it does not reach problematic

*TABLE 3.1* ■ **EVIDENCE FOR NONSOCIAL REINFORCEMENT**

1. No social consequences are apparent.
2. Problem behavior does not decrease when social contingencies are withdrawn.
3. Problem behavior decreases when sensory effects of behavior are attenuated.
4. If a Premack contingency involving the authorized access to engage in the problem behavior is put in place, the behaviors required to access such an event increase in probability.

**TABLE 3.2 ■ ANALYSIS OF DIRECT REINFORCEMENT EFFECTS OF STEREOTYPIC BEHAVIOR**

| Motivating Operation | Behavior | Maintaining Contingency (direct) | Future probability of behavior under MO |
|---|---|---|---|
| Relative deprivation of sensory event | Engages in stereotypic behavior | Produced immediately, abolished deprivation state | More likely |

levels because it does not consume one's entire purpose for the day. However, for persons with disabilities, such a stereotypic behavior pervades the entire day and conflicts with the individual engaging in a wide variety of alternate activities and behaviors.

Table 3.2 depicts the relationship between the sensory event being in a relative deprivation state (see first column A, Motivating Operation) and the occurrence of the self-stimulatory behavior (second column). Note that the maintaining contingency is the direct result the behavior produces (third column). Any effect of the behavior in the social environment from the occurrence of this behavior is inconsequential. The staff or teacher may admonish the client or child after the behavior, however, such a social event is not the purpose of this behavior, even though it may appear to be a reliable contingency of the behavior. It is the sensory result of the stereotypic behavior that will make such a form of behavior occur again when the motivational conditions are present. Sensory events that can be produced directly through various behaviors are auditory, visual, tactile, gustatory, and olfactory stimuli.

Many ritualistic (stereotypic) behaviors appear to produce their own immediate kinesthetic reinforcer. Such behaviors often occur independent of the reaction from the social environment. Addictive behaviors, such as smoking and drinking, may also be maintained as a result of their immediate sensory effect. Although this may not describe how such behaviors were developed in the first place, it can explain why such behaviors are still maintained even when the original purpose is no longer functional. Certainly, for smokers at certain age ranges, social reinforcement and peer acceptance of smoking has diminished tremendously in the last decade. Yet some people continue to smoke despite the removal of peer reinforcement (and known health risks). Why? For smokers who began the habit years ago, the act of smoking often has its own *built in* reinforcer.

Table 3.3 provides some questions to consider when entertaining direct access to immediate sensory stimuli as a hypothesis.

In Question 1, you should consider whether a 1:1 relationship exists between the behavior and the sensory event. What is the desired sensory event (Question 2)? In some cases, it may be easy to determine the probable sensory reinforcer. For example, someone who sings in the shower is probably reinforced with the auditory result of vocal production in an enclosed area. However, in other cases, it may be difficult to discern what automatic sensory event is the reinforcer. If necessary, an experimental analysis that presents condi-

**TABLE 3.3 ■ QUESTIONS TO CONSIDER**

1. Is there a reliable (every single occurrence) relation between the specific behavior and immediate production of the hypothesized desired sensory event? What is the specific form of the behavior?

2. What seems to be the auditory, visual, tactile, kinesthetic, or gustatory sensation that seems to be the maintaining contingency?

3. What evidence supports the hypothesis that a sensory event is the maintaining contingency? Does this behavior occur across a variety of situations when the client is in a deprived state relative to the sensory event? In other words, does the client engage in this behavior (usually) irrespective of context?

tions where the sensory effect is ameliorated or eliminated may be the most effective manner of determining such.

Question 3 addresses the evidence that points to a hypothesis of direct access to sensory reinforcement. If the problem behavior is sensory reinforced, it will often occur across most contexts (possibly excluding contexts where punishing consequences have affected the rate). For many clients who engage in self-stimulatory behavior, they engage in such behaviors irrespective of context. If a client engaged in hand flapping only in the context of certain staff, and not others, or when alone, such a pattern of stereotypic behavior would seem to point to a socially mediated access or escape function. Perhaps some examples of subcategory 1.1 DA: sensory reinforcer will clarify direct access functions representative of this category.

*Talking Is Good?* I (E.C.) observed a client at a residential facility for persons with disabilities talking loudly to herself while pushing a laundry cart across a parking lot. I looked around and did not see any staff or other people. How can anyone talk or engage in conversation when there is not an audience with which to interact? A traditionally trained mental health professional may surmise that such vocal behavior is directed at an imaginary person. The client is carrying on a conversation with someone in her mind, who is responding back to her. Although one cannot see what is transpiring inside her cortex, these professionals assume the existence of such on the basis of the carried on conversation. Hence, the client is considered to be experiencing auditory hallucinations.

Is there an alternate explanation? Can such a behavior be maintained in the absence of an audience? Vocal discourse may produce its own reinforcer, that is, auditory (hearing one's voice) or kinesthetic effect on vocal cords. Certainly, this phenomenon is present in infants who babble for long periods, testing out their newfound ability to generate a sensory effect by vocal production. As I observed this person pushing the laundry cart by herself, that certainly seemed a plausible hypothesis.

How can one determine whether sensory reinforcement is maintaining the client's vocal behavior? If this behavior occurs when staff are not physically present, and such behavior does not result in their subsequent attention, its function does not seem to be socially mediated. In contrast, if particular staff attend to her in certain ways upon hearing her talking to herself, then subcategory 1.1 DA is probably not an accurate diagnosis for this client.

Failure to diagnose this as a behavior maintained by sensory reinforcement when indicated may lead to the design of an ineffective treatment strategy. If the vocal discourse produces direct access, attempts to alter staff behavior may prove of little utility in changing the behavior (Table 3.4). A treatment strategy that involved "ignoring the behavior" would have no effect at all on the rate of this behavior. Intervention of problem behaviors within

*TABLE 3.4* ■ **DIAGNOSIS OF VOCAL DISCOURSE IN THE ABSENCE OF OTHERS**

| Diagnosis | 1.1 DA: sensory reinforcer |
| --- | --- |
| Target behavior(s): | Vocal discourse with no audience |
| Function: | Production of kinesthetic and/or auditory sensory stimuli |
| Target behavior likely under following contexts: | When by self, away from staff |
| Target behavior unlikely under following contexts: | When in presence of staff |
| Rule out: | Socially mediated access functions (2.1 SMA; 2.3 SMA) or socially mediated escape function (4.1 SME) |

this category should be aimed at "weaning her off" of sensory reinforcement or bringing it under control in certain contexts that are not as public (see Chapter 4).

*The Voices Make Me Laugh.* Here is a similar real-life circumstance. A man, for no apparent reason, would occasionally just burst out laughing as if he had just heard the funniest joke in the world. During an intake at a psychiatric center, he told the professional conducting the assessment that he heard voices in his head. These voices would tell him funny stories and jokes. As a result, this individual was diagnosed with schizophrenia, with "hearing voices" a prime reason for such a diagnosis.

Does he really hear voices? Many mental health professionals would say "yes," explaining that such voices are a product of his hypothesized neuro-chemical deficits. His mind makes him actually hear voices. Of course, no one can absolutely posit that he does hear voices because the only person who can accurately determine such is this man. The only data regarding this phenomenon is his self-report, which has obvious problems with validity. Is it possible that such a behavior, laughing independent of social input, could be a behavior maintained by reinforcement? As he became a client at our (K.S.) Community Re-Entry Project at the University of the Pacific, we would have to answer that question.

How would a functional target behavior analysis proceed with such a behavior? First, it was not our intention that we actually try to figure out if some internal auditory stimuli were present (currently impossible to deduce). Our primary goal was to determine whether the behavior could be socially mediated. To rule out staff (or peer) attention as a possible maintaining contingency, we collected data on the laughing incidents under two conditions: (1) how often he burst out laughing when there were people close by and (2) how often he laughed when he was too far away from people for them to notice him laughing and interact with him. If adult attention were maintaining such a behavior one would expect to see him engage in this laughter when he was near people, but not involved in social interactions. In addition, if he did engage in such a behavior when away from people, such behavior would recruit their attention.

Therefore, we examined two related sets of data under each condition. We examined the number of times he laughed and the total number of minutes he laughed. We found that in this person's case, if he was left alone and not interrupted, the probability of this behavior was far greater than in the presence of people. In addition, it was noted that such laughter was not frequently resulting in staff attention. In fact, he was perfectly content to be alone while bursting out into laughter. Given this information, it seemed unlikely that his outbursts of laughter were maintained by social attention. This caused us to suspect that for this person, laughing itself was reinforcing (Table 3.5).

Could laughing without someone providing a comical situation be a behavior that produces reinforcement in the absence of people? It is similar to the process that many of

#### TABLE 3.5 ■ DIAGNOSIS OF LAUGHING BEHAVIOR

| Diagnosis | 1.1 DA: sensory reinforcer |
|---|---|
| Target behavior(s): | Inappropriate laughing in absence of social circumstance provoking laughter |
| Function: | Production of kinesthetic and/or auditory sensory stimuli |
| Target behavior likely under following contexts: | When by self, away from staff |
| Target behavior unlikely under following contexts: | When staff are close by |
| Rule out: | Socially mediated access function (2.1 SMA) or socially mediated escape function (4.1 SME) |

us go through related to singing in the shower or talking to ourselves. When we sing in the shower, there is generally no one else present to provide attention. Singing in the shower also does not terminate or avoid some aversive situation. Further, most of us would not say that a voice in our head told us to sing in the shower. Therefore, we are left with the only possible function being self-stimulation. So whether it is laughing, singing, or talking to oneself, try to *discriminate where you do these self-stimulatory behaviors,* but once you are alone, go ahead, I will not tell!

## DISCUSSION QUESTIONS

What would you surmise would be the conditions under which laughing at inappropriate times would be maintained by social attention? How would you conduct a trigger analysis of such a context?

*Time Out Does Not Work?* A landmark study in the field of applied behavior analysis involved a study of the effectiveness of time out procedures with stereotypic behavior (Solnick, Rincover, & Peterson, 1977). It provided evidence that some behaviors produce their own reinforcer. A 6-year-old girl with autism engaged in tantrum behavior. The initial assessment did not reveal the function of this behavior. *(Remember this was 1977, and the state of practice and research was not yet investigating behavioral function of target problems.)* The researchers tested the effectiveness of time out on tantrum behavior during instructional sessions. In contrast to a baseline, the results were surprising. Time out did not decrease tantrum behavior. How could that be?

The researchers noted that when this girl was sent to time out, she engaged in stereotypic behavior, that of weaving her fingers in a pattern. Such behavior was obviously discouraged during instruction. Hence, time out was the perfect opportunity to engage in such a behavior. Solnick and colleagues (1977) then decided to conduct a second study. These researchers would test a hypothesis about why time out did not produce a change in tantrum behavior. In the follow-up study, time out was still a contingency for this girl's tantrum behavior during instruction. However, the efficacy of time out was investigated under two different conditions. In one condition, the stereotypic behavior occurring in time out was left unabated. In a second experimental condition, such behavior was prevented by immediately restraining her hands upon the initial hand weave. Therefore, in this condition, the sensory effect of such stereotypic behavior was prevented.

The results proved an important point. If time out resulted in free access to stereotypic behavior (and sensory reinforcement), then time out was ineffective at reducing tantrum behavior. However, when such a sensory effect was eliminated, time outs reduced tantrum behavior. In 1977, these researchers uncovered the possibility that stereotypic behavior was probably automatically reinforced in many clients with such a problem.

*Pica: The Classic Case of Sensory Reinforcement.* A client sticks inedible things in his mouth and gnaws on them (commonly called pica). Many naive personnel may ascribe such behavior of a client to some form of social attention. When asked why the client does that, a staff person responds, "He knows that it upsets me in that I have to go and get it out of his mouth. He likes to see me work." Putting aside for the moment the employee's work habits, the purpose of the behavior often has nothing to do with staff. One would not ascribe a baby's gnawing or mouthing a particular object as a behavior intended to upset his mother or care provider. The same may hold true in this case.

If pica behavior in a particular client is producing its own sensory reinforcer, what could that possibly be? Mouthing of inedible objects produces oral stimulation (probably similar to gum chewing for some people), a sensory event that is the direct result of the behavior. If pica (in this particular case) is serving a direct access function, then oral sensory stimulation might be the reinforcer. One should see that such behavior occurs at a consistent rate when left unabated. Attempts to stop it often are met with the client finding contexts in which access to the reinforcer is "under the radar" of the staff. In other words, the client becomes sneaky in engaging in this behavior.

Table 3.6 illustrates the contextual conditions and function of pica serving a direct access function.

In some cases, pica may be socially mediated. However, the form of the behavior is of such a nature that sensory reinforcement should be initially considered when reviewing behavioral assessment data. To rule out social mediation of this behavior, examine the relationship between engaging in pica and socially mediated positive or negative reinforcers. For example, when the client engages in pica, is he removed from some environment reliably? Is pica a more efficient behavior in getting such a result than other behaviors?

*I Like to Bang Against Plexiglas.* A hypothetical adult client with developmental disabilities slaps his hand against the Plexiglas window. Data reveal that this behavior occurs multiple times a day, and he targets the Plexiglas window rather than the stucco wall next to the window. Staff may try to keep him away from the window, but he continues to seek opportunities when they are not as vigilant. When they are not looking, he runs to the Plexiglas window and strikes it with open hand. Staff attribute this client's destructive behavior toward property to the adult attention he receives upon its exhibition. The staff will scold him and redirect him back to his couch. They will often report, "He likes negative attention. We tell him to stop, but that seems to be what he thrives on, since he goes and does it again at every opportunity."

If such were true, then removing attention would result in the extinction of window slapping from this client. However, removal of such staff attention does not decrease this daily pattern of behavior. Could it be that such behavior is maintained by the direct result it produces? When this client hits the window, a sound of some decibel level is produced. If such a sound is unique to hitting this particular Plexiglas window, it may be this sensory reinforcer that is the controlling variable. Maybe it is not the sound that is created, but rather, it is the unique kinesthetic feel of hitting Plexiglas with one's bare hand. Hitting the wall would not produce the same sensation, which explains why he targets the window.

The functional treatment strategy will not rely on socially mediated contingencies, such as ignoring the behavior. To reiterate, ignoring a problem behavior that is sensory reinforced will probably be ineffectual, or make matters worse.

**TABLE 3.6 ■ DIAGNOSIS OF PICA BEHAVIOR**

| Diagnosis | 2.1 DA: sensory stimuli |
|---|---|
| Target behavior(s): | Pica |
| Function: | The gnawing on objects for the stimulation to the mouth, possibly gustatory (taste) or kinesthetic |
| Target behavior likely under following contexts: | When it has been awhile since engaging in gnawing behavior (establishing operation) |
| Target behavior unlikely under following contexts: | Sustained access just prior (abolishing operation) |
| Rule out: | Socially mediated access functions (2.1 SMA) or socially mediated escape functions (SME 3.1, 3.2, 3.3) |

**DISCUSSION QUESTIONS**

Describe the scenario under which such a behavior as hitting Plexiglas would be a function of negative reinforcement? What would staff have to do when he bangs Plexiglas?

### (1.2) DA: Tangible Reinforcers

When you want a drink of juice, you may ask someone to get it for you if you are in his or her home. But when you are in your own home, you walk to the refrigerator, pull out the juice bottle, pour it in a cup, and drink. Such a chain of behaviors is reinforced, under the motivational condition of wanting juice, by ingesting the liquid refreshment. For many people, direct access to tangible reinforcers is available to them when they engage in acceptable behaviors, such as walking to the refrigerator. In contrast, some clients cannot simply go get something out of the refrigerator whenever they desire some food or drink item. Attempts to engage in such behaviors results in their being prevented from direct access of reinforcers. When such appropriate behaviors are denied or restricted, undesirable behaviors may occur. Table 3.7 illustrates the contextual conditions for this subcategory.

Note that the desired item, activity, or event is currently unavailable to the client and is in a state of relative deprivation prior to the occurrence of the behavior (first column). Given a deprivation state with respect to the item or event, this motivating operation establishes the value of a chain or sequence of behaviors that can produce the item. The chain of behaviors that can result in obtaining the desired item or activity becomes more probable (next two columns). The direct access to this reinforcer that such behavior produces abates the deprivation state. As a result of this abolishing operation, the behavior becomes more likely when the deprivation state reaches a similar point in the future. Note again that any social consequence for this behavior is tangential and not the maintaining variable. The staff may scold the child, place her in time out, or engage in other discipline practices. Such practices have nothing to do with the purpose of the behavior. Further, in light of the efficiency of the direct access behavior in producing reinforcement, such attempts to "punish" the behavior may fail.

If a client wants a piece of chocolate cake and is told "not till after dinner," pilfering a piece of cake undetected becomes an effective manner of getting cake. Do you have clients who eat their food at mealtime and then begin grabbing the food off their neighbor's plates? If they are adept at pulling this off reliably, such a chain of stealth and swift behaviors becomes strengthened while at the group mealtime. Do they do this for your "negative" attention? Probably not. Your comments regarding their behavior are tangential and inconsequential to the true purpose of this behavior. They would probably be elated if you would turn around and ignore them! They would then have a chance to devour a sufficient amount of someone else's dinner without interruption.

Table 3.8 presents some questions to consider in evaluating a behavior as a 1.2 DA: tangible reinforcer diagnosis. First, the target behavior must have a reliable and frequent

*TABLE 3.7* ■ **ANALYSIS OF DIRECT REINFORCEMENT EFFECTS**

| Motivating Operation | Behavior | Maintaining Contingency | Future probability of behavior under MO |
|---|---|---|---|
| Relative deprivation of tangible item | Chain of behaviors occurs | Tangible item produced immediately at the end of the chain, abolished deprivation state | More likely |

---

### *TABLE 3.8* ■ **QUESTIONS TO CONSIDER FOR A 1.2 DA DIAGNOSIS**

1. Is there a reliable, somewhat frequent, direct relation between the problem behavior and getting a desired item or activity? Describe the chain of behaviors.

2. Are the target behaviors more likely to produce the desired items/activities than appropriate behaviors? Are other attempts to access these items or events thwarted?

3. Are the direct access problem behaviors thwarted? If so, how often is the client successful?

4. Are there any special contexts (e.g., during shopping trips, while at home) that make these behaviors more likely?

---

relation between the desired tangible reinforcer and its occurrence (Question 1). In the chain of behaviors, it is the last response step in the chain that produces the tangible reinforcer.

In addition to the reliable relation between chain of behavior and direct production of reinforcer, you should note whether other behaviors are more or less successful in obtaining the desired event (Question 2). Question 3 examines the rate of reinforcement for the problem behavior. The ability of a chain of behaviors to produce the tangible reinforcer under sufficient motivational conditions determines the probability of such behaviors. Question 4 attempts to discern if there is any special context for such behavior, such as shopping trips or other occasions where a special tangible reinforcer is available.

*Breakfast Is Down the Corner.* Stealing is a great example of a behavioral pattern that can be maintained by direct access to the desired tangible items. It also is often maintained by social peer attention, as is often the case with juvenile delinquents. Knowing which motivating operation is in effect can lead to a more functionally derived treatment strategy. A foster family I (E.C.) was involved with had several children, all coming from the same mother. One of the boys (Roberto, who was 9 years old at the time) was stealing money and various things from family members as well as from classmates at school. This was apparently a behavioral pattern he picked up early in life when he was with his biological mother. I was told that when the children wanted breakfast, they were told (facsimile of conversation), "The mini-mart is down the street, get to it." His biological mother felt her children should fend for themselves, hence his early exposure to shoplifting. Once this state of affairs was uncovered, they were removed from their mother. But you can imagine that with insufficient consequences for being caught, and continued practice, Roberto became quite adept at being a frequent usurper of other people's possessions.

Prior to my involvement, the foster father had tried many strategies to deter stealing. These included pleading with him, discussing society's prohibition against stealing, appealing to his better judgment, trying to induce guilt and shame over stealing others' possessions, and grounding him. It would be essential to design a plan that made stealing items not functional (in terms of keeping items). Additionally, getting desired items should be addressed via appropriate channels. If the behavior is maintained because of the items it directly produces, then a program that addresses that function should designate an alternate venue for getting desired items. Reinforcing the absence of stealing would seem to be the way to go in this case.

The plan I came up with involved planting items around the house in conspicuous spots to monitor stealing. I called this the *planted item technique,* borrowed from researchers Switzer, Deal, and Bailey (1977). Each day the father would place several items, including money, in designated places (unannounced to Roberto). This allowed his father to systematically track stealing by checking each place.

Roberto was informed of the plan the night before it was to go into effect. If all the items remained in their place at the end of the day and there were no other reports of stealing, Roberto received $.50 for the day. However, if something was missing, the punishing consequences involved the following: (1) return item(s) stolen, (2) lose the stipend amount for that day, and (3) pay a penalty equal to double the value of the item(s) taken. Note that this plan had consequences for stealing as well as for not stealing. I believe the father also threw in early bedtime as well.

As you can imagine, his rate of stealing went down. Stopping this behavior had a profound impact on Roberto's relationship with both of his foster parents. Probably one of the nicest outcomes of changing Roberto's behavior happened on one of my visits to the home. His foster mother reported to me an incident in which she was so particularly proud of him. Roberto had returned some planted money to her, saying he found it (planted item) and that she must have lost it. Now that is how you develop a moral compass, a conscience in a child who lacked an upbringing that instilled such values. About a year and a half later, Roberto was still reported to not have a problem with stealing.

*Food Scavenging!* Some clients in residential and inpatient facilities have a target behavior listed on their habilitative plan as *scavenging*. In the case of students with severe disabilities, such may be listed on their individualized educational plan (IEP). Selecting items off the floor and placing them in one's mouth is a chain of behaviors that can serve a direct access function. The food ingestion would seem to be the terminal reinforcing event for the chain of behaviors involved in scavenging. If one scavenges the floor after people have eaten, some of the items procured may be ingested as food (see Table 3.9).

The same behavioral phenomenon exists with some clients who ingest cigarette butts that are thrown on the floor or ground after being smoked. They scavenge areas looking for cigarette butts and will resist staff attempts to physically refrain them from picking up the cigarette butt off the floor. If you believe that this scavenging behavior is socially mediated, try ignoring such attempts to scavenge in an in-vivo experiment. If the rate stays high or increases, you obviously have not removed the maintaining contingency. You may also receive a "thank you" from the client for allowing unrestricted access to the desired event.

## Category 2.0: Socially Mediated Access (SMA)

Problem behaviors that serve this type of function access positive reinforcement through the behavior of another individual. Such events as social attention and interaction from teachers, peers, staff, or parents are socially mediated. However, obtaining preferred food items, toys, or activities can also be mediated through the behavior of another person. In contrast to the prior category, the client's behavior produces positive reinforcement by someone else presenting the desired item or event to the client or child. Within this major category are the following subcategories: 2.1 SMA: adult/staff attention; 2.2 SMA: peer attention; 2.3 SMA: tangible reinforcers; and 2.4 SMA: other.

**TABLE 3.9 ■ 1.2 DA DIAGNOSIS OF SCAVENGING BEHAVIOR**

| Diagnosis | 1.2 DA: tangible reinforcer |
| --- | --- |
| Target behavior(s): | Scavenging (picking items off the ground and ingesting them) |
| Function: | Access tangible reinforcer |
| Target behavior likely under following contexts: | Access to desired item(s) on the floor |
| Target behavior unlikely under following contexts: | Areas where food on the floor is improbable |
| Rule out: | Socially mediated function (2.1 SMA) |

## ARE CERTAIN DISORDERS MORE LIKELY TO BE DIAGNOSED WITH SOCIALLY MEDIATED FUNCTIONS?

No, not to the extent that there is any empirical evidence supporting such a contention. For example, to say that persons with intermittent explosive disorder are more likely to have aggressive behavior that is functioning to access adult or peer attention is in opposition to the content of this book. The social environment of each individual determines how certain behaviors affect other people as well as the physical environment. One person with this disorder may yell and scream when he is at work. Other employees leave him alone at these times. The function may be avoidance of social interaction at times when it is not desired. Unfortunately, frequent exhibition of such behavior will inevitably result in being fired (long-term consequence). In another person with the same psychiatric disorder, the function of verbal and sometimes physically aggressive behavior may be in the context of his spouse, for example, when she talks on the phone to her friends and does not pay enough attention to him. Such behavior may be maintained by recruiting desired attention.

The role of a traditional mental disorder diagnosis in a function-based diagnostic classification system is irrelevant at best. While such a diagnosis may be useful in other treatments such as medication, its utility in a behaviorally based system is nonessential. It could often be counterproductive if it sways professional personnel from examining behavioral function.

### (2.1) SMA: Adult/Staff Attention

"He does it for my attention! He even likes negative attention." Although not all problem behaviors function to access attention, as some people would have us believe, in some circumstances, it is true. Problem behaviors that successfully access teacher, parent, or care provider attention are strengthened when the child or client is in need of such attention. Concurrently, other behaviors in the child or client's repertoire that are less effective or efficient in producing such desired events become weakened. For children, attention from parents, teachers, care providers, or staff at facilities can serve as the maintaining contingency for behavior (both appropriate and inappropriate). For clients in facilities, staff attention is sometimes the maintaining variable in target undesired behavior. A descriptive analysis for this subcategory is given in Table 3.10.

Table 3.10 illustrates that behaviors that serve this function occur when attention is relatively unavailable (column A). This sets up the conditions for the client to be motivated to obtain such (given someone who is discriminative for the reinforcement of some behavior(s). The occurrence of the behavior (column B) at some frequency or duration produces the desired form of attention (column C-1), thus making it functional under those antecedent conditions. The direct result of the client or child's behavior on the physical environment is inconsequential as a consideration in the maintenance of the behavior (column C-2).

What form of behavior results in attention is determined by the specific social environment. For example, in one situation, a smile from a man may evoke eye contact and a smile back from an interested female walking past this man. However, the same smile from this man has no effect on another woman whom he sits down next to. Later on, the same behavior from this man results in a frown of disgust from a married woman in the restaurant.

### TABLE 3.10 ■ CONTEXT FOR BEHAVIOR SERVING AN ATTENTION FUNCTION

| A | B | C-1 | C-2 |
|---|---|---|---|
| Note if attention is on lean schedule at certain times (consider client's motivating operation) and person | Behavior occurs (at some frequency and/or duration) | Adult attention (delivered in some form) | Inconsequential, has no effect on strengthening behavior |

If the smile produces a fair number of acceptable social responses, this man is more likely to smile than exhibit other behaviors when seeking someone's attention.

Problem behaviors maintained by adult attention can take many forms, from innocuous minor behaviors such as giggling, to behaviors that cause great disruption, such as severe tantrums, aggression to others, and running away. For attention to be a maintaining contingency, the problem behavior should reliably produce teacher attention, and this temporal relationship should be observed. For example, in the face of a child wanting attention, the problem behavior becomes more effective or efficient at getting the adult's attention than other behaviors, either desirable or undesirable. Table 3.11 specifies factors to examine when considering an adult attention hypothesis.

This maintaining contingency involves a reliable relation between the problem behavior and the access to desired attention (Question 1). Other more acceptable behaviors are less likely to result in attention (Question 2). Although the target problem behaviors may have to occur at some frequency and duration (Question 3), they are more successful at getting attention than other more acceptable behaviors (Question 2). Let's examine possible examples of problem behavior representative of this diagnostic category.

*I Want Your Attention, NOW!* A hypothetical student, Dolly, is referred for consultation as a result of whining and tantrum behavior in a primary elementary grade class. The teacher reports to you that this student is simply immature for her age. Dolly spends part of her day in general education and the remainder in a special education resource room. The general education teacher states that these tantrum behaviors can occur unexpectedly—"whenever Dolly is in a bad mood. You never know when she is in a bad mood!"

You schedule a consultation visit and prepare to identify the context under which tantrum behaviors occur. Using direct observation and an A-B-C descriptive focused analysis, you view the following in a 50-minute period of teacher lecture and independent seatwork. Tantrum behavior did not occur during teacher-delivered instruction. Rather, it occurs during seat work. Dolly would work for a while without any problems. However, the context for tantrums seems to involve the following. Dolly raises her hand to obtain teacher attention. When Dolly requests teacher attention by raising her hand, such requests frequently go ignored for some period of time because the teacher is often working with someone else. Hand raising is not an effective or efficient manner to get the teacher's attention at these times. This is not making a social judgment, but rather an empirical observation. However, when Dolly hits her desk with her hands while concomitantly whining and complaining, the teacher first tells her to stop. However, shortly thereafter, the teacher comes to her desk to "find out what all the fuss is about." With this offering of help by the teacher, Dolly then proceeds to calm down and begin her seat work (and the teacher provides her help and encouragement).

When this student wants the teacher to come over to her, what are her options? Raise her hand? Selecting that option results in a longer protracted wait. Bang on the desk? That option produces faster results; hence, that form of behavior becomes strengthened under the conditions of wanting teacher attention.

**SMA or DA?**
*Narrated PowerPoint Presentation*

### TABLE 3.11 ■ QUESTIONS TO CONSIDER FOR A 2.1 SMA DIAGNOSIS

1. Is there a reliable, somewhat frequent relation, between the problem behavior and teacher, staff, or parent attention? What is the form of the behavior?

2. Are the target behaviors more likely to produce attention than acceptable appropriate behaviors?

3. What type of reinforcement schedule is it on? How often and long do such behaviors sustain before attention is given?

In this case, there is another question one has to ask and answer. Why is teacher attention in some form of deprivation in the general education class, but not in the resource room (tantrum behaviors not reported to be a problem in this setting). Observation of the two classrooms will reveal the reason. You realize that in this student's resource room there maybe 6–11 children at any one time. Therefore, needing teacher attention is not as lengthy a wait as in the general education class. In the general education class, 25 other students have needs as well. Dolly's access to teacher attention is markedly less. Hence she engages in behaviors that are hard to ignore, but unfortunately will result in her loss of placement in mainstream settings. Table 3.12 summarizes this functional analysis and diagnostic information.

*I Am on the Phone!* How many times have you seen (or been the recipient of) a child screaming, "Mom, I need to talk to you!" while Mom is on the phone or engaged in conversation? Interrupting behaviors occur because they are more successful under those conditions than other more desirable behaviors. The child may tug on Mom's shirt, but to no avail. However, a loud scream produces several responses from Mom. Let's look at a scenario depicting what transpires that makes screaming an adaptive response for this child when mom is busy with someone else.

*Child:* Mom, I need you *(in conversational tone while pulling on her shirt).*

*Mom:* Wait just a minute, I am on the phone with your sister. She is at the dentist.

*Child:* *(after several minutes go by):* Mom, I need to get some juice. I am losing my voice from lack of liquid.

*Parent:* Hold on, I will only be another minute.

*Child:* *(several minutes go by, child screams):* Well I will just get it myself. I have to do everything myself. Nobody cares about me!

*Mom:* OK, I am coming *(and terminates conversation).*

As you can see, the child escalates her demanding when minor forms do not result in the mom's attention (which is very often the case). Ignoring these minor forms then makes the screaming bout at the end more likely, with the mom terminating the conversation shortly and attending to the child. The child's level of screaming under conditions where she wants attention has just been strengthened. Of course, many more scenarios similar to this play out over time to develop a reliable relation between the form of screaming and accessing the mom's attention (see Table 3.13).

### TABLE 3.12 ■ DIAGNOSIS OF DOLLY'S BEHAVIOR

| Diagnosis | 2.1 SMA: adult attention |
|---|---|
| Target behavior(s): | Whining and tantrum behavior (includes crying, pleading, falling to the floor while crying) |
| Function: | Access teacher's attention and help on seat work, other behaviors such as raising hand are less effective at getting attention |
| Target behavior likely under following contexts: | During seat work in larger classes |
| Target behavior unlikely under following contexts: | During teacher presentations or being in smaller class |
| Rule out: | Socially mediated escape functions (4.2 and 4.3 SME) |

*TABLE 3.13* ■ **DIAGNOSIS OF INTERRUPTING BEHAVIORS**

| Diagnosis | 2.1 SMA: adult attention |
|---|---|
| Target behavior(s): | Interrupting behaviors (includes crying, whining, pleading, tugging at parent's shirt or blouse) |
| Function: | Access parent's attention, other behaviors such as waiting a period of time are less effective at getting parent's attention while busy |
| Target behavior likely under following contexts: | While mom is on phone or engaged in conversation with someone else |
| Target behavior unlikely under following contexts: | At other times |
| Rule out: | Socially mediated access functions (2.2 and 2.3 SMA) |

## DISCUSSION QUESTIONS

What should parents do about this problem of attention-getting behavior with their children? How do you not attend to such forms of behavior? What might happen if you do not attend to minor forms of attention getting? (See the DRO replacement behavior option for the answer.)

*A Pinch Here, a Pinch There.* An adult male client with severe mental retardation who has no vocal speech would pinch people as they passed by him. It was easy for me (E.C.) to discern who this client was upon entering the building without anyone pointing him out. As I entered the building I could see him sitting at a table. Nothing striking there, right? Upon observation, adult staff at his day treatment program would near his table area and then move in a semicircle away from him in order to get to the other side. Now you know why it was easy to figure out who this client was without someone pointing him out.

Occasionally, even with staff winding a long arc around his area, he would be successful in pinching people. If someone got too close, he would *dart out* of his seat and pinch that person. Of course, new persons on the floor had to be warned about such a behavior in order to engage in the protocol for avoiding him. As you could imagine, this "imposed circle of avoidance" made attention even more desired from this client's perspective. As staff became more successful at avoiding him, the rate of attention from staff became less and less. The more successful staff persons were at avoiding him on a given day, the greater his deprivation of adult interaction.

To compound matters, the staff was instructed to engage in the following contingency upon being pinched by this client. "Say 'No pinching.'" Then proceed to teach him what to do instead. Grab his hand, shake it, and say, "This is what we are supposed to do." The program designer probably thought that this would teach him how to initiate acceptable social interactions with staff. Instead of pinching, he would offer to shake hands. Wrong on that count. Let's examine all the behavioral contingencies in place for this client. When he simply sits in his seat, people avoid him so that he will not pinch. Nothing in the program design mentions to catch him when he is not pinching and prompt the acceptable behavior! But, when he does pinch, he gets some brief interaction with people in this correction procedure (see Table 3.14). Pinching successfully ensures him staff attention as the staff adhere to this program. Pinch away!

*"I Will Kill Myself!"* When someone in a mental health facility makes this statement, his or her environment is guaranteed to change. Protocol requires that a number of staff

*TABLE 3.14* ■ **PINCHING AS A 2.1 SMA DIAGNOSIS**

| Diagnosis | 2.1 SMA: adult attention |
|---|---|
| Target behavior(s): | Pinching others |
| Function: | Access staff person's attention; under conditions where people avoid physical proximity to him other behaviors are less effective at getting their attention |
| Target behavior likely under following contexts: | During day treatment where client is set apart from others, particularly as an initial part of chain accessing staff attention |
| Target behavior unlikely under following contexts: | When given frequent attention/interaction (probably) |
| Rule out: | Socially mediated escape functions (4.2 and 4.3 SME) |

interactions, interviews, and assessments be conducted to determine the dangerousness of such a verbal statement. Such traditional assessments often revolve around determining whether the person is depressed to such a level that killing oneself is an option they might entertain. Of course, all instruments that could be used for committing suicide are made inaccessible. Staff members are intensely vigilant in these circumstances to ensure that such items are not attainable. Such efforts are certainly mandatory in the case of protecting life.

Could a functional analysis be of utility in separating out those persons whose life is in immediate danger from others? What possible behavioral function could such threats serve? Could such threats to kill oneself be under control of social reinforcers? If so, why would some people need to go to this extreme (stating they are going to kill themselves) to get such reinforcers? Although not discounting the possibility that some people obviously commit suicide because they feel (at that time) life may not be worth living, a functional analysis of verbal statements may prove useful in designing treatment.

Let us take the case of someone who has just lost a spouse through an abrupt death. In their state of depression, they contact a mental health crisis center. Contingent upon saying that suicide is an option as a result of their grief, they immediately interact with many different professional people (e.g., doctors, nurses, social workers, front-line support staff, therapists, etc.). In a time of need, these professional people are very supportive and caring, and the client possibly begins to reevaluate their life in new ways. As this person's mental health is evaluated as improving, the client sees these people less and less over time. For some people that may not be a problem because they have other people in their social network to return to. People with friends and relatives can be provided the care and support one needs to face difficult life-altering circumstances. But what about those people who have lost the one friend they had? Whom do they return to? If there is no one left, or their relatives live far away, they return to emptiness (in terms of social network). For these people, getting "better" results in a significant decrease in social interactions (adult/staff attention). The better they are, the less contact they have with people.

It is important to address why a functional analysis is just as essential as traditional diagnostic evaluations of persons in this circumstance. A traditional view begins with the assumption that verbalizing the statement "I feel I might kill myself" is a symptom of depression or low self-esteem. Given that view, the professionals involved will "pull-out all stops" to make this person less depressed. They will probably provide antidepressant medications and increased professional services (including individual and group therapy). What this regimen establishes has both a short- and long-term ramification. First, after receiving such services the person does feel better, that is, less depressed. That is the short-term result, which is essential. However, what also is established is that such statements are very effective in recruiting social interaction when desired. Such interaction becomes more desired once the client is released if social interaction is less available for him in the community. The longer the client goes without engaging in social interactions with people from his world, the more likely such statements can occur. This process, in effect, establishes a cyclic pattern of improvement and worsening. The functional utility of such statements in accessing attention, as well as the person's loss of attention from professionals as he gets better, needs to be considered if we are to develop more effective interventions for people diagnosed with mental illness.

If mental health systems take such a possible function into account, would it replace the current system? Absolutely not! People who say they are going to commit suicide need attention. It is currently impossible to determine who is likely to follow through with this threat and when. However, what a functional analysis will add to the comprehensive treatment of these people is the concurrent development of a social network for them when they leave the facility. Perhaps developing conversational skills as well as social trips to local community centers while they are inpatients would be therapeutic. Making new friends and contacts would be a treatment objective. Professionals would spend as much time in developing this person's new circle of friends as they would in triaging the presenting complaint. In short, giving this person many reasons to live is the best long-term approach, one encumbered by a functional analysis of the maintaining contingencies.

*Will Steal for Social Attention.* I (K.S.) was referred a 12-year-old female living in a foster home. The psychiatric staff were considering putting her on psychotropic medications due to her diagnosis of kleptomania. The referral was to determine if she could control herself in this matter or if it was it purely *neurological* (hence the need for medication as the only effective solution). This young woman would steal daily, often items that were of no real value to her. Among the items reported to have been stolen were a broken pencil, other students' school work, a kitchen egg timer, and even a pair of dentures! Now most people would assume that the reinforcer for stealing is the access to the desired item (i.e., 1.2 DA: tangible reinforcer).

In this case, that diagnosis did not fit. The items she stole were not items used by her. They served no purpose in her life. So why might someone steal items that were useless to her? I asked one of the staff persons, "What does she do with these items?" The staff person's reply was, "She leaves them on her desk in her room. I think she must be psychotic or something. She does not have any sense to hide them. She leaves them where she knows I will find them."

Could it be that this person desires to get caught? But why would someone want to get caught? Is such a purpose best explained by invoking an existential crisis theory? When I asked staff what happened when she got caught, the reply was illuminating. "I punish her by giving her long lectures on how bad it is to steal, but it just isn't working, I think she has low self esteem and wants to be punished" (there you go, an existential crisis). Perhaps she is a masochist!

Can an analysis of environmental contingencies support another explanation (one rooted in some form of reality)? Perhaps she desires attention, in whatever form. Consider this hypothesis. If she had minimal ability to initiate interactions, she might be forced to rely on another behavior to interact with people. Her stealing did not seem to be a function of access to tangible reinforcers. It also did not occur under conditions that would promote escape or avoidance behavior. Rather, it was her most effective way to access adult attention. Using this information, fill out Table 3.15.

### (2.2) SMA: Peer Attention

This diagnostic category encompasses problem behaviors that gain desired peer attention, particularly when peer approval is a powerful reinforcer. This function exists more

### TABLE 3.15 ■ DIAGNOSIS OF STEALING CASE

| Diagnosis | |
| --- | --- |
| Target behavior(s): | |
| Function: | |
| Target behavior likely under following contexts: | |
| Target behavior unlikely under following contexts: | |
| Rule out: | (2.2) SMA: peer attention |

frequently in school settings with adolescents (e.g., class clown phenomenon) but can be operable with other clients where peer attention is a desired event.

In order for peer attention to function as a maintaining contingency for target problem behavior, peer attention has to be available. Given that children, adolescents, and adults can transmit information regarding the display of behavior, peers can either be physically present (e.g., in the classroom at the time of the behavior) or be able to be informed of the incident.

Behaviors that gain desired peer attention become strengthened, particularly in social environments where peer approval is a powerful reinforcer. Problem behavior maintained by peer attention might be hard to detect because the approval or attention of peers may not occur immediately. In fact, with older children, some problem behaviors are reinforced by peers at a later time when they find out about the misbehavior (e.g., aggressive or disruptive behavior). Some adults engage in behavior that recruits peer attention or approval as well (e.g., man or woman who "brags" about sexual conquests to buddies, or brags about other phenomenon that recruit approval from peers).

This maintaining contingency involves a reliable relation between the problem behavior and the access to desired peer attention. Other more acceptable behaviors are less likely to result in attention. Although the target problem behaviors may occur some time before certain peers become aware of the incident or behavior, the delayed result still maintains the behavior. Teacher or adult attention may occur much closer to the problem behavior but may not be a factor in its maintenance. Very often, an incorrect hypothesis about such behaviors in this subcategory being maintained by adult attention leads to an ineffective strategy. The following examples illustrate this point.

*Everyone Loves a Clown (Except the Teacher).* An example of problem behavior maintained by peer attention is a hypothetical junior high school special education student, Billy. He is referred for a functional behavioral assessment for his verbally inappropriate behavior toward teachers. Following is a sample of what transpires during an incident of inappropriate verbal behavior during a pre-algebra class.

*Teacher:* Who can tell me what a linear equation is?

*Billy: (somewhat covertly, although within earshot of other students)* What a bore.

*Teacher:* Billy do you have something to contribute to this discussion?

*Billy:* I said what a core concept! *(other students start giggling)*

*Teacher:* Perhaps you would like to teach this core concept.

*Billy:* What for! *(class breaks out laughing, Billy is sent to the principal's office)*

It is not difficult to surmise that such behavior is resulting in peer attention. When Billy makes such comments to the teacher, he gets the attention and approval of his fellow classmates. For a trip to the principal's office, he now becomes the most popular kid in the class. He has peers wanting to hang out with him during recess and at lunch. Such reinforcement can often override the power of designated discipline strategies such as dismissal from class. It is important to diagnose these problems as 2.2 SMA: peer attention in order to provide effective intervention.

It is important to note that while some people may view the teacher's attention as the maintaining variable, such is not the case. Without peer attention that followed teacher attention, the level of the problem behavior would be much weaker. This is not to say that the teacher's response to Billy's initial smart remark did not provide the perfect forum for this student. It set the stage for peer attention to become more pronounced.

Suppose the teacher attended to other behaviors of this student that do not result in peer attention, such as raising his hand to be recognized. Would such have an effect on inappropriate verbal behavior? Many people, naive to an understanding of behavioral function, would vehemently respond with "Yes." From what you know now, why would a change in his behavior probably not happen?

## DISCUSSION QUESTIONS

Would you conduct an analogue assessment to determine whether it is adult attention or peer attention that is maintaining the problem behavior? What are some problems in testing this choice between diagnostic categories in Billy's case? Is an in-vivo treatment hypothesis strategy more adept at answering this question?

*Class Clown: It's Elementary.* A hypothetical second grade student engages in a number of inappropriate behaviors, such as sticking her tongue out at the teacher (when she's not looking), dropping her pencil, and making faces. Despite the fact that the teacher admonishes her for engaging in such behaviors, the peer reinforcement for such behaviors is far stronger than the admonishment she receives. She becomes the most popular student on the playground during recess. Subsequently, the rate of these behaviors is maintained at a high level as a result of their ability to get peers to attend and laugh with her.

### (2.3) SMA: Tangible Reinforcer Hypothesis

We have all seen children at the supermarket whine, cry, and throw a tantrum. Are they possessed by demons? Many people will comment that they probably want something from their parents. Very often, they are right. They have assessed the motivational condition correctly. What is also true is that this set of behaviors has been successful in the past in obtaining such desired items or activities.

Given deprivation with respect to the item or event, this antecedent context sets up the motivational condition for behaviors that are successful at getting the item. As a result of the adult's mediation of such behaviors, they become more probable. Unlike the direct access category, the client's target behavior does not directly produce the item. When the behavior occurs at some level or duration, it is mediated by someone, usually an adult, providing the item contingent upon the behavior. The delivery of this reinforcer makes such target problem behavior much more likely when the same or similar antecedent context appears in the future.

Therefore, target problem behaviors that function to access a desired tangible item, object, event, or activity under conditions where the client needs such are strengthened.

Further, other behaviors (perhaps more desirable) in the child's or client's repertoire that are ineffective or inefficient at producing such events become weakened.

In many cases, target behaviors functioning in this subcategory are usually misdiagnosed for problems maintained solely by adult attention (2.1 SMA). This can easily happen if one simply watches the first socially mediated event following the target behavior. For example, let us say that a student in a special day class for mild disabilities refuses to line up for adaptive physical education (P.E.). When she does this, the teacher quickly moves to her. The teacher is now in close proximity to the student and may say something. If one assesses that the first social event that occurred subsequent to the behavior is the maintaining variable, one would diagnose this problem as a 2.1 SMA, given a reliable relation between these events during adaptive P.E. However, after some protracted discussion, the teacher bribes the student to get in line by allowing her to carry her favorite doll while she goes to P.E. Now you know the whole story!

The problem in accurately diagnosing behavior problems in this category is that the delivery of the desired event or item will also coincide with adult attention. This is always true because access to the item is socially mediated. However, one should recognize that adult attention is an incidental variable and that access to the item, activity, or event is the "driving force" for the behavior. This can be tested in an in-vivo hypothesis test comparing two conditions. In half the sessions, present *only* attention and praise for this student when she gets in line. In the other sessions, provide the desired item if she gets in line within a certain time. If the item is the power behind the maintaining contingency, guess what condition will result in her getting in line more frequently?

The problem behavior may have to occur over some period of time before the adult provides the event or activity. In the case of children, the care provider or parent may initially attempt to ignore such behavior and not "feed into it." The parent refuses to give the child what he or she wants. Such initial attempts at ignoring the behavior do not result in the problem behavior ceasing. Rather, the problem escalates in form and duration. As a result of the child's behavior worsening, the adult, under pressure (and wanting to stop the behavior at all costs), gives the child the object or activity. It is essential to detect such a shaping of different forms of problem behavior and durations by the parent's response to both the initial form as well as the more severe form.

Sometimes the presentation of the tangible reinforcer is done in a manner that looks like the teacher, parent, or care provider is reinforcing appropriate behavior (e.g., "If you're quiet for 5 seconds, then I'll let you go outside and play"). The child engages in appropriate behavior and subsequently is given the desired item. However, one should realize that the entire chain of problem behaviors has led to the client's access to the item. It is not simply a matter of what behavior occurred prior to the delivery of the item! Table 3.16 presents questions to pose when considering this diagnostic subcategory.

This maintaining contingency involves a reliable relation between the problem behavior and the access to the desired item or event (Question 1). Other more acceptable behaviors are less likely to result in designated reinforcement (Question 2). Although the target problem behaviors may have to occur at some frequency or duration (Questions 3), they are more successful at getting the desired item or event than other more acceptable behaviors (Question 2). This aspect of subcategory 2.3 SMA is particularly relevant for the analysis of behavioral function. To reiterate, attention and other events may occur in the interim between behavior onset and delivery of socially mediated tangible reinforcement. Do not assume the events that are temporally closer to reinforcement are maintaining the behavior! Rather, in some cases, it is the ultimate delivery of the tangible reinforcer that is the driving force behind the client's behavior. Let's examine possible examples of problem behavior serving this diagnostic category.

**TABLE 3.16 ■ QUESTIONS TO CONSIDER FOR A 2.3 SMA DIAGNOSIS**

1. Is there a reliable, somewhat frequent relation between the problem behavior and socially mediated access to the tangible item or event? What is the form of the behavior?

2. Are the target behaviors more likely to produce access to the item or event than appropriate behaviors?

3. What type of reinforcement schedule is it on? How often or how long do such behaviors sustain before the item is given?

*Elopement.* A client was frequently running naked down the driveway of a residential facility. Staff reported that this occurred at least twice a week. Several staff would follow her and try to talk her into coming back. Obviously being naked will result in adult attention, both from staff and passersby. But such attention alone did not seem to explain this periodic nude display in the neighborhood. The staff indicated that this client was perfectly capable of accessing attention from staff, multiple times during a given day. Further, on a streaking day, her access to attention would be comparable to other days, suggesting that such was not in a deprived condition at the time of the behavior.

I (K.S.) was tasked with determining what happens that makes her engage in such a behavior. She obviously returned to the facility at some point in time. Perhaps how the staff "bribe" her back might provide a clue. I asked how they got her to return to the inside of the facility (and put clothes on). Their reply was that they had to offer her a soda if she returned.

Can the access to soda be so powerful that it makes this client shed her clothes and run down the driveway naked? It must be that access to sodas via other means (i.e., behaviors) is pretty difficult. Apparently, simply running out of the facility with clothes on did not set the conditions for getting a soda. The following is a facsimile of an interview with staff to get at this information.

*Keven:* What else does she do to get a soda?

*Staff:* Oh, she is not allowed to have sodas. She is on a restricted diet. She asks for sodas all the time and we tell her that she cannot have one, as it is not on her diet plan.

*Keven:* What does she do when she gets a soda?

*Staff:* Oh she guzzles it down, belches, and smiles.

Can you see that access to a soda, under the rigorous diet plan, becomes a deprived event? Further, acceptable behavior such as requesting a soda is not functional. Hence, the streaking behavior becomes functional under the motivational condition where getting a soda is highly sought by this client. Solving this problem now becomes easy. A quick conversation with the dietitian resulted in her being able to have one soda per day. The results of such a strategy confirmed my hypothesis. Once she had one soda each day, she did not streak down the driveway.

*Milton, the Pincher.* The stated relationship between Milton pinching people and getting a walk would make pinching more probable when he wants a walk. Hence, pinching behavior would be diagnosed with a 2.3 SMA category: tangible reinforcer. We would contend that pinching other people is a functional behavior when Milton desires a walk. Also, unfortunately other more appropriate behaviors are not more functional in Milton getting a walk (Table 3.17).

*TABLE 3.17* ■ **MILTON, THE PINCHER**

| Diagnosis | 2.3 SMA: tangible reinforcer |
|---|---|
| Target behavior(s): | Pinches staff |
| Function: | Accesses walk with staff (walk is the driving force because he cannot go on a walk outside unless accompanied by staff) |
| Target behavior likely under following contexts: | When he has been without a walk for an entire day |
| Target behavior unlikely under following contexts: | When he is taken for a walk early in the afternoon |
| Rule out: | Socially mediated escape function (4.1 SME) and socially mediated access function (2.1 and 2.2 SMA) |

## DISCUSSION QUESTIONS

In Milton's case, how would you determine that the walk is the maintaining contingency and not simply attention? How would you conduct an in-situ treatment hypothesis strategy to separate these two variables that occur together (i.e., in order to get a walk Milton has to have the staff attend to him)?

*I Don't Like What I Am Wearing!* Some students with severe disabilities may soil their clothes, even though they are capable of independent toileting, to get a change of clothes (i.e., change to preferred clothes). Other students learn to rip or tear their clothes for the same purpose (i.e., they will be given more preferred clothing articles to wear once their old clothes are torn). As long as the student gets new clothes contingent on these behaviors, ripping or soiling clothes will continue to occur under conditions where the student desires a change of clothing. Although the teaching staff's behavior is understandable, it certainly presents you with a plausible function for this behavior. Your turn to fill out Table 3.18.

*I Am Hungry Now.* A hypothetical adult with profound mental retardation exhibits a frequent and sometimes intense form of aggressive behavior toward staff, particularly before lunch. She will hit and attempt to bite them. A functional analysis may reveal that such behavior may be maintained by staff providing edibles and other food reinforcers to the client upon such behavior once she is calmed down. They may even state, "If you calm down, I will give you a cracker or candy bar." Although some staff may not realize that such a contingency is strengthening aggressive behavior, it is the entire scenario that is reinforced, not simply "calm behavior." Such forms of aggressive behavior become highly likely as the initial part of the entire chain when this client is hungry.

*TABLE 3.18* ■ **DIAGNOSIS OF CLOTHES-WEARING CASE**

| Diagnosis | |
|---|---|
| Target behavior(s): | |
| Function: | |
| Target behavior likely under following contexts: | |
| Target behavior unlikely under following contexts: | |
| Rule out: | |

To complicate matters, aggressive behavior may not eventually result in food every day. On some days, no food may be offered. The staff may report that they do not give her food when she is aggressive (forgetting the times when it is used to calm her down). Of course, you realize that delivery of food does not have to occur with every incident. Rather, some intermittent delivery of food can maintain such behavior, especially if other behaviors are more unsuccessful at getting food than self-abuse. For example, her attempts at going to the refrigerator in the class to get food are met with opposition and redirection to the couch. Going to the refrigerator and attempting to get food never works! Aggression at least works some of the time. This client may learn who is more likely to give food conditional upon her aggressive behavior and then focus her efforts on those staff. Of course, the individual must want food in the first place (motivational condition) to set up the context for food-seeking behaviors to become functional.

*He Likes to Be Restrained.* This real-life case illustrates how a chain of events that begins with a client being restrained for aggressive behavior can end in a tangible reinforcer. Often with clients who frequently engage in behaviors that terminate in restraint, personnel will claim they like being restrained. But an analysis of the events that transpire subsequent to the restraint may be an eye-opening revelation as to true function.

In the mid-1980s, I (E.C.) was hired as a consultant for a training program for people with developmental disabilities. This program was set up for some clients just coming out of the state institution in a wave of depopulation taking place during that time period in California. These clients had some of the most disruptive and challenging behaviors of the persons leaving the state institution, and this agency wanted to serve such persons (given a higher rate of reimbursement for handling such difficult behavior problems). It was not uncommon for a client to have to be physically restrained as a result of his potentially dangerous behavior. The restraint would occur at a point where the client's behavior had escalated so that danger was imminent. The staff was well-trained in this procedure and executed it in a safe and efficient manner when needed. Over time, some clients only needed to be restrained every once in awhile. In contrast, other clients were involved in a prone containment just about every day.

One client in particular was brought to my attention. His rate of episodes where he had to be restrained was quite high. The facilities behavioral specialists reasoning was that restraint should always function as a punisher because no one in their right mind could actually like that. Therefore, their explanation of his behavioral episodes, involving aggression and property destruction, was that he was just "going off." Unfortunately, when he got to this level of aggression and property destruction, there was no alternative except to restrain him. I thought, "Could there be a competing consequence? What could he possibly be getting out of the restraint process so that accessing this tangible item or event would override the aversive aspect of the restraint?" The answer? Coffee!

Here was a typical scenario. As reported by staff, he would be restrained when his state of aggressive behavior reached the danger point. Directives to engage in more appropriate behavior were fruitless in some situations. It was as if he *wanted* to be restrained. Two or more staff persons would put him in a prone containment in a safe manner, preferably on a soft surface. As he calmed down, they began a process of releasing him progressively, until he was standing erect again. They would then have him sit in a chair. As a method to calm him down further, he was given lots of attention from staff, soothing comments, and *coffee*. The proof that coffee was the smoking gun was the following piece of information I obtained after viewing this phenomenon with my own eyes. Prior to the incident, if he asked for coffee, he was told he could not have any until lunch because he just had some for breakfast. Now do you see the competing consequences? Act up, get restrained; 15–20 minutes later, get coffee. Don't act up, but ask nicely, no coffee.

*Lays Potato Chips: Bet You Can't Have Just One.* A hypothetical client with schizophrenia in a day treatment program engages in property destruction. How does such a behavior relate to getting potato chips? The road to extra potato chips is long and winding, but the payoff is at the end. During snack time, after this client has finished her food, she will sometimes attempt to get up and get more snack items, particularly when the snack item is potato chips. This attempt is rebuffed by staff (i.e., direct access behavior is ineffective). They get in front of her and direct her verbally, and sometimes physically, back to her chair. She may then scream and holler, in which case staff move her away from the dining table. She then knocks items off the adjacent table or any other surface that is in need of redecorating. As a consequence for such behavior, she is placed in time out. Looks like none of these behaviors result in extra potato chips, right? Suppose that after the time out, *sometimes* staff give her a half a bag if she was quiet during her time out (as an incentive not to create havoc while in time out). Now you see the whole chain of events and how such a behavior as property destruction can serve a food-accessing function. One has to get to time out in order to have the possibility of payoff. Whatever behaviors result in staff giving her a time out will become more probable under the current environmental conditions. This analysis is depicted in Table 3.19.

## Category 3.0: Direct Escape (DE)

The behavioral function of this major category is that these escape (and avoidance) behaviors directly terminate (or completely avoid) an aversive event. For example, you feel an itch on your leg, which produces a certain level of discomfort. This antecedent context sets up the motivational condition for some behavior to relieve the aversive state—the itch. You scratch that area in a certain manner that causes the minor discomfort to disappear for a while (termination of aversive event). Your scratching of the itch brought about its removal directly.

Direct escape functions can often be operable when clients are involved in situations or activities involving task demands. If a client is being presented with a nonpreferred task or demand (establishing the value of escape), then leaving the area directly produces at least a temporary cessation of the demand or task. Note that this behavior is successful in at least temporarily postponing the engagement with the task. Depending on what staff do after the behavior, determine whether such behavior will result in temporary postponement of the work task or permanent removal. If staff begin to prevent the client from walking away from the area, another behavior may take its place. The client may learn that in order to be successful in getting away, one cannot simply walk away because staff will prevent the client from getting away. He must now run from the area in order to be successful.

Other contexts that may generate direct escape behaviors are aversive social or physical environments. Many people find noisy areas an intrusion, and given sufficient exposure

### TABLE 3.19 ■ DIAGNOSIS OF 2.3 SMA

| Diagnosis | 2.3 SMA: tangible reinforcer |
| --- | --- |
| Target behavior(s): | Property destruction in the form of knocking items off of surfaces |
| Function: | Accesses extra bag of potato chips after time out |
| Target behavior likely under following contexts: | When she has been denied an extra bag by being redirected back to dining table |
| Target behavior unlikely under following contexts: | Other than mealtime in the evening |
| Rule out: | Socially mediated escape function (4.1 SME) and socially mediated access function (2.1 and 2.2 SMA) |

to such, engage in a behavior that withdraws themselves from such an event. Leaving the noisy area for a quiet area is sometimes an option for many of us. However, under the same conditions, clients or students leaving the area without notice can constitute a behavior problem in facilities and educational institutions. The function is the same; however, we can get away with that, and they often receive additional consequences.

The same holds true for clients that want to escape crowded or odorous environments. In this category, the form of the escape behavior results in a direct termination of the aversive event or stimulus. Leaving or running away from the scene produces the direct termination of the aversive event. Leaving the area may be more tolerated by staff or care providers if the client accompanied such behavior with an assertive verbal indication, such as, "I am feeling a little bothered by the noise. I would like to leave for a while." However, when leaving is not accompanied by such a verbal request, it often becomes a problem behavior for staff that requires intervention.

Students who are faced with instructional tasks can engage in escape behaviors when the tasks are relatively long and difficult. Such a context sets up the motivating condition for escape or avoidance behaviors. Often such escape behaviors are of a form that involve the teacher responding in a certain manner to such a behavior that temporary escape is produced. Most escape behaviors during instructional conditions are socially mediated. This probably is a function of the social environment being more attuned to direct escape behaviors and preventing them (e.g., having door closed to class) or ameliorating their effect (immediately returning them to their seat). But socially mediated escape behaviors are more insidious in their ultimate environmental effect (see the following example).

## DON'T JUST GET UP, HIT SOMEBODY!

A hypothetical student with severe disabilities gets out of his seat during group instruction time and sits next to the computer. He is immediately brought back by staff. Further, to prevent such an episode from recurring, the teacher places an aide right next to this student so that the aide can stop the escape early in its genesis. Over a brief period of time, this student learns the futility of just getting up and walking out. Hence, such direct escape behavior becomes less likely.

However, the aversive condition has not been diminished. He is still faced with the task. His motivation to engage in some behavior that results in escape from this task is still relevant. He then hits another student during this group instruction time. The teacher immediately directs her aide to guide him to the time-out area to teach him "We do not hit in this class!" With such a contingency, the rate of this student's hitting peers during group time increases to a daily occurrence. Is this teaching him a lesson? Yes, it is! When you want out, hit someone.

## DISCUSSION QUESTION

What reinforcement operation explains why the teacher in this hypothetical scenario may continue to use time out despite its function?

The subcategories under direct escape functions (in addition to the other category) are 3.1 DE: unpleasant social situations; 3.2 DE: relatively lengthy task, chore, instruction; 3.3 DE: relatively difficult task, chore, instruction; and 3.4 DE: aversive physical stimuli.

### (3.1) DE: Unpleasant Social Situations

This diagnostic category encompasses problem behaviors that directly terminate the child's engagement or interaction in unpleasant social situations (unpleasant relative to that child). A client is at a work station with a number of other clients. One of the other clients engages in screaming and other tantrum-type behavior. This client runs to the corner of the room, and then eventually goes out the door. The motivating condition for this set of behaviors was an aversive social situation, that is, the other client next to him screaming. This client terminates his presence by leaving the area. Perhaps such a behavior had been learned over many years of similar circumstances where screaming clients often follow up such bouts with another disruptive behavior, that is, they start hitting other people.

Direct escape behaviors that can occur under unpleasant social situations can include leaving the facility, home, or classroom without permission; running away; or moving to another area. Many direct escape behaviors often involve the client's response to the administration of a discipline procedure, such as leaving the time-out area. For example, a child does something wrong during recess and is taken to the principal's office. While unsupervised, he leaves. Leaving the area would not be considered a behavior that is maintained because of adult attention! Rather, its ability to directly terminate the unpleasant event is what maintains it in the future. Perhaps his stays will be more closely supervised if he continues such behavior when sitting in the office.

Table 3.20 illustrates that the motivating operation for this subcategory of problem behaviors is the presence of an aversive or unpleasant situation (first column). One must take into account that *aversive* is a relative term for that individual client, at that point in time. What is aversive or unpleasant to one person may not be to another. Further, the same situation may be less aversive to an individual on Monday than it was for her last Sunday.

Such a context sets up the motivational condition for behaviors that escape (or avoid) such aversive events. The behavior becomes functional in that circumstance when it is successful at direct escape or avoidance of that situation. Note that in categories where the escape of the aversive situation occurs directly as a function of the behavior, the social consequences that follow such behavior are tangential and inconsequential. Table 3.21 presents some questions that are relevant for discerning such a diagnosis of 3.1 DE: unpleasant social situations.

This maintaining contingency involves a reliable direct relation between the problem behavior and the escape or avoidance of the unpleasant social situation (Question 1). Other more acceptable behaviors are less likely to result in escape (Question 2). Although the target problem behaviors may have to occur at some frequency and due to staff preventing such from escaping (Question 3), they are more successful at terminating the undesired social situation than other more acceptable behaviors (Question 2).

*Running Away From the Facility.* A hypothetical client living in a group home facility for female adults with mental disorders and disabilities wants to go to the mall on Saturday. In this facility, clients must earn outside community privileges on the weekend through a point system. If a client earns a certain level of points by Friday, by behaving

**TABLE 3.20 ■ BEHAVIOR ANALYSIS OF DIRECT NEGATIVE REINFORCEMENT EFFECTS**

| Motivating Operation | Behavior | Contingency (C-2) | Future probability of behavior under MO |
|---|---|---|---|
| Presence of aversive social situation | Engages in problem behavior | Aversive event terminated immediately, removes aversive state | More likely when aversive event is present in the future |

### TABLE 3.21 ■ QUESTIONS TO CONSIDER FOR A 3.1 DE DIAGNOSIS

1. Is there a reliable, somewhat frequent, direct relation between the problem behavior and termination of the undesired social situation? What is the form of the escape behavior?

2. Are the target behaviors more likely to produce escape from the situation than other more appropriate behaviors to terminate a social interaction?

3. What type of reinforcement schedule is it on? Is the client thwarted in his/her attempts to directly terminate the social situation? How long do such escape behaviors sustain before the aversive or unpleasant event is terminated?

appropriately, following staff directions, and completing designated chores, she can earn a trip to the mall with the rest of the clients on Saturday afternoon. Further, other weekend community activities are also available to the clients who earn the prerequisite number of points. However, if a client does not earn the required points for that week, that client has to stay back while the remaining clients go on their community outing. To make such a consequence even more unpleasant, the client staying in the facility has to do extra, nonpreferred chores during this time.

When this client does not earn enough points, she leaves the facility on Friday night or early Saturday morning. In the past 4 months, she has left the facility unauthorized five times. Four of these fives occasions were on weekends where she would *not* have earned community privileges. What is the reason for this potentially dangerous behavior? If she does not earn the points needed, she resorts to leaving on her own and avoiding chores and staying back. The primary consequence of leaving is simply to be brought back to the facility when found. Can you see how such a behavior will continue to occur under these conditions (i.e., not earning enough points)? As she becomes more skilled at navigating life outside the facility on her own, other contingencies become operable. In addition to escaping an aversive condition, she also enjoys some activities that are only available outside the facility. Such powerful results make leaving the facility more likely each weekend (Table 3.22).

### (3.2) DE: Relatively Lengthy Task, Chore, Instruction

This diagnostic category encompasses behaviors that postpone or terminate the child's or client's engagement with an instructional task, chore, or demand.

The value of escape is established because the task or chore is lengthy in duration. *Lengthy* is a relative term. What may be lengthy to you may be of short duration to me. Such a context sets up the motivational condition for behaviors that escape (or avoid) such

### TABLE 3.22 ■ RUNNING AWAY AS A 3.1 DE DIAGNOSIS

| Diagnosis | 3.1 DE: unpleasant social situation |
| --- | --- |
| Target behavior(s): | Leaving the facility unauthorized |
| Function: | Escapes/avoids nonpreferred chores and staying at home while others are on community outing |
| Target behavior likely under following contexts: | When client has not earned enough points for community outing |
| Target behavior unlikely under following contexts: | When client has earned enough points for community outing |
| Rule out: | Socially mediated access functions (2.1, 2.2, 2.3). In 2.3 SMA: see if she gets something after coming home that she would not have gotten, e.g., extra TV time for a couple of nights |

aversive events. The behavior becomes functional in that circumstance when it is successful at direct escape or avoidance of that situation. The social consequences of such behavior are inconsequential. In many cases, such social responses following the behavior are often misdiagnosed as the primary function of the behavior. If escape is produced directly, what the teacher does or says after this result is not the driving force behind the behavior. Such teacher responses are inconsequential to the maintenance of the behavior, although they may further enable the direct escape behavior.

In this subcategory, the child (or client) is capable of performing the assignment or task, but the duration of the instructional activity required is above his level. For example, a student can perform at adequate levels addition and subtraction problems involving carrying and borrowing. If he is given only five of these to do, no problem behaviors emerge. He finishes these and then proceeds to something else (hopefully of higher probability). However, when he is given 50 to do, he gets out of his seat, digs into his backpack looking for something, and performs other such avoidance behaviors. "Daydreaming" during seat work time is an example of a behavior that directly produces disengagement with the instructional material.

The professional attempts to analyze the antecedent conditions inherent in such target behaviors. In addition, she also looks for contexts where assignment completion occurs. Examining how effective such possible direct escape behaviors are in the presence of lengthy tasks allows for a more accurate prescription to this problem. Manipulating the *difficulty* of the task is not the answer. Some form of altering task *length* is one component of a functional behavior analytic strategy.

Many teachers would report they reinforce appropriate behavior. However, the controlling effects of lengthy instructional periods may make termination of instruction a contingency that is more powerful than the use of praise and teacher attention as contingent events for appropriate behavior. Lengthy instructional periods, both in general and special education, would seem to be a prevalent context for problem behaviors, as the following example illustrates.

## THE CASE OF "WACKY CONTINGENCIES" IN THE CLASSROOM

One might assume that appropriate behavior (e.g., staying on task, doing one's work) is routinely reinforced in the classroom. When asked, most teachers would reply, "Of course I reinforce good behavior." But what do they mean when they say, "reinforce good behavior"? Let us look at a typical series of events in the classroom and examine whether reinforcement is delivered for appropriate behavior, such as assignment completion.

At 9:00, the teacher hands out the math assignment to all the children in the classroom. The math period on the daily lesson schedule is slated for 9:00 to 10:00 A.M. At 10:00, the students are slated for a 10-minute recess period before the advent of another instructional period. Let us examine closely what happens to two different students, Jacque and Jeanette, in this hypothetical math class during a day in September. Both students are given similar assignments and have similar abilities. Both students also would rate math work as a less preferred task to other more interesting activities.

At 9:00, the teacher hands out the math assignment sheets, which consist of 25 calculation problems, and requests that the students begin working on their assignment. Jacque, disliking the assignment, says to himself, "I'm not sure I like this but I'll work hard and get it done. Then I'll get something else to do." Jacque proceeds to work hard on the math assignment. Jeanette has similar thoughts, except she tells herself, "I'm not ready to do this yet so I think I will go sharpen my pencil and get my papers organized and get ready for the next period, which is more to my liking." Subsequently, Jeanette does a minimal amount of work on the assignment, looking for every opportunity to do something other than the math problems.

Shortly after the period has started, Jacque has completed his work and goes up to the teacher and turns in his paper. The teacher remarks, "Jacque, what a wonderful job you've done. This is an exceptional paper. I'm so proud of you, and I know your parents would be proud of you also. Now lets see how you do on this one (as she gives him another sheet)." (In the teacher's mind, she is telling herself—"that's the way to reinforce him for his work, I really gave him lots of praise. He'll probably want to do a really great job on that new math sheet.") Meanwhile, the teacher notes that Jeanette has not even finished the fourth problem on the assignment. She scolds Jeanette, and tells her that if she doesn't finish her math assignment that she'll have to do the same sheet over again tomorrow (the teacher notes to herself—I'll not praise Jeanette for her performance).

One may be tempted to laugh or discount this as an unusual situation, but it is all too frequently the case across many classrooms. Why is this a wacky contingency? The teacher certainly praised Jacque for completing his assignment! Can one say that reinforcement occurred for appropriate behavior? To answer that question, one has to examine multiple consequent events for completing the assignment. When Jacque finished the assignment, he received praise and more work! Note that the completion of the assignment results in more work. Jacque does not receive any additional reinforcer or incentive for completing his work, but rather is given more work (a nonpreferred task). Also, note that Jeanette's failure to complete the assignment merely resulted in the work being postponed until the next day's math period. Both children get the same amount of recess. Therefore, recess is not a contingent event that is based on assignment completion. Rather, it is time based, that is, when it is time for recess apparently everyone goes, irrespective of the amount of work done.

Under these conditions, what can we predict for the future? Jacque may learn that finishing work usually results in more work. One can imagine what will happen to his work production over time. He eventually begins to complete his assignment less frequently. Jeanette learns to put up with scolding and disparaging remarks but still gets recess like everyone else. She is described by her teacher as a student who doesn't care about reinforcement (because she obviously doesn't do her work to receive the teacher's praise).

What is the wacky contingency? Complete your work—get more! Fail to complete your work—get less! Fix that and you will be very successful in having many students become more adept at completing their assignments in school.

Table 3.23 presents questions to pose when considering this diagnostic subcategory. This maintaining contingency involves a reliable direct relation between the problem behavior and the escape or avoidance of the lengthy task (Question 1). Other more acceptable behaviors are less likely to result in escape (Question 2). The target problem behaviors may have to occur at some frequency, due to staff preventing such from escaping (Question 3). However, they are more successful at terminating the lengthy task than other more acceptable behaviors (Question 2). This function needs to be distinguished from the next subcategory in that the child's ability to perform the task (accurately) is adequate. However, the length of time required to engage in the task is the factor, making escape from the instruction or chore a powerful motivating condition.

*I Need a Break.* A hypothetical student with severe disabilities is given a task, which she completes. On days when she is given small amounts of work, followed by a break, the staff report she is not a problem. However, on days when there is more work, staff report that she lays her head down more on the table. Staff ascribe such behavior to the possibility that she did not get enough sleep the prior night. She lays there for 5–10 minutes and then gets up. Some days she lays her head down a little longer. School staff want to speak to her mom about her sleep habits. Unfortunately, the information relayed does not seem to

---

### *TABLE 3.23* ■ QUESTIONS TO CONSIDER FOR A 3.2 DE DIAGNOSIS

1. Is there a reliable, somewhat frequent, direct relation between the problem behavior and termination of the client's involvement in the task or chore? What is the form of the escape behavior?

2. Are the target behaviors more likely to produce escape from the instructional tasks or chore than other more appropriate behaviors?

3. What type of reinforcement schedule is it on? Is the client thwarted in his/her attempts to directly terminate his/her engagement in the task?

support their contention. Rather, she is more likely to engage in that behavior when the instructional task lasts longer than 20 minutes. Would you say she has learned how much work she wants to do in one stretch?

*Making Many Beds.* Some adult clients have problems when required to complete a chore. One can observe that the difficulty of the task is not the issue. The client can perform the requisite steps of the chore; it is the length of the chore. A hypothetical client was given a position at a hotel as a maid. This was perceived as a "good fit" because the residential staff reported that she was able to make her bed every morning.

Several weeks after her start, she was let go for not performing her duties. Although she was able to make a few beds, and made them up to standard, the problem was in the lack of completing all her assigned rooms. Realize that if you work for a hotel in supported employment, you must make many beds. This duration mismatch created an aversive condition for that client. She would hide from the supervisor or fall asleep on one of the beds. Taking her own extended breaks directly escaped the lengthy task, and also got her fired. To say that she engaged in avoidance behaviors because she wanted to get fired would be fallacious. She would be perfectly happy only having to do a few beds a day and still be employed. The easiest explanation is not always the correct one.

## DISCUSSION QUESTIONS

Would you guess that some nondisabled workers have similar problems? Why?

### (3.3) DE: Relatively Difficult Task, Chore, Instruction

This diagnostic category encompasses problem behaviors that directly terminate the task or chore, with such escape responding motivated by the difficulty of the task or chore. The aversive state is created because the task or chore is relatively difficult. Difficult is a relative term. What may be difficult for you may be easy for me (and vice versa). Such a context sets up the motivational condition for behaviors that escape (or avoid) such aversive events. The behavior becomes functional in that circumstance when it is successful at directly escaping or avoiding difficult tasks or instructional demands. Note that the social consequences that follow such behavior are inconsequential in terms of strengthening the behavior (column C).

Table 3.24 presents questions to pose when considering this diagnostic subcategory. This maintaining contingency involves a reliable direct relation between the problem behavior and the escape or avoidance of the relatively difficult task (Question 1). Other more acceptable behaviors are less likely to result in escape (Question 2). Although the target problem behaviors may have to occur at some frequency and due to staff preventing such from escaping (Question 3), they are more successful at terminating the task than other more acceptable behaviors (Question 2).

Much *passive* off-task behavior is direct escape from task engagement. One can only avoid the task in a passive manner for so long before teacher admonishment. If longer breaks from work are desired, you will have to do something that removes you more permanently from the classroom. To reiterate an earlier point, students who are faced with difficult material will often engage in behaviors that are socially mediated. The more disruptive, the more likely the student will get removed from the instructional situation.

**TABLE 3.24 ■ QUESTIONS TO CONSIDER FOR A 3.3 DE DIAGNOSIS**

1. Is there a reliable somewhat frequent direct relation between the problem behavior and termination of the relatively difficult task? What is the form of the escape behavior?

2. Are the target behaviors more likely to produce escape than other more appropriate behaviors to terminate the client's engagement in the difficult task?

3. What type of reinforcement schedule is it on? Is the client thwarted in his/her attempts to directly terminate his/her engagement in the task? How long or often do such behaviors have to occur before they are successful?

*Instructional Mismatch.* In school settings, a child's engagement with the instructional task is aversive to her, primarily because she is not capable of performing the task accurately or fluently. Children who are given academic tasks that are way above their current level face this on a daily basis. For example, giving a child a seat work task involving decimal problems may be appropriate for her grade level. However, if she is only capable of adding and subtracting single-digit numbers, an aversive context is generated. This content level *mismatch* creates the conditions for escape or avoidance as a powerful motivative condition. This is a sure prescription for developing an aversion to math time, that is, constantly expose the child to material she has very little chance of succeeding with. In these cases, the child may engage in behaviors that avoid attending to the instruction or task, such as daydreaming, reading comic books, and so on.

## DISCUSSION QUESTIONS

Explain how instruction and problem behavior are inextricably intertwined. When students fail repeatedly with their class assignments, what condition does that set up?

### (3.4) DE: Aversive Physical Stimuli

If you mistakenly put on clothes that are too tight, you would remove these clothes and put on other clothes. Such a chain of behaviors is functional in that it produces the termination of the aversive event directly. Suppose you are prevented from changing clothes because personnel see such as your wanting to "control your environment"? Would you resort to behaviors deemed maladaptive? If you are faced with this daily, you probably would. Except that such behaviors are not necessarily maladaptive, but rather functional if the result is a change in clothes (see Table 3.25).

What are some other examples of direct escape behaviors terminating an aversive event? People often leave an area that smells, put a coat on when it is cold, take a break when one has been working too long, and so forth. Although such behaviors are certainly

**TABLE 3.25 ■ QUESTIONS TO CONSIDER FOR A 3.4 DE DIAGNOSIS**

1. Is there a reliable somewhat frequent direct relation between the problem behavior and direct removal of the aversive physical event? What is the form of the escape behavior?

2. Are the target behaviors more likely to produce removal of the stimulus than other more appropriate behaviors?

3. What type of reinforcement schedule is it on? Is the client thwarted in his/her attempts to directly terminate the aversive stimulus? How long or frequent do such behaviors have to occur before achieving their desired result?

understandable, with some clients the manner in which they escape the aversive physical situation is unacceptable.

The differentiation between this subcategory and the previous categories is the imposition of a discrete physical stimulus that the client finds aversive. This may be differentiated from the prior aversive stimuli or events in that the stimulus is applied directly to the client. Upon hearing a loud noise coming from your smoke alarm, you may generate a chain of behaviors that eventually results in disabling the connection between the battery and the smoke alarm. It is the last step that is performed that produces the direct cessation of the noise, hence negative reinforcement.

The following are some examples of problem behaviors in this subcategory.

*Nude Clients.* Some clients in residential and educational programs periodically or frequently engage in ripping or tearing their clothes off. Although the suggestion that such behavior is maintained by social attention is pertinent, that does not always turn out to be a correct diagnosis. What might be an alternate maintaining contingency for some clients? If the clothes she is currently wearing are less desired, or if she is used to some other fabric (e.g., cotton, silk, etc.), the motivational condition exists for escape behavior. Ripping her clothes off produces a direct effect on clothes removal.

In many of these cases involving clients who rip off their clothes, why does an alternate, more acceptable behavior not occur? Such behaviors may not be present in the repertoire of the client (see Chapter 4 on diagnosis of replacement behaviors). It may also be the case that such behaviors are in the repertoire of the client but not reinforced by staff. Suppose a client is capable of taking his clothes off appropriately *but staff block attempts to undress?* Such an acceptable behavior is not functional. Similarly, requesting different clothes that are not as comfortable is either not in the repertoire, or such requests fall on deaf ears.

Although clothes tearing can result in adult attention (whatever is said or done), one must not always assume that such attention is the maintaining variable. Although nudity will certainly result in attention, the primary function is direct escape from the nonpreferred clothes. If the client was allowed to change into new clothes, he probably would not run around the unit nude. An analogue test for this hypothesis would be to allow the client to change into new clothes when he signals his desire (may have to be taught) for several weeks. Then for the next several weeks, do not prompt or reinforce his request to change clothes.

Misdiagnosing this problem as an adult attention function (subcategory 2.1 SMA) would lead to an ineffective treatment. Attending to this client when he is clothed and not attending to him when he is nude would do little or nothing to solve the problem. In fact, it may lead to longer durations of nudity because ignoring would elicit no response on the part of staff to get him dressed!

*Head Bang From a Toothache?* A young man with multiple disabilities was unable to speak and had a history of engaging in mild head slapping behavior. The staff were instructed to simply interrupt him when he engaged in self-abuse and redirect him to his assigned task. They guessed that he was doing this to obtain attention because he kept doing it. Their next plan was for such behavior to be placed on extinction, that is, removal of staff attention.

Unfortunately, the intensity of the head slapping increased. If their hypothesis was correct, the removal of attention should have resulted in a decrease in this behavior. Concurrently, another behavior that will be more successful in getting attention would have increased. Such did not occur with this treatment regimen (wrong diagnosis!). The young man proceeded to bang his head to the point that his mouth was bleeding and the side of his face was swollen. Another hypothesis needed to be entertained. Upon being brought

**TABLE 3.26 ■ HEAD BANGING AS A 3.4 DE DIAGNOSIS**

| Diagnosis | 3.4 DE: aversive physical stimuli |
| --- | --- |
| Target behavior(s): | Slapping self on face |
| Function: | Directly terminates pain temporarily |
| Target behavior likely under following contexts: | In presence of tooth pain |
| Target behavior unlikely under following contexts: | When tooth pain is not felt |
| Rule out: | Socially mediated access functions (2.1, 2.3) and socially mediated escape functions (4.1, 4.2, 4.3) |

into the case, I (K.S.) immediately sought medical attention. Upon examination of the mouth area, it was discovered that this young man had developed an abscessed tooth. It is very likely that this abscessed tooth was quite painful. The face slapping was hypothesized to have directly alleviated some of the pain caused by this abscess, at least temporarily. When dental treatment was rendered, two subsequent phenomena resulted. First, the treatment successfully reduced the abscess. Equally important, the self-abusive behavior ceased completely (Table 3.26).

## Category 4.0: Socially Mediated Escape (SME)

Socially mediated escape (SME) problem behaviors remove or postpone aversive events. It contrasts with the previous category of direct escape behaviors in that the child or client's behavior does not directly terminate the aversive event. Rather, the negative reinforcer is removed through the behavior of another person, that is, parent, staff, care provider, teacher, or peer.

Within this category are the following subcategories—4.1 SME: escape of unpleasant social situations; 4.2 SME: escape of relatively long tasks or chores; 4.3 SME: escape from difficult tasks or chores; and 4.4 SME: aversive physical stimuli. Note that the same aversive events that served as antecedent conditions for direct escape behaviors can also serve as the motivational conditions for socially mediated escape. However, the difference is in the manner in which escape or avoidance is produced. A tantrum cannot directly remove a child from an unpleasant social situation (its only effect is on sound wave production in the area). Rather, it can serve as a communication to her parent to mediate the situation. Upon hearing her child throw a tantrum, the parent interprets such as a message that the child is unhappy in the current situation and thereby removes her. When the child appears more pleased at getting away from this situation, the parent stores this information away for the next tantrum.

### (4.1) SME: Escape of Unpleasant Social Situations

This diagnostic subcategory encompasses problem behaviors that terminate the child's engagement or interaction in relatively unpleasant social situations (unpleasant relative to that child). The antecedent and motivational conditions match the DE subcategory of the same circumstance, unpleasant social situations. These would not usually be instructional conditions unless the social circumstance itself (e.g., child sits next to someone who teases her) makes the instructional setting aversive, not the instruction. The presence of the aversive social situation sets up the motivational condition for the client to engage in escape or avoidance behavior that is socially mediated. The form of such behaviors is determined by how successful and reliable such behaviors are at getting a person to terminate an already existing event or postpone the advent of an upcoming aversive event.

**TABLE 3.27 ■ QUESTIONS TO CONSIDER FOR A 4.1 SME DIAGNOSIS**

1. Is there a reliable, somewhat frequent relationship between the problem behavior and termination of the undesired social situation? What is the form of the escape behavior?

2. Are the target behaviors more likely to produce escape from the situation by an adult, staff person, teacher, or parent than other more appropriate behaviors to terminate a social interaction?

3. What type of reinforcement schedule are they on? How long or frequent do such behaviors sustain before the aversive or unpleasant event is terminated by someone?

Table 3.27 presents the questions to ask when considering this diagnostic subcategory. This maintaining contingency involves a reliable relation between the problem behavior and the escape or avoidance of the unpleasant social situation (Question 1). Other more acceptable behaviors are less likely to result in escape (Question 2). Although the target problem behaviors may have to occur at some frequency or duration (Question 3), they are more successful at terminating the undesired social situation than other more acceptable behaviors (Question 2).

*Hiding.* A child, about 5 years of age, was referred to me (K.S.) due to his hiding in dangerous locations in his house (once he was found in the oven). What would be the circumstance that would generate such hiding behavior? Through interview and descriptive analysis, the antecedent for such behavior appeared to be his foster mother attempting to discipline him. When he had engaged in some unwanted behavior, his foster mother would call to him (from another room). She asked him to come to her so she could reprimand him.

As you can imagine, her tone of voice would be different than if she simply wanted to talk with him. Her tone of voice was the cue for this child. Upon hearing her command for him to come, he would find the nearest place to hide; this could be inside kitchen cabinets, under furniture, or in the garden shed. The process of searching for him was so tedious and aversive that it altered the mother's response. By the time she found him, she was so relieved, she would sometimes hug him instead of reprimand him. His behavior of hiding was quite effective in escaping any further, more intense, reprimand from his mother.

*Spinning.* I (K.S.) received a referral for a middle-aged man in a locked psychiatric unit with a diagnosis of schizophrenia. He had an unusual way of getting the doctors and nurses to quit talking to him. When they approached and began to interact with him, he would simply stretch out his arms and begin to spin in circles. Anyone within arms' distance would be struck. This behavior was quite successful in getting not only the doctors and nurses to avoid him, but also all of the other patients (Table 3.28).

**TABLE 3.28 ■ SPINNING BEHAVIOR AS A 4.1 SME DIAGNOSIS**

| Diagnosis | 4.1 SME: unpleasant social situation |
| --- | --- |
| Target behavior(s): | Spinning in circles |
| Function: | Avoiding undesired staff interaction |
| Target behavior likely under following contexts: | Staff approaching him and attempting to talk to him |
| Target behavior unlikely under following contexts: | When left alone by staff |
| Rule out: | Socially mediated access functions (2.1, 2.3) |

## DISCUSSION QUESTIONS

What FBA data would indicate that spinning behavior serves a 1.1 DA: sensory reinforcer function? If a trigger analysis found that he spun around only 30% of the total times staff approached him, what would you set up as a test of a diagnosis of 1.1 DA?

*Shut Up and Leave Me Alone!* A client diagnosed with paranoid schizophrenia had been living in a locked psychiatric facility for 15 years (Schock, Clay, & Cipani, 1998). He had a lengthy history of hitting other people, primarily in the context of their initiating and maintaining an interaction with him. To say that his regard for small talk was not very high is an understatement! The collection of baseline data was not pursued due to the dangerousness of the behavior. However, an analysis of the possible function of this client's aggression from records and interview seemed to indicate that hitting the other person resulted in his being left alone. The termination of the social situation as a result of hitting someone was hypothesized as the maintaining variable. Instead of saying, "Please leave me alone!" he would hit the other resident, which then produced the desired result of being left alone (Table 3.29).

Developing an alternate behavior (instead of aggression) that would hopefully have the same function was required before he arrived at his new residential facility. His continued persistence at ending conversations by hitting people would probably make his stay at the community-based facility a short one. Prior to his arrival, I (K.S.) and my staff decided to develop and reinforce a new behavior that would terminate a conversation and not involve hitting. The staff taught him to use the phrase, "Shut up and leave me alone!" We considered a more acceptable phrase, for example, "I do not want to talk to you anymore," or "Please leave me alone." However, those forms of protest may not have had the desired effect in the current facility. Residential staff persons might consider such a verbal request as a possible sign of needing help and continue trying to pry the client for information. Subsequently, he would be "forced" to hit that person to be left alone. Hence, more acceptable protests would be unable to reliably terminate the interaction, making such protests less functional than aggression. The selected target statement seemed like there would be no misinterpretation of its intent on the audience. Data over a 6-month period bore this out. The target verbal statement occurred regularly, while aggression did not.

*Back to Level 1.* Aggressive behavior can be a socially mediated escape behavior, particularly when it occurs as a chain of events under conditions where a punisher is

*TABLE 3.29* ■ **SHUT UP AND LEAVE ME ALONE!**

| Diagnosis | 4.1 SME: unpleasant social situation |
| --- | --- |
| Target behavior(s): | Hitting other clients/staff |
| Function: | Avoiding undesired social interaction or continued conversation |
| Target behavior likely under following contexts: | At the beginning of conversation or after some time elapses |
| Target behavior unlikely under following contexts: | When left alone or short interactions |
| Rule out: | Socially mediated access functions (2.1, 2.3) |

administered by staff for a client's previous target behavior. For example, let us say a child at a residential facility does something wrong (i.e., a proscribed target behavior) and is moved down one level on the point system. As a result of being told he has been moved back to Level 1, he profusely swears at the staff person and begins kicking things, slamming doors, and throwing books against the wall. *(Note to reader: Do not take this as our approval of level systems of reinforcement. They are not our preference in behavioral intervention.)*

Why does he engage in such a tirade? Such behaviors do not appear to be functional. The staff do not grant him his wish to go back to his previous level despite his verbal tirade. Perhaps it is what transpires after the staff intervene. Suppose someone in higher authority, hearing the commotion, meets with the child to calm him down. In the process of engaging in conflict resolution tactics, this authority figure makes a deal with the child regarding his return back to Level 2. What effect does such a negotiation have on the future probability of these reactions by this child to loss of reinforcement? Can such a negotiation be the maintaining contingency for this child's behavior when he is punished by staff and loses Level 2 privileges? Would this child have been offered a special deal had these raucous behaviors not happened? I think he will be more likely to act out in future situations where the only manner of ameliorating the consequence of his behavior is to knock things around.

This scenario may be quite familiar to people who work in facilities and group homes. It is sanctified as a clinical procedure and goes by the name of *crisis management*. What looks like a good way of handling an explosive situation in the short run (because the child stops intense tantrum behavior) is not beneficial in the long run because, as a result, these children have more frequent crises requiring the clinical expert to come in and render the situation manageable. This is done by negotiation of consequences. Of course, such negotiation ameliorates the escalation of the child's disruptive behavior at the time, but what is never studied or considered is the long-term effect of these frequent negotiations. How effective do you think the originally designed consequences will be in decreasing the initial target behaviors over several weeks or months?

*Avoidance Functions.* Many problem behaviors that occur under noninstructional conditions can be a response to the administration of a discipline procedure. In this manner, the occurrence of the target behavior may be strengthened more for its avoidance capability than for its immediate escape function. For example, a child does something wrong during recess and is taken to a time-out area. The child yells at the teacher, "I'm not going!" As the teacher escorts him to time out, the child attempts to fight with and resist the teacher. He hits and kicks the teacher, resulting in an exacerbation of consequences. He is then sent home for assaulting a teacher on the playground. Why do such behaviors occur while the child is being escorted to time out? Aggression in this context gets reinforced if the adult is less likely to implement time out for fear of stirring up a situation like the last time out. When aggression, or the threat of it, conditions the social environment in that fashion, it becomes an effective avoidance behavior under threat of discipline.

### (4.2) SME: Relatively Lengthy Task, Chore, Instruction

This diagnostic category encompasses behaviors that postpone or terminate the child's or client's engagement with an instructional task, chore, or demand. The analysis in Table 3.30 depicts the relationship between the antecedent context, the behavior, and the contingency produced, which makes the escape behavior more probable under similar antecedent contexts.

The value of escape is established because the task or chore is lengthy in duration (first column). Lengthy is a relative term. What may be lengthy to you may be of short duration to me. Although some of us may not mind cutting the front lawn if it takes 15 minutes,

*TABLE 3.30* ■ **RELATIVELY LENGTHY TASK**

| Motivating Operation | Behavior | Maintaining Contingency (C-1) | Future probability of behavior under MO |
|---|---|---|---|
| Relatively lengthy task | Throws a tantrum by swearing, kicking property, etc. | Task is removed, aversive condition is terminated by some person | More likely under the same or similar motivating operation |

we may not be comfortable with a lawn that is 4 acres (that's why riding lawn mowers have a certain market share). In this subcategory, the child is capable of performing the assignment or task, but the duration of the instructional activity required is too long. Under this motivational condition, the problem behavior occurs. As a result, staff remove, ameliorate, or eliminate the task presented. Again, as with all socially mediated behaviors, the direct result of behavior is inconsequential in terms of stimulus control. The maintenance of the behavior is not determined by such a contingency being reliably produced.

Another point needs to be made in diagnosing this subcategory. Many professionals naive to functional analysis believe they can determine the purpose of the child's behavior by asking the child (or client) "Why do you do that?" Any professional report that uses the client's statement to such a question as the sole basis for a diagnosis of behavioral function should not be taken seriously. Although the history of psychotherapy is one of accepting client self-report at face value, such a methodology cannot be relied on in a science-based approach!

Here is an example of the lack of utility of such questioning. When these children are asked why they don't complete their work or assignment or engage in inappropriate behaviors, they often respond with "I am bored." Personnel then believe that through this self-revelation, the causative agent of the problem behavior has been discovered. This contention is ill-conceived on several grounds.

First, behavior analysis requires that controlling variables be identified through reliable and valid measurement. The reliability and validity of the client's self-report cannot be ascertained. Asking the client why she did something does not give us a "window" into the person's motivation. One can certainly question the correspondence between what someone says and what someone does. The field of psychology that relies on self-report as a valid measure of motivation is often ineffectual in changing behavior, particularly when there is a weak correspondence between saying and doing. To understand motivation, one must study and analyze the observable, reliably measured events surrounding the behavior. Hence, an FBA will always require that someone's *motivation* to behave in a certain fashion be understood from a scientific measurement of variables in the environment. Second, this explanation does not lead one to understand how off-task and disruptive behaviors are functional. In fact, if boredom was the causative agent behind the child's performance, then the treatment should be providing more challenging work. I will take bets on how well that works in getting the child to perform better in class.

Examining how effective such possible escape behaviors are in the presence of lengthy tasks allows for a more accurate treatment prescription to this problem. In this subcategory, manipulating the difficulty of the task is not the answer. Some form of altering task length would be a primary component of a functional behavior analytic strategy. The "Case of the Wacky Contingency" presented earlier illustrates why such a context is existent in many school classrooms across the country.

This subcategory can also be diagnosed with tasks or chores outside of a classroom setting. Some clients have problem behaviors when required to complete a chore. It is not a difficult chore for this client; the client can perform the requisite steps of the chore. Rather, it is the length of the chore that establishes the value of escape. One may be able to wash

---

**TABLE 3.31 ■ QUESTIONS TO CONSIDER FOR A 4.2 SME DIAGNOSIS**

1. Is there a reliable somewhat frequent relationship between the problem behavior and termination of the lengthy task(s), chore(s), or instruction? What is the form of the escape behavior?

2. Are the target behaviors more likely to produce escape from the situation by an adult staff person or parent than other more appropriate behaviors to terminate a social interaction?

3. What type of reinforcement schedule is it on? How long or frequent do such escape behaviors sustain before the aversive task, chore, or instruction is terminated by someone?

---

several dishes in a sink at home. However, if you work for a restaurant, you must wash many dishes, pots, and pans. This duration *mismatch* thus creates an aversive condition for that client, which sets the stage for behaviors that temporarily or permanently escape from the task. It is to be distinguished from the next behavioral function in that the child's ability to perform the task (accurately) is adequate, but the length of time is the factor making escape from instruction a powerful motivating operation.

The questions in Table 3.31 should be posed when considering this diagnostic subcategory. This maintaining contingency involves a reliable relation between the problem behavior and the escape or avoidance of the lengthy tasks, chores, or assignments (Question 1). Other more acceptable behaviors are less likely to result in escape (Question 2). Although the target problem behaviors may have to occur at some frequency and duration (Question 3), they are more successful at terminating the undesired lengthy tasks than other more acceptable behaviors (Question 2).

## DISCUSSION QUESTIONS

How would you conduct an analogue assessment to determine whether the problem behavior occurs during instruction because of length of assignment? Instructional difficulty?

*Hitting the Table and Social Mediation.* A hypothetical student with severe disabilities will hit the table during instruction on a regular basis. Your observations may reveal that such behavior, particularly the lengthier and more intense it is, results in the teacher removing him to another area. Although the short-term result is one of stopping the behavioral episode (which encourages the teacher to believe she is on the right path), the long-term effect of such action is disastrous! The teacher is unwittingly developing such disruptive behavior as functional when the student does not want to continue in the instructional session. You have observed that hitting the table becomes highly likely when the instructional session goes beyond 6 minutes. Especially in light of the fact that there is no definitive criteria for instructional session length, hitting the table with some force inevitably occurs at some point in the teacher's lesson. Although some people ascribe such behavior to the child's mental retardation, you now know better. You realize that the social environment has a big part in maintaining and probably exacerbating self-injury as a socially mediated escape behavior.

What would be an analogue or in-vivo test to determine if length of task is the controlling variable in this case? In alternating fashion, the teacher would present one of two conditions during the instructional period in which this behavior occurred. In the first condition, on alternating days, the student would receive a short assignment. In the second condition, the student would receive a lengthy assignment (other days). An analogue test would mimic the controlling variables by removing the task, contingent on the exhibition of the problem behavior. The task would be terminated for a short period of time (e.g., 1 minute). An in-vivo test would involve the same two conditions except the break would be contingent on completing the assignment in whatever condition was operable at the time, that is, lengthy versus short.

*"I'm Bored".* A student is referred for property destruction, tantrums, and oppositional behaviors in the class. Your interview with the teacher and observations in the class reveal that when the student is given a lengthy assignment, she initially whines and complains, stating "I'm bored." However, another more challenging task of similar length is met with this same complaint. When she is redirected back to work, she engages in more severe objections (tantrums and oppositional behavior) and eventually gets mad enough that she throws objects at the floor and wall. This results in the teacher removing the child to the corner until she can behave properly and do her work! Note the effect of the child's throwing-objects behavior: the child's termination of her engagement in the assignment for some period of time. Although the student can work for 15–20 minutes without a problem, working for 1 hour is just too much (Table 3.32). Hence, the child has learned how to get a 5-minute break. Throw something!

*Going Gandhi.* A young teenager, in and out of home placement could do any task or chore you wanted her to do. However, her actual performance left something to be desired. The group home staff constantly reported that she did not finish her chores. They ascribed it to her oppositional and lazy attitude, claiming she had a personality disorder. Her opposition would not be in a form involving aggression or destructive behavior. She did not yell or scream. I (K.S.) observed the staff in one interaction with her. They were attempting to get her to get up, clean her room, take her medications, and come eat breakfast. She got up and went to a chair in the living room, and then she refused to move, refused food, refused medications, and refused to talk to anyone. She simply sat there, in protest, quietly like Gandhi.

An analogue test was set up to determine what could be the possible reason for not completing chores that were easy for her to perform under direction. In one condition, I assisted her in a simple task of room cleaning. If I gave her one-step tasks, she completed the task. All she seemed to need was one-step commands and contingent verbal praise after completing each step. However, when given a multiple-step direction she did not complete the task. This was true even when offered praise and tangible reinforcement. During these tests it appeared that she was simply unable to complete the task. However, the same task could be accomplished if it was broken down into its unit components and performed one step at a time. Lengthy tasks were a no go at this time. Breaking them up into small units, and doing one at a time, solved the problem (Table 3.33).

### TABLE 3.32 ■ 4.2 SME DIAGNOSIS FOR THROWING BEHAVIOR

| Diagnosis | 4.2 SME: lengthy instructional task |
| --- | --- |
| Target behavior(s): | Throws objects at wall, tantrum behavior |
| Function: | Removed to corner or some other area, away from work |
| Target behavior likely under following contexts: | Lengthy tasks |
| Target behavior unlikely under following contexts: | When given shorter amounts of work followed by contingent intermittent breaks (i.e., completes work) |
| Rule out: | Socially mediated access functions (2.1, 2.2) and socially mediated escape function (SME 2.3) |

*TABLE 3.33* ■ **4.2 SME DIAGNOSIS**

| Diagnosis | 4.2 SME: lengthy task |
|---|---|
| Target behavior(s): | Verbal opposition to engaging in chores/task |
| Function: | Removed from work area |
| Target behavior likely under following contexts: | Given list of tasks |
| Target behavior unlikely under following contexts: | Given assistance with short task |
| Rule out: | Socially mediated access functions (2.1, 2.3) and socially mediated escape function (4.3) |

*Enough Is Enough.* A student with severe disabilities is given a task, which she completes. She gets out of her seat, but at that time, an instructional aide tells her to go back to her seat so that she can work on another task. She reluctantly complies, finishes part of it, and then attempts to leave her seat again. As she leaves her seat, the aide admonishes her to finish. She hits herself at this point, and the aide comes over to her and tells her to stop. She hits herself again, right in front of the aide. The aide then moves her to another area of the room with a different activity. If you were this child, what would you do the next time you felt you did enough work on a particular task or activity and wanted to change activities? Table 3.34 depicts this function.

*I Need a Break, My Brain Is Swelling.* A mainstreamed fourth grade student in a regular class is given a reading assignment in a social studies text. The teacher has reported to you that this child will frequently throw a tantrum during class assignments. The teacher has suggested that maybe he does not belong in her class because it is too difficult for him. Your observation reveals that he reads about three pages during a reading assignment. He also is able to answer the questions correctly. He then decides to take a break and gets out some toy cars he brought from home. The teacher sees him playing, admonishes him, and gives him another reading assignment. He argues with the teacher, with no success, and then throws his social studies book on the floor. The teacher sends him to the principal's office for defiant and disruptive behavior. The teacher decries, "That will teach him not to play in my classroom." The child goes to the principal's office and sits in the seat outside of the office with one of his cars in his pocket. You fill in the rest of the story!

Your turn to fill out Table 3.35.

*TABLE 3.34* ■ **4.2 SME DIAGNOSIS, VERBAL OPPOSITION**

| Diagnosis | 4.2 SME: lengthy task |
|---|---|
| Target behavior(s): | Verbal opposition to engaging in chores/task |
| Function: | Removed from work area |
| Target behavior likely under following contexts: | Given list of tasks |
| Target behavior unlikely under following contexts: | Given assistance with short task |
| Rule out: | Socially mediated access functions (2.1, 2.3) and socially mediated escape function (4.3) |

*TABLE 3.35* ■ **DIAGNOSIS OF VERBAL OPPOSITION CASE**

| Diagnosis |
| --- |
| Target behavior(s): |
| Function: |
| Target behavior likely under following contexts: |
| Target behavior unlikely under following contexts: |
| Rule out: |

*The 20-Minute Child.* A child hits the desk to temporarily terminate the presentation of an instructional task. This scenario illustrates that the hitting-the-desk incident terminates instruction by the teacher, removing the instructional demand and subsequently "dealing" with the problem behavior. Note that the aggressive behavior is negatively reinforced by the teacher in that another stimulus condition is presented in the place of the task, for some period of time. Yelling and screaming can also accompany aggressive behavior intended to remove aversive events, often occurring before or during the aggressive acts.

Aggressive behavior results in the teacher removing the child to the corner until she can behave properly and do her work. Note the effect of the child's throwing-objects behavior: removal of the (aversive) assignment for some period of time. Although the student can work for 15–20 minutes without a problem, working for 1 hour is just too much. Hence, the child has learned to get a 5-minute break (i.e., throw things).

*Socially Mediated Escape of Independent Seat Work.* Some children who are deemed to have *minimal impulse control* when using a more traditional diagnostic classification, are found to throw tantrums and kick objects, desks, and other children (who are close by) when it is time to do seat work. Or they verbally refuse to complete the assignment. Note that turning to the *minimal impulse control* explanation does not give the slightest hint on what to do behaviorally. Perhaps medication interventions are apparent with this explanation. However, a behavioral intervention for minimal impulse control does not exist!

A functional diagnosis is far more useful in offering an explanation and route for intervention. If these behaviors serve to throw the teacher off track by dealing with these behaviors instead of pressing on with instruction, such behaviors can be maintained by serving a socially mediated escape function. Although some students may be fine when working under close supervision, they cannot function adequately when more independence is required. The treatment strategy would attempt to do two things: (1) not allow such tantrum behaviors to postpone or ameliorate the seat work task requirements, and (2) select another more appropriate behavior that replaces the tantrum behavior to terminate seat work and get close supervision. Perhaps after completing some independent seat work, the child can get his chair moved closer to the teacher's area *(hey, a contingency, what a good idea).*

## (4.3) SME: Relatively Difficult Task, Chore, Instruction

This diagnostic subcategory encompasses problem behaviors that terminate the task or chore, with such escape responding motivated by the difficulty of the task or chore. In the presence of difficult tasks, chores, or assignments, the target problem behavior occurs. It is maintained in its particular form by its ability to escape or avoid such relatively difficult tasks.

In school settings, the child's engagement with the instructional task is aversive to her, primarily because the child is not capable of performing the task accurately or fluently. This lack of skill sets the stage for escape from or avoidance of those instructional situations and conditions. This function occurs frequently with children who are given academic tasks that are way above their current level. This is a sure prescription for developing an aversion to school work, that is, constantly expose the child to material she has very little chance of succeeding with. In these cases, the child may engage in the problem behaviors to avoid all school work because such work is often something she is unsuccessful at.

The questions in Table 3.36 should be posed when considering this diagnostic subcategory. This maintaining contingency involves a reliable relation between the problem behavior and the escape or avoidance of the difficult task, chore, or instruction (Question 1). Other more acceptable behaviors are less likely to result in escape (Question 2). Although the target problem behaviors may have to occur at some frequency or duration (Question 3), they are more successful at terminating the undesired condition than other more acceptable behaviors (Question 2).

*Self-Injury Often Escapes Instruction.* Very often, problem behaviors, such as self-abuse, can function to remove instructional tasks or materials because the teacher has to stop instruction to deal with the behavior. Imagine seeing a student hitting herself repeatedly when faced with a task demand. Contingent upon this flurry of hits, the teacher attempts to hold her hands, thereby preventing her from hitting her face. But one must note what stimulus change gets affected in addition to physical contact. Instruction stops! As a result of the ability of the child's self-abuse to terminate an instructional demand, hitting her head becomes more probable in the future when she is presented with the same or similar tasks.

What would be an analogue or in-vivo test to determine if difficulty of task is the controlling variable? In alternating fashion, the teacher would present one of two conditions.

In half of the sessions, the student would receive easy material. Such easy tasks would be determined by previous student performance demonstrating mastery levels of performance. For example, if the student is currently reading at the third grade level as identified by achievement tests, an easy assignment would be first or possibly second grade reading texts.

In the other half of the sessions, the student would receive a difficult task or assignment. This could probably be accomplished by assigning reading material from the everyday work she does (third grade level). An analogue test would mimic the controlling variables. Therefore, in both conditions contingent on the exhibition of the problem behavior, the task would be terminated for a short period of time (e.g., 1 minute). An in-vivo test would involve the same two conditions, except the break would be contingent on completing the assignment in whatever condition at the time, that is, difficult versus easy.

With some children who engage in self-injury the form of their response and intensity defies one's sensibilities. Such episodes of protracted hitting to their face and body of severe intensity perplex both lay people and professionals. In watching an episode of protracted

---

### TABLE 3.36 ■ QUESTIONS TO CONSIDER FOR A 4.3 SME DIAGNOSIS

1. Is there a reliable somewhat frequent relationship between the problem behavior and termination of the difficult task, chore, or instruction? What is the form of the escape behavior?

2. Are the target behaviors more likely to produce escape from the situation by an adult staff person or parent than other more appropriate behaviors to terminate the task?

3. What type of reinforcement schedule are they on? How long do such escape behaviors sustain before the aversive or relatively lengthy task, chore, or instruction is terminated by someone?

length and intensity, is not uncommon for even professionals to claim that the child is biologically driven to such episodes, that is, his brain made him do it, and he is not responsible for his actions. The overriding contention is that such behavior cannot be explained by any learning conditioning history.

Can a conditioning history be the explanation for such severe forms of self-injury? Unfortunately, minor forms of self-abusive behavior are often exacerbated unintentionally over time. Over the course of several or many months, the severity of the child's self-injury (e.g., head hitting) may intensify as a result of the parents or teachers trying to ignore the minor forms of self-abuse. These severe forms of self-injury become even more powerful in their ability to alter the environment. In addition to producing an escape from the aversive context, the possibility of such behaviors also impacts the likelihood of task demands being made (avoidance function as well). As repeated attempts to ignore some forms of self-injury are displayed, the requirement for the intense forms to occur and produce escape is more evident. At some point in this longitudinal process, the child's repeated self-injury has left scars. Further, she has become too unmanageable for her current educational placement, and her placement is changed to a more restrictive setting. In many cases, over time, her social environment becomes more respectful of such a destructive capability that very few (if any) demands are placed on her. Also over time, her tolerance for such painful blows has been enhanced, as a result of this gradual incremental approach to powerful strikes to the face and body. If you simply observe the child after years of "practice" altering her social environment, you might conclude that she is driven by some innate mechanism to abuse herself.[1]

*Difficult Tasks.* Other students engage in a variety of problem behaviors that escape difficult tasks. A student may initially complain about difficult material and subsequently engage in a number of verbal complaining statements such as, "This is too hard, I can't do this. I don't know how to do this." If the teacher does not provide relief by presenting an alternate activity or making that task less difficult, the complaints may increase in intensity, or new problem behaviors give rise, for example, the student gets out of her seat or engages in disruptive behavior with other students. Of course, such behaviors are immediately effective in temporarily halting the student's engagement with the assignment. It is important to note that the student's initial complaining of the difficulty of the task was not reinforced. Therefore, the student had to engage in other (more serious) behaviors in order to produce the desirable result: escape from the difficult assignment (see Table 3.37).

This brings up an interesting question about current practice regarding the stipulation of using the core curriculum for students with various disabilities.

**TABLE 3.37 ■ 4.3 SME DIAGNOSIS, DIFFICULT TASK**

| Diagnosis | 4.3 SME: difficult instructional task |
| --- | --- |
| Target behavior(s): | Complaining followed by more "active" attempts to escape instruction |
| Function: | Temporary disengagement in task |
| Target behavior likely under following contexts: | Difficult material |
| Target behavior unlikely under following contexts: | Easy material |
| Rule out: | Socially mediated access functions (2.1, 2.3) and socially mediated escape function (4.2) |

## ACCESS TO THE CORE CURRICULUM FOR ALL?

These examples and the nature of this diagnostic category bring up an interesting question related to the current vogue of placing many special needs students in the core curriculum as a preferred practice. What this function presents as a probable outcome is the following: Presenting instruction and assignments that are grade levels above a student's current level of functioning is often a prescription for serious behavior problems. In light of that, does a decision to place a student on the general education curriculum affect how he will behave in class? You bet! Instruction and behavior are intertwined. When students are incompetent at the material, such is an existent condition that breeds behavior problems, irrespective of where the child is served. Hopefully this makes people reevaluate the "mainstreaming at all costs" philosophy. Looking good and doing good can be two distinct entities!

*Difficult Chores.* Let us say a client in a residential treatment program engages in loud tantrum behavior every morning when she is asked to make the bed. Such behaviors do not occur for afternoon chores such as taking out the garbage, or even vacuuming, which she likes. However, making her bed is always a headache for her and staff, who have to prod her through it. One program staff person suggested that she might have problems with bed making because it was a chore done in the morning. Perhaps she is not a morning person! They then changed the time she could make her bed to the afternoon. This solution had no effect on the rate or severity of the tantrum behavior. In examining the client's performance of this task, she often required corrective prompts on many of the aspects of making a bed, such as the corner tuck and straightening out the bed sheet. Bed making took her twice as long as it should have because she frequently had to correct the errors she made. Could this be why bed making is so aversive to her? It is not that bed making is a morning task, rather it is the difficulty of the bed making chore. Once the client becomes more adept at making the bed and quicker at completing it, the behavior problems will decrease. As difficulty decreases (due to effective teaching), so do problem behaviors.

Your turn to fill out Table 3.38.

### (4.4) SME: Aversive Physical Stimuli/Events

The questions in Table 3.39 should be posed when considering this diagnostic subcategory. This maintaining contingency involves a reliable relation between the problem behavior and the escape or avoidance of the aversive physical stimulus (Question 1). Other more acceptable behaviors are less likely to result in escape (Question 2). Although the target problem behaviors may have to occur at some frequency or duration (Question 3), they are more successful at terminating the undesired condition than other more acceptable behaviors (Question 2).

*TABLE 3.38* ■ **DIAGNOSIS OF DIFFICULT TASK CASE**

| Diagnosis |
| --- |
| Target behavior(s): |
| Function: |
| Target behavior likely under following contexts: |
| Target behavior unlikely under following contexts: |
| Rule out: |

*TABLE 3.39* ■ **QUESTIONS TO CONSIDER FOR A 4.4 SME DIAGNOSIS**

1. Is there a reliable somewhat frequent relation between the problem behavior and removal of the aversive stimulus? What is the form of the escape behavior? What is the relative aversive physical condition?

2. Are the target behaviors more likely to produce a socially mediated escape from the physical stimulus than other more appropriate behaviors?

3. What type of reinforcement schedule are they on? How long or frequent do such escape behaviors sustain before the aversive stimulus is terminated by someone?

*Here's Something You Cannot Ignore!* A previous example illustrated how some clients rip their clothes off to directly terminate an aversive stimulus. In this example, let us stipulate that staff are fairly efficient at chain interruption, thereby blocking direct attempts to rip clothes off and receive new clothes. Similarly, requesting different clothes falls on deaf ears. However, when this hypothetical client urinates in his pants, guess what happens? He is cleaned up and gets new clothes. Because staff cannot allow the client to remain in soiled clothing for very long, what behavior is functional in getting new clothes? Soiling one's clothes!

## HOW DOES ONE TRANSLATE BEHAVIORAL ASSESSMENT DATA INTO A FUNCTION-BASED DIAGNOSTIC CATEGORY?

How does a professional evaluate the different sources of data collection to come up with a diagnostic classification of the target problem behavior? There are no hard and fast rules. In Chapter 2, we presented and rated the accuracy of the different methods of collecting functional analysis data. Therefore, depending on which data source is available, the professional evaluates the data, looking for evidence of a certain function.

It seems to us that in some cases, diagnosing a problem behavior is an iterative process. You may initially surmise that screaming, in the case of a client who refuses to do a chore, is 4.2 SME: relatively lengthy tasks/chores. However, after an analogue assessment, the data do not bear that out. There were insignificant differences between long and short duration chores. Further, evidence brings you to suspect that adult attention is the culprit. Using a descriptive focused analysis reveals that such screaming brings hugs and praise from the staff as well as an occasional tangible reinforcer if he promises that he will be good and do his chore. It also reveals that other behaviors are not successful in getting hugs. Hence, the differential diagnosis more pertinent is either (or both) 2.1 SMA: adult attention or 2.3 SMA: tangible reinforcer.

As you can see, it is a lot like playing detective. Unfortunately, there is not an algorithm for determining functions of problem behavior. Although analogue assessments and in-vivo hypothesis testing will reliably give you the best information, we believe it is up to the behavior-analytic clinician to put the evidence together and come up with a best fit hypothesis.

## MULTIFUNCTIONAL BEHAVIOR

The diagnostic categories in this chapter illustrate how different behaviors can serve different purposes. However, just as different behaviors can serve the same function, so too can one behavior (or topographically similar) serve different functions. Under some antecedent conditions, a particular behavior can serve a given environmental function. However, under other antecedent conditions, the same behavior serves a different function.

Perhaps a chart can illustrate how the same behavior in form can serve different environmental functions (Table 3.40). Let's use a hypothetical female client in a day treatment program for adults with varying types of developmental disabilities. This client engages in aggressive behavior under several different contexts, with different motivational conditions present.

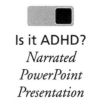

Is it ADHD?
*Narrated PowerPoint Presentation*

*TABLE 3.40* ■ **ILLUSTRATIONS OF MULTIPLE FUNCTIONS AGGRESSIVE BEHAVIOR CAN SERVE**

| Target Behavior | DA Functions | SMA Functions | DE Functions | SME Functions |
|---|---|---|---|---|
| Aggression to others | None | Access to tangible reinforcers (2.3) | None | Escape from aversive tasks, escape from social punishment |

Aggression can exert such a powerful effect on the social environment that it can be the most efficient behavior in some people's repertoire under a variety of MOs. It can be efficient at producing adult attention in some circumstances, whereas it can also be adaptive when the person wishes to access some tangible reinforcer under conditions of deprivation. Further, it occurs under varied aversive contexts and effectively functions to escape or avoid such.

In Table 3.40, note that one function of this client's aggressive behavior is 2.3 SMA. In the morning, she hits staff when it is time to put her clothes on. The aggressive behavior toward staff occurs after she and they have argued for some time about wearing the clothes selected for her by the morning staff. Hitting occurs when staff attempt to get her to dress, following some period of arguing, with the selected clothes. On some occasions, when the client hits, some staff will let her choose which clothes to wear if she promises not to hit them again. The differential diagnosis for this client's aggressive behavior would be 2.3 SMA: tangible reinforcer. When she cannot select her favorite clothes to wear in the morning, she is more likely to hit staff. Further, hitting is a behavior that intermittently results in getting the desired clothing. Aggression appears to serve a socially mediated function under this condition.

However, scatter plot data indicates that not all aggressive behavior occurs during the morning ritual. This client also is aggressive when she requests to go outside the house and is refused. Her aggressive behavior is occasionally reinforced by the same staff who handle her in the morning routine. Again, these staff have learned that the best way to not generate further aggression on her part in these circumstances is to "give in." This crisis management approach may work for them. However, other staff who are not reinforcing such behavior are really getting the brunt of her aggressive behavior. As a result of the initial form of hitting failing to produce the desired event, she escalates her level of aggression. In some cases, her aggression reaches a level where it is unsafe for everyone, and she is restrained. This context also depicts a differential diagnosis of 2.3 SMA: tangible reinforcer under the condition of wanting to go outside and being initially denied.

This client also has some frequency of being noncompliant with staff around chores. The contingency for noncompliance is a brief time out. Aggression also occurs in this context. When placed in the time out chair, she will sometimes leave the time out chair to hit the residential staff. In other cases, staff get hit by her on the way to the time-out chair. Under the conditions of time out, aggressive behavior is illustrative of subcategory 4.1 SME: escape from unpleasant social events. The client's aggression will be maintained when being placed in time out given two factors: (1) such behavior temporarily postpones the advent of the time out (as they struggle to get her to the chair) and (2) such behavior reduces the likelihood of such a social consequence, that is, time out, being used in the future (avoidance function). Table 3.41 depicts the diagnostic categories.

Multifunctional behavior problems require a differential set of contingencies for the different sources of stimulus control. In other words, the procedures to be used when the target problem behavior occurs will vary with the context. Suppose a client in an inpatient unit screams when someone steps in front of the TV. The screaming occurs even if the other resident is just passing by, not standing in front of the TV. You diagnose this problem as a 2.1 SMA: adult attention because the screaming will reliably bring staff to the area to

**TABLE 3.41 ■ DIFFERENTIAL DIAGNOSIS OF CLIENT'S AGGRESSIVE BEHAVIOR**

(1.0)  Direct access (DA): None

(2.0)  Socially mediated access (SMA)

   2.3 SMA: tangible reinforcers, preferred clothing

   2.3 SMA: tangible reinforcers, preferred activity outdoors

(3.0)  Direct escape (DE)—none

(4.0)  Socially mediated escape (SME)

   4.1 SME: unpleasant social situations, removal from time out

remove the client who is in front of the TV. The treatment contingencies would involve the extinction of the screaming along with the reinforcement of an alternate behavior, such as requesting the client to move. If that is unsuccessful, the client makes the request to staff that they move the client (instead of screaming). However, contingent on screaming, the staff will now not move the client. Depending on the strength of the replacement behavior, the staff may also turn off the TV as an additional contingency for screaming.

If the same client also screams when he is asked to clean up his dinner plate and silverware and place them in the kitchen, the function of this behavior may best fit subcategory 4.2 SME: escape from lengthy task, chore. In this case, staff will not remove the client from the area; rather, they will require him to stay until he completes his task. Screaming will not result in removal. Hence, staff must perform different repertoires depending on what the antecedent conditions is. Here is an example of a real-life case involving two different functions for an unusual behavior: diving onto the floor.

*Diving Onto the Floor.* Roy was a 48-year-old man who had been residing in locked psychiatric treatment centers for several years prior to his admission to our facility (K.S.). He had also briefly lived in several different care homes, none for longer than 3 months. He had numerous problematic behaviors, including making delusional statements, elective mutism, and catatonia. One of the primary reasons for his discharge from the group homes, however, was diving on the floor and refusing to get up. On some occasions, he injured staff by diving into them.

Once he arrived at our facility, my staff and I observed that sometimes he would dive to the floor and pretend to be asleep. In these incidences, he would lay on the floor while ignoring staff requests, until staff left the area. He would then immediately get up and engage in his usual activities. Certainly such incidents seemed to be escape from some aversive event that staff were presenting. However, there were other times when he seemed to desire their attention. On these occasions, once the staff left the area he would get up, run full speed, and dive headfirst into the nearest staff person's feet. In one scenario, it appeared that the diving on the floor functioned to escape demands, but in the other scenario it appeared to function to access staff attention. Except for the result of the latter being diving into a specific person, the topography of each type of scenario was that of diving on the floor.

I ruled out the possible physical result of the behavior, that is, the physical sensation obtained when skimming across the floor, as the controlling contingency. We focused on an analysis of the socially mediated effects of the diving behavior. Hence the A-B-C data in Table 3.42 only reports socially mediated effects.

My staff and I repeated the A-B-C descriptive analysis of the diving behavior across several days. On some occasions Roy would simply lie on the floor for a short time, then get up and resume his activities. However, during some of the observations, after lying on the floor for a short period of time he would get up, run full speed, and dive into a staff person. Diving into a person was always preceded by diving to the floor, but not every event of diving to the floor was followed by diving into a person.

**TABLE 3.42 ■ DESCRIPTIVE ANALYSIS FOR "DIVING" BEHAVIOR**

| | A | B | C |
|---|---|---|---|
| 9:45 A.M. | Sitting in day room; no staff interaction for 45 minutes | Got up, walked toward staff, dove onto floor at their feet | Staff walked away |
| 10:00 A.M. | Laying on floor; staff in next room | Got up ran into other room and dove into staff person | Multiple staff intervene to direct him away form the staff he dove into and talk with him Physical contact with staff person |
| 10:15 A.M. | In medication area staff asks him to sit in chair to take his blood pressure | Dove to floor and closed his eyes | Staff prompted him to get up and then left the area |
| 10:20 A.M. | Laying on floor; no one close by | Gets up and goes to day room and sits down | No demand; no staff interaction. Back to sitting in day room |
| 10:25 A.M. | Sitting in day room. Staff asks him to come get his blood pressure taken. | Dives to the floor and closes his eyes | Staff prompt him to get up and then leave the area |

The descriptive observation data we collected appeared to support two different functions for diving to the floor. One function appeared to be escape from an uncomfortable event or unpleasant task. For example, requests by staff to have his blood pressure checked, requests to attend therapy in groups, and requests to talk with a social worker, doctor, or anyone he did not already know all routinely resulted in a dive to the floor. Under this set of conditions he was likely to get off the floor quickly if the staff left the area and did not repeat the prompt.

The other function appeared to be to access staff attention. My staff noted that the behavior of diving into a staff person revolved around the number of prompts given to get up. If staff repeatedly prompted him to get up and attempted to talk with him while he was on the floor, he would sometimes get up and return to his previous activity. However, if staff delivered a single prompt to get up and then left the area, he seemed more likely to get up and dive into people.

Given the need to quickly and very accurately determine the function of this behavior we tested the staff observations by conducting an experimental analysis. We developed three test conditions. One condition was in effect each day. The conditions were presented sequentially until each had been in place four times. One trial consisted of exposure to all three conditions. In order to expedite the assessment process we collected data on two different behaviors in each condition. The first behavior was diving to the floor. The second behavior was diving into people. This design allowed us to simultaneously test both behaviors across three conditions.

In the *first condition* we tested the effects of task demand. In this condition the value of staff attention was kept at low levels by providing staff attention to Roy about every 15 minutes independent of any behavior on his part. The value of escape from task demands was established by a second staff making requests for Roy to complete tasks that had been associated with diving to the floor during the A-B-C data collection. In this condition if Roy dove to the floor the staff making demands would leave, and the staff providing attention would continue talking with him as if the behavior had not occurred. A high rate of diving to the floor, and not diving into people, would support the contention that the function of the behavior is escape from relatively unpleasant tasks. Conversely, a low rate would tend to rule out that it functioned to produce escape from relatively unpleasant task demands

In the *second condition,* we tested the effects of deprivation of staff attention. In this condition the value of escape from task demands was kept at low levels by ensuring no requests or demands were presented to Roy during the session. The value of staff attention was established by staff avoiding any unnecessary interaction with Roy. In this condition if Roy dove to the floor the staff would continue to ignore the behavior and still make no demands. If he attempted to dive into staff the behavior would be blocked, and Roy would be redirected to another area. A high rate of diving into people would provide support for an attention function for this topography.

In the *third condition,* we set up a control condition for both attention and unpleasant tasks by ensuring that the establishing operation for both was minimal or nonexistent. In this condition the value of escape from task demands was kept at low levels by ensuring no requests or demands were presented to Roy during the session. The value of staff attention was kept at low levels by providing staff attention to Roy continuously, independent of any behavior on his part. If Roy dove to the floor the staff would continue to provide noncontingent attention and still make no demands. If he attempted to dive into staff his behavior would be blocked and redirected to another area, and the noncontingent delivery of attention would continue.

A low rate of both diving behaviors would indicate that the motivating variables were a deprivation of attention (diving into people) and unpleasant tasks (diving on the floor). If such were the case, I would have possibly revisited the hypothesis of a direct reinforcement function. Table 3.43 shows the rate of occurrence of diving to the floor and diving into people as a function of each test condition.

A review of the data for condition one indicated that although he did dive on the floor, he did not dive into people. Because we had reduced the value of staff attention by providing it noncontingently in this condition, we could be reasonably sure that diving on the floor did not result in an increase in staff attention. This data provided support for the hypothesis that diving onto the floor was not maintained by staff attention. Given that there was a high level of demands in this condition, we had reasonable evidence that escape was a maintaining function of diving to the floor. Additionally, when the demand was removed contingent on diving to the floor, Roy stood up and returned to his previous activity.

The data from condition two requires a bit more explanation. In condition two we reduced the value of escape from demands by ensuring that no task demands were made. We increased the value of attention by not interacting with him. In this condition we were reasonably sure that the diving to the floor and diving into people were *not* maintained by escape. In each of the trials diving into people appeared to be the second part of a chain of behavior that started with diving on the floor, and then after some short period of time he would get up and dive into a staff person. In this condition diving to the floor was never followed by simply getting up and returning to his usual activity. A return to his usual activity only occurred after some level of staff interaction. In the third condition,

*TABLE 3.43* ■ **RATE OF DIVING BEHAVIOR ACROSS CONDITIONS**

| | Condition 1—Task Demands and Noncontingent Staff Attention | | Condition 2—No Task Demands and No Staff Attention | | Condition 3—Noncontingent Staff Attention and No Task Demands | |
|---|---|---|---|---|---|---|
| | Diving on the floor | Diving into people | Diving on the floor | Diving into people | Diving on the floor | Diving into people |
| Trial 1 | 2 | 0 | 1 | 1 | 0 | 0 |
| Trial 2 | 3 | 0 | 2 | 2 | 0 | 0 |
| Trial 3 | 1 | 0 | 1 | 1 | 0 | 0 |
| Trial 4 | 4 | 0 | 1 | 1 | 1 | 0 |

the zero rates of both of the targeted behaviors provides evidence that attention and escape accounted for the all of the occurrences of both topographies of the diving behaviors and that diving was not maintained by direct reinforcement.

We made the following conclusions based on this test data.

1. When Roy was asked to do tasks (even when already receiving attention) he would dive to the floor and remain there until the staff presenting the demand left the area. He did not dive into other people. The result was the demand was removed. (Escape function)
2. When Roy was not asked to do a task and staff did not interact with him he would dive to the floor, and when staff continued to ignore him he would eventually get up and dive into the nearest staff person. The result was an increase in attention. (Attention function)
3. When we made no demands and talked with him he did not dive to the floor and did not dive into people. The diving behaviors did not occur when attention was already available and no demands were presented. (Ruled out direct reinforcement as maintaining contingency—possible sensory effects produced by grinding body against floor.)

Probably of greatest practical significance, the data from the third condition generated an effective temporary intervention to immediately reduce both topographies of the diving behavior while we developed a plan to teach Roy more acceptable behaviors to escape demands and access staff attention.

## DISCUSSION QUESTIONS

1. Why would a behavior that has both SMA and SME functions be difficult for staff to treat?
2. How would you make it easier for the staff to discriminate which motivating operation was at strength at any given moment?
3. Describe a procedure for discriminating that a behavior has multiple functions.

## SUMMARY

There are four major function-based diagnostic classifications of problem behavior. Direct access behaviors are maintained at high levels because they directly access the positive reinforcer. Socially mediated access problem behaviors produce a positive reinforcer indirectly, through the behavior of another person. Direct escape behaviors remove or avoid aversive events directly. Socially mediated escape problem behaviors remove or avoid aversive events or conditions indirectly, through the mediation of another person's behavior.

Within each major category, there are subcategories reflecting the same functional relationships as the major category. The subcategories delineate specific reinforcers, such as access to adult attention or escape from difficult tasks. This function-based diagnostic classification system can be used to determine the specific functional treatment strategy for the problem behavior.

### Note

1. There is a disorder, Lesch-Nyhan, that is hypothesized to automatically produce self-injury.

# Replacement Behavior Options

## 4

This chapter will examine the role of replacement behaviors in treating client problem behaviors. Steps to identify possible replacement behaviors, as well as the delineation of replacement behavior options for problem behaviors serving one of the four major diagnostic categories, are presented. Clinical examples are used to illustrate each replacement behavior option.

## WHAT IS A REPLACEMENT BEHAVIOR?

When treating problem behaviors, one must decrease the target unacceptable behaviors while selecting an alternate desirable behavior, termed a replacement behavior, for specific reinforcement. A replacement behavior serves the same environmental function as a problem behavior. Therefore, a replacement behavior cannot be designated without an understanding of the target behavior's function under specific antecedent contexts. The selected replacement behavior must be capable of producing the same reinforcer as the problem behavior in the identified contexts. The hypothetical example depicted in Table 4.1 illustrates how an alternate, more appropriate form of behavior can replace the current function of the problem behavior.

The designation of the three possible replacement behaviors in Table 4.1 stipulates that each replacement behavior must result in the delivery of the reinforcer. For example, in the first replacement behavior, requesting the toy (from another child) must produce the desired toy at some high level of probability. One cannot simply announce that requesting behavior is an alternate replacement behavior for this child instead of grabbing a toy. Without ensuring that reinforcement will ensue for requesting behavior, the target behaviors may still be more functional than the designated means for obtaining reinforcement. If the requests are not honored reliably, requesting behavior will not function effectively to access reinforcement. Requesting then becomes a less probable behavior under these circumstances. Meanwhile other behaviors will be exhibited in an attempt to get the toy.

Further, the prior functional target behavior, that is, grabbing the toy from another child, must not be allowed to succeed. Such behavior, when exhibited, must result in immediate removal of the toy from the target child. Further, the loss of access to that toy (and others) for a period of time must be invoked. This contingency for grabbing behavior must be in place in order for any potential replacement behaviors to have a chance at becoming functional. Allowing this child to grab a toy from a child without such a contingency dooms the development of alternate behaviors to failure. The removal of the *toy must be immediate! If* the adult argues with the child, this contingency is considerably weakened, and grabbing toys from other children becomes strengthened relative to more appropriate behaviors.

Similarly, sharing the toy upon request (second example) has to also be honored if it is going to take the place of grabbing a toy. Further, the target child's enjoyment of the sharing of the toy must parallel the reinforcing magnitude of playing with the toy in isolation. Sharing versus playing alone, even with the same toy, are not the same events. Hence, the reinforcing potency of the sharing context needs to be evaluated as being as powerful as playing alone. If it is not as pleasurable, engaging in a request to share will probably not replace grabbing the toy.

Finally, teaching the child to wait for a period of time before getting the desired toy will be effective only if grabbing the toy never (or rarely) produces access to the toy. Therefore, the previously stipulated contingency for toy grabbing must be in place. In addition, the ability to delay gratification often needs to be systematically developed. This plan

*TABLE 4.1* ■ **EXAMPLE OF ALTERNATE REPLACEMENT BEHAVIORS**

**Problem Behavior:**

Under the conditions of wanting a toy that another child is using, the target child gets the toy from the other child (consequence) by grabbing the toy (behavior problem) and running away with the toy (1.2 DA: direct chain to tangible reinforcers).

**Goal:**

Decrease the target inappropriate behavior, that is, grabbing the toy and running away with the toy. Increase an alternate appropriate behavior given the same context.

**Possible Appropriate Replacement Behaviors:**

1. *Requesting toy* Desired Contingency:

Child gets the toy from another child (consequence) by asking nicely if he can play with the toy, and other child gives the toy upon request. The request needs to be honored for such a replacement behavior to be naturally maintained. Further, grabbing the toy results in loss of access to the toy immediately, by adult removing the child from the toy and play area.

2. *Offering to play together* Desired Contingency:

Child shares the toy with another child (consequence) by asking nicely if he can play with the toy with that child. The request to share the toy needs to be honored for such a replacement behavior to be naturally maintained. Again, grabbing the toy results in loss of access to the toy immediately, by adult removing the child from the toy and play area.

3. *Getting another toy, while waiting for wanted toy to become available* Desired Contingency:

Adult specifies time period each child wanting a certain toy will have, e.g., 2 minutes. The target child waits or gets another toy during the interim period. When it is his turn to play with the desired toy, he is given access by adult requiring the other child to relinquish the toy, and the target child gets a certain amount of time with the toy, e.g., 2 minutes.

would probably require a progressive manner of teaching "waiting behavior." Such plans are covered in the behavioral plans section of this book.

Suppose the same reinforcer—access to a toy—is accessed through an adult via tantrum behavior? The diagnostic category for this target behavior is 3.1 SMA: tangible reinforcer. What might be some of the options for an alternate replacement behavior? Table 4.2 illustrates two possible alternate replacement behavior options for the designated SMA function of the target behavior of tantrums, that is, access to the toy. In the first option, an appropriate request will replace the tantrum behavior in terms of toy access function. If the child throws a tantrum, he does not get the toy. If he requests the toy in an appropriate tone of voice, he gets the toy.

*TABLE 4.2* ■ **EXAMPLE OF ALTERNATE REPLACEMENT BEHAVIORS FOR TANTRUM BEHAVIOR**

**Problem Behavior:**

In the absence of having a desired toy, the child gets the toy from the caregiver (consequence) by throwing a tantrum for several minutes (behavior problem).

**Goal:**

Decrease the target inappropriate behavior, i.e., tantrum behavior. Increase an alternate appropriate behavior given the same context.

**Appropriate Replacement Behaviors:**

1. *Request toy from caregiver* Desired Contingency:

The child is given the toy by the caregiver (consequence) after an appropriate request is made for the toy. The request needs to be honored for such a replacement behavior to be naturally maintained. Further, the child engaging in tantrum behavior results in a period of time where the desired toy is made not available.

2. *Finish task or chore first* Desired Contingency:

The child is given the toy by the caregiver (consequence) after the child completes the task or chore assigned (Premack contingency). Completing the chore needs to be honored as requisite for accessing the toy. Further, tantrum behavior sets up a period of time whereby the desired toy is not available.

*TABLE 4.3* ■ **THE STEPS TO IDENTIFYING REPLACEMENT BEHAVIORS**

- Identify the diagnostic category of problem behavior by assigning it to one of the four major diagnostic categories (and sub-categories) presented in Chapter 3.
- Identify the specific reinforcers that result from the occurrence of the problem behavior (Chapter 3), under the prevailing motivational conditions and antecedent contexts.
- Designate an alternate appropriate behavior(s) that *will be made* to produce the same function as the problem behavior in the identified antecedent social contexts, whether naturally or contrived.
- If the problem behavior serves more than one function, identify the different functions for each antecedent context and repeat above steps for each unique source of stimulus control.

In the second option, performing a required chore is a conditional event prior to getting the toy. Completing a chore becomes the chain of behaviors required to access the toy (Premack contingency). It is again essential that completion of the task results in accessing the toy, while ensuring that the tantrum behavior does not produce the toy (or minimally, produces the toy less effectively and efficiently than completing the chore; see Table 4.2). Note how both examples select an alternate appropriate behavior that can serve the same function (i.e., produce the same reinforcer) as the problem behavior. Once the replacement behavior is developed in the client's repertoire, it will replace the function or purpose of the problem behavior. This will occur only if the dual contingency exists in the environment. The replacement behavior achieves reinforcement, while the target problem behavior is significantly less functional, or nonfunctional, in achieving the desired result. Table 4.3 presents the steps to utilize in identifying a functional replacement behavior.

## DISABLE ONE FUNCTION, ENABLE ANOTHER

Too often, many naive attempts at developing a replacement behavior involve simply specifying that some selected behavior should replace the target behavior. People who espouse such declarations do not seem to grasp or comprehend the nature of behavior with respect to antecedent and consequent stimuli. To accomplish the successful transition from a currently functional target problem behavior becoming nonfunctional and a currently nonfunctional appropriate behavior becoming functional, social control over the maintaining contingencies is required!

MOs &
Aggression
*Narrated
PowerPoint
Presentation*

Target behavior                 *Eliminate or disable current function*
Replacement behavior       *Enable and enhance desired environmental function*

For example, a referral is made for someone who hits people on the shoulder while sitting on the couch and watching TV in a group home for persons with disabilities. One of the program managers decides that the replacement behavior should be to have this client put his hands in his pockets. That certainly sounds good because it is a state of affairs that is incompatible with hitting people on the couch. However, it offers little in the way of understanding *why* (i.e., maintaining contingency) the hitting behavior occurs. Suppose the hitting occurs because the person next to the target client is talking, and hitting him makes him shut up. Is it reasonable to expect this client will keep his hands in his pockets the next time his listening to the TV program is interrupted? I believe the hands will come out of the pocket and deliver the shot that produces cessation of talking from his neighbor. Then the hands will probably go back into the pockets.

In summary, the behavior analyst needs to produce two changes in the client or child's environment. First, the target behavior's current function needs to be disabled or severely impaired by manipulating those current contingencies. Equally important, the alternate appropriate behavior needs to be enabled in producing the desired environmental function previously produced by the target behavior under relevant motivational conditions.

In this chapter, we present several options for reinforcing a replacement behavior or set of behaviors. Your determining what the maintaining contingencies are for the problem behavior as well as the current strength of the potential replacement behavior is at the heart of designing an effective functional treatment. The following material presents several replacement behavior options for each major diagnostic category for problem behavior: 1.0 DA, 2.0 SMA, 3.0 DE, and 4.0 SME. Of course, removal of the maintaining reinforcer is implicit within each of these options.

## REPLACEMENT BEHAVIOR OPTIONS FOR DA PROBLEM BEHAVIORS

There are four replacement behavior options when treating a target problem behavior that is maintained by direct access to positive reinforcement. All four options require the chain interruption strategy as a component to address client attempts to engage in the prohibited target behavior, or actually engaging in the behavior when unauthorized.

*Alternate Direct Access Form option:* Identify an alternate, more acceptable form of behavior (one that is not as inappropriate or dangerous) that directly produces the same specific reinforcer.

*Access mand (request) option:* Identify a requesting behavior (mand) that would allow staff to mediate such a request or choice by providing the client with a more appropriate setting (area) in which to engage in the problem behavior (if the problem behavior is not dangerous, but is merely inappropriate in form).

*Omission Training option (differential reinforcement of all other behaviors, or DRO):* Identify a length of time that you want the individual not to perform the target direct access behavior, that is, the nonoccurrence of behavior for a set time period, contingent upon which provides access to the specific reinforcer (either by request or by direction of staff).

*Premack Contingency option (engagement in lower probability behaviors as the contingency for access to a specific reinforcer):* Identify a regimen of tasks that, when completed, allows the client to access the specific reinforcer (Premack Principle).

### Chain Interruption Strategy

Chain interruption involves interrupting or blocking the performance of the behavior at its earliest onset. In conjunction with the differential reinforcement of the identified replacement behavior, a chain interruption strategy as a contingency is essential for DA problem behaviors. In order for the problem behavior to be ameliorated, it must be weakened in its ability (i.e., disabled) to directly contact the sensory or tangible reinforcer.

Although many professionals espouse the deployment of developing a replacement behavior, they often overlook what must be done to behaviors that produce positive (or negative) reinforcement directly. If the client is not prevented from engaging in the direct access behavior, then the desired sensory or tangible reinforcer is contacted ad lib. The replacement behavior option will thus be rendered less functional (i.e., less effective and efficient). As a result, the client will not engage in that designated replacement behavior to access reinforcement.

Therefore, it is essential that you interrupt the target behavior before it contacts reinforcement, or at least before a certain amount is acquired. For example, if the client is mouthing inedible objects because of the oral stimulation it produces, such a direct relationship would need to be greatly impeded via chain interruption or blocking. Attempts to physically stop the client from placing the object in his mouth are necessary. If the client is stopped only after he has gnawed on the object for a while, it is too late! Sensory reinforcement has already been achieved. Impeding such a response–reinforcer relationship is critical to the success of any treatment plan.

The staff must become more vigilant in detecting the initial parts of this behavior and interrupting it. Their efforts may be met with the client becoming more stealthy in engaging in this behavior. However, the effort to make such a direct access to positive reinforcement function more arduous will be essential for the selected replacement behavior to become functional. The replacement behavior option must successfully access sensory reinforcement, while the target problem behavior is obstructed frequently. If staff can fulfill that requirement, the replacement behavior option will increase in frequency while the DA problem behavior will decrease.

Concurrent with the chain interruption strategy targeting the direct access problem behavior, a strategy for developing or increasing an alternate replacement behavior needs to be designed. Each of the following four options may be considered. In some cases, one option may be more suited for a specific context and setting than others. This needs to be a clinical decision.

## Alternate Direct Access Form Option

In some cases, it is possible to identify an acceptable replacement behavior that varies slightly in topography from the problem behavior but still produces directly the same desired result. In a prior example, a client with severe mental retardation ran to the door, swung it wide open, and ran outside. The maintaining reinforcer for this direct access chain of behaviors was getting to go outside. A more acceptable alternate behavior can be walking out the door (not running), and then exiting with staff supervision. Engaging in any previous form of exiting would result in staff stopping him and delaying his access to outside until the replacement behavior occurs. The rearranged contingencies are delineated in Table 4.4.

Suppose we determine that sticking inedible things in one's mouth is maintained by a direct access to the ingestion of edible items. A replacement behavior that alters the form to be more acceptable while maintaining the same access to the reinforcer is illustrated in Table 4.5.

*TABLE 4.4* ■ **REARRANGED CONTINGENCIES**

**Maintaining Contingency for Target Behavior:**

1.2 DA: tangible reinforcer

**Contingency Plan for Target Behavior (chain interruption):**

If the client engages in the target behavior (runs outside), he will be stopped and brought back immediately to the start point. He will be required to wait a period of time, for example, 1–2 minutes, before being prompted to perform the alternate behavior. Of course staff have to be close to catch any inappropriate exiting behavior immediately, upon which they will perform this regimen.

**Contingency Plan for Replacement Behavior:**

If the student signs "out," he will be allowed to go outside if he walks appropriately. Student may need staff to prompt such behaviors in contrast to running, as well as massed trials of practice (if replacement behavior diagnosis is inept repertoire).

### *TABLE 4.5* ■ **ACCEPTABLE FORM**

**Maintaining Contingency for Target Behavior:**

1.1 DA: sensory reinforcer

**Contingency Plan for Target Behavior:**

If the student attempts to stick inedible items in his mouth, he will be physically prevented from achieving such a result, if possible. Additionally, a 3-minute removal from environment (place him in a chair where access to any object is precluded) should be effected before prompting the replacement behavior. The function of this 3-minute time out is to make such attempts less functional and more arduous in getting edible items (i.e., disabling the function).

**Contingency Plan for Replacement Behavior:**

If the student walks over to his basket where there is foods he may eat in peace. This option would be considered for clients who do not have problems with weight, such as obesity.

The following case examples are further illustrations of the use of this replacement behavior option.

*Pushing and Shoving.* A client was referred to me (E.C.) for behavioral consultation as a result of his pushing and shoving staff in order to get to the refrigerator. He lived in a residential facility with five other adults with autism. You probably think he is going into the refrigerator to get something out to eat or drink. Such was not the case. Once he opened the refrigerator, he would check to see if the lunch bags for the next day were made and placed in their correct space.

Why would he push and shove staff in order to get to the refrigerator? This behavior was the result of staff preventing him from engaging in his obsession with "checking on the lunches." Simply walking over to the refrigerator to check out the lunch bags would only result in his being sent back to the living room area. He thereby learned to become both quicker and more aggressive in achieving his goal of getting to the refrigerator. You can see that pushing or shoving staff and running past them when they were not looking was more functional in this circumstance, given the staff's predilection toward preventing access to the refrigerator.

The replacement behavior identified for this client was walking appropriately to the refrigerator. He was taught to engage in such behavior, with the result being un-obstructed access to the refrigerator. Given his previous history, this behavior had to be prompted for a while. If he walked appropriately to the kitchen, he was allowed to open the refrigerator door and check out the sack lunches. If he ran, pushed, or shoved anyone, he would not get to open the door at that time and was required to return to the area where the running began. He was then to demonstrate the appropriate walking behavior, which resulted in his being allowed to open the refrigerator door. Of course, pushing and shoving would decrease once such behaviors only postponed his access to the refrigerator.

*Unique Sensory Reinforcer.* Replacing the function of the problem behavior may sometimes be difficult with a problem behavior diagnosed as 1.1 DA: sensory reinforcer. A more acceptable form that does not produce direct access to the positive reinforcer will not *replace* the problem behavior's function. Although you may think that the two are equivalent, in the eyes of the client they are not. Here is a case in point.

In the early 1980s, a client was referred to me (E.C.) for a behavioral plan for an extremely revolting and undesirable behavior. In her day treatment program, she would grab feces left in the toilet bowl from her own use or someone else's and squish it in her hands.

The first plan set up at the program was to prevent her from doing this. The day treatment aides were to restrain her from engaging in such a behavior. Unfortunately, this plan did not work to make her value the activity less. In fact, it seemed to only deprive such an event and make the motivational condition to access it stronger. Such an increased desire on the client's part to get to the bathroom further compounded the staff's problem in managing her. Use of the bathroom by other clients was a signal to her that the desired activity may be available. She would then dash to the toilet to determine whether something was left in the toilet bowl from the last user. Because she was now being prevented from going to the bathroom at these times, she began to engage in aggressive and disruptive behavior toward staff when they tried to restrain her from engaging in this behavior. Further, she became more capable of discerning times when staff would be less vigilant and a mad dash to the bathroom might pay off. When another client was engaged in tantrum behavior and staff were involved in some extensive management procedure, she would dart toward the bathroom. Hence, another client's problem resulted in staff having to deal with two problems.

My analysis of this behavior supported a direct access function (1.1 DA: sensory event). The client seemed to like the sensation of squishing the feces in the toilet bowl. I am not sure why this was pleasurable to her, but it certainly seemed that the behavior was producing its own reinforcer. The replacement behavior that was targeted for reinforcement involved the same form of the behavior. When she completed a designated number of tasks, she earned a specified amount of free time. She was then allowed to go to the bathroom and squish feces! However, prior to going to the bathroom, disposable rubber gloves were placed on her hands. She then engaged in the squishing behavior, with the gloves on. When her free time elapsed, she took the gloves off and disposed of them in the garbage can in the bathroom. She then washed her hands thoroughly before going back to the work area. She resumed her work on tasks to earn more free time. Data indicated that the rate of running to the bathroom to "check it out" reduced to zero, as did the wrestling matches with the staff. Her work production was maintained at high levels.

Why was this form chosen and not something else? Suppose we had set up a program that allowed her to squish play dough instead? That certainly would be more appropriate than the squishing feces in her hands, even with gloves on. However, squishing play dough may not have resulted in the same sensory reinforcer. Therefore, allowing her access to play dough *may not have been* equivalent from her perspective. Hence, such a contingency may have had no effect on the rate of the target behaviors, that is, running to the bathroom unauthorized to squish feces with one's bare hands.

In the designated plan, the form of the replacement behavior left the sensory reinforcer intact, for the most part. Despite the repugnant aspect of this behavior, the designed program had two critical effects. First, it did remove sanitary concerns in regards to the sensory maintained behavior. Second, it resulted in a reduction of the target behavior occurrence to zero for many days. Contrast this with the result obtained when staff tried to obstruct her access to the reinforcer: frequent incidents of aggression and running to the bathroom. Finally, her obsession with this ritual decreased over time until it was not something she chose to do during earned free time.

*Don't Jump!* The client mentioned earlier who jumped out of his wheelchair could also have accessed floor time in another manner. If a graded platform was built, he could have been taught to hoist himself up on the top of the platform and then gradually slide down (similar to a children's slide on the playground). This option would have been easier on the staff. Getting into his wheelchair might have been achieved by a reverse process, that is, him moving himself up the graded platform.

## MAINTAINING CONTINGENCY FOR TARGET BEHAVIOR: 1.2 DA: TANGIBLE REINFORCER

### Plan for Target Behavior

If the client shows signs of attempting to jump out of the wheelchair, he will be physically prevented for a period of 5 minutes subsequently.

### Contingency Plan for Replacement Behavior

With some initial prompting, the client is taught how to wheel his chair over to the platform and engage in a series of physical movements that result in his propping himself onto the platform, and then gradually traversing down the platform safely.

### Access Mand (Request) Option

In some cases, it may be possible to teach the individual to request permission to engage in the desired activity (a mand). A request or mand need not be vocal; it could be a manual sign or gesture, such as pointing to a symbol or picture. The only requirement on the form of the request is that it is reliably translated by the receiver of the message.

This option is particularly suited where the form of the behavior is not dangerous or unhealthy but is unacceptable in some context. Contingent upon a request, staff can then provide an appropriate place for the student or client to engage in the behavior. For example, some stereotypic or self-stimulatory behaviors can be treated effectively by teaching the client to request (vocally or nonvocally) the opportunity to engage in those behaviors. Contingent upon this request, the staff can then direct the client to a private area. One must make sure that the request is honored by staff in a timely manner, especially in the beginning of the program. If the request is not honored, or is delayed to a significant extent, then requesting behavior will not be functional. One would expect that the request will never fully be able to compete with engaging in the stereotypic behavior ad lib. It is therefore important that the dual contingency be operable. The following contingency box illustrates this requirement.

## MAINTAINING CONTINGENCY FOR TARGET BEHAVIOR: 1.1 DA: SENSORY REINFORCER

### Contingency Plan for Target Behavior (chain interruption)

Interrupt initial chain of stereotypic behavior. Removal for several minutes from any opportunity to perform such behavior (chain interruption).

### Contingency Plan for Replacement Behavior

Prompt client to request (in whatever designated form) access to desired activity or event. Contingent upon request, provide client access to desired activity in a designated setting. With some behaviors diagnosed as 1.1 DA (e.g., masturbation, nose picking), the area should be private, away from others seeing him.

How would this replacement behavior option be used? Suppose a client frequently runs out of her residential facility and lacks safety skills involving roads and cars. She leaves the facility simply to get outside. Such is not an unreasonable behavior because one can only stay inside for so long before wanting to have a change in scenery. However, her unauthorized and spontaneous leaving the facility without staff supervision is a definite serious problem, given her inability to navigate roads and cars safely.

Suppose the client is taught to request an outside activity with staff supervision by signing "walk." When she wants to go outside, she would be prompted to sign "walk." The staff would then take her hand and let her guide them to the area she wished to go to. This allows her to get outside the house, but with the necessary staff supervision.

---

**MAINTAINING CONTINGENCY FOR TARGET BEHAVIOR: 1.2 DA: TANGIBLE REINFORCER**

**Contingency Plan for Target Behavior (chain interruption)**

If the client engages in the target behavior (runs outside), she will be brought back immediately and required to wait a period of time, for example, 1–2 minutes, before being prompted to perform requesting behavior. If she is caught running before getting outside, the same contingency is in effect.

**Contingency Plan for Replacement Behavior**

If she signs "walk," she will be allowed to go outside if she walks appropriately with staff. Staff should prompt such behaviors initially to replace running outside, as well as massed trials of practice (if replacement behavior diagnosis is inept repertoire).

---

The following are some more illustrations of the mand option with prior clinical examples:

*I Need a Change of Clothing.* A client rips off his clothes occasionally because he doesn't like the clothes he has on. Rather, he prefers other clothes. You can see that reinforcing a request for new clothes, or allowing him to choose which clothes to wear in the morning for work or school, is more preferable from a management perspective than the current "clothes ripping" behavior.

---

**MAINTAINING CONTINGENCY FOR TARGET BEHAVIOR: 1.2 DA: TANGIBLE REINFORCER**

**Contingency Plan for Target Behavior (chain interruption)**

If the client begins to engage in the initial forms of the target behavior (tearing at clothes), he will be physically stopped (immediately) and required to wait a period of time, for example, 1–2 minutes, before being allowed to engage in an alternate behavior.

**Contingency Plan for Replacement Behavior**

If the student signs "new clothes," he will be allowed to procure a choice of clothes to wear. The student may need staff to prompt such a request immediately when forced to wear undesired clothes, as well as massed trials of practice (if replacement behavior diagnosis is inept repertoire).

---

One should realize that developing these specific communicative behaviors will only be functional if the 1.2 DA: tangible reinforcer diagnosis was accurate. Suppose clothes ripping is maintained because the client likes the "feel" of ripping clothes? Would a decelerative effect be obtained on clothes ripping behavior? Probably not! In fact, this program might provide "more fuel to the fire!"

*Privacy Please.* A client with mental retardation engages in masturbation out in the public, open area of a residential facility. Teaching him to request privacy via a signal allows staff to mediate this request. He is brought to his bedroom area, where the door is closed. Of course, he is not allowed to engage in public displays any more, and such attempts are immediately stopped by removal of the opportunity for a designated time. As the staff become excellent at thwarting his public attempts, the requesting privacy becomes more attractive. Exhibiting such a request provides unhindered access to genital stimulation. His behavior changes as a function of differential reinforcement. Public displays undergo extinction, while requests for privacy increase. Everyone is happy!

## Omission Training (DRO) Option

Allowing a client free unrestricted access to the desired reinforcer, contingent upon a request, is certainly a good first strategy to use in many cases. Developing a mand for accessing a reinforcer is certainly more preferable than denying access to the reinforcer with concomitant side effect behaviors. Obstructing the client's access to the bathroom in the prior example resulted in generating other more disastrous behaviors, while not solving the initial problem. Therefore, teaching the client to mand for a desired reinforcer should have the effect of removing problem behaviors whose function was to access the prohibited reinforcer.

Unfortunately, in some circumstances, such a manding strategy as the replacement behavior option may run into trouble. Let's take a student in an educational program who frequently engages in stereotypic behavior of touching the floor five times each side with his left and then right hand. The teacher decides to develop a requesting option that allows her to sign "play." Contingent upon signing "play" she is allowed to touch the floor in an area of the classroom designated for such behavior (to develop setting stimulus control).

Such a plan may not reduce the frequency of stereotypic behavior to a more acceptable level. Suppose the client requests permission to engage in stereotypic behavior every 2 minutes? She is requesting it so often it is to the point where the teacher cannot get the student to complete any instructional task! What do you do then? Obviously, a client who frequently requests to engage in stereotypic behavior would pose a problem for most school or work environments. In many cases, developing requesting behaviors to access sensory or tangible reinforcement should also be combined with other replacement behavior options. Such an additional strategy should gradually reduce the level of accessing the reinforcer to a more manageable reasonable level. I have termed it, "weaning them off of frequent reinforcement."

One treatment option of choice for these circumstances is omission training. Omission training is also referred to as the differential reinforcement of other behavior (DRO). In omission training, the client is taught to forgo engaging in the target behavior that is producing reinforcement for a designated amount of time. Fulfilling this requirement is the contingency for authorized access to the sensory or tangible reinforcer (Mazaleski, Iwata, Vollmer, Zarcone, & Smith, 1993). By beginning with a small amount of time, termed the DRO interval, the client learns to reliably delay gratification. Contingent upon success being obtained with small DRO intervals, the interval is gradually increasing. Therefore, the client learns to forego the reinforcer for longer periods of time in a progressive manner. This develops greater self-control in regard to the client's baseline level of access, where she previously required immediate gratification. Additionally, a chain interruption procedure is deployed contingent upon the behavior, with a restarting of the full DRO interval.

This replacement behavior option does not develop a specific *replacement* behavior. Hence, it is often not considered by many as a replacement behavior option. However, a replacement behavior does not have to be a single unitary form! A replacement behavior can consist of a chain of behaviors that accesses reinforcement (also see Premack Contingency Option). This replacement behavior option does not develop a systematic chain of behaviors. Rather, a variety of interim behaviors probably occur across the DRO interval. The replacement behavior is the absence of the target behavior, or the occurrence of any other behavior. The topography of such a chain of behaviors varies with each delivery of reinforcement, with one common element: absence of the target behavior.

*Talking Is Good When it Occurs in the Right Context!* Remember the client with disabilities who talked loudly to herself while pushing a laundry cart across a parking lot? This behavior was hypothesized by me (E.C.) to produce its own auditory (hearing one's voice) or kinesthetic stimulation (sensory effect on vocal cords). If a review of antecedent context data reveals that such vocal discourse occurs at a consistent rate during staff absence, what can be done to bring it under more acceptable conditions? When is vocal behavior acceptable? When you talk to other people! When is it OK to talk to oneself without raising suspicions that one is delusional? When it is done as a song!

If vocal behavior produces its own reinforcer, what can compete with that? In some cases, I (E.C.) have used a microphone (Mr. Mike) that enhances the auditory production of voice. How would omission training work? The use of Mr. Mike to talk or sing can be earned when this client achieves the absence of talking-to-self behavior in the designated DRO interval. Of course, the client would need to be monitored for instances where she would engage in self-talk in public, with the following contingency rendered for such occurrences.

## MAINTAINING CONTINGENCY FOR TARGET BEHAVIOR: 1.2 DA: SENSORY REINFORCER

### Contingency Plan for Target Behavior (chain interruption with reverse Premack)

If the client engages in the target behavior (self-talk in public), she will be brought inside immediately and required to engage in a nonpreferred task. Subsequently, she will be allowed to engage in prior activities with the DRO interval being reset.

### Contingency Plan for Replacement Behavior

If the student does not talk to herself while in public for the entire DRO interval, she is provided a designated amount of time on Mr. Mike as soon as possible after achieving success. Later in the program, it may be possible to provide points when she succeeds in a DRO interval and allowing an exchange of points after she has met two or three DRO intervals.

## Premack Contingency Option

A common question that comes up when discussing the development of a durable and spontaneous requesting repertoire is, "Do you have to give the reinforcer every time it is requested?" The response is, "Yes, in the initial phase of the program." In order to build a new behavior, all basic behavioral texts will indicate this as a must! But this may create some problems. Does this require that parents, teachers, and staff should provide a designated item or activity whenever a client requests it? If people do this, it will create demand machines. Children and clients will spend too much time requesting food and other reinforcers.

Although the answer to the first question is still "Yes," the ramification of such a strategy does bring up a dilemma. For most of us, we have learned how to delay gratification for some period of time on many activities and events we find reinforcing. A client or child who constantly requests food and particular kinds of food items may be engaging in unhealthy behavior patterns, to say the least!

What can be done for such cases? How will the child learn to be reasonable in regards to her access to reinforcing items and events? The answer lies in utilizing the Premack contingency. In this option, before a client can request a reinforcer and receive it, certain tasks have to be completed. At work, many people must wait for 1.5–2.0 hours before taking their coffee break *(there is an implicit assumption here that certain work requirements are fulfilled in the interim, however incorrect that may be)*. In the case of school settings, the teacher or principle would require that certain academic or instructional tasks be completed by the student prior to the student requesting access to certain reinforcers.

The Premack contingency could be tagged on to the requesting replacement behavior option delineated previously to begin to develop *delay of gratification* skills. The Premack contingency requires some low probability behavior (e.g., completion of a task) to occur prior to the client being allowed to request access to the high probability behavior, that is, the desired sensory reinforcer. In this manner, the occurrence of the target problem behavior can be under control of both designated times (after tasks are completed) and settings (engaging in the behavior in certain nonpublic or nontraining areas). The task completion criteria for accessing the positive reinforcer can be progressively altered as a function of the success of the program in producing the contingency.

Table 4.6 illustrates how the Premack contingency option contrasts with the other replacement behavior options detailed previously. The target behavior is stereotypic hand-flapping and is maintained by the direct sensory result it produces.

The first replacement behavior option treats this problem behavior by developing a request/mand by the client to engage in the stereotypic behavior. The request need not be vocal for individuals incapable of speaking. The staff can then provide a place where he can engage in such behavior for a designated period of time. This option may not reduce the client's desire to access the activity, but it will certainly provide a nonpublic forum for engaging in this behavior.

Omission training could be added on to the requesting program at some point. The client would request access to the behavior, and then a DRO interval would be set up. This would be short in the beginning and progressively lengthened. *If* the client engages in the target behavior prior to the lapse of the DRO interval, chain interruption procedures are deployed. Further, the DRO interval is reset for the full length.

Similar to omission training, the Premack contingency option will eventually reduce the frequency of accessing the reinforcer. In contrast to omission training, the Premack contingency requires some performance on designated tasks as the conditional event for reinforcement of the requesting behavior. Again, chain interruption procedures are utilized should the client attempt to access the sensory or tangible reinforcer without prior authorization. Such unauthorized attempts also can be punished by increasing the number of tasks required contingent upon the attempt to access the reinforcer prematurely (see "Reverse Premack Principle").

**TABLE 4.6 ■ CONTRASTING REPLACEMENT BEHAVIOR OPTIONS FOR 1.1 DA: SENSORY REINFORCER**

| Alternate Form | Probably not Applicable |
| --- | --- |
| Requesting behavior option | Client signs, says, or points to picture icon requesting access to stereotypic behavior |
| Omission training | Client goes without engaging in stereotypic behavior for some period of time and then is allowed request to engage in hand flapping in a designated area for a designated period of time |
| Premack contingency | Client performs designated number of tasks and then is allowed to request to engage in hand flapping in a designated area for a designated period of time |

## REPLACEMENT BEHAVIOR OPTIONS FOR SMA PROBLEM BEHAVIORS

There are five replacement behavior options when treating a problem behavior that is maintained by socially mediated access to positive reinforcement. With all SMA problem behaviors, withdrawal of reinforcement (extinction) for the occurrence of the target behavior is a requisite for making the alternate behavior functional.

*Direct Access to tangible reinforcer:* Developing or strengthening a chain of behaviors that produce the desired tangible reinforcer directly.

*Access mand (request) option:* Identify a requesting behavior (mand) that would allow staff to mediate such a request or choice by providing the client with the desired person's attention or tangible reinforcer.

*DRL group contingencies for peer attention:* Designating a lower rate of the target behavior (differential reinforcement of low-rate behavior), which is the criterion for providing a powerful reinforcer to the group. The target rate may be for either the individual client's behavior or a group's level of behavior or performance.

*Omission Training option:* Identify a length of time that you want the individual not to perform the target behavior, that is, the nonoccurrence of target behavior for a set time period. Contingent upon the client not engaging in the target behavior in the DRO interval, access to the desired adult or staff attention or tangible reinforcer is provided.

*Premack Contingency option (lower probability behaviors as the contingency for access to the reinforcer:* Identify a regimen of tasks that, when completed, allows the client to access the reinforcer (Premack Principle).

### Extinction

With socially mediated access problem behaviors, there is usually no need for a chain interruption strategy, unless the problem behavior can be dangerous to the client or others (e.g., self-abuse, aggression, property destruction). In those cases, simply for safety requirements, a chain interruption procedure delineated in the previous section should be used. With other SMA behaviors, there is no need to physically interrupt the behavior. Simply not providing the positive reinforcer contingent upon the problem behavior will be sufficient to facilitate its demise.

In cases of SMA problem behaviors, extinction is necessary. *Extinction* is defined as the removal of the functional reinforcer contingent upon the target behavior occurring. Given that problem behaviors in this category are maintained by the behavior of others, it becomes obvious how the reinforcer will have to be removed. People will have to behave differently when the target behavior occurs!

In order for a replacement behavior to *replace* the target behavior function, it is critical to ensure that the target behavior no longer results in the delivery of the socially mediated reinforcer. To implement extinction, one must be able to tolerate the occurrence of the target behavior (Iwata, 2006). Staff, parents, care providers, and teachers need to refrain from the delivery of the reinforcer for the problem behavior, whether it be adult attention or a tangible item or event. Peer reinforcement of the previously reinforced target behavior needs to be removed, but the mechanism is somewhat different than with other socially mediated reinforcers.

All the functional behavioral treatment plans would require that the maintaining reinforcer for the target problem behavior be eliminated, or at least weakened (i.e., disabled). If complete elimination of the contingency is not plausible (humans will be humans), then there needs to be a significant disabling of the previous temporal and reliable relationship. The weakening of the relationship can be based on the contingency being less reliable than the one that exists for the replacement behavior.

For example, let us say that the tantrum behavior of an adolescent in a group home results in getting the desired reinforcer within 5 minutes of the tantrum onset, 70% of the time. To disable this relationship, tantrum behavior should not produce the desired reinforcer at all. This designation would be specified in the behavioral plan. Once the plan is enacted, we can hope for a 0% relationship between tantrums and access to socially mediated reinforcers. However, in human service and educational settings, perfect performance is something to strive for, but not always the case. However, if the staff or teachers are able to remove the delivery of the reinforcer for 80% of the tantrums, they have significantly disabled the functional ability of tantrums to produce reinforcement. In addition, if doing a simple chore in 5 minutes results in 100% access to the reinforcer, the previous relationship between tantrums and reinforcement has been further weakened. Given that data, the most efficient behavior for accessing desired reinforcers is doing a designated 5-minute chore.

In summary, complete removal of reinforcement is preferred. However, if complete removal of the positive reinforcer is not viable, weakening the maintaining contingency can result if the replacement behavior "pays off" at a greater level or amount. If the replacement behavior results in a greater and more frequent reinforcement schedule than the target behavior, the change in client behavior should occur. Making the replacement behavior easier to perform is a strategy. Concurrently, making the target behavior less efficient at accessing the desired reinforcer is also requisite. Making the occurrence of the target behavior serve as a mand for a nonpreferred regimen of tasks can also be an adjunct complementing extinction. I (E.C.) have termed this reversal of conditional probabilities typical of reinforcement operations the *Reverse Premack Principle*.

**Using Reverse Premack**
*Narrated PowerPoint Presentation*

### REVERSE PREMACK PRINCIPLE

Another method of disabling the function of the target behavior is to have such a behavior serve as a mand for a regimen of nonpreferred tasks. In other words, the occurrence of a higher probability behavior (target behavior) is followed by the client engaging in a behavior of lower probability, thus setting up a punishment contingency (Premack, www.psych.upenn.edu/-premack/essays/reward.html).

For example, engaging in tantrum behavior to access a tangible reinforcer is a high probability behavior under the motivational conditions where access to the event is in a relative state of deprivation. A functional treatment would rearrange the contingencies for getting the tangible reinforcer by removing the reinforcer for the target behavior (disabling this function) and scheduling it for an alternate replacement behavior (enabling this function). To further disable the previous target behavior's function, the environment also imposes an activity that is of lesser probability contingent upon its occurrence. Therefore, not only is the maintaining reinforcer temporally removed from the target behavior, but a lesser probability activity is imposed. In this manner, the contingencies enabling the replacement behavior are made even more potent, and the contingencies disabling the target behavior are also more powerful.

### Direct Access to Tangible Reinforcer

In some cases, if appropriate, the client can be taught to access directly the tangible reinforcer that was maintaining the problem behavior. Teaching a client to pour his own drink instead of throwing a tantrum (to have someone else get it for him) is obvious once the function of tantrum behavior is discovered.

*I Want a Sandwich, Please.* A client with developmental disabilities would throw a tantrum and yell loudly when hungry, and staff on an intermittent basis would provide food to him contingently (LaVigna, Willis, & Donnelan, 1989). Teaching him to make his own sandwiches and snacks negated the need for tantrums when he was hungry. Note that the behavioral effects of the tantrums and the sandwich making behavior are the same, but one alternate is obviously more desirable than the other.

---

**MAINTAINING CONTINGENCY FOR TARGET BEHAVIOR: 2.3 SMA: TANGIBLE REINFORCER, FOOD ITEM**

**Contingency Plan for Target Behavior**

If the client throws a tantrum and yells loudly, he will not receive food.

**Contingency Plan for Replacement Behavior**

If the student makes his own sandwich, he can proceed to eat it.

---

## Access Mand (Request) Option

In this replacement behavior option, the desired reinforcer, whether it be adult attention or access to a tangible reinforcer, is provided by staff upon an appropriate request. Concurrently, the previous function of the target behavior is negated through extinction. As an example, let's look at how this differential reinforcement process would work for a child with autism who falls on the floor. The FBA data point to the maintaining contingency as access to tangible reinforcer (2.3 SMA: tangible reinforcer). Currently falling on the floor is followed by teacher attention in the form of cajoling her to get up, rubbing her shoulders as an incentive to get up, and finally getting her favorite picture book out and showing her the pictures while cajoling her up to sit at the table (Bingo!). The plan calls for a nonvocal request (i.e., raise hand) to serve as the behavior that will bring the teacher or aide over to her with the book and begin showing her the pictures (Table 4.7). This replacement behavior would now substitute for dropping on the floor as a means to get attention.

Note that in this example the request for the book is designated as the replacement behavior. Such a request will now result in an adult interacting with her while looking at the book. If access to the book is the maintaining contingency for the student's target behavior, then reinforcing requests at 100% levels negates the function of the target behavior.

Let's examine how such a replacement behavior ameliorates the prior function of the target behavior. Previously, book reading was delivered when this child dropped to the floor. Now such behavior only results in a postponement of this activity. The extinction plan might be designed so that the exhibition of the target behavior results in a time period where access to the book is withheld. The request for the book would be reinforced only after this extinction period. However, if hand raising occurs prior to the target behavior, it immediately produces this event. To reiterate, disable one function, enable another!

---

*TABLE 4.7* ■ **TARGET AND REPLACEMENT BEHAVIORS**

| Reinforcer | Undesired Form (Target Behavior) | Alternate Replacement Behavior |
| --- | --- | --- |
| Adult reads/shows student favored book | Drops to the floor | Request (raises hand) for adult to bring book |

### MAINTAINING CONTINGENCY FOR TARGET BEHAVIOR: 2.3 SMA: TANGIBLE REINFORCER, BOOK READING ACTIVITY

#### Contingency Plan for Target Behavior

If the student drops to the floor, she will not receive the book reading activity for 5 minutes after getting up and sitting back down in her seat.

#### Contingency Plan for Replacement Behavior

If the student raises her hand, she will immediately receive the desired activity for a 3-minute period (unless first contingency is in place). Such behavior may need to be prompted in the beginning, particularly if replacement behavior diagnosis is inept repertoire.

Realize that requesting will be functional only if you are correct in your analysis. If this child's dropping to the floor is the result of getting a book, making it more profitable to request the book than drop will prove effective. If this is not a correct diagnosis, that is, the reinforcer maintaining the dropping behavior is not the book reading activity, this plan will be ineffective. Developing a request to access a book reading activity with an adult may eventually occur, but it will not significantly affect the student's target behavior. Why? A misdiagnosis means that the primary purpose of dropping to the floor was not to get the book reading activity, but rather something else. A wrong diagnosis leads to a wrong replacement behavior, which then leads to an ineffective treatment.

*A Pinch Here, a Pinch There.* How would this replacement behavior option be used to treat the client's pinching behavior I (E.C.) observed from the previous chapter? Because pinching is currently maintained because of the staff interaction, this contingency needs to be rectified. Pinching should obviously result in no (or little) staff interaction. However, a sign for communication by this individual (e.g., signing "me") would result in someone coming over and shaking his hand and talking with him for a while. Replacing access to social interaction from the target behavior to a request for interaction will switch the schedule of reinforcement in favor of the more appropriate behavior. It is quite plausible that the signing response will need to be shaped and prompted frequently before becoming more spontaneous.

### MAINTAINING CONTINGENCY FOR TARGET BEHAVIOR: 2.1 SMA: ADULT ATTENTION

#### Contingency Plan for Target Behavior

If the student pinches a staff member, he will not receive any attention for 5 minutes subsequently.

#### Contingency Plan for Replacement Behavior

If the student signs "me," he will immediately receive the desired social interaction activity for a 3-minute period. Such behavior may need to be prompted in the beginning, particularly if the replacement behavior diagnosis is inept repertoire.

*A Request for Food to Replace Self-Injury.* In the previous chapter, a hypothetical student with severe disabilities exhibits an unacceptable level of self-abusive behavior. Your observations revealed that the teacher was unwittingly developing self-abuse in the child as a functional behavior when the student wanted food. Because this student is unable to vocally request food, how would one replace self-injury with requesting behavior? Simply teach the student how to sign (or use other nonvocal system) indicating a request for food at times when he wants food. The staff would reinforce such behaviors with food while self-injury undergoes extinction. Therefore, self-abuse becomes less probable under the motivational condition, being weakened by its inability to access food, while signing becomes stronger.

---

### MAINTAINING CONTINGENCY FOR TARGET BEHAVIOR: 2.3 SMA: TANGIBLE REINFORCER, FOOD ITEMS CONTINGENCY

#### Plan for Target Behavior

If the student engages in self-injury, a chain interruption procedure will be used (to include restraint for a specified period of time), and he will not receive any food item for 3 minutes subsequently. In addition, a *Reverse Premack Principle* would be instituted during the 3 minutes of nonaccess.

#### Contingency Plan for Replacement Behavior

If the student signs "food," he will immediately receive the desired food item, in small quantity, with an opportunity to continue requesting to get more (until a designated amount has been consumed). Such behavior may need to be prompted in the beginning, particularly if the replacement behavior diagnosis is inept repertoire (discussed in a later section).

---

### DRL Group Contingencies for Peer Attention

Removing peer reinforcement requires a different mechanism. One cannot often successfully instruct peers to ignore the behavior (remove reinforcement) so the target student will behave more appropriately. What is in it for them? To remove peer reinforcement for problem behavior, it is necessary to tie the access to contrived reinforcers for the group to the child's exhibition of target problem behavior. In many cases a group criterion level can be designated, for example, the class cannot go over five disruptive incidents in the morning in order to earn 10 minutes of extra recess after lunch. Here are some examples.

*Everyone Loves a Clown (Except the Teacher).* Let's take the case of a hypothetical junior high school special education student, Billy. Billy engages in frequent verbally inappropriate behavior toward teachers. Subsequent to such behavior the class laughs, girls smile, boys nod their heads, and all have a good time. He has peers wanting to hang out with him during recess and at lunch. Unfortunately, this is exacerbated even when Billy is disciplined by being sent to the principal's office. How can one make his peers responsible for not feeding into this behavior?

A group contingency involves the setting of a contingency in which the group accesses (or not) a group reward, contingent upon the behavior of the group performance. As an example, the following contingency can be enacted with extra peer conversation time at the end of the period as the reinforcer. If the class stays at or below a certain level of inappropriate comments (taking into account Billy's rate), the whole class earns conversation time. If the class goes beyond the designated number of allowed inappropriate comments, they lose out. Do you think that peer reinforcement for Billy's inappropriate verbal behavior will still be forthcoming? Fill in the following box.

**MAINTAINING CONTINGENCY FOR TARGET BEHAVIOR: 2.2 SMA: PEER REINFORCEMENT**

**Contingency Plan for Target Behavior**




**Contingency Plan for Replacement Behavior**




*Do Not Argue!* Simply asking Antonio and his sister to stop arguing, separating them, and intermittently sending them to their rooms did not work. There were great bouts of verbal abuse inflicted upon each other during these arguments. Antonio and his sister were foster children living in a two-parent household. Like many other parents, these foster parents (actually his grandmother and grandfather) attempted to figure out who started the argument and why. This strategy often led down the path of no return. Hence, the referral for my (E.C.) behavioral intervention services to address this problem behavior as well as others that were occurring at school.

Why do children argue? Arguing is usually maintained by the listener's response. One cannot argue with a wall, but one can attempt to have the last word with another human being. Sometimes the arguments between Antonio and his sister were about silly things. Other times they were about who gets what TV show or favored item or activity. After collecting behavioral assessment data, my behavioral specialist (R.P.) designed a plan to address this interlocking dynamic. It was obvious that we were going to discontinue attempting to find out who started it as a method.

Therefore, rather than deal with the incident as a CSI specialist, the designed intervention simply counted each argument against both children (delineated in Cipani, 2004). An argument was counted when both children said something to each other in a negative or derogatory tone. With behaviors that are maintained by peers, it is essential to allocate consequences to all concerned. Individual contingencies for the one who started it, even if such could be ascertained, are often ineffective. To remove peer reinforcement, one has to make the contingency affect all those involved during the incident.

R.P. taught the grandmother how to use early bedtime as a contingency for unacceptable levels of arguing on a given day. In our DRL contingency, if Antonio and his sister had two or fewer arguments in a given day, then they both go to bed at their normal 8 o'clock time period. However, three or more arguments resulted in earlier bedtime. The data on average frequency of arguments between Antonio and his sister follows. Table 4.8 shows what it did for Antonio.

Note that in the first 2-week period (3/8–3/17), the average daily rate of arguing was 1.5. This translates to the two children rarely having three arguments because you know what kicks in if that happens. Apparently these two children really liked staying up until 8 P.M. The effect on behavior becomes even more pronounced in the weeks to follow. The period from 4/21–5/14 did not have one incident of arguing behavior. There are not too many families that can boast that, especially those with children who were

*TABLE 4.8* ■ **AVERAGE FREQUENCY OF ARGUING ACROSS BASELINE AND CONSEQUENCE TIME PERIODS**

| Baseline | 3/8–3/17 | 3/18–3/27 | 3/28–4/12 | 4/13–4/19 | 4/21–5/4 | 5/5–5/14 |
|----------|----------|-----------|-----------|-----------|----------|----------|
| 3.0 | 1.5 | 0.75 | 0.50 | 0.25 | 0 | 0 |

previously experiencing severe difficulty in dealing with each other without taunting and arguing.

It is important to note that arguing might still produce the desired listener response, yet the punishment contingency overrides this relationship. While the discriminative stimuli for verbal aggression were present, a concurrent contingency involving removal of a reinforcer, contingent upon the verbal arguments, successfully competed with the behavior's functionality.

The "Good Behavior Board Game" is an excellent example of a group-oriented contingency for a student's target behavior that is maintained by peer attention. It measures the class rate of defined disruptive behaviors in 10-minute intervals. If the class reaches the behavior goal for a given interval, their board piece moves up one space on the maze. Reinforcement is provided every few spaces via a treasure box. For further information, consult the text *Classroom Management for All Teachers: Plans for Evidence-Based Practice* (Cipani, 2008).

## Omission Training Option

The use of the omission training option for SMA problem behaviors is similar to the previous application for DA behavior problems. If the client goes without engaging in the target problem behavior for a designated period of time, the delivery of the desired reinforcing event occurs. The occurrence of the target behavior only results in the postponement of the reinforcer, in that the DRO interval is extended. For example, if a DRO interval is set at 4 minutes, the delivery of the reinforcer is contingent on the client not performing the target behavior for that period of time. The client can engage in a variety of other behaviors, but the functional reinforcer is only conditional upon the absence of the target behavior during the 4-minute DRO interval. However, if the behavior does occur within the 4-minute period, the DRO interval is reset for the full time period contingent upon the occurrence. The following examples illustrate this dual contingency.

*Waiting to Get New Clothes.* Omission training can be added as a component to a requesting option for socially mediated access problem behaviors. A previous example involved a client who would rip his clothes off to get staff to bring him new clothes. How would omission training be used to decrease the clothes ripping behavior? Perhaps the behavior analyst might consider building in a certain amount of time to elapse without the target behavior occurring following a request for a change of clothing. Initially, the length of the DRO interval would be small to promote success in the beginning of the program. The DRO interval would be gradually increased once the client has learned to tolerate the nonpreferred clothes for some small period of time. Further, ripping his nonpreferred clothes during the DRO interval would result in a resetting of the DRO interval back to zero. Remember, extinction of the previously reinforced response has to occur. When the DRO interval elapses, the client would be allowed to request, in whatever manner, more preferred clothes. In this gradual progressive manner, the client is being taught how to delay gratification for longer periods of time.

**MAINTAINING CONTINGENCY FOR TARGET BEHAVIOR: 2.3 SMA: TANGIBLE REINFORCER, FOOD ITEM**

**Contingency Plan for Target Behavior**

If the client rips his clothes, he will not be given preferred clothes. Further, the DRO interval is reset. If he engages in a tantrum subsequent to not getting new clothes, the DRO interval is reset after the tantrum behavior has subsided.

**Contingency Plan for Replacement Behavior**

If the student signs "shirt please," a wait interval (DRO) is designated. Following the lapse of the designated DRO interval, he will receive the desired clothing item. The DRO period should be short in the beginning (e.g., 2 minutes). It can be progressively lengthened with success.

*Get to the Student Quicker.* What about the student who bangs her desk to get the teacher to come over to her when she needs help (see "I want your attention, now!")? This scenario from the prior chapter found that the behavioral function of this target behavior was a quicker access to teacher help and attention. When this student wanted the teacher to come over to her, raising her hand was not as effective or efficient as banging on the desk. Banging on the desk produced faster results. Hence, that form of behavior was strengthened under the conditions of wanting teacher attention and the teacher being with other students.

Of course, waiting and raising one's hand appropriately are the alternate replacement behaviors that are desirable. But as long as banging the desk produces attention quicker, the alternate behaviors do not have a chance of competing with this behavior. Hence, a DRO would provide a consequence to the target behavior that further disables its ability to access the positive reinforcer. The rearranged contingencies should be as shown in the following box.

**MAINTAINING CONTINGENCY FOR TARGET BEHAVIOR: 2.1 SMA: ADULT ATTENTION, TEACHER HELP**

**Contingency Plan for Target Behavior**

If the student bangs on desk, there is a delay in teacher attention for 3 more minutes with each incident.

**Contingency Plan for Replacement Behavior**

If the student raises her hand (request for help) and waits up to 30 seconds, the teacher will come over and provide help. The wait period can be progressively extended with repeated success at prior wait periods (however, the DRO interval for the target behavior should also be proportionally lengthened).

*How Long Should the DRO Interval Be?* Unfortunately, in some cases, an interval length for the DRO is not determined by baseline data. Rather, the naive program designer may arbitrarily set the DRO interval at some value he perceives as fair, such as 5 minutes. This arbitrary decision can often lead to program failure. The DRO interval should be set as a function of the baseline data. The baseline data collected should allow for the user to determine the average interval of nonoccurrence of the target behavior.

*TABLE 4.9* ■ **FOUR SESSIONS OF DATA**

| Date | Frequency of Target Behavior | Duration of Data Session (in minutes) | Average Nonoccurrence Interval Length (in minutes) |
|------|------|------|------|
| 11/1 | 5 | 50 | 10 |
| 11/1 | 8 | 48 | 6 |
| 11/2 | 10 | 50 | 5 |
| 11/3 | 10 | 30 | 3 |

This can be achieved simply by dividing the length of the data collection session by the frequency of target behavior. Table 4.9 provides this analysis for four sessions of data collection.

One can see that the average nonoccurrence interval ranged from a low of 3 minutes to a high of 10 minutes (best session). Therefore, selecting a DRO interval of 20 minutes would probably result in the student not earning the desired reinforcer very often (or not at all). Setting it at 1 minute would be comparatively easy. Setting it at 5 minutes would be reasonable. If this data was not available, an arbitrary selection might be 20 minutes or more. Setting it at 20 minutes would probably result in continued failure. Hence, the client rarely, if ever, earns reinforcement. She is then forced to go back to the target behavior to access reinforcement, or some other behavior that is equally unacceptable.

## Premack Contingency Option

In this option, the desired reinforcer is produced following the client's successful compliance to a designated regimen of tasks or demands. In a school setting, getting free time would be contingent on performing a certain number of tasks. During free time, the student would be allowed to access desired events and activities.

*Lays Potato Chips: Bet You Can't Have Just One.* As you will recall, the client with schizophrenia in a day treatment program engages in property destruction to get another bag of potato chips. Such behavior is functional in that subsequent to the programmed time out for this behavior, she is sometimes given another bag of chips. Although such behavior does not result in a second bag of chips every time, it is more successful in getting seconds than simply asking staff. Obviously, engaging in property destructive behaviors needs to be seriously weakened in its ability to get potato chips. However, simply programming extinction for such behaviors may make the client engage in other more inappropriate behaviors that access this reinforcer. If left to chance, behaviors that may naturally develop may be as bad (or worse) than property destruction, such as self-abuse and aggression to others. Selecting an acceptable replacement behavior and training the staff to reinforce this behavior with extra chips is essential.

This case poses a significant problem. Her desire for more potato chips is after she has already had a bag. One could just reinforce her request for an additional bag of chips. However, such a contingency may lead to increased unacceptable levels of eating potato chips. She may satiate at six bags per mealtime! Simply reinforcing requesting behavior is often not a practical plan with food items.

However, requiring her to perform certain tasks to get another quarter bag of chips may prove useful. She would be required to complete three tasks and then be allowed to request chips. What if she wants more? She would be required to perform another six tasks before being allowed to mand for chips successfully. In these types of plans increasing the performance requirement with each delivery makes the client want the chips less and less.

### MAINTAINING CONTINGENCY FOR TARGET BEHAVIOR: 2.3 SMA: TANGIBLE REINFORCER, FOOD ITEM

#### Contingency Plan for Target Behavior

If the client engages in property destructive behavior, she will not be given more potato chips following the planned time out. Rather, following the time out, she is given the opportunity to perform the following replacement behavior. Also, a chain interruption procedure should be in place for property destructive behavior, followed by removal from the area to a time out.

#### Contingency Plan for Replacement Behavior

If the student requests more chips, she can complete three task demands, and then she earns a quarter bag of chips. She can repeat this until one additional bag is consumed. The number of tasks required to earn chips can be progressively increased by three tasks with each new request.

*Why Does the Premack Contingency Work With SMA Diagnoses?* The Premack principle designates a relationship between a high-probability behavior and a low probability behavior. In using the specific reinforcer maintaining the SMA problem behavior as the requirement for the Premack contingency, one can increase the probability of that set of behaviors as the replacement behavior. But what is the point of the arbitrary selection of tasks as the replacement behavior?

It is often the case that the social environment has made it too easy for some children or clients to get certain events or reinforcers. Therefore, access of such events occurs at unreasonable levels. To want someone's attention is not a sin, but it surely is tough to accommodate when it is demanded every few minutes. Although this may be an acceptable state of affairs for infants, as children get older they have to be weaned off of such frequent and lengthy attention from their parent. Unfortunately, some children do not undergo such conditioning and learn to engage in disruptive and disastrous behaviors to continually access attention or preferred items or activities.

To reduce the client's constant desire for a given reinforcer, a Premack contingency is well suited. Requiring the performance of a less preferred event as a condition for access to reinforcement is a strategy that will eventually wean them off of frequent access. I have viewed several clinical applications of the Premack contingency that resulted in the client not requesting the event as often to access reinforcement. Further, the problem behavior also is no longer occurring.

Table 4.10 contrasts four replacement behavior options for self-injurious behavior involving a socially mediated access function, 2.3 SMA: tangible reinforcer of food.

The self-injurious behavior (SIB) of a child accesses food under conditions when the individual is hungry. Teaching appropriate requests to get a variety of food items from adults or others in the environment is a behavior that could replace the SIB in this case. A second option would be to build the chain of direct access behaviors, for example,

**TABLE 4.10 ■ CONTRASTING REPLACEMENT BEHAVIOR OPTIONS FOR A 2.3 SMA DIAGNOSIS**

| | |
|---|---|
| Requesting behavior option | Client signs/says/points to picture icon requesting food |
| Alternate form reinforcement | Client gets food item and prepares it to eat |
| Omission training | Client goes without engaging in self-injury for some period of time and then is allowed to request food |
| Premack contingency | Client performs designated number of tasks and then is allowed to access food item (possibly after a request has also occurred) |

going to the refrigerator, selecting an item, and eating it. Skills in preparing her own foods would also be appropriate here.

A third option is omission training. The client would have to go a period of time without self-injury before a request for food is honored. Of course, self-injury does not access food as was previously the case. Finally, a Premack contingency option would require the client to perform several tasks before a request for food is reinforced. The latter two strategies are useful in gradually weaning the client off her frequent need for such reinforcers.

## REPLACEMENT BEHAVIOR OPTIONS FOR DE PROBLEM BEHAVIORS

There are four replacement behavior options when treating a problem behavior that is maintained by direct escape of negative reinforcement. A chain interruption procedure (delineated in a prior section of this chapter) is necessary when the direct escape problem behavior is about to occur or is in the process of escaping. Chain interruption would involve stopping the child or client from directly escaping the aversive condition or stimulus. If chain interruption is not used, it is unlikely that a designated alternate escape behavior will be able to compete with the problem behavior's ability to effectively and efficiently terminate the aversive event.

*Alternate direct escape form:* Identify an alternate acceptable behavior that also produces escape from the aversive situation. Such a behavior should not be inappropriate or dangerous but does directly and immediately produce escape from the aversive condition in a more socially desirable manner.

*Escape mand (protest or negotiation behavior):* The protesting or negotiating response is mediated by teacher, staff, or others by their removing or postponing the aversive condition from the client or removing the client from the aversive condition.

*Tolerance training option (DNRO or differential negative reinforcement of other behaviors):* Identify a length of time that you want the individual not to perform the behavior, that is, he waits appropriately to be removed from the aversive event. The nonoccurrence of the target behavior for the DNRO interval period provides for the child or client to escape or avoid the aversive event (either by request or by direction of staff).

*Premack Contingency option (lower probability behaviors as the contingency producing escape).* Identify a regimen of tasks that, when completed, allows the client to escape the aversive condition or situation (Premack Principle utilized in an escape fashion).

### Alternate Direct Escape Form

In some cases, a more acceptable alternate form of escape behavior can be identified and developed. Such a behavior must be just as capable of producing escape from the aversive situation as the target problem behavior. This is the same principle that was used for direct access problems except that the alternate form now produces direct escape. Many problem behaviors with young children may fall into this category. For example, spitting food out is unacceptable, yet everyone occasionally has food in their mouth that they find extremely distasteful. There are acceptable and unacceptable ways to remove food from your mouth. The acceptable behavior is for the child to use a napkin or go to the bathroom and spit out the food (see Table 4.11).

*TABLE 4.11* ■ **REPLACEMENT BEHAVIOR—MORE ACCEPTABLE FORM MAINTAINED BY NEGATIVE REINFORCEMENT**

| Reinforcer | Undesired Form | Desired Form |
| --- | --- | --- |
| Removing unpleasant taste in mouth | Spits out food (wherever) | Spits out food into napkin/hand, throws in wastebasket |

*Night Waking Problems.* Some children have problems at night time sleeping by themselves in a dark room. They often wake up and go into their parents' bed. This pattern then becomes another problem, especially when it occurs frequently. The behavior of getting into the parents' bed is directly reinforced by the termination of an aversive event, that is, being alone in the bed at night when it is dark. If the aversive event is being in the dark at night, perhaps some other alternate behavior that eliminates that condition might be feasible. Teaching the child to turn on the light whenever he or she wakes up would be an alternate replacement behavior. If darkness is the only aversive event, turning on the light would remove the aversive event without getting into the parents' bed. However, if getting into the parents' bed is also a function of some positive reinforcers, other contingency arrangements would be needed.

*Nude Clients.* This replacement behavior option can apply to clients who frequently engage in ripping or tearing their clothes off. If such behavior is maintained by the direct removal of nonpreferred clothing, simply allowing them to change clothes or select their own clothing would do the trick! Of course, if such a behavior is maintained by social attention this strategy would be ineffective in reducing the rate of clothes ripping. However, if the clothes the client is currently wearing are less desired, or they are used to some other fabric (e.g., cotton, silk, etc.), this direct escape alternative form is well suited.

If the client is not capable of self-dressing, then this behavior may have to be taught (i.e., prompted and shaped) in order for it to be a useful replacement behavior. Other clients may not have previously changed clothes spontaneously because such behavior was (or would be) thwarted or punished by staff. Increasing their independent changing of clothes may just require a simple differential reinforcement plan—let them do it in a private area.

---

### MAINTAINING CONTINGENCY FOR TARGET BEHAVIOR: 3.1 DE: DIRECT ESCAPE, NONPREFERRED CLOTHES

#### Contingency Plan for Target Behavior

If the student engages in clothes ripping or tearing behavior, a chain interruption procedure will be used. The client will then be required to perform three nonpreferred tasks under staff supervision (reverse Premack).

#### Contingency Plan for Replacement Behavior

If the student chooses his own clothes from a sample of acceptable clothing, he will be allowed to wear it. If he changes his clothes without engaging in any problem behavior he will be allowed to wear those clothes. He can change no more than three times in a given time period each day.

---

### Escape Mand

The client's ability to terminate or avoid an undesired social or instructional condition can also be enhanced by developing two types of communicative skills: verbal protests and negotiating skills. Saying in a calm voice "I prefer not to do that" instead of screaming to avoid an aversive task is certainly more preferable from the standpoint of the caregiver or staff. However, if the client is incapable of appropriate protesting behavior, then other forms of protest occur under conditions where escape behavior is likely. Unfortunately, these alternatives are often undesirable from the standpoint of the staff, parent, or teacher.

Appropriate protesting skills are often not in the repertoire of many clients who have severe skill deficits.

In some cases protesting skills are not viable. For example, when the client or student is required to complete some assigned task that is essential for the client's well-being, protesting the task probably should not lead to termination of the request. However, negotiation skills may be appropriate for this circumstance and should be developed. Negotiating for a smaller amount of an assigned task or for a shorter period of time to engage in the activity can often be successful and produces escape earlier than if negotiation had not been undertaken. Some examples might help illustrate this replacement behavior option.

*How About Only Five Pages Please?* Suppose an FBA reveals that a student engages in a variety of procrastination behaviors (goes to bathroom, lies down, watches TV) when the homework assignment is relatively lengthy. Simply allowing her to protest doing any homework would not be feasible. However, reducing the number of pages to read before a short break would seem to be more reasonable. Perhaps the student can be taught to negotiate with her parent the number of pages she must read before she takes a break. If the student commits to following through, the parent agrees to allow a short break following completion of the agreed upon task.

## MAINTAINING CONTINGENCY FOR TARGET BEHAVIOR: 3.1 DE: DIRECT ESCAPE, SCHOOL HOMEWORK ASSIGNMENTS

### Contingency Plan for Target Behavior

If the student engages in direct avoidance of doing homework at the scheduled time, a chain interruption procedure will be used that involves terminating any event the client is currently engaged in immediately, other than sitting at the table with books out.

### Contingency Plan for Replacement Behavior

If the student, while at the table, negotiates a certain amount of the homework assignment to be done prior to taking a break, the parent authorizes such a plan and provides a break if the agreement is upheld.

In developing appropriate forms of negotiation, the verbal form should contain elements of a request instead of a refusal. For example, "How about if I—," is an appropriate form of verbal behavior. In contrast, "I won't do this" is likely to result in lack of results from the staff person, teacher, or parent. Certainly negotiating the time or amount of a task is a much better alternative to the previous manner of dealing with the situation, that is, doing all kinds of things to avoid sitting at the table and studying.

*Can I Do My Household Task at 4 P.M.?* With regard to household tasks that people find unpleasant, negotiating the time at which they will be completed may be the solution for some clients. With some clients, staff have to constantly remind them to complete their chores. Such reminders and prompts often end in arguing, yelling, and sometimes worse, behavioral problems on the part of the client. Negotiating with the client a time in which a task will be completed allows the individual to postpone the aversive event until a time when other more preferred activities are not interrupted. This strategy *would not be* useful for some clients who detest ever doing the task or chore. The selection of a replacement behavior for them would require a different option, such as the Premack contingency.

---

## MAINTAINING CONTINGENCY FOR TARGET BEHAVIOR: 3.2 DE: DIRECT ESCAPE, LENGTHY CHORE

### Contingency Plan for Target Behavior

If the client engages in direct avoidance of doing a chore, without negotiating an agreed upon time, a chain interruption procedure will be used. This procedure involves immediately terminating whatever the client is currently engaged in and requiring him to perform the chore immediately. Further, the ability to negotiate the time the task is to be done the next day is removed as a consequence, and the task will be initiated immediately after school.

### Contingency Plan for Replacement Behavior

If the client negotiates a certain time when he will initiate and complete his assigned chore, the parent authorizes such a plan and does not constantly remind the client, providing the contract is upheld (i.e., chore is completed by agreed upon time).

---

### Tolerance Training (DNRO) Option

The previous two options involve a replacement behavior that allows the child or client to escape or certainly ameliorate an aversive condition. However, in many circumstances, one may not simply be able to opt out of a social or instructional situation. For example, if an elementary grade student did not want to do go to large assemblies, it is unacceptable to simply opt out. However, keeping him there for over 15 minutes results in frequent disruptive behavior until he is removed for being too disruptive. Therefore, a more reasonable option may be to allow the child to leave the assembly when he goes without the target behavior for a reasonably shorter period of time. The child would have to tolerate the assembly for a designated period of time before being allowed to opt out. For example, if the child stays in the assembly for at least 10 minutes without engaging in the target behaviors, he could then leave.

In tolerance training, you identify a length of time for the nonoccurrence of behavior (DNRO interval). When this criterion is met, you terminate the child or client's involvement in the social or instructional situation. In this manner, you are developing an individual's tolerance for a nonpreferred event. With success at lower DNRO intervals, you can progressively increase the DNRO interval required to escape, thus increasing the individual's tolerance to aversive events of some duration.

*I Need a Break.* Remember the student with severe disabilities who lays her head on the table when asked to complete lengthy tasks? The use of tolerance training could provide such a reinforcer contingent on not doing such a behavior for a designated period of time. Let us say that the teacher has collected baseline data. The average length of time this child would go before putting her head on the table was 7 minutes (range of 3–10 minutes). With this baseline data, one can be guided to select a reasonable initial standard for reinforcement. The program designed thereby sets the DNRO interval at 6 minutes. If she does not lay her head down on the table for 6 minutes, she earns the right to do so for a 6-minute period and take a break. If she engages in the behavior prior to the timer elapsing, a chain interruption strategy is used. The teacher will immediately prompt her to pick her head back up. Additionally, the teacher will reset the DNRO interval length. Of course, with success, the DNRO interval could be progressively increased. Fill in the following box.

**MAINTAINING CONTINGENCY FOR TARGET BEHAVIOR**

**Contingency Plan for Target Behavior**

**Contingency Plan for Replacement Behavior**

## Premack Principle (Escape)

Again, the Premack contingency can be utilized, but under this option the completion of a designated number of tasks results in escape and avoidance of further tasks for some period of time. Where can a Premack contingency be useful? Some adult clients with disabilities are either at an employment setting or working in a site that is getting them ready for employment. In some of these cases, the actual task or job is not the problem. Rather, it is the fact that the client may not be used to working for lengthy periods of time without a break. The client's inability to work for a designated period of time produces an uncomfortable (aversive) situation for them. Hence, they engage in behaviors that are aimed at getting away from the tasks, that is, escape behaviors. If such behaviors occur often enough or are of a severe or dangerous nature, their placement is jeopardized.

The Premack contingency would progressively build this client's stamina for working continuously, possibly in a noncompetitive site beforehand. Initially, the break may need to come sooner (i.e., shorter number of tasks required to complete) than the criterion level (e.g., 2 hours). Setting up a Premack contingency would be effective in eventually reducing the number of behavior problems that previously terminated the work task directly, such as leaving the area.

A note of caution on the use of the Premack Principle for escape-motivated problem behaviors. Rearrangement of contingencies may not be the sole solution to problems that occur during certain academic tasks. In many cases, children are very inept at performing the assigned tasks. Simply arranging a contingency is not the answer. They will continue to find such tasks aversive as long as their competence in completing such tasks is lacking. It is not the purpose of this manual to go into great detail on instructional procedures; however, do realize that good teaching procedures are usually at the heart of problems that occur with instructional tasks that are relatively difficult for the child.

*Psychotic Student?* A junior high school–aged student in a residential and day treatment program for severe emotionally disturbed children engaged in a number of disruptive (termed *psychotic* by some staff) behaviors. During baseline, his work production on assignments was extremely low. Off-task behavior was ignored; this student frequently was allowed to avoid completing any work. An FBA pointed to such behaviors as effective in escape and avoidance of his engagement of academic tasks.

The rearranged contingencies I (E.C.) set up were the following. In order to leave his seat and engage in free time activities, this student was required to complete a minimal amount of math work in one period, a minimal amount of reading in another period, and a minimal amount of writing in another period. Failure to do so resulted in his inability to get out of his seat to go "play." Failure to complete any assigned work at school resulted in the work being sent home and being finished prior to any TV time (this contingency was invoked several times). With success the amount of material was increased progressively in all three periods.

*I Need a Break.* A Premack contingency can also be used with the student who lays her head on the table. The contingency for laying her head on the table would still involve chain interruption. In addition to being required to pick her head up, she would also have to begin the designated number of tasks all over again. For example, if she was required to perform five tasks to earn a break, and she engaged in the target behavior after three tasks were accomplished, she would have an additional five tasks to complete in order to get a break (Reverse Premack Principle). If she completes five tasks in a row without putting her head down, she would be authorized to take a 6-minute break where she could put her head down. Putting her head down on the table unauthorized is quickly interrupted and leads to a further postponement of break time.

Note that with this dual contingency, completing five tasks "right off the bat" is far more efficient in getting an authorized substantial break than simply taking it unauthorized. The contingencies are stacked in favor of completing one's work without taking an unauthorized break. Taking a break only leads to a postponement of the substantial break period. With success, the number of tasks required for a break could be progressively increased. Fill in the following box.

---

**MAINTAINING CONTINGENCY FOR TARGET BEHAVIOR**

**Contingency Plan for Target Behavior**

**Contingency Plan for Replacement Behavior**

---

There are several considerations when utilizing the Premack option for escape-motivated behaviors. Once the student has finished the assigned tasks, he or she gets free time for a designated period of time. It is unacceptable for the teacher or staff to provide additional tasks in this break period. Second, one needs to make certain that the student is capable of performing the assigned tasks. Third, start with a small number of tasks initially to ensure you don't burn out the student before he or she is able to finish those tasks.

## REPLACEMENT BEHAVIOR OPTIONS FOR SME PROBLEM BEHAVIORS

There are three replacement behavior options when treating a problem behavior that is maintained by socially mediated escape of negative reinforcement. Extinction of the target problem behavior is essential. The termination of the aversive event by staff, teachers, parent, or care providers must not occur when the target behavior is exhibited. If the schedule of negative reinforcement of the target behavior is not weakened, the replacement behavior will probably not be able to compete with the target behavior under motivational conditions that give rise to escape or avoidance behavior.

*Alternate direct escape form:* Identify an alternate acceptable behavior that also produces escape from the aversive situation. Such a behavior should not be inappropriate or dangerous but does directly and immediately produce escape from the aversive condition in a more socially desirable manner.

*Escape mand (protest or negotiation behavior):* The protesting or negotiating response is mediated by teacher, staff, or others by their removing or postponing the aversive condition from the client or removing the client or child from the aversive condition.

*Tolerance Training option (DNRO, or differential negative reinforcement of all other behaviors):* Identify a length of time that you want the individual not to perform the behavior. The nonoccurrence of the target behavior for a set time period provides escape or avoidance of the aversive event (either by request or by direction of staff).

*Premack Contingency option (lower probability behaviors as the contingency for escape from the negative reinforcer).* Identify a regimen of tasks that, when completed, allows the client to escape the aversive condition or situation (Premack Principle utilized in an escape fashion).

## Extinction Burst for SME Problem Behaviors

How resistant to extinction will a given target problem behavior be? In applied settings, an inherent requirement of the professional behavior analyst is to consider the possibility that the target problem behavior may occur in bursts when an extinction condition is imposed. Problem behavior under intermittent schedules of escape that serves an SME function can pose a tremendous problem for implementation of a treatment plan requiring an extinction condition. The durability of target behavior under a trigger analysis can be used to assess possible extinction burst effects with escape maintained behavior (Rolider, 2003).

In this assessment method, the therapist presents the aversive condition for a period of time in a brief session. In some cases, it might be necessary for the staff person who has stimulus control over the behavior to be involved in the session, especially if the problem behavior has not generalized to different people. During the session, the aversive condition is maintained while the rate and duration of the problem behavior is recorded. For example, if a client hits himself when he is asked to put his clothes in the hamper, the session would be conducted by providing this request. If necessary, the request could be re-presented on a fixed time schedule for the length of the session. Assessment sessions with SME problem behaviors would seem to require less time, especially if the behavior occurs readily when the MO is presented. The session would end with the final withdrawal of the request and a change to another activity.

Specify a uniform limited time for each assessment session, such as, 2, 5, 10, or 15 minutes. The length of time should be in relation to the probable frequency of behavior. Remember, with extinction during these sessions, one may get an exacerbation of the rate and intensity of the problem behavior, as well as possible other disruptive behaviors. Therefore, for high frequency behaviors, a short time period should provide sufficient evidence of the problem's initial operant level under extinction. If necessary, a control condition could be deployed, which would be the absence of the aversive event.

Here is an example of a trigger analysis of a possible extinction burst for an SME problem. A hypothetical inpatient adult in a large institution for developmental disabilities engages in property destruction about three to four times a month. He will throw chairs and objects and kick furniture during these tirades. The board-certified behavior analyst Ms. Carr believes that such behavior is functional under conditions of lengthy tasks or chores. Prior to the destructive behavior he will chant repeatedly about his dislike of certain chores assigned to him during the day. He will state, "I cannot do it! I cannot do it." This verbal behavior (most likely a mand) seems to be part of the behavioral chain that involves property destruction at the end of the tirade (also a mand). Ms. Carr decides to deploy the trigger analysis assessment method with this chanting behavior. She realizes that conducting a rate analysis of property destruction is not suitable given the disruptive nature of this behavior to the environment. Therefore, the session will be terminated if he throws chairs or objects or becomes aggressive to the staff person conducting the session. The session will also be terminated if he kicks furniture. Demands to engage in some chore will be presented each minute on a fixed time schedule (1 minute). Three sessions of hypothetical data are delineated in Table 4.12.

For SMA problem behaviors, the deprivation condition hypothesized to be the relevant MO for the problem behavior is produced. The time before the assessment session would deprive the event or item from the client to ensure the MO is in effect. If this pre-session deprivation is insufficient to create a strong MO, then it might be necessary to provide the item or activity at the onset of the session and then abruptly remove it. The occurrence of the target behavior during this assessment *should not* result in the delivery of the reinforcer.

Let's use a hypothetical child with autism to illustrate this analysis for SMA problems. You observe that this child screams at his mother to turn on the TV cartoon channel in the morning. You see that extinction is the functional approach for solving this problem, but you are unsure how long this child might scream if extinction will be deployed. You determine that a lengthy extinction burst might not result in treatment fidelity and want to discern if extinction is an ecologically feasible procedure to deploy. To obtain this data, the therapist asks the mom to delay turning on the TV for 5 minutes when the child sits down on the couch to watch TV. An interval recording method is selected to quantify the screaming behavior.

---

### PROTOCOL FOR TRIGGER ANALYSIS SESSION

*Target behavior:* Screaming
*MO-EO:* Withholding of favorite TV channel
*Trigger analysis:* Removal of TV for a 5-minute period in the beginning of the morning.
*Method of Measurement:* 10-second interval recording system, partial interval method of scoring within intervals
*Protocol for implementing test session:* When it is time for the child's favorite cartoon to come on, and he is sitting on the couch waiting for you to turn on the TV, delay turning on the TV for 5 minutes. You should use an oven timer to monitor the length of time. Do not turn on the TV during this time. Every 10 seconds, indicate on the data sheet whether the child screamed in a given interval by marking an x next to that designated interval. If the child begins engaging in destructive behaviors, note these and end the session, and mark the interval where that occurred. The percentage of occurrence would only be computed on the intervals up to that point.
*Control Sessions:* Deprivation of item or event is not conducted, session length matched to trigger analysis (absence of MO-EO)

---

*TABLE 4.12* ■ **THREE SESSIONS OF HYPOTHETICAL DATA**

| Session | Length of Session (minutes) | Number of Chants per Minute | Session Stopped? When? |
|---------|------------------------------|------------------------------|------------------------|
| 3/10 | 3 | 3 | No |
| 3/10 | 2 | 4 | Yes, after second demand |
| 3/10 | 3 | 7 total | Yes, within 20 seconds |

You obtain data across a 5-day period for each of the two conditions: test and control. The following percentage of occurrence of screaming (10-second intervals partial interval recording system) was obtained for the trigger analysis when the mom delayed the TV time by 5 minutes for the five days: 100, 83, 100, 100, 83. The last session was stopped early due to destructive behavior. When the TV was not withheld the percentage of intervals where the child screamed was zero percentage. Based on this data, you surmise that a functional approach needs to consider the aversive condition that may arise with extinction imposed for screaming behavior.

*Use in Evaluating Treatment Effects.* This method of assessment can also be valuable in evaluating functional treatment effects. Again the trigger analysis identifies the rate of the problem behavior, given the presence of the relevant MO and extinction for the target behavior. Collecting data using this assessment method can be particularly apt if it is difficult for staff to collect continuous data on the target behavior and alternate replacement behavior. The same procedural elements of the trigger analysis are deployed, except that the display of the replacement behavior identified in the treatment program would result in the removal of the aversive event (unpleasant social situation, lengthy task or chore, aversive physical stimulus, or difficult task or chore). This can provide excellent data in determining whether the intervention program has been successful in ameliorating the problem behavior while increasing the probability of the replacement behavior under the MO.

## Alternate Direct Escape Form

This option can also be applied for escape behaviors that are socially mediated (i.e., SME). The client or child is taught how to perform a series of acceptable behaviors that result in direct termination of the aversive events (Table 4.13).

The following examples might help illustrate this replacement behavior option.

*Nude Clients.* How would this replacement behavior option apply to a client who engages in tantrum behavior until staff intervene? Simply allowing him to change clothes or select his own clothing would do the trick! If the clothes the client is currently wearing are clothes that are less desired, or he is used to some other fabric (e.g., cotton, silk, etc.), this direct escape alternative form is well suited.

If the client is not capable of selecting clothes or self-dressing, then this behavior may have to be taught (i.e., prompted and shaped) in order for it to be a useful replacement behavior. In some cases the chain of behaviors is already acquired but does not currently occur under the motivating operation. These clients do not spontaneously change clothes when uncomfortable because such a chain of behavior was (or would be) thwarted or punished by staff. Increasing their independent changing of clothes may just require a simple differential reinforcement plan, that is, let them do it in a private area. Staff have to be directed to allow such behavior when it occurs.

*TABLE 4.13* ■ **REPLACEMENT BEHAVIOR—MORE ACCEPTABLE FORM MAINTAINED BY NEGATIVE REINFORCEMENT**

| Reinforcer | Undesired Form | Desired Form |
| --- | --- | --- |
| Terminating unpleasant social Interaction | Yells and screams until staff intervene | Leaves area |

## MAINTAINING CONTINGENCY FOR TARGET BEHAVIOR: 4.4 SME: SOCIALLY MEDIATED ESCAPE, AVERSIVE STIMULUS

### Contingency Plan for Target Behavior

If the student engages in tantrum behavior, he will not receive new clothes. Rather, after a short period of time following cessation of tantrum, he will be prompted to go and select new clothes and put them on. Over time, prompts for the sequence of behaviors needed to produce this outcome will be faded until he performs this independently under the conditions of wanting new clothes to wear.

### Contingency Plan for Replacement Behavior

If he changes his clothes without engaging in any problem behavior he will be allowed to wear those clothes. He can change no more than three times in a given time period each day.

### Escape Mand (Protest or Negotiation Behavior)

This option can also be applied for escape behaviors that are socially mediated (i.e., SME). Again, two types of acceptable communicative responses to deal with aversive social situations are protesting behaviors and negotiating skills. The following examples might help illustrate this replacement behavior option.

*"I'm Bored"*. This child had learned how to get a 5-minute break by throwing things. Baseline data reveals that she will engage in such property destructive behaviors once or twice in a half day. How could the teacher make throwing things ineffectual while reinforcing an alternate more appropriate behavior? Suppose the student could request a 5-minute recess? Would that impact the student's frequency of throwing things?

Here are the basics of the contingencies. In any given morning, this student is given only two recess cards that she can use. The same applies for afternoons. Whenever she needs to have a break, she can simply pull out one of her two cards, give it to the teacher, and set the timer for 5 minutes. Subsequently, after the break she returns to work. If she goes without a tantrum for a morning or afternoon period and also uses only two or fewer cards per morning, she earns five points. The following chart depicts the contingencies for target and replacement behavior.

## MAINTAINING CONTINGENCY FOR TARGET BEHAVIOR: 4.1 SME: SOCIALLY MEDIATED ESCAPE, SCHOOL ASSIGNMENTS

### Contingency Plan for Target Behavior

If the student engages in tantrum and property destructive behavior, any break cards left are immediately removed for the remainder of the morning or afternoon session. If she cannot be stopped from continuing to throw materials, she will be removed from the area for the protection of other students and placed in time out until she calms down. Following time out, she is told that she has extra work to do during recess at the principal's office area (Reverse Premack Principle). Further, she does not earn five points and has to return to the assignment during the class period.

### Contingency Plan for Replacement Behavior

If the student uses a recess card, she can take a 5-minute recess break. Any period (morning or afternoon) when the student does not go over her recess cards and has no tantrums, she earns five points toward a selected Friday video at her parents' home that evening. She has to earn 30 points by Friday afternoon in order to earn the Friday video (i.e., no more than two opportunities where she did not earn points).

*Enough Is Enough.* The same methodology can be used for students with severe disabilities when problem behavior is maintained by socially mediated escape of tasks. This student hits herself in the head and face when she is pressed to continue the task (4.2 SME: lengthy task, chore, or assignment). In the past, when she engaged in this behavior, she was then moved to another activity, whereupon such self-injury ceases. If you were this child, what would you do the next time you felt you did enough work on a particular task or activity and wanted to change activities? Under the current social arrangement, you would continue hitting yourself! The following chart illustrates how self-injury can be disabled as a functional behavior while enabling protesting as functional in the same circumstance.

---

## MAINTAINING CONTINGENCY FOR TARGET BEHAVIOR: 4.2 SME: SOCIALLY MEDIATED ESCAPE, LENGTHY TASK/ACTIVITY

### Contingency Plan for Target Behavior

If the student engages in self-injury the current activity is maintained. Staff would prompt the student to perform the communicative replacement behavior.

### Contingency Plan for Replacement Behavior

If the student performs the protest behavior, the staff change the activity. Such behavior may have to be prompted in the beginning prior to the self-injury for it to occur in the presence of the student's motivational condition to escape the activity. This is assuming that, in most cases, the replacement behavior is not currently in the repertoire of the student (see inept repertoire in next section).

---

Table 4.14 depicts how protesting behavior can function as an effective replacement behavior with an SME problem behavior. The four different subcategories of socially mediated escape are used to illustrate how protesting behavior can produce an escape of the relevant aversive event.

## Tolerance Training Option

In many circumstances, protesting an instructional task or required event is not feasible. For example, if an elementary grade student does not want to do math today, it is unacceptable

---

*TABLE 4.14* ■ **PROTESTING BEHAVIORS ACROSS DIFFERENT SME CATEGORIES**

**Target behavior: Self-injury**
**Hypothesized Maintaining Contingency: 4.1 SME, 4.2 SME, 4.3 SME, and 4.4 SME**

| | |
|---|---|
| 4.1 SME: unpleasant social situation—another student tantrums in a class for students with autism | Student raises hand when he feels uncomfortable, and staff remove him from the area where all the screaming is going on. |
| 4.2 SME: lengthy task—student is in a 30-minute storytime | Student signs "enough," and staff take him out of the story time and have him engage in play skills training. |
| 4.3 SME: difficult task—student is presented with a vocal language task in which he is only capable of making four sounds | Student signs "help," and the teacher helps him sign the word instead of pressing him for vocal response. (Note: in this case the Premack option is better suited.) |
| 4.4 SME: aversive stimulus— student is given a peanut butter sandwich that has meat on it | Student raises hand to alert teacher of need to communicate, points to the peanut butter sandwich, and signs "No." Teacher then removes sandwich and, upon inspection, sees the problem. |

to simply opt out. To allow the child to escape whenever she says "I don't feel like doing this today, sorry, it is not in the cards" would not be in the child's long-term best interest. Although such a strategy may significantly reduce the level of problem behaviors in math period for this child, it would affect the child's progress on math content. Therefore, protesting is not always an acceptable alternate replacement behavior.

For these circumstances there is a better option. In tolerance training, the task is terminated when a certain time interval passes in which no target behaviors occur. Therefore, escape from the aversive condition is conditional upon "not doing the behavior" for some designated period of time. To use tolerance training, identify a reasonable DNRO interval to begin the program based on baseline data. If the client is successful in not engaging in the target behavior for that period, the parent or staff allows the client to leave the activity and engage in a more preferred event.

*Out-of-Seat Behavior.* Many young children have difficulty staying in their seat for a protracted period of time. Although most of these children learn over time to tolerate sitting in a seat or desk, or sitting on a carpet square in preschool, some children do not. They frequently get up, wander around, and disrupt the learning environment. A program called Grandma's Rule for increasing in-seat behavior (Cipani, 2004, 2008) uses the basic strategy of tolerance training to progressively develop continuous in-seat behavior.

After deriving the average in-seat interval from baseline data, the DRO interval is set at the average in-seat interval. If the child does not get out of her seat once during the interval, the child earns several minutes of out-of-seat time (hence the Premack contingency). If the child gets out of her seat unauthorized during this time, the child is returned to the seat and the timer is reset for the full DRO interval. As the number of times the DNRO interval is reset decreases, the length of the DNRO interval can be progressively increased. For further information on how such a plan can be used in school and home settings, please consult the book *Classroom Management for Al Teachers: Plans for Evidence-Based Practice* (Cipani, 2008).

---

### JUST BECAUSE IT SOUNDS GOOD DOES NOT MEAN IT WILL WORK!

Curriculum modification as an antecedent positive behavioral intervention strategy is often recommended. Its indiscriminate use can have little or no effect on some target behaviors whose function is unrelated to the task or instruction. For example, if the target behavior's function is one of accessing adult attention (i.e., a diagnosis of 2.1 SMA: adult attention), then modifying the curriculum is not clinically indicated and is probably superfluous. Changing the curriculum will have an inconsequential effect on the rate of the target behavior. In contrast, modifying the curriculum is clinically indicated when the target behavior is diagnosed as 4.3 SME: if the curriculum modification removes the source of the difficulty in the current instructional material. Behavioral interventions should be prescribed as a function of the controlling variables for the particular target behavior, not haphazardly.

Tolerance training would be effective only if a child's out-of-seat behavior is the result of the lengthy condition of instruction (or being required to sit for lengthy periods). If task difficulty is the condition driving the behavior (3.3 DE: difficult tasks, chores assignments), then curriculum modification is needed in addition to tolerance training or another replacement option. The question for SME problem behaviors occurring during instruction should be "Is it too long or too difficult (or both)?"

---

*The 20-Minute Child.* This hypothetical child hits the desk to temporarily terminate the presentation of a lengthy instructional task. When this child hits the desk, the teacher deals with the problem behavior, thus temporarily terminating the instructional assignment. If an FBA reveals that this temporary halt to task engagement is maintaining the behavior (4.2 SME: task duration), then such a contingency obviously needs to be disabled, while a more appropriate behavior needs to be enabled to produce escape.

First, the teacher would no longer deal with the target behavior, thus interrupting the instructional time period. What would occur contingent on the target behavior is the resetting of the DNRO interval to the full amount. With this contingency, the target behavior no longer results in teacher mediation of temporary escape. Rather, the target behavior only serves to lengthen the instructional period. What happens when this child goes the entire interval without engaging in target behavior? The teacher would then allow him to terminate his engagement of the current task and spend a designated amount of time on a more preferred task. This plan strengthens one set of behaviors (i.e., nonoccurrence of target behavior), while weakening another behavior (target behavior) by selectively producing escape from task. Fill in the following box.

---

**MAINTAINING CONTINGENCY FOR TARGET BEHAVIOR**

**Contingency Plan for Target Behavior**


**Contingency Plan for Replacement Behavior**

---

Now fill in the box if the diagnosis was 4.3 SME: difficult task, chore, or instruction.

---

**MAINTAINING CONTINGENCY FOR TARGET BEHAVIOR**

**Contingency Plan for Target Behavior**


**Contingency Plan for Replacement Behavior**

---

*I Need a Break, My Brain Is Swelling.* How would tolerance training apply to the tantrum behavior of the mainstreamed fourth grade student? Remember, the teacher has reported that this child will frequently throw a tantrum during class assignments. He reads about three pages during a reading assignment, in approximately 4–7 minutes. He then decides to take a break and gets out some toy cars he brought from home. The teacher sees him playing and admonishes him. Subsequent to that he begins to throw a tantrum. In the following box, specify the contingencies that would be in effect for the target behavior of tantrums (4.2 SME: lengthy assignment). Keep in mind that not completing the assignment and taking his own break is intimately tied to the tantrum. You may need to convince the teacher that his engagement in relatively lengthy reading assignments may have to be progressively shaped over a period of time. No plan will take him from reading three pages in 4 minutes one day to reading for 1.5 hours continuously a week after treatment.

---

**MAINTAINING CONTINGENCY FOR TARGET BEHAVIOR**

**Contingency Plan for Target Behavior**

**Contingency Plan for Replacement Behavior**

---

### Premack Principle (Escape)

The Premack contingency can also be utilized for socially mediated escape behavior. The completion of a designated number of tasks results in escape and avoidance of further tasks or chores for some period of time. The use of a Premack contingency is well suited as a strategy for developing increased persistence at work or in school. A break from work or school assignments can be progressively developed until the persistence needed for most jobs or classrooms is achieved.

This strategy would require the client to complete a small number of designated tasks. Once these are completed to criterion, the client is allowed to take a break from work. Setting up a Premack contingency would be effective in eventually reducing the number of behavior problems that previously terminated the work task directly.

The following examples depict the use of this contingency for 4.0 SME category of problem behaviors.

*I Need a Break, My Brain Is Swelling.* How would the Premack option apply to the tantrum behavior of the mainstreamed fourth grade student? The contingencies that would be in effect for the target behavior of tantrums (4.2 SME: lengthy assignment) as well as the replacement option are delineated in the following box.

## MAINTAINING CONTINGENCY FOR TARGET BEHAVIOR: 4.2 SME: LENGTHY TASKS

### Contingency Plan for Target Behavior

Contingent upon tantrum behavior, another assignment will be added to the student's task assignment board (Reverse Premack Principle).

### Contingency Plan for Replacement Behavior

A set number of tasks/assignments is issued at the beginning of the independent seat work session. When the student completes all the tasks he earns the remainder of the time to engage in more preferred activities (listed on a menu chart). Once the period is up, the same contingencies are put in effect for the next content instructional session.

## SUMMARY

This chapter presented replacement behavior options for each of the four major categories of problem behavior. The next chapter provides a further delineation of these replacement behavior options with a clinical hypothetical example illustrating the process from functional behavioral assessment to the diagnosis of the problem behavior's function to functional treatment using the designated replacement behavior option.

# Functional Behavioral Treatment Protocols

In this chapter, the material presented in Chapter 4 is expanded to provide a treatment protocol for each replacement behavior option delineated for 2.0 SMA and 4.0 SME target behaviors. The treatment protocols for 1.0 DA and 3.0 DE are the same as the 2.0 SMA and 4.0 SME protocols, respectively, except for some minor variations in the procedures for dealing with the occurrence of the target behaviors. These variations are explicated in each replacement behavior option.

For 2.0 SMA target behaviors, the following protocols are presented in this chapter:

- Alternate Direct Access Form
- DRL Group Contingencies for Peer Attention
- Omission Training (Differential Reinforcement of Other Behaviors, or DRO)
- Noncontingent Reinforcement (NCR) with Extinction
- Premack Contingency Option
- Access Mand (Request) Option

For 4.0 SME problem behaviors, the following protocols are presented in this chapter:

- Premack Contingency Option
- Tolerance Training Option (or Differential Negative Reinforcement of All Other Behaviors)
- Escape Mand (Protest or Negotiation Behavior) Option
- Alternate Direct Escape Form
- Noncontingent Escape (NCE)

Both the 2.0 SMA and 4.0 SME sections also contain a protocol for a treatment program called *noncontingent reinforcement.* This program was not delineated in the prior chapter because it does not readily address the function of the target behavior or the development of the replacement behavior (not one specified). Rather, it works as a result of altering the motivational condition of the client in one of two ways. In the case of target behaviors maintained by positive reinforcement, the rate of the target behavior is reduced by abolishing the value of the reinforcer for the client. The specific reinforcer is presented noncontingently according to a time schedule. In the case of target behaviors maintained by negative reinforcement, the NCE program alters behavior by removing the aversive stimulus that generates escape behavior. In both cases it may also establish the conditions for extinction by disrupting the contingent pairing of the target behavior and the reinforcer.

All the protocols in this chapter, with the exception of NCR/NCE, contain a functional arrangement of treatment contingencies. The target behavior's function is disabled, while the replacement behavior's function to the relevant reinforcer is enabled.

## 2.0 SMA FUNCTIONS: ALTERNATE DIRECT ACCESS FORM

### Brief Description

In this replacement behavior option, the desired reinforcer is produced by the client engaging in a chain of behaviors that produces the item or event, independent of anyone else's assistance.

To implement a direct access replacement option program, you must determine what chain of behaviors can directly produce the reinforcing items or event. If the person can fluently perform the requisite chain of behaviors, a simple rearrangement of contingencies is required. Performance of the designated chain of behaviors is allowed to produce the reinforcer, whereas previously it was probably disabled. Concurrently, extinction of the target behavior (i.e., socially mediated) is programmed.

If the person does not currently possess the direct access behavior, the behavior must be shaped to produce an effective response (see inept repertoire diagnosis in Appendix A). In some cases, the entire chain of behaviors may have to be taught. In other cases, a few components of the chain may be lacking.

In some cases the client can perform the chain of behaviors, but not fluently (i.e., with acceptable speed and accuracy). If that is the case, fluency training is required. Once the client has acquired fluent performance of the chain of behaviors, differential reinforcement as delineated in this program is implemented. The use of differential reinforcement disables the target behavior's function, while enabling the function of the direct access behavior.

The advantage of this replacement behavior option is that it allows the client to independently obtain reinforcing items without reliance on other people or having to use communication or social skills. The direct access option develops a specific chain of behaviors that will continue to be functional for the client over time. Once these behaviors are acquired they can be utilized in other situations through the process of shaping and generalization.

### Terms

*Trigger analysis:* Setting up all the context conditions hypothesized to occasion the target behavior, and documenting the occurrence (or lack thereof) of the target behavior and the direct access replacement behavior.

### Apparatus

Data sheets—See Form 5.1, "Simple Frequency Data with Rate Formulas"
Reinforcing items or events—The specific tangible items or event that have been identified as the maintaining reinforcers. These will be made available for direct access and must be readily available without assistance from other people.

### Baseline Measurement

There are two different pieces of information you need to obtain. First, you need to determine how often the target behavior is occurring under relevant conditions. Additionally, the frequency of occurrence of the proposed direct access replacement behavior under the same conditions is needed.

The frequency measure is best suited for both these requirements. You (or the designated staff person) simply count each time the client engages in the target behavior as well as each time the client performs the direct access behavior under the same conditions (see Form 5.1). When considering this option, baseline rates for the direct access replacement behavior are typically at or near zero.

## Trigger Analysis (see Form 5.2)

1. Set up (contrive) or wait for (capture) a situation in which the person is very likely to want access to the desired item or event. You must ensure that the motivational conditions are as strong as possible. This can be contrived through temporary deprivation of the desired items.
2. Present a stimulus that signals that the item is now available to the person.
3. Observe the persons behavior, and record if the target behavior or the chain of direct access replacement behavior occurs.
4. Record the time taken to initiate the first response.
5. Record the time taken to complete the chain of behaviors and obtain reinforcement.
6. If the replacement behavior was attempted (or performed) record which steps were completed and any prompts required to facilitate the performance of the steps.
7. Record if the reinforcing item or event was provided by the staff or care provider.
8. Repeat steps 1–4 at least six more times.
9. Graph or display the data across all baseline sessions.

## Direct Access Procedures

If the baseline data indicates that the person is not performing the direct access behavior, start by teaching the behavior using discrete trials. If the baseline data indicates that they are able to perform the behavior, then skip to incidental teaching.

### Discrete Trials

1. Present a prompt for the person to perform the first step in the task.
2. Provide reinforcement contingent on completing the behavior or chain of behaviors.
3. If the person does not complete the task or engages in the target behavior, provide an additional prompt to help them complete the next step.
4. Provide reinforcement, preferably access to the reinforcing item or event you want the person to directly access with this behavior.
5. Record data.
6. On each successive trial, shape more independent responding by reducing the level of prompt provided.
7. Once the person is performing the task without the need for additional prompts, change to incidental teaching method.

### Incidental Teaching

1. Observe for conditions under which the person would usually engage in the target behavior.
2. If the person directly accesses an item or event, allow them to do so.
3. If the person does not access the item or event, provide a prompt to engage in the direct access behavior.
4. If the person does not complete the task or engages in the target behavior, do not provide access to the reinforcer (extinction), instead provide an additional prompt to help them complete the next step.

5. On each successive trial, shape more independent responding by reducing the level of prompt provided.
6. Record data.

### Ensure Access to Reinforcement!

It is critical that the desired reinforcer be available on a continuous schedule (every time) while the person is learning to perform the direct access replacement behavior (or chain of behaviors).

If the rate of the direct access replacement behavior becomes too high with ad lib access, you may consider setting up a Premack contingency as an additional option to reduce the rate of access.

*If utilizing this behavior option for Direct Access behaviors (1.0 DA): Utilize the same baseline and treatment procedures as above, except that chain interruption would occur instead of extinction when the target behavior is displayed.*

## How It Works

When the client or child is motivated to access a particular item or event, and they can do so directly, it will become functional very quickly. The direct access behavior will probably produce the item or event at a higher rate and more reliably than the target behavior, which required other people to be involved. There is no reliance on ancillary skills, such as initiating a social interaction or making a request.

### Hypothetical Example

#### I Want a Sandwich, Please

Bill is a person with developmental disabilities living in a group home, and he was referred for services due to "tantrums and yelling." Mr. Hewlet was assigned the case and began the assessment process by reviewing the data the group home staff were keeping. He then proceeded to interview the staff of the home to understand the definitions of the targeted behaviors and gain information about the conditions under which the behavior occurred.

The data for the previous week are displayed in Example Form 5.1A.

Mr. Hewlet needed to determine if the frequency counts were a reliable measure of the referred target behavior. He asked the staff to describe what the target behavior looked

---

### EXAMPLE FORM 5.1A ■ SIMPLE FREQUENCY DATA

■ CLIENT: Bill

CHART STARTED: _____

**Day/Month/Year**

■ BEHAVIOR: Tantrums/yelling
■ Total Observation Time: ___ MIN (__, ___-minute session/day)        Session length: ___ min
■ Number of Days: 7
■ Place an X on the appropriate day box each time the behavior occurs

| | 1 : | 2 : | 3 : | 4 : | 5 : | 6 : | 7 : | Totals |
|---|---|---|---|---|---|---|---|---|
| Target Behavior | xxxx | xxxxx | xxx | xxxxx | xxxx | xxxxx | xxxxxx | |
| Daily Rate | 4 | 5 | 3 | 5 | 4 | 5 | 6 | 32 |

like the last time it happened and if there was much variation across occurrences. The staff reported that the behavior was the same each time. Bill would walk around the house and sit at the dinning room table briefly. He then would get up and walk around the house stomping his feet, briefly sit back down at the table, and then begin to yell loudly with no specific content. The staff indicated that Bill would briefly stop yelling while sitting at the table if the staff sat and talked with him. However, Bill would resume yelling after a short period of time. The staff further commented, "you know it would not be so bad if he didn't always have these fits when I am busy preparing meals."

Mr. Hewlet suspected that the timing of Bill's target behaviors might have something to do with the function of the behavior. He asked if the behavior happened at any time other than right before meals. The staff replied, "Oh yes, sometimes it happens when I am preparing the snacks." Further questioning revealed that the behavior only happened around times when food was provided and that the yelling and tantrum behaviors stopped as soon as Bill accessed food. One of the staff did indicate that sometimes she would provide him with a little bit of food prior to meals "to take the edge off." She could then get back to preparing the meal for everyone in the house. She indicated that she did not like to do this, but sometimes it was the only way to get him to stop long enough for her to prepare the meal. Mr. Hewlet now knew that the target behaviors at least intermittently accessed a tangible item and were more likely at times when Bill was likely to have been food deprived (hungry). He was sure that the behaviors served a socially mediated access function. Mr. Hewlet asked if Bill ever engaged in the target behaviors when no other people were around. The staff indicated the target behaviors only occurred around the staff and only at meal and snack times. There was no difference in his target behaviors regardless of which staff were working, and the behavior occurred when staff were interacting with him and when they were not. This latter piece of information seemed to rule out a target behavior diagnosis of 2.1 SMA: staff attention. There was no difference in his target behaviors if peers were present or not, which would tentatively rule out 2.2 SMA: peer attention. With this information Mr. Hewlet was reasonably sure that the behavioral diagnosis would be 2.3 SMA: tangible reinforcer, food item (see Table 5.1).

Mr. Hewlet asked the staff if they had ever seen Bill prepare his own food. The staff replied "no, we do all that for him." Further questioning indicated that there were no house rules that prohibited clients from preparing their own food. Mr. Hewlet decided that in this case perhaps it would be most effective to simply teach Bill to prepare his own food item when he was hungry. He found out from the staff that Bill's favorite food was a peanut butter and jelly sandwich. However, no one knew if Bill had the skill to prepare a sandwich for himself. Mr. Hewlet set up a simple trigger analysis to find out what skill Bill had in making his own sandwich.

Mr. Hewlet placed all the needed materials for making a peanut butter and jelly sandwich on the counter in the kitchen. At the same time staff were preparing a snack,

**TABLE 5.1 ■ YELLING OR TANTRUM DIAGNOSTIC TABLE**

| Diagnosis | 2.3 SMA: tangible reinforcer, food item |
| --- | --- |
| Target behavior(s): | Yelling/tantrum |
| Function: | Access food item |
| Target behavior likely under following contexts: | Waiting for meals and snacks |
| Target behavior unlikely under following contexts: | While eating and immediately after eating |
| Rule out: | 2.1 SMA: staff attention<br>2.2 SMA: peer attention |

Mr. Hewlet said "Bill, come over here and make yourself a peanut butter and jelly sandwich." He then gestured to the sandwich making items. Bill stopped walking, looked at Mr. Hewlet and then at the peanut butter jar, smiled, and proceeded to the kitchen. Mr. Hewlet observed Bill's efforts at sandwich making and was pleasantly surprised to find out that Bill not only was quite fluent in sandwich making but also cleaned up after himself! Mr. Hewlet repeated these trigger analysis trials on five more occasions with the same result (see Example Form 5.2).

If Bill had not been able to complete the task Mr. Hewlet would have completed a Task Analysis and developed a plan to teach him the skill using a combination of Discrete Trial Training, Incidental Teaching, Chaining, and Behavioral Fluency. Mr. Hewlet now could develop a simple contingency plan that he knew would eliminate the tantrums and yelling. This plan would enable the alternative replacement behavior, while disabling the target behavior.

Based on the trigger analysis, Mr. Hewlet developed the following contingency. If Bill tantrums or yells loudly he will not be provided food of any kind until the target behaviors had been absent for 2 minutes. If he prepares his own sandwich, he is free to eat it. He is to have free access to the sandwich making materials 30 minutes before snacks and meals. Staff will continue taking data on tantrums and yelling and also record if he has prepared and consumed any food independent of staff (see Example Form 5.3).

The plan was implemented and was very effective, as can be seen on the completed Example Form 5.1B data sheet. The function of the target behavior of tantruming or yelling was quickly disabled, and the function of the direct access behavior of making and eating a sandwich was enabled and maintained by the naturally occurring environmental contingencies.

---

### EXAMPLE FORM 5.1B ■ SIMPLE FREQUENCY DATA

■ CLIENT: **Bill**

CHART STARTED: _____
Day/Month/Year

■ Target Behavior: **Tantrum/yelling**
■ Direct Access Replacement Behavior: **Making and eating a sandwich**
■ *Number of Days: 7*
■ Place an X on the appropriate day box each time the behavior occurs

| | 1 | 2 | 3 | 4 | 5 | 6 | 7 | Totals |
|---|---|---|---|---|---|---|---|---|
| Target Behavior | xx | x | | | | | | |
| Daily Rate | 2 | 1 | 0 | 0 | 0 | 0 | 0 | 3 |

■ Total occurrences observed: **3**

| | 1 | 2 | 3 | 4 | 5 | 6 | 7 | Totals |
|---|---|---|---|---|---|---|---|---|
| Direct Access Behavior | xxx | xxxxx | xxxxxx | xxxxx | xxxxxx | xxxxxx | xxxxx | |
| Daily Rate | 3 | 5 | 6 | 5 | 6 | 6 | 4 | 35 |

■ Total occurrences observed: **35**

## EXAMPLE FORM 5.2 ■ TRIGGER ANALYSIS TRIAL DATA

### TRIGGER ANALYSIS TRIAL INSTRUCTION

■ Client name: **Bill**

■ Antecedent set up:

■ Motivation for the reinforcing item will be assured by: **Doing trigger analysis 30 minutes before a meal**

■ Availability of the reinforcing item will be indicated by: **A verbal prompt and the sandwich making items being out on the counter**

■ Type and sequence of prompts to be used: **Verbal, then gestural, then graduated guidance if needed**

■ Preferred response: **Prepares and eats a peanut butter and jelly sandwich with no assistance and cleans up afterwards**

■ Conditions regarding access to the reinforcing item:

    ■ How much: **1 Sandwich**

    ■ How long: **N/A**

| Step | Description |
|------|-------------|
| 1 | **Initiates sandwich making** |
| 2 | **Gets bread** |
| 3 | **Opens peanut butter and jelly** |
| 4 | **Gets knife and spreads peanut butter and jelly** |
| 5 | **Assembles sandwich** |
| 6 | **Cleans area** |
| 7 | **Consumes sandwich** |

■ I = Independent    P = prompted    N = did not complete

| | Date | Time Start | Time End | Step | | | | | | | % comp |
|---|---|---|---|---|---|---|---|---|---|---|---|
| Trial | | | | 1 | 2 | 3 | 4 | 5 | 6 | 7 | |
| 1 | | 11:30 | 11:40 | P | I | I | I | I | I | I | 86% |
| 2 | | 4:30 | 4:35 | P | I | I | I | I | I | I | 86% |
| 3 | | 4:30 | 4:36 | P | I | I | I | I | I | I | 86% |
| 4 | | 11:30 | 11:35 | P | I | I | I | I | I | I | 86% |
| 5 | | 11:30 | 11:32 | P | I | I | I | I | I | I | 86% |
| 6 | | 11:30 | 11:34 | P | I | I | I | I | I | I | 86% |

■ Independent completion rate: Whole task (completed/possible): <u>0/6</u>

■ Prompted completion rate: Whole task (completed/possible): <u>6/6</u>

■ Time to complete task:

    ■ Longest <u>10 min</u>

    ■ Shortest <u>2 min</u>

    ■ Average <u>5.33 min</u>

*EXAMPLE FORM 5.3* ■ **DIRECT ACCESS: SIMPLE PLAN**

### Direct Access: Plan

- Person served: **Bill**
- Target Behavior: **Yelling and tantrums**
- Behavioral diagnostic category: **2.3 SMA: tangible reinforcer, food item.**
- Direct access behavior: **Making own sandwich**
- Designated time Period(s): **Any**
- Rate of Target behavior:  Baseline **4.6 per day**  Target **0**
- Rate of Direct access behavior:  Baseline **0**  Target **3 per day**
- Initial form or task analysis of direct access behavior: **Assemble and consume a peanut butter and jelly sandwich with the items already available on the kitchen counter**
- Reinforcing item/event to be directly accessed: **Food items**
- When and how will it be made available: **initially all items to assemble a sandwich will be left out on the kitchen counter and will be made available to Bill 30 minutes before each snack and meal**
- How to respond to the target behavior: **Remove all food items until Bill has stopped engaging in the target behaviors for 2 minutes. Then prompt Bill to the kitchen area where the sandwich making items are located. Prompt him to assemble a sandwich if he does not independently do so.**
- How to build the direct access replacement behavior: **Prompt Bill to the kitchen area where the sandwich making items are located. Prompt him to assemble a sandwich if he does not independently do so.**
- Types of prompts to be used:
  ☒ Visual    ☒ Vocal    ☐ Written    ☒ Touch    ☐ Graduated Guidance
- When to use prompts: **Visual prompt in the form of items used to prepare sandwich should be out at all times; vocal prompt to make a sandwich should be given if Bill is walking toward the table around meal times; a touch prompt should be used to direct Bill to the area of the sandwich making materials if the verbal prompt was ineffective**

## What If?

*What if the person refuses or is unable to complete the direct access behavior?*

This would require teaching the person the skill first. If they were unable to acquire the skill, then some environmental set up would be needed to allow them a way to access the reinforcer directly. If that were still not possible an alternative might be to use noncontingent reinforcement.

*What if the direct access behavior results in the person getting the reinforcer at too high a rate?*

If this occurs the simplest solution would be to implement a Premack contingency. In using a Premack contingency, the person could still directly access the reinforcer, but the complexity or duration of the behavior required prior to access could be increased. This would require more effort on the part of the client to access the reinforcer and thereby reduce the frequency of access.

*What if the person can do the direct access behavior, but they are too slow?*

If the person is simply taking too long to complete the task you should consider fluency training or DRH (differential reinforcement of higher rates of behavior). In fluency training the focus is on breaking the task down into the individual movements required to complete each step of the overall task, and then increasing the speed of movement of each component rather than focusing on accurate performance of the entire task. Accuracy of the entire task develops as each component can be performed quickly, accurately, and without hesitation.

DRH focuses on differentially reinforcing the person performing the behavior faster. The faster they do the behavior, the greater the pay off. Both methods are effective at speeding up slow performances.

## Forms: Direct Access

5.1 Simple Frequency Data with Rate Formulas
5.2 Direct Access Trigger Analysis Trial Data Sheet
5.3 Direct Access: Simple Plan

---

### FORM 5.1 ■ SIMPLE FREQUENCY DATA WITH RATE FORMULAS

■ Client: _____        CHART STARTED: _____

Day/Month/Year

■ Behavior: _____

■ Total Observation Time: __MIN__ (__, ___-minute session/day)        Session length: __min__

■ Number of Days: __

■ Place an X on the appropriate day box each time the behavior occurs

| | 1 : | 2 : | 3 : | 4 : | 5 : | 6 : | 7 : | Totals |
|---|---|---|---|---|---|---|---|---|
| Target Behavior | | | | | | | | |
| Daily Rate | | | | | | | | |

A. Total Minutes Observed: __

B. Total occurrences observed: __ Rate/minute = B/A $\underline{\quad/\quad}$ = ____

C. Range (low) __ to (high) __, Avg = __ Rate/hour = (B/A)60 ($\underline{\quad/\quad}$)60 = ____

| | 8 : | 9 : | 10 : | 11 : | 12 : | 13 : | 14 : | Totals |
|---|---|---|---|---|---|---|---|---|
| Direct Access Behavior | | | | | | | | |
| Daily Rate | | | | | | | | |

A. Total Minutes Observed: __

B. Total occurrences observed: __ Rate/minute = B/A $\underline{\quad/\quad}$ = ____

C. Range (low) __ to (high) __, Avg = __ Rate/hour = (B/A)60 ($\underline{\quad/\quad}$)60 = ____

### FORM 5.2 ■ DIRECT ACCESS TRIGGER ANALYSIS TRIAL DATA SHEET

■ Client Name: _____

■ Antecedent set up: _____

■ Motivation for the reinforcing item will be ensured by: _____
_____

■ Availability of the reinforcing item will be indicated by: _____
_____

■ Type and sequence of prompts to be used: _____
_____

■ Preferred response: _____
_____

■ Conditions regarding access to the reinforcing item:
    ■ How much: _____
    ■ How long: _____

| Step | Description |
|------|-------------|
| 1 | |
| 2 | |
| 3 | |
| 4 | |
| 5 | |
| 6 | |
| 7 | |

■ I = Independent    P = prompted    N = did not complete

| | Date | Time Start | Time End | Step | | | | | | | % Comp |
|---|------|-----------|----------|---|---|---|---|---|---|---|--------|
| Trials | | | | 1 | 2 | 3 | 4 | 5 | 6 | 7 | |
| 1 | | | | | | | | | | | |
| 2 | | | | | | | | | | | |
| 3 | | | | | | | | | | | |
| 4 | | | | | | | | | | | |
| 5 | | | | | | | | | | | |
| 6 | | | | | | | | | | | |
| 7 | | | | | | | | | | | |
| 8 | | | | | | | | | | | |
| 9 | | | | | | | | | | | |
| 10 | | | | | | | | | | | |

■ Independent completion rate: Whole task (completed/possible): __/__

■ Prompted completion rate: Whole task (completed/possible): __/__

■ Time to complete task:

■ Longest _____ Shortest _____ Average _____

*FORM 5.3* ■ **DIRECT ACCESS: SIMPLE PLAN**

■ Person Served: _____

■ Target Behavior: _____

■ Behavioral Diagnostic Category: _____

■ Direct Access Behavior: _____

■ Designated Time Period(s): _____

■ Rate of Target behavior:                    Baseline _____    Target _____

■ Rate of Direct access behavior:          Baseline _____    Target _____

■ Initial form or task analysis of direct access behavior: _____

_____

■ Reinforcing item/event to be directly accessed: _____

■ When and how will it be made available: _____

■ How to respond to the target behavior: _____

■ Types of prompts to be used:
  ☐ Visual          ☐ Vocal          ☐ Written          ☐ Touch          ☐ Graduated Guidance

■ When to use prompts: _____

## More Information

Dattilo, J., & Camarata, S. (1991). Facilitating conversation through self-initiated augmentative communication treatment. *Journal of Applied Behavior Analysis, 24,* 369–378.

Mithaug, D. K., & Mithaug, D. E. (2003). Effects of teacher-directed versus student-directed instruction on self-management of young children with disabilities. *Journal of Applied Behavior Analysis, 36,* 133–136.

Thompson, R. H., & Iwata, B. A. (2000). Response acquisition under direct and indirect contingencies of reinforcement. *Journal of Applied Behavior Analysis, 33,* 1–11.

Vaughn, B. J., & Horner, R. H. (1997). Identifying instructional tasks that occasion problem behaviors and assessing the effects of student versus teacher choice among these tasks. *Journal of Applied Behavior Analysis, 30,* 299–312.

## 2.0 SMA FUNCTIONS: DRL GROUP CONTINGENCIES FOR PEER ATTENTION

### Brief Description

One cannot often successfully instruct peers to ignore the target problem behavior of a particular peer so that the targeted person will behave more appropriately. It is necessary to implement a group contingency that results in the group's reinforcement being contingent upon the lowering of the rate of the target behavior for the group as a whole. This option, differential reinforcement of lower rates of behavior (DRL), involves providing a reinforcer to a group of students or clients for achieving a group criterion. The reinforcer is presented following a specified period of time during which the identified target behavior for the entire group occurs at or below a prespecified level (termed the *behavioral standard*).

In this SMA option, reinforcement is provided to the entire group only when the rate of a target behavior for the whole group, during a specified period of time, is lower than a prescribed limit, for example, the class cannot have more than five disruptive incidents in the morning in order to earn 10 minutes of extra recess after lunch. By using a group contingency we establish the motivation for the peer group to ignore the person engaged in target behaviors. Once the group meets the initial behavioral standard, we systematically change the standard over time to shape the rate of target behavior to a final criteria level. This allows for more frequent contact with the reinforcing event initially and generally speeds the learning process.

To implement a group DRL program, determine what level of the target behavior is acceptable for the group as a whole (behavioral standard). Next, measure the target behavior across the entire group during a specified interval of time. The group's frequency of occurrence of the target behavior is compared with the behavioral standard. If the group's frequency of behavior is above the standard, reinforcement is withheld. If the group's frequency is at or below the behavioral standard, reinforcement is provided to the group.

The advantage of using a DRL procedure is that it is relatively easy to implement, and it specifically focuses on the reduction but not total elimination of the target behavior. It is not designed to teach any new behavior but alters the rate or intensity of already existing behaviors. The disadvantage with any group contingency is that it may also result in inappropriate forms of counter control by peers toward a targeted individual.

## Terms

*DRL interval:* The length of time during which the group must maintain the occurrence of the target behavior below the behavioral standard to earn the group reinforcer.

*Behavioral standard:* The level of behavior that is considered acceptable. This is set as a function of baseline data on the group's rate of behavior.

*Changing criterion:* The process of systematically changing the behavioral standard to successively lower rates that approximate the final criteria.

*Final criteria:* The terminal behavioral standard. This is the goal. When reached, it will indicate that the DRL has been a success and no further reduction in target behaviors is warranted.

## Apparatus

Timing device—This can be a kitchen timer, alarm clock, computer with alarm feature, Palm Pilot, tape recorder with beeps at designated intervals, or a calendar, depending on the length of the schedule of reinforcement. The purpose is to prompt the staff person, teacher, or parent to provide the reinforcer.

Data sheets—See Form 5.5, "Simple Frequency Data on Group and Individual Behaviors".

Reinforcing items or events—If tangible items will be utilized, a sufficient supply must be available.

## Baseline Measurement

1. Determine that the target behavior is maintained by peer reinforcement (i.e., 2.2 SMA: peer reinforcement).
2. Operationally define or pinpoint the target behavior being observed, with specific criteria for onset and offset of behavior (if not readily evident).
3. Determine the observation period possibly by reviewing scatter plot or A-B-C data to identify periods of time when the target behavior is highly likely or at the specific time of day or event in which you would like to reduce the level of the target behavior.
4. Construct the data sheet to reflect the length of the observation period, trying to keep the length reasonably similar across multiple sessions (see Form 5.4).
5. During observation, record the occurrence of the target behavior for the whole group (if desired use special notation for specific individuals of interest).
6. Repeat step 5 until the observation period ends.
7. Sum the total number of occurrence's for the entire group, and enter on the data sheet.
8. Collect this data for at least five more baseline sessions, and graph the data.

## DRL Procedures

1. Determine the final criteria for the behavioral standard for the group, as well as for the individual client or student.
2. From baseline data, calculate the mean level of occurrence for the group.
3. Determine your initial behavioral standard and DRL interval. (The initial standard and interval should be equivalent to baseline levels.)
4. Set the timing device to the initial interval.
5. When the designated time period elapses deliver the designated reinforcer to the group if the group's behavior did not exceed the behavioral standard.
6. If the group's frequency of the target behavior exceeds the behavioral standard, do not provide the reinforcer.
7. As occurrences decrease, gradually change the criterion of the behavioral standard until you reach the final criteria.

### Changing the Criterion

The behavior analyst can change the behavioral standard in a stepwise fashion such that it is closer to the final criteria as a function of client performance. A good general rule is to change the behavioral standard by 10% at each step, when the designated criterion level of performance met.

## How It Works

The group contingency DRL removes peer reinforcement for the child or client's target behavior. This is accomplished by tying the group's access to tangible reinforcers to a lowered rate or intensity of target behavior. The social environment *enabled* the target behavior of the individual by frequently providing the desired peer attention contingent upon its occurrence. The DRL schedule *disables* this function by providing reinforcement to the group only if the target behavior occurs relatively infrequently (i.e., below a preset standard). Peers will be less likely to provide attention when the individual engages in the target behavior because the individual's frequency of target behavior now partly determines reinforcement rate and magnitude for the whole group. Peer reinforcement for the target behavior is consequently removed. It is possible that such peer reinforcement might shift to other behaviors not directly targeted. This can be remedied by including the new behaviors in the DRL contingency.

### Hypothetical Example

### Class Clown

Billy is a junior high school special education student. He engages in frequent verbally inappropriate behavior toward teachers. Subsequent to such behavior the class laughs, girls smile, boys nod their head and all have a good time. He has peers wanting to hang out with him during recess and at lunch. When Billy is "disciplined" by being sent to the principal's office, it actually increases the attention he gets from his peers.

Mrs. Jones, the principal, after constantly seeing Billy in her office for referrals, discusses the case with Billy's teacher, Mr. Smith, who is in his first year of teaching. Mrs. Jones believes Billy does these behaviors for teacher attention. She advises him to ignore students when they do things like this or he will continue to have problems managing his classroom.

### Teacher

Mr. Smith returned to his classroom. He decided to try out the principal's advice and ignore Billy's silly behaviors in the hopes that such behaviors would extinguish. Mr. Smith

*TABLE 5.2* ■ **VERBAL INAPPROPRIATE BEHAVIOR**

| Day | Class | Billy | Total Class | Total Billy |
|---|---|---|---|---|
| 1 | xxxxxxxxxxxxxxx | xxxxxx | 15 | 6 |
| 2 | xxxxxxxxxxxx | xxxxxxxx | 12 | 8 |
| 3 | xxxxxxxxxxxxx | xxxxxxx | 13 | 7 |
| 4 | xxxxxxxxx | xxxxxxxxxx | 9 | 10 |
| 5 | xxxxxxxxxxxx | xxxxxxxxxxxxx | 13 | 13 |

considered the specific examples of Billy's behavior that were inappropriate so that he could pinpoint a definition of the behavior. He identified the following behaviors as components of the target behavior:

1. Low volume statements that were audible to the class but not the teacher.
2. Facial and hand gestures not related to answering academic questions.
3. Comments that resulted in other students attending to Billy rather than classroom instructions.
4. Direct verbal refusals to complete academic tasks.

With this definition, Mr. Smith took baseline data for 1 week. He did this by simply counting the frequency of verbally inappropriate behavior (as he had defined it). Mr. Smith also decided to keep a frequency count of the same behaviors across the rest of the class. The data he collected is presented in Table 5.2.

Mr. Smith reviewed the data and considered what might be maintaining Billy's behavior. He noticed that the behavior occurred when there were task demands as well as during free time. Mr. Smith concluded that it probably was not an escape-maintained behavior. He noticed that the behavior never resulted in Billy getting an item such as food or a book, so it was not maintained by access to a tangible item.

He decided that he would ignore Billy's inappropriate verbal behavior and instead only attend to Billy when he was participating in class. He decided to apply this same contingency to the class as a whole for 1 week, and he obtained the data presented in Table 5.3.

Mr. Smith was pleasantly surprised at the effect his attention had on most of the class. He also noticed that his attention had no apparent effect on Billy's behavior. He could now safely rule out a diagnosis of 2.1 SMA: adult attention. A more fitting diagnosis for Billy's behavior was 2.2 SMA: peer attention (see Table 5.4).

Great! But now what? How do you change the behavior of the whole class? How can one make Billy's peers responsible for not "feeding into" this behavior? Mr. Smith decided that he would definitely need to set up a group contingency to address this problem's function in getting peer attention. A group contingency would tie everyone's "lot" together. Either everyone earns the reinforcer, or no one earns it!

*TABLE 5.3* ■ **INAPPROPRIATE VERBAL BEHAVIOR (EXTINCTION TRIAL)**

| Day | Class | Billy | Total Class | Total Billy |
|---|---|---|---|---|
| 1 | xxxxxxx | xxxxxxxxx | 7 | 9 |
| 2 | xxxxx | xxxxxxxx | 5 | 8 |
| 3 | xxxxxx | xxxxxxxxx | 6 | 9 |
| 4 | xxxxx | xxxxxxxxxxx | 5 | 11 |
| 5 | xxxxxxx | xxxxxxxxxxx | 7 | 11 |

### *TABLE 5.4* ■ VERBALLY INAPPROPRIATE BEHAVIOR TOWARD TEACHERS DIAGNOSTIC TABLE

| Diagnosis | 2.2 SMA: peer attention |
|---|---|
| Target behavior(s): | Verbally inappropriate behavior toward teachers |
| Function: | Access peer attention |
| Target behavior likely under following contexts: | Peers present in structured setting with teacher |
| Target behavior unlikely under following contexts: | Individual meetings with teacher. No peers present |
| Rule out: | 2.1 SMA adult attention<br>4.0 SME |

Mr. Smith's class was a very social group. Given a choice of activities they would certainly choose to have time to talk in class with each other. He decided to set up the following group contingency. The class would earn extra peer conversation time at the end of the period if the class stayed below a certain level of inappropriate verbal comments. Mr. Smith developed the following plan (see Example Form 5.4).

Mr. Smith implemented the plan by explaining to the class that he would be counting the number of verbally inappropriate behaviors. He gave examples of such behaviors to the class. He let the class know that if they could stay below the behavioral standard they would earn 10 minutes of free time at the end of the class period. He also let them know that he would be the only and final authority in regards to their score with respect to the standard.

### *EXAMPLE FORM 5.4* ■ GROUP CONTINGENCY DRL: SIMPLE PLAN

■ Group: **3rd period class**
■ Individual (if any): **Billy**
■ Target Behavior: **Verbally inappropriate behavior**
■ Replacement Behavior: **On task verbal responses**
■ Designated time period for contingency: **Entire class period**
■ Baseline Data (sessions or days): **5 days**

| Day/session | Group | Individual | Total group | Total Individual |
|---|---|---|---|---|
| 1 | xxxxxxx | xxxxxxxxx | 7 | 9 |
| 2 | xxxxx | xxxxxxxx | 5 | 8 |
| 3 | xxxxxx | xxxxxxxxx | 6 | 9 |
| 4 | xxxxx | xxxxxxxxxxx | 5 | 11 |
| 5 | xxxxxxx | xxxxxxxxxxx | 7 | 11 |
| | | Mean Frequency | 6 | 9.6 |

■ Initial Behavioral Standard: **15 or fewer events of verbally inappropriate behaviors.**
■ Criteria for adjusting standard up: **5 consecutive class periods meeting the behavioral standard will result in a reduction of allowed verbally inappropriate behaviors by 1 statement per class period.**
■ Criteria for adjusting standard down: **5 consecutive class periods not meeting the standard. New standard will be set at the mean level of occurrence for the whole class including Billy's data.**
■ Reinforcement to be delivered: **10 minutes of free time for conversations at the end of the class period.**

**EXAMPLE FORM 5.5 ■ SIMPLE FREQUENCY DATA ON GROUP AND INDIVIDUAL BEHAVIORS**

■ Student: Billy
          CHART STARTED: _____
■ Group: **3rd period**
          **Day/Month/Year**
■ Behavior: **Verbally Inappropriate behavior**
■ Session length: <u>**90 min**</u>
■ Number of Days: <u>**21**</u>
■ Place an X on the appropriate day box each time the behavior occurs

|        | 1 | 2 | 3 | 4 | 5 | 6 | 7 | Totals |
|--------|---|---|---|---|---|---|---|--------|
| Group  | 6 | 5 | 2 | 2 | 1 | 1 | 1 | 18 |
| Client | 9 | 11 | 14 | 16 | 14 | 11 | 12 | 87 |

|        | 8 | 9 | 10 | 11 | 12 | 13 | 14 | Totals |
|--------|---|---|----|----|----|----|----|--------|
| Group  | 2 | 3 | 2 | 2 | 2 | 2 | 2 | 15 |
| Client | 9 | 8 | 6 | 4 | 4 | 3 | 2 | 36 |

|        | 15 | 16 | 17 | 18 | 19 | 20 | 21 | Totals |
|--------|----|----|----|----|----|----|----|--------|
| Group  | 1 | 2 | 1 | 2 | 1 | 2 | 1 | 10 |
| Client | 2 | 1 | 1 | 1 | 1 | 1 | 2 | 9 |

Additionally, any event of bullying or threatening any of their classmates would result in the immediate loss of the 10 minutes of free time. He then led a brief discussion on how each person in the class might help to meet the behavioral standard.

Mr. Smith continued recording data as listed in Example Form 5.5.

In reviewing the data, Mr. Smith noted that initially the class reduced their verbally inappropriate behavior, but Billy's actually increased to an average of about 12 times per day. Billy's rate of target behavior appeared to have peaked at 16 incidents on day 4 and declined rapidly on the following 4 days. Mr. Smith attributed this increase to an extinction burst. He surmised that this occurred because the rest of the class no longer attended to Billy when he made inappropriate statements. By the 9th day of the intervention the class had met the criterion to increase the behavioral standard, so Mr. Smith changed the standard to 14 or fewer events of verbally inappropriate behavior. The class continued to meet the standard, and Mr. Smith continued to change the standard as they progressed.

## What If?

*What if the behavior does not decrease (or gets worse) with the group contingency DRL?*

As in the example, there may be a brief increase as the client adjusts to the new contingencies. If you have diagnosed the function correctly, it should decrease within a few sessions or days. If it persists longer than this consider a more intensive assessment as you may have misdiagnosed the function of the behavior. Consider also that it may be a multiple function behavior and that the initial diagnosis was simply incomplete in that it only diagnosed one function.

*What if the group becomes abusive to one of the group members?*

This can be an issue in using group contingencies. One can set up an additional criteria as Mr. Smith did. If an abusive incident occurs even once, it results in an immediate loss of the reinforcing item or event. If you have a group that tends to be abusive to each other, you might also consider a group contingency relative to increasing socially appropriate interactions as your first step. After that is successful, consider targeting verbally inappropriate behavior.

### Forms: Differential Reinforcement of Other Behaviors With Extinction

5.4 Group Contingency DRL: Simple Plan
5.5 Simple Frequency Data on Group and Individual Behaviors

---

### FORM 5.4 ■ GROUP CONTINGENCY DRL: SIMPLE PLAN

- Group: _____
- Individual (if any): _____
- Target Behavior: _____
- Replacement Behavior: _____
- Designated time period for contingency: _____
- Baseline Data (sessions or days): _____

| Day/session | Group | Individual | Total group | Total Individual |
|---|---|---|---|---|
| 1 | | | | |
| 2 | | | | |
| 3 | | | | |
| 4 | | | | |
| 5 | | | | |
| | | Mean Frequency | | |

- Initial behavioral standard: _____
  _____
- Criteria for adjusting standard up: _____
  _____
- Criteria for adjusting standard down: _____
  _____
- Reinforcement to be delivered: _____
  _____

## FORM 5.5 ■ SIMPLE FREQUENCY DATA ON GROUP AND INDIVIDUAL BEHAVIORS

■ Client: _____        CHART STARTED: _____

■ Group: _____        Day/Month/Year

■ Behavior: _____

■ Session length: __min

■ Number of Days: __

■ Place an X on the appropriate day box each time the behavior occurs

| | 1 : | 2 : | 3 : | 4 : | 5 : | 6 : | 7 : | Totals |
|---|---|---|---|---|---|---|---|---|
| Group | | | | | | | | |
| Client | | | | | | | | |

| | 7 : | 8 : | 9 : | 10 : | 12 : | 13 : | 14 : | Totals |
|---|---|---|---|---|---|---|---|---|
| Group | | | | | | | | |
| Client | | | | | | | | |

| | 15 : | 16 : | 17 : | 18 : | 19 : | 20 : | 21 : | Totals |
|---|---|---|---|---|---|---|---|---|
| Group | | | | | | | | |
| Client | | | | | | | | |

| | 22 : | 23 : | 24 : | 25 : | 26 : | 27 : | 28 : | Totals |
|---|---|---|---|---|---|---|---|---|
| Group | | | | | | | | |
| Client | | | | | | | | |

| | 29 : | 30 : | 31 : | 1 : | 2 : | 3 : | 4 : | Totals |
|---|---|---|---|---|---|---|---|---|
| Group | | | | | | | | |
| Client | | | | | | | | |

## More Information

Cipani, E. (2004). *Classroom management for all teachers: 12 plans for evidence based practice.* Upper Saddle River, NJ: Pearson Prentice Hall.

Dietz, S. M., & Repp, A. C. (1973). Decreasing classroom misbehavior through the use of DRL schedules of reinforcement. *Journal of Applied Behavior Analysis, 6,* 457–463.

Deitz, S. M., & Repp, A. C. (1974). Differentially reinforcing low rates of misbehavior with normal elementary school children. *Journal of Applied Behavior Analysis, 7,* 622.

Lennox, D. B., Miltenberger, R. G., & Donnelly, D. R. (1987). Response interruption and DRL for the reduction of rapid eating. *Journal of Applied Behavior Analysis, 20,* 279–284.

Singh, N. N., Dawson, M. J., & Manning, P. (1981). Effects of spaced responding DRL on the stereotyped behavior of profoundly retarded persons. *Journal of Applied Behavior Analysis, 14,* 521–526.

Wright, C. S., & Vollmer, T. R. (2002). Evaluation of a treatment package to reduce rapid eating. *Journal of Applied Behavior Analysis, 35,* 89–93.

## 2.0 SMA FUNCTIONS: OMISSION TRAINING (DIFFERENTIAL REINFORCEMENT OF OTHER BEHAVIOR, OR DRO)

### Brief Description

In differential reinforcement of other behavior, or DRO, the specific maintaining reinforcer is contingent on the absence of the target behavior in a given period of time. DRO is one of the simplest of all behavior reduction procedures. One could view a DRO as a reinforcement system that allows the person to earn specific reinforcement by engaging in a host of varying behaviors as long as the target unacceptable behavior does not occur.

To implement a DRO program, you would determine if the target behavior occurred during a specified interval of time. If it occurred, reinforcement is withheld, and the interval (called the DRO interval) is reset for the full length of time. If the target behavior did not occur during the DRO interval, specific reinforcement (i.e., the functional reinforcer) is provided at the end of the DRO interval. By structuring the contingencies in this way, engaging in any behavior other than the targeted behavior pays off better. Concurrently, the target behavior's functional relation to reinforcement is disabled.

The advantage of using a DRO procedure is that it is easy to implement and specifically focuses on the reduction of the unwanted behavior. It is not designed to teach any new behavior or to target any specific behavior for an increase. The advantages generally outweigh the disadvantages with this procedure. It has been one of the most widely used reductive procedures for unwanted behaviors.

### Terms

*Interbehavior interval:* The length of time that passes between the end of one targeted behavior and the beginning of the next occurrence of the targeted behavior.

*DRO interval:* The length of time for which the person must abstain from engaging in the target behavior in order to earn the reinforcer.

*Thinning the schedule of delivery of maintaining reinforcer:* The process of gradually reducing the delivery of the reinforcer so that more time elapses between each delivery.

### Apparatus

Timing device—This can be a kitchen timer, alarm clock, computer with alarm feature etc, a tape recorder with beeps at designated intervals, or a calendar, depending on the length of the schedule of reinforcement. The purpose is to prompt the staff person, teacher, or parent to provide the reinforcer when the DRO interval elapses.

Data sheets—See Form 5.6 "Simple Frequency Data With Formulas."

Reinforcing items or events—If tangible items or activities have been identified as the maintaining reinforcers and will be delivered on a DRO schedule, a sufficient supply must be available.

### Baseline Measurement

1. Identify the target behavior to be observed and its function.
2. Operationally define or pinpoint the behavior being observed, with specific criteria for onset and offset of behavior (if not readily evident).
3. Determine the observation period, possibly by reviewing scatter plot or A-B-C data to identify periods of time when the target problem behavior is highly likely.
4. Construct the data sheet to reflect the length of the observation period, trying to keep the length reasonably similar in multiple baseline sessions.
5. During the observation period, record any occurrence of the target behavior.
6. Sum the occurrences across the session, and enter them on the data sheet.
7. Divide the session length by the total frequency of target behavior (see following examples) to arrive at the interbehavior interval for that session.

8. Continue observing client and target behavior for at least four more baseline sessions.
9. Graph or display the interbehavior interval across all baseline sessions noting the range and mean.

## Calculating the Interbehavior Interval

Table 5.5 contains data on the frequency of hitting (target behavior) for a hypothetical client. All observations sessions were 120 minutes in length. The observations were conducted over 5 days.

Using the data from Table 5.5 to calculate the interbehavior interval for the entire 5 days of observation, we would simply take the total number of minutes we conducted observations and divide that number by the total number of occurrences of the target behavior. In this case:

600 total minutes ÷ 18 total occurrences of behavior = an interbehavior interval of 33.33 minutes

If we were to calculate the interbehavior interval for day 1 it would be:

120 minutes ÷ 2 occurrences of behavior = an interbehavior interval of 60 minutes

If we were to calculate the interbehavior interval for day 5 it would be:

120 minutes ÷ 6 occurrences of behavior = an interbehavior interval of 20 minutes

## DRO With Extinction Procedures

1. From your baseline data, calculate the interbehavior interval.
2. Determine your schedule of delivery of the maintaining reinforcer. (The initial schedule should be set so that reinforcement occurs at or more frequently than the average interbehavior interval, e.g., initial interval set at 20% below the average interbehavior interval. Mean interbehavior interval of 300 seconds would yield an initial schedule of reinforcement that occurred every 240 seconds.)
3. Obtain a supply of the tangible reinforcer to be delivered (if dealing with 2.3 SMA: tangible reinforcer).
4. Set the timing device to the initial delivery schedule.
5. When the timer goes off deliver the reinforcer to the person if the person has not engaged in the target behavior for the entire time prior to the timer going off, and then reset the timer.
6. If the client engages in the target behavior during the interval, do not provide the reinforcer, but rather reset the timer for the full DRO interval. (extinction)
7. Thin the schedule of reinforcement.

## Thinning the Schedule of Delivery of Maintaining Reinforcer

The schedule of reinforcement is thinned when the target behavior goal is achieved. When the goal is achieved, the behavior analyst can increase the length of the DRO interval and set a new target behavior goal. The steps for thinning the schedule follow.

TABLE 5.5 ■ FREQUENCY OF HITTING AND INTERBEHAVIOR INTERVALS

|  | 1 | 2 | 3 | 4 | 5 | Totals |
|---|---|---|---|---|---|---|
| Hitting | xx | xxx | xxxxx | xx | xxxxx x | 18 |
| Interbehavior interval | 60 min | 40 min | 24 min | 60 min | 20 min | 33.33 min |

1. When the target behavior goal is achieved, increase the length of the interval between reinforcement by 5%–10%. For example, if the DRO interval was 5 minutes, and the target behavior goal was met, then the new schedule for delivery might be set at 5 minutes, 30 seconds.
2. With each week of success in achieving the target behavior goal, the schedule of delivery is thinned by progressively increasing the DRO interval by 10%.
3. If the target behavior occurs at a rate higher than the goal consistently over a given week, consider returning to the previous schedule of reinforcement. (If you have made several attempts at thinning the schedule but are unable to get past a particular DRO interval, it may be best to keep the schedule at that level while incorporating another functional behavior treatment option.)

*If utilizing this behavior option for* Direct Access behaviors (1.0 DA): *Utilize the same baseline and treatment procedures as above, except that chain interruption would occur instead of extinction when the target behavior is displayed.*

## How It Works

The DRO, or omission training, works as a result of altering the schedule of delivery of an identified maintaining reinforcer in favor of behaviors other than the target behavior (see Borrero & Vollmer, 2002, regarding Matching Law). Previously, the exhibition of the target behavior was functional. The social environment *enabled* the function of the target behavior by frequently providing the desired positive reinforcer contingent upon its occurrence. The DRO schedule *disables* this function by further postponing the delivery of the reinforcer with an occurrence of the target behavior, that is, the interval is reset. Therefore, doing anything other than the target behavior is a more efficient path to accessing the reinforcer.

### Hypothetical Example

### Milton the Pincher

Milton was a person diagnosed with schizophrenia who had developed the behavior of frequently pinched other clients. Mrs. Symthe, a staff member on the unit, believed that Milton pinched other clients as the result of his schizophrenia. She claimed that he has an inability to control his impulses, and therefore, behavioral intervention efforts will not prove fruitful. Mr. Delgadillo, the behavioral consultant, believed differently. He was determined to identify the maintaining reinforcer of the pinching and produce an intervention that addressed such a function.

Mr. Delgadillo started by interviewing the inpatient staff members. He asked the following questions:

1. What was he doing, or what was going on before he engaged in the pinching?
2. What did he specifically do? What did the pinching look like?
3. What happened after he pinched? What did staff do? How did they react?

Unfortunately, the answers that staff provided did not point clearly to the function of the pinching behavior. Some staff reported that Milton pinched when he was left alone, some reported that he pinched when it was noisy, and other staff reported that Milton pinched when asked to complete a task. They were all relatively consistent in reporting how the pinching behavior looked (form or topography), so Mr. Delgadillo was reasonably certain they were all observing and reporting on the same behavior. In regards to what happened after the pinching behavior, again the answers were quite varied. One staff person indicated that pinching gets Milton out of doing certain tasks. Another indicated that she thought Milton pinched so that he could "be the center of attention." Because no clear antecedent conditions and no clear function could be determined from the interviews, Mr. Delgadillo decided to set up an A-B-C chart for him and the staff to collect data during a 2-week period. Table 5.6 is a representative sample of such data.

*TABLE 5.6* ■ **A-B-C OBSERVATION SUMMARY OF PINCHING BEHAVIOR**

| Antecedent Conditions | Target Behavior | What Happened? | What Was Natural Result of Behavior? |
|---|---|---|---|
| 1. Sitting in the art therapy room and asked to paint. | Pinched peer. | Separated and counseled and taken outside for a walk at his request. | Sensation produced when pinching someone else's skin. |
| 2. Watching TV in the day room. Finally settled down after perseverating on going outside all morning. The public defender came to talk to another client. | Pinched visitor. | Separated, counseled, and taken outside to walk and relax. | Sensation produced when pinching someone else's skin. |
| 3. Short of staff, more noisy than usual. He asked to go for a walk and was told that we could not go today. | Pinched his preferred staff. | Nonpreferred staff immediately took him out of the building to walk until he "seemed calm." | Sensation produced when pinching someone else's skin. |
| 4. During psychiatrist rounds, Milton perseverated on going for a walk with staff. Doctor asking him about how he was doing. | Pinched doctor 3 times, last one very hard. | Restrained, then taken for a walk to help him calm down before seeing the doctor again. | Sensation produced when pinching someone else's skin. |
| 5. Sitting in the dayroom playing cards with his preferred staff. Another client became agitated, and staff were attempting to prompt the other client to go outside for a walk. | Smiled and began pinching his staff repeatedly, unresponsive to redirection. To stop pinching. | Another staff person prompted him to use his calming strategy and go for a walk with her. He waved at his preferred staff, continued smiling, and went out for a walk. | Sensation produced when pinching someone else's skin. |

Mr. Delgadillo examined the A-B-C descriptive data in Table 5.6 and then set about answering the question, "What are the common elements in all five events involving pinching?" While some of the incidents involved a demand placed on Milton, other situations did not involve any demands (see incidents 2 and 5). It did not appear that pinching was functioning to escape demands. However, to test whether escape from a task or taking a walk with staff was the function of pinching, Mr. Delgadillo set up a simple test. He took Milton for a walk, and then arranged for the doctor to evaluate Milton immediately upon their return. The evaluation by the doctor was chosen as it had been one of the demand situations during which Milton had engaged in pinching. Milton did not pinch and in fact was very cooperative with the doctor's assessment. Mr. Delgadillo repeated this test using several different task demands. Each time he replicated this test, he obtained the same result. When Milton was given a walk a priori, he handled the subsequent task demands with no problem. Mr. Delgadillo was now fairly certain that Milton's behavior served a socially mediated access function. But was it attention or tangible contingencies that maintained the pinching behavior?

Mr. Delgadillo reviewed the data and found that the pinching behavior did not subside when staff were talking with Milton. Further, Milton was observed to have excellent social skills in that he was very adept at starting and maintaining conversations with both staff and peers. From this information Mr. Delgadillo ruled out 2.1 SMA: staff attention and 2.2 SMA: peer attention.

Mr. Delgadillo had previously noted that in all five cases he observed the eventual outcome was that Milton went for a walk outside of the unit with a staff person. Mr. Delgadillo determined the most likely hypothesis is that pinching is being maintained by socially mediated access to a tangible reinforcer, in this case, going for a walk (2.3 SMA: tangible reinforcer, walking outside the unit).

Why would staff engage in such a response to pinching? The staff response made sense to them at the time, in that they judged Milton to be in a state of anxiety, particularly

### TABLE 5.7 ■ PINCHING STAFF DIAGNOSTIC TABLE

| Diagnosis | SMA 2.3: tangible reinforcer |
|---|---|
| Target behavior(s): | Pinches staff |
| Function: | Accesses walk with staff (walk is the driving force because he cannot go on a walk outside unless accompanied by staff) |
| Target behavior likely under following contexts: | When he has been without a walk for an entire day |
| Target behavior unlikely under following contexts: | When he is taken for a walk early in the afternoon |
| Rule out: | Socially mediated escape function (4.1 SME) and socially mediated access function (2.1 and 2.2 SMA) |

when around other clients. They would therefore take him out for a walk to calm him down. While on the walk, Milton appeared calmer, and he stopped pinching. Facility staff thereby interpreted their use of a walk as an anxiety reductive procedure and believed this practice was clinically sound.

However, Mr. Delgadillo's assessment led to an alternate hypothesis. Milton's pinching (of other people) is a functional behavior when he desires a walk. The exhibition of such a behavior greatly increases the chances that staff will take him out. Unfortunately other more appropriate behaviors did not appear to be as effective in getting a walk (see Table 5.7).

Having formulated a diagnosis of pinching as 2.3 SMA: tangible reinforcer in the form of a walk, Mr. Delgadillo procured a summary of the unit's reliable data on the occurrence of target behaviors, including times and dates of occurrence. Data was collected over a 4-hour session (240 minutes) each day. Unit records indicated that Milton was pinching people about three times per hour (see Example Form 5.6).

The interbehavior interval was calculated by determining the

Total Minutes Observed (1200 minutes) ÷ Total Frequency target behavior occurred (58 occurrences) = average interbehavior interval (20.7 minutes)

With this data in hand, and an understanding of the function of the pinching behavior, Mr. Delgadillo formulated an intervention plan (see Example Form 5.7). Having

### EXAMPLE FORM 5.6 ■ FREQUENCY COUNT DATA SHEET

■ Condition: <u>Baseline</u> or ~~Treatment~~      Recording Method: frequency/session length

■ Client: Milton      CHART STARTED: _____*6-21*_____

     **Day/Month/Year**

■ Behavior: **Pinching**

■ Total Observation Time: **1200 MIN (1, 240**-minute session/day)      Session length: <u>240 min</u>

■ Number of Days: <u>5.</u>

| | 1 | 2 | 3 | 4 | 5 | Totals |
|---|---|---|---|---|---|---|
| Pinching | xxxxxxx | xxxxxxxxxxx | xxxxxxxxxxxxx | xxxxxxxx xxxxxxxx | xxxxxxxxxxx | 58 |
| Daily Rate | 1.75/hr | 2.75/hr | 3.25/hr | 4/hr | 2.75/hr | 2.9/hr |
| Interbehavior interval | 34.29min | 21.82min | 18.46min | 15min | 21.82min | 20.69min |

A. Total Minutes Observed: <u>1200</u> Interbehavior interval = *A/B* <u>1200/58</u> = <u>20.69 min</u> Rate/hour = (B/A)60 (<u>58/1200</u>)60 = **2.9/hr**

**EXAMPLE FORM 5.7 ■ DIFFERENTIAL REINFORCEMENT PLAN**

**Differential reinforcement with extinction: Plan**

- Person Served: **Milton**
- Target Behavior: **Pinching**
- Behavioral diagnostic category: **2.3 SMA category; tangible reinforcer**
- Target Rate: **0 events per week**
- Designated time Period(s): **8a to 12 noon**
- Baseline data across five times/sessions:
  1. ___7___
  2. ___11___
  3. ___13___
  4. ___16___
  5. ___11___
- Rate of target behavior:            Baseline _**2.9/hour**_    Target _**0**_
- Interbehavior interval:                 Baseline _**20.7 min**_    Target _**24hours**_
- Initial schedule of Differential reinforcement:
    - **_X_** Fixed time schedule every _**15**_ minutes/~~hours/days~~

                        OR

    - ___ Variable time schedule on average every ___ minutes/hours/days
- Reset Timer: ___ End of each interval
    - **_X_** End of each interval AND if target behavior occurs
- Reinforcer(s) to be used:
  1. **Walk outside with staff**
  2. _____
  3. _____
  4. _____
  5. _____
    - Special instructions for delivery of reinforcer(s):
      **If pinching occurs immediately reset the timer to 15 minutes and record data.**
- Criterion for Increasing amount of time between reinforcers: **When pinching behavior occurs in <1% of intervals observed for three consecutive days. Increase time DRO interval by 10%.**
- Criterion for Decreasing the amount of time between reinforcers: **If pinching behavior occurs in more than 5% of observed intervals for three consecutive days decrease DRO interval by 1 minute.**
- Criterion for withholding the scheduled reinforcer delivery: **Occurrence of pinching.**

determined that the pinching behavior occurred about every 20 minutes, he set the initial DRO interval to 15 minutes to ensure that Milton was very likely to obtain reinforcement in the form of outside walks more often under this plan.

Prior to implementing the program Mr. Delgadillo informed the staff that an extinction burst would probably occur and that they should be prepared for this event. He also made sure to be on the unit during the implementation of the program so that he could help to support the staff and to assure them that the program was implemented correctly. The program was implemented, and the data was collected and is presented in Figure 5.1.

As Mr. Delgadillo expected, and as can be seen in Figure 5.1, the DRO was successful in reducing the occurrence of pinching behavior. It is interesting to note that as Mr. Delgadillo predicted, on 6/26 the pinching behavior worsened. This is a familiar and expected pattern when using extinction. It is called an extinction burst. Following this burst (increase in rate from prior level) the pinching behavior steadily and quickly declined. Because

**Frequency of Pinching Per Day**

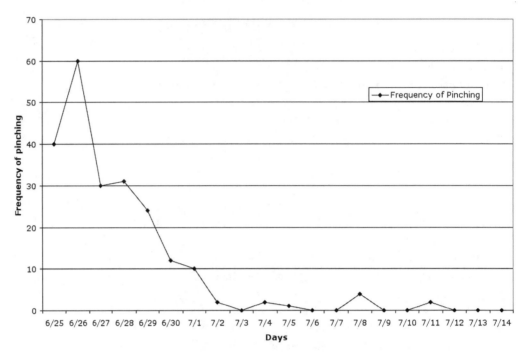

***Figure 5.1*** ■ Frequency of pinching behavior.

Mr. Delgadillo had let the staff know what to expect they were prepared for this and stuck with the plan. By 7/14 the behavior had met the criteria for thinning the DRO schedule, so Mr. Delgadillo increased the interbehavior interval by 10% such that reinforcement was now delivered every 17 minutes. Mr. Delgadillo continued this thinning process until the pinching behavior was no longer occurring and Milton was going on walks with a staff person once in every 24-hour period.

### What If?

*What if the behavior does not decrease (or gets worse) with DRO?*

When using DRO with extinction, an initial worsening of the target behavior is very possible. The technical term for this is an *extinction burst.* As the name implies, it is a brief and often intense increase in the target behavior. Such a result is often the case when the target behavior no longer produces the maintaining reinforcer. However, one should see a dramatic decrease in the target behavior within 3 sessions or days. If the behavior continues at a high rate for longer than that you will need to confirm that the item or event you are using is actually reinforcing for the person (i.e., is the functional reinforcer). The other possibility is that the DRO interval is simply too long for the person to contact the reinforcer at a high enough rate to enable the nonoccurrence of target behaviors as functional. In this case, shortening the DRO interval is an option you should consider. If this is still ineffective you should consider starting with noncontingent reinforcement (see NCR option).

*What if I cannot ignore some of the target behaviors?*

If the target behavior has life-threatening consequences and cannot be ignored, you can program a DRO without extinction. In this case all the elements of the DRO would be the same with the exception that when the target behavior occurs we will continue to respond to it as we have in the past. This will make the behavior change process somewhat slower because the difference in level of reinforcement will not be as great. This can be countered to some extent by shortening the DRO interval, thus increasing the density of reinforcement for all other behaviors.

## Forms: Differential Reinforcement of Other Behaviors With Extinction

5.6 Simple Frequency Data With Formulas
5.7 Differential Reinforcement of Other Behavior With Extinction: Simple Plan
5.8 Formulas for Calculating Rate of Targeted Behavior and Interbehavior Interval
5.9 Formulas for Determining Increases or Decreases in Frequency of Differential Reinforcement

---

### FORM 5.6 ■ SIMPLE FREQUENCY DATA WITH FORMULAS

■ Client:                                CHART STARTED: _____
                                                                   Day/Month/Year

■ Behavior: _____
■ Total Observation Time: __MIN__ (__, ___-minute session/day)        Session length: __min__
■ Number of Days: __
■ Place an X on the appropriate day box each time the target behavior occurs

|  | 1 : | 2 : | 3 : | 4 : | 5 : | 6 : | 7 : | Totals |
|---|---|---|---|---|---|---|---|---|
| Target Behavior |  |  |  |  |  |  |  |  |
| Daily Rate |  |  |  |  |  |  |  |  |
| Interbehavior interval |  |  |  |  |  |  |  |  |

A. Total Minutes Observed: __ Interbehavior interval = $A/B$ __/__ = ___
■ Rate/hour = (B/A)60 (__/__)60 = ___

|  | 8 : | 9 : | 10 : | 11 : | 12 : | 13 : | 14 : | Totals |
|---|---|---|---|---|---|---|---|---|
| Target Behavior |  |  |  |  |  |  |  |  |
| Daily Rate |  |  |  |  |  |  |  |  |
| Interbehavior interval |  |  |  |  |  |  |  |  |

A. Total Minutes Observed: __ Interbehavior interval = $A/B$ __/__ = ___
B. Total occurrences observed: __ Rate/minute = B/A __/__ = ___
C. Range (low) __ to (high) __, Avg = __ Rate/hour = (B/A)60 (__/__)60 = ___

*FORM 5.7* ■ **DIFFERENTIAL REINFORCEMENT OF OTHER BEHAVIOR WITH EXTINCTION: SIMPLE PLAN**

■ Person Served: _____

■ Target Behavior: _____

■ Behavioral diagnostic category: _____

■ Target Rate: _____

■ Designated time Period(s): _____

■ Baseline data across five times/sessions:      1. _____
                                                  2. _____
                                                  3. _____
                                                  4. _____
                                                  5. _____

■ Rate of target behavior:            Baseline _____    Target _____

■ Interbehavior interval:             Baseline _____    Target _____

■ Initial schedule of Differential reinforcement:

    ■ ___ Fixed time schedule every ___ minutes/hours/days

                  OR

    ■ ___ Variable time schedule on average every ___ minutes/hours/days

■ Reset Timer:

    ■ ___ End of each interval

    ■ ___ End of each interval AND if target behavior occurs

■ Reinforcer(s) to be used:           1. _____
                                      2. _____
                                      3. _____
                                      4. _____
                                      5. _____

    ■ Special instructions for delivery of reinforcer(s):

    _____

    _____

    _____

■ Criterion for increasing amount of time between reinforcers:

_____

■ Criterion for decreasing amount of time between reinforcers:

_____

■ Criterion for withholding the scheduled reinforcer delivery:

_____

---

*FORM 5.8* ■ **FORMULAS FOR CALCULATING PERCENTAGE OF INTERVALS OF TARGETED BEHAVIOR AND INTERBEHAVIOR INTERVAL**

■ *Interbehavior Interval:* This formula will help you determine on average how much time passes between the occurrence of targeted behaviors (Interbehavior interval). Use this information to help set the frequency of noncontingent reinforcement.

    ■ **Total Minutes Observed ÷ Total Behavior Occurrences Observed = Average interbehavioral interval**

■ *Rate:* This formula will help you to determine the how often the behavior occurs in a given amount of time. Use this formula if you have different lengths of observation periods to allow for ongoing comparison of data.

    ■ **Number of occurrences of behavior ÷ Length of observation In minutes = rate of behavior per minute**

    ■ **Rate per hour = (rate per minute) 60**

    ■ **Rate per day = (rate per minute) 1440**

*FORM 5.9* ■ **FORMULAS FOR DETERMINING INCREASES OR DECREASES IN FREQUENCY OF DIFFERENTIAL REINFORCEMENT**

■ *Formula for 10% increase in time between reinforcement.*
■ Current reinforcement interval $\times$ 1.10 = (10% increase in time)
■ *Formula for 5% increase in time between reinforcement.*
■ Current reinforcement interval $\times$ 1.05 = (5% increase in time)
■ *Formula for 10% decrease in time between reinforcement.*
■ Current reinforcement interval $\times$ 0.90 = (10% decrease in time)
■ *Formula for 5% decrease in time between reinforcement.*
■ Current reinforcement interval $\times$ 0.95 = (5% decrease in time)

## More Information

Borrero, J.C., & Vollmer, T.R. (2002). An application of the matching law to severe problem behavior. *Journal of Applied Behavior Analysis, 35,* 13–27.

Barton, L.E., Brulle, A.R., & Repp, A.C. (1986). Maintenance of therapeutic change by momentary DRO. *Journal of Applied Behavior Analysis, 19,* 277–282.

Carole C., Miltenberger, R., Maki, A., Barenz, R., Jurgens, M., Sailer, A., et al. (2004). A comparison of response cost and differential reinforcement of other behavior to reduce disruptive behavior in a preschool classroom. *Journal of Applied Behavior Analysis, 37,* 411–415.

Cowdery, G.E., Iwata, B.A., & Pace, G.M. (1990). Effects and side effects of DRO as treatment for self-injurious behavior. *Journal of Applied Behavior Analysis, 23,* 497–506.

Goetz, E.M., Holmberg, M.C., & LeBlanc, J.M. (1975). Differential reinforcement of other behavior and noncontingent reinforcement as control procedures during the modification of a preschooler's compliance. *Journal of Applied Behavior Analysis, 8,* 77–82.

Haring, T.G., & Kennedy, C.H. (1990). Contextual control of problem behavior in students with severe disabilities. *Journal of Applied Behavior Analysis, 23,* 235–243.

Harris, S.L., & Wolchik, S.A. (1979). Suppression of self-stimulation: Three alternative strategies. *Journal of Applied Behavior Analysis, 12,* 185–198.

Heard, K., & Watson, T.S. (1999). Reducing wandering by persons with dementia using differential reinforcement. *Journal of Applied Behavior Analysis, 32,* 381–384

Lindberg, J.S., Iwata, B.A., Kahng, S., & DeLeon, I.G. (1999). DRO contingencies: An analysis of variable-momentary schedules. *Journal of Applied Behavior Analysis, 32,* 123–136.

Luce, S.C., Delquadri, J., & Hall, R.V. (1980). Contingent exercise: A mild but powerful procedure for suppressing inappropriate verbal and aggressive behavior. *Journal of Applied Behavior Analysis, 13,* 583–594.

Marcus, B.A., & Vollmer, T.R. (1996). Combining noncontingent reinforcement and differential reinforcement schedules as treatment for aberrant behavior. *Journal of Applied Behavior Analysis, 29,* 43–51.

Martinez, S.S. (1977). Comparison of extinction, DRO 0-sec, and DRO 6-sec in the elimination of imitative responding under discrete-trial paradigms. *Journal of Applied Behavior Analysis, 10,* 315.

Mazaleski, J.L., Iwata, B.A., Vollmer, T.R., Zarcone, J.R., & Smith, R.G. (1993). Analysis of the reinforcement and extinction components in DRO contingencies with self-injury. *Journal of Applied Behavior Analysis, 26,* 143–156.

McCord, B.E., Iwata, B.A., Galensky, T.L., Ellingson, S.A., & Thomson, R.J. (2001). Functional analysis and treatment of problem behavior evoked by noise. *Journal of Applied Behavior Analysis, 34,* 447–462.

Piazza, C.C., Fisher, W.W., Hanley, G.P., Hilker, K., & Derby, K.M. (1996). A preliminary procedure for predicting the positive and negative effects of reinforcement-based procedures. *Journal of Applied Behavior Analysis, 29,* 137–152.

Repp, A.C., Barton, L.E., & Brulle, A.R. (1983). A comparison of two procedures for programming the differential reinforcement of other behaviors. *Journal of Applied Behavior Analysis, 16,* 435–445.

Repp, A.C., & Deitz, S.M. (1974). Reducing aggressive and self-injurious behavior of institutionalized retarded children through reinforcement of other behaviors. *Journal of Applied Behavior Analysis, 7,* 313–325.

Rolider, A., & Van Houten, R. (1985). Movement suppression time-out for undesirable behavior in psychotic and severely developmentally delayed children. *Journal of Applied Behavior Analysis, 18,* 275–288.

Thompson, R.H., Iwata, B.A., Hanley, G.P., Dozier, C.L., & Samaha, A.L. (2003). The effects of extinction, noncontingent reinforcement, and differential reinforcement of other behavior as control procedures. *Journal of Applied Behavior Analysis, 36,* 221–238.

Vollmer, T.R. (1999). Noncontingent reinforcement: Some additional comments. *Journal of Applied Behavior Analysis, 32,* 239–240.

Vollmer, T.R., Iwata, B.A., Zarcone, J.R., Smith, R.G., & Mazaleski, J.L. (1993). The role of attention in the treatment of attention-maintained self-injurious behavior: Noncontingent reinforcement and differential reinforcement of other behavior. *Journal of Applied Behavior Analysis, 26,* 9–21.

Woods, D.W., & Himle, M.B. (2004). Creating tic suppression: Comparing the effects of verbal instruction to differential reinforcement. *Journal of Applied Behavior Analysis, 37,* 417–420.

## 2.0 SMA FUNCTIONS: NONCONTINGENT REINFORCEMENT (NCR) WITH EXTINCTION

### Brief Description

In noncontingent reinforcement, or NCR, the specific maintaining reinforcer is presented noncontingently following a given period of time. Reinforcement is provided even if the behavior has or is occurring. The NCR plan reduces the rate of behavior by reducing the client's motivation to access the reinforcer. Hence, the motivation to engage in a behavior that produces such a reinforcer is also altered. This method is similar to methods termed response independent reinforcement or time-based delivery of stimuli with known reinforcing properties (Vollmer, 1999).

In NCR *with extinction,* the specific maintaining reinforcer is presented following a given period of time. There is one caveat to this time-based delivery. The reinforcer is withheld if the person is engaging in the target behavior at the time of the scheduled delivery. It is provided once the target behavior ceases. To implement this option for SMA problem behaviors, you need to determine how frequently to provide the reinforcer. You deliver the reinforcing item based on that time schedule, unless the target behavior is occurring at a scheduled delivery. If the target behavior is currently occurring you would withhold the reinforcer until the target behavior had subsided for some brief period of time.

The advantage of using an NCR procedure is that it is easy to implement and quickly alters the target behavior by reducing the client's deprived condition relative to the reinforcer. NCR procedures generally do not teach or strengthen any new replacement behaviors. They alter the rate of the target behavior by simply removing the motivation underlying the targeted behavior. Generally, NCR will be used in conjunction with other replacement behavior options that are designed to teach specific replacement behaviors. NCR may not be useful in situations where frequent access to the maintaining reinforcer is impractical or not feasible.

### Terms

*Schedule of reinforcer delivery:* This refers to the interval schedule of noncontingent delivery for the maintaining reinforcer to be made available to the client or child.

*Interbehavior interval:* The length of time that passes between the end of one targeted behavior and the beginning of the next occurrence of the targeted behavior.

*Thinning schedule of delivery of maintaining reinforcer:* The process of gradually reducing the delivery of the reinforcer so that more time elapses between each delivery.

*Partial interval method of recording:* An interval recording strategy that involves observing whether a behavior occurs or does not occur during specified time periods. Partial interval recording requires the observer to record the occurrence of the behavior (in the respective interval) if it occurs in any part of the interval. If a behavior occurs several times within an interval, it is recorded as occurring only once within that interval. If a behavior occurs for a long period of time it is recorded during each interval in which it occurred, even if it was for only for part of a given interval. For example, a person may bang his head 10 times in one interval but only once in another interval.

*TABLE 5.8* ■ **PARTIAL INTERVAL DATA**

| Interval | 1 | 2 | 3 | 4 | 5 | 6 | 7 | 8 | 9 | 10 |
|---|---|---|---|---|---|---|---|---|---|---|
| What you would record | | X | X | | X | X | X | | | X |
| Actual frequency of behavior | 0 | 1 | 5 | 0 | 2 | 1 | 5 | 0 | 0 | 1 |

*TABLE 5.9* ■ **PARTIAL INTERVAL DATA LONG DURATION**

| Interval | 1 | 2 | 3 | 4 | 5 | 6 | 7 | 8 | 9 | 10 |
|---|---|---|---|---|---|---|---|---|---|---|
| What you would record | X | X | X | | | | | | | |
| Actual Duration of | |------------------------| | | | | | | | |

Both intervals will be marked to indicate that the behavior occurred, despite the difference in the number of head bangs that occurred in both intervals. The illustration in Table 5.8 indicates the partial interval recording in the top row (designated by an X) with the actual frequency presented in the bottom row.

Table 5.9 is another example of a partial interval recording system with a behavior that is of long duration. Let's say a client's target behavior is yelling. The client is observed to initiate yelling in the middle of interval 1. He finally stopped in the middle of interval 3. In the partial interval system, yelling behavior would be recorded as occurring in intervals 1, 2, and 3.

## Apparatus

Timing device—This can be a kitchen timer, alarm clock, computer with alarm feature, tape recorder with beeps at designated intervals, or a calendar, depending on the length of the schedule of noncontingent reinforcement. It's purpose is to prompt the staff person, teacher, or parent to provide the reinforcer.

Data sheets—See Form 5.10 "Partial Interval Data, 30-Minute Intervals" and Form 5.11 "Partial Interval Data, 2-Minute Intervals"

Reinforcing items or events—If tangible items or activities that have been identified as the maintaining reinforcers are to be delivered on a NCR with extinction schedule, a sufficient supply must be available.

## Baseline Measurement

Baseline measurement consists of determining the interbehavior interval for the target behavior. To accomplish this, a partial interval method is used for recording the occurrence of the target behavior. Partial interval methods of recording are useful when dealing with behaviors that may be difficult to keep track of or when staff persons have many other duties besides collecting data.

### Steps to Collect Baseline Data Using Partial Interval Recording

1. Identify the target behavior to be observed.
2. Operationally define or pinpoint the behavior being observed.
3. Determine the observation period, possibly reviewing scatter plot or A-B-C data to identify periods of time when behavior is highly likely.
4. Determine the length of the observation period and divide the observation period into equal interval blocks (keeping these the same across baseline sessions).
5. Construct the data sheet.
6. During observation, enter date and time of day on data sheet and set timing device for interval length.
7. At the end of each interval, if the target behavior occurred at all, place an X in the corresponding interval on the data sheet.
8. Repeat step 7 until the observation period ends.

**EXAMPLE OF PARTIAL INTERVAL DATA**

- Recording Method: Partial interval
- Interval Length: 2 minutes
- CLIENT: _____ Arthur _____      CHART STARTED: _____ 2-1 _____

                                                                                    Day/Month/Year

- BEHAVIOR: _____ XXX _____
- Total Observation Time: **50 MIN (1, 10-minute session/day)**      Session length: **10 min**
- Number of Days: **5.**

          ☐ Behavior did **NOT** occur                    ☒ Behavior **DID** occur

**Day of the month/Start time**

| Interval # | Day 1<br>10:30 | Day 2<br>12:10 | Day 3<br>1:10 | Day 4<br>2:15 | Day 5<br>2:45 |
|---|---|---|---|---|---|
| 1 |   | X | X | X | X |
| 2 | X | X |   | X | X |
| 3 |   | X | X |   |   |
| 4 | X |   |   | X |   |
| 5 |   | X | X | X | X |
| total | 2 | 4 | 3 | 4 | 3 |

- **Grand total = 16 intervals with target behavior over a possible 25 intervals**
- **Inter-behavior interval = 50 min./16 intervals with behavior = 3.125 minutes**

9. Sum the total number of intervals in which a target behavior occurred, and enter that number on the data sheet.
10. Continue observing client and target behavior for at least four more baseline sessions.

For example, the staff person records partial interval data on the rate of occurrence of the targeted behavior on the following data sheet. Observations are made five times per day, for 10 minutes. If the behavior occurs within a given 2-minute interval, an X is placed on that respective interval. Therefore, the following data sheet for 1 day of observation reveals a grid, involving five intervals per observation across five observation sessions.

*Recording Method: Partial Interval*

As you can see, in the first observation period (column marked day 1), the client engaged in the target behavior only during the second and fourth interval during the entire 10-minute observation. During the next observation period, he engaged in the target behavior in intervals 1, 2, 3, and 5. The totals at the bottom of each column are out of a possible of 5 intervals that the behavior can be recorded. Summing across the row labeled "total" yields 16 intervals in which the target behavior was recorded as having occurred (against a total of 25 intervals for 5 days of observation). With this ratio 16/25, one can compute the percentage of occurrence, in this case 64% of intervals.

The interbehavior interval can also be calculated by dividing the number of minutes of observation for the week (50) by the number of intervals that the target behavior occurred (16), which yields an average interbehavior interval of 3.125 minutes. In other words, the target behavior occurs about every 3 minutes. In this example it is important to note that the rate of target behavior is relatively stable across the five observation periods. If it were more variable, one should examine what factors were different at each observation to account for the variability in rate of occurrence.

## NCR With Extinction Procedures

1. From baseline data, calculate the interbehavior interval.
2. Determine your schedule of delivery of the maintaining reinforcer. (The initial schedule should be set so that reinforcement occurs at or more frequently than the shortest interbehavior interval, for example, initial interval set at 80% of the average interbehavior interval.)
3. Obtain a supply of the reinforcer to be delivered.
4. Set the timing device to the initial delivery schedule.
5. When the timer goes off, deliver the reinforcer to the person if the person has not engaged in the target behavior for 5 to 10 seconds prior to the timer going off.
6. Reset the timer.
7. If the client has engaged in the target behavior prior to the timer going off, then withhold the reinforcing item until the target behavior stops for 10 seconds. (extinction)
8. Record data on data sheet.
9. Thin the schedule of reinforcement.

### Thinning the Schedule of Delivery of Maintaining Reinforcer

The schedule is thinned when the target behavior goal is achieved. When the goal is achieved, increase the length of the interbehavior interval and set a new target behavior goal. The steps for thinning the schedule follow.

1. When the target behavior goal is achieved with the program, increase the length of the interval between deliveries by 5%–10%. For example, if the length of time between noncontingent delivery was 5 minutes and the target behavior goal was met, the new schedule for delivery might be set at 5 minutes, 30 seconds.
2. With each week of success in achieving the target behavior goal, the schedule of delivery is increased progressively by 10%.
3. If the target behavior occurs at a rate higher than the target behavior goal consistently over a given week, consider returning to the previous schedule of reinforcement.
4. If you have made several attempts at thinning the schedule but are unable to get past a particular rate of reinforcement, it may be best to keep the schedule at that level while incorporating another functional treatment program.

*If utilizing this behavior option for* Direct Access behaviors (1.0 DA): *Utilize the same baseline and treatment procedures as above, except that chain interruption would occur instead of extinction when the target behavior is displayed.*

## How It Works

1. By eliminating the client's motivation for a particular reinforcing item or event. When there is no motivation for the item or event there is no reason for the person to do any of the behaviors that previously produced that reinforcer.
2. By disrupting the learned contingency between the client's unwanted target behavior and the reinforcing event. That is, the reinforcing event happens on some time schedule and is withheld if the unwanted behavior occurs, so the person may learn that the unwanted behavior is no longer needed to get the reinforcer.

*TABLE 5.10* ■ **SUMMARY OF A-B-C OBSERVATIONS PHYSICAL AGGRESSION**

| Antecedent Conditions | Target Behavior | What Did Aide Do? | What Was Natural Result of Behavior? |
|---|---|---|---|
| 11:40 By self, not interacting with others. | Hit peer. | Aide came over and told her to apologize and "play nice." | Inconsequential. |
| 11:51 on the periphery of an activity with several other children. | Kicked another child. | Aide took Kim aside and explained why it is important to cooperate with other children, then they played a game together with other children, with aide providing lots of praise for Kim. | Inconsequential. |

### Hypothetical Example

Mr. K, a behavioral consultant, was asked to help find a way to reduce the amount of aggressive behavior exhibited on the playground by a kindergarten student named Kim. The teacher and playground supervisor felt that Kim engaged in such behavior because she was immature for her age and her parents "spoiled her at home." Mr. K began the consultation by operationally defining the behaviors. The target behaviors were defined as: using any body part to make physical contact with any body part of another person with sufficient force to be judged as intentional. Examples include hitting, biting, and kicking other children. What would not be counted as aggression was incidental contact from the play activity, such as bumping into someone, falling on someone during running, and so forth.

Baseline data was collected, and a functional assessment was completed by observing Kim on the playground as well as collecting A-B-C data. This data was used to perform a descriptive analysis of the various forms of Kim's aggressive behavior. The following data from one observation period on 6/21 reflects the contextual data surrounding Kim's aggressive behavior on the playground. Because the hypothesis was a socially mediated event, the last column is marked inconsequential (see Table 5.10).

From the A-B-C data, in Table 5.10 it was determined that Kim's aggressive behavior was maintained by socially mediated access to staff attention (2.1 SMA: adult attention). In this case one of the teachers volunteer aides, Ms. State, was inadvertently maintaining this behavior (see Table 5.11).

If Kim went longer than 4–8 minutes without "playing" with any of the other children during recess, she would hit, bite, and kick other students close to her to get Ms. State to stop playing with other children and come to the area. In some cases, she would remove Kim and spend time counseling her on how to interact with other students. The desired event appears to be the aide's prompting of play with the other children and simultaneously playing with Kim in the process.

*TABLE 5.11* ■ **PHYSICAL AGGRESSION DIAGNOSTIC TABLE**

| Diagnosis | 2.1 SMA: adult attention |
|---|---|
| Target behavior(s): | Physical aggression |
| Function: | Access adult attention |
| Target behavior likely under following contexts: | Anytime Kim goes longer than 8 minutes without playing with another student |
| Target behavior unlikely under following contexts: | While interacting with the teachers aide, Ms. State |
| Rule out: | 2.2 SMA: peer attention<br>4.1 SME: unpleasant social situations |

*EXAMPLE FORM 5.11A* ■ **PARTIAL INTERVAL DATA**

- ■ Condition: <u>Baseline</u> or ~~Treatment~~
- ■ Recording Method: Partial interval
- ■ Interval Length: 2 minutes
- ■ CLIENT: *Kim*

CHART STARTED: _____ **7/5** _____

**Day/Month/Year**

- ■ BEHAVIOR: Physical aggression
- ■ Total Observation Time: <u>100 MIN</u>

Session length: <u>20 min</u>

☐ Behavior did **NOT** occur          ☒ Behavior **DID** occur

**Day of the month**

| Interval # | Interval end time | 7/5 | 7/6 | 7/7 | 7/8 | 7/9 |
|---|---|---|---|---|---|---|
| 1 | 2 | | x | x | | |
| 2 | 4 | x | | | | x |
| 3 | 6 | | | x | x | |
| 4 | 8 | | x | | | x |
| 5 | 10 | | | | x | |
| 6 | 12 | | | x | x | x |
| 7 | 14 | | | . | | |
| 8 | 16 | x | x | | | x |
| 9 | 18 | | | x | x | x |
| 10 | 20 | | | | | |
| | Total | 2 | 3 | 4 | 4 | 5 |

Mr. K needed an adequate analysis of the rate of this behavior during playground periods. He collected baseline data from the 5th through the 9th of the following month. Example Form 5.11A illustrates the recording of the behavior in 2-minute intervals with a partial interval recording system.

In graphing the data from Form 5.11, it appeared that there was an increasing trend in the occurrence of the unwanted behavior (2, 3, 4, and 5 intervals on consecutive days) (see Figure 5.2).

Mr. K could have calculated the interbehavior interval on the cumulated data, and it would have looked like this:

100 minutes ÷ 18 intervals with aggression = 5.56 Minutes

In order to increase the likelihood of getting a positive effect quickly, Mr. K calculated the interbehavior interval based on the session with the most occurrences, thus ensuring that the rate of noncontingent reinforcement was higher than the rate of reinforcement she was currently receiving for aggressive behaviors.

Mr. K counted the total number of minutes of the observation (20) and divided it by the total number of intervals in which aggression occurred (5). This gave him an average interbehavior interval of 4 minutes.

20 minutes ÷ 5 intervals with aggression = 4 Minutes

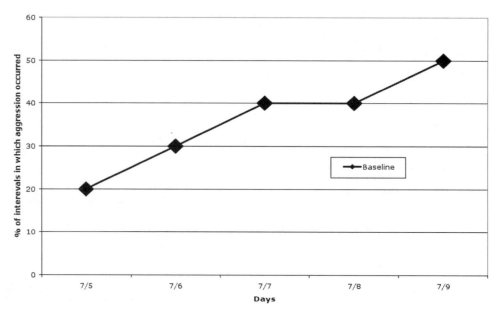

**Kim Aggression Baseline**

*Figure 5.2* ■ Aggressive behavior.

Mr. K decided to start with an NCR schedule that required the aide to prompt and help Kim play with the other children on a set schedule, hopefully prior to her engaging in aggression (see Example Form 5.12).

Mr. K then started the intervention on the 12th of the month. The data are presented in Example Form 5.11B.

We can present the same data in graphical format to more easily see the trends (see Figure 5.3).

Based on the data that no aggression had occurred for 3 consecutive days, Mr. K changed the schedule to 1 minute of social interaction every 3.5 minutes.

3 Minutes (Current schedule) × 1.10 (10 percent increase) = 3.3 minutes

(Note: Because the time frames were relatively short, and Mr. K knew that his timing device would make it difficult to track anything smaller than half a minute, he rounded up to 3.5 minutes.)

There was one event of aggression on the first day of the new schedule but no further occurrences for 3 days after that. Mr. K continued this process until the schedule had been thinned to every 10 minutes. After consultation with the teacher and teachers aide as to the feasibility, Mr. K decided to keep the NCR schedule at this level while they taught Kim some new behaviors that she could use to request the teachers aide to provide social interaction. Kim continued to have no events of physical aggression during the acquisition of a simple request for attention, in this case "Please play with me."

It was noted that Kim could make the request quite well during training but was not using it during recess. Mr. K surmised that the noncontingent reinforcement that was keeping the aggression from occurring did so by eliminating the motivation to do any behavior that functioned to produce adult attention. He therefore began thinning the schedule of noncontingent reinforcement 10% following every 3 consecutive days with <1% intervals having an occurrence of aggression.

Upon reducing the noncontingent delivery of reinforcement, Kim began to use the requesting behavior she had previously learned. Mr. K continued to collect data and thin

*EXAMPLE FORM 5.11B* ■ **PARTIAL INTERVAL DATA**

- ■ Condition: ~~Baseline~~ or **Treatment**
- ■ Recording Method: Partial interval
- ■ Interval Length: 2 minutes
- ■ CLIENT: *Kim*

CHART STARTED: ___**7/12**___

**Day/Month/Year**

- ■ BEHAVIOR: Physical aggression
- ■ Total Observation Time: 100 MIN

Session length: **20 min**

☐ Behavior did **NOT** occur      ☒ Behavior **DID** occur

**Day of the month**

| Interval # | Interval end time | 7/12 | 7/13 | 7/14 | 7/15 | 7/16 | 7/17 | 7/18 | 7/19 | 7/20 | 7/21 | 7/22 | 7/23 | 7/24 |
|---|---|---|---|---|---|---|---|---|---|---|---|---|---|---|
| 1 | 2 | | | | | | | | | | | | | |
| 2 | 4 | x | | | | | | | | | | | | |
| 3 | 6 | x | | | | x | | | | | | | | |
| 4 | 8 | | | | | | | | | | | | | |
| 5 | 10 | x | | | | | | | | | | | | |
| 6 | 12 | | | | | | | | | | | | | |
| 7 | 14 | | | | | | | | | | | | | |
| 8 | 16 | | | | | | | | | | | | | |
| 9 | 18 | | | | | | | | | | | | | |
| 10 | 20 | | | | | | | | | | | | | |
| | Total | 3 | 0 | 0 | 0 | 1 | 0 | 0 | 0 | 0 | 0 | 0 | 0 | 0 |

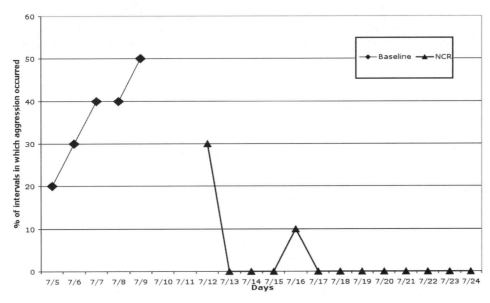

**Kim Partial Interval Aggression**

*Figure 5.3* ■ Partial interval aggression data.

***EXAMPLE FORM 5.12*** ■ **NONCONTINGENT REINFORCEMENT WITH EXTINCTION: SIMPLE PLAN**

■ Person Served: **Kim**

■ Target Behavior: **Physical Aggression**

■ Target Behavior Goal: **Aggression in less than 1% of observed intervals**

■ Designated time Period(s): **Lunch playground period 25 minutes per day**

■ Baseline data across five times/sessions:

1. __2__
2. __3__
3. __4__
4. __4__
5. __5__

■ % of intervals in which target behavior occurred:   Baseline **40%**   Target **<1%**

■ % of intervals in which reinforcement occurred:   Baseline _____   Target _____

■ Interbehavior interval:   Baseline **4 min**   Target **15 min**

■ Initial schedule of non-contingent reinforcement:

■ _X_ Fixed time schedule every _3_ minutes and at the outset of the playground activity.

OR

■ ___ Variable time schedule on average every ___ minutes/hours/days

■ Reinforcer(s) to be used:

1. Prompting of play behavior with other children by Ms. State, Ms. State to interact for 1 min
2. _____
3. _____
4. _____
5. _____

■ Special instructions for delivery of reinforcer(s):

**Ms. State is primary deliverer of prompt and social interaction. If she is not available it may be done by another person. The other person should have some interactions with Kim prior to the playground period.**

■ Criterion for increasing amount of time between reinforcers: **When aggressive behavior occurs in <1% of intervals observed for 3 consecutive days, increase time between delivery of noncontingent reinforcement by 10%.**

■ Criterion for decreasing the amount of time between reinforcers: **If aggressive behavior occurs in more than 5% of observed intervals for 3 consecutive days, decrease time between delivery of noncontingent reinforcement by 1 minute.**

■ Criterion for (extinction) withholding scheduled reinforcer delivery: **If aggressive behavior has occurred within 5 seconds of the scheduled delivery of reinforcement or is currently occurring, do not provide the reinforcer until the aggressive behavior has stopped for 30 seconds.**

the schedule of noncontingent reinforcement until the targeted interbehavior interval of 15 minutes.

Mr. K then discontinued the noncontingent reinforcement delivery but continued to take data for 1 month to ensure that the new behavior would continue to be effective in obtaining social attention.

## What If?

*What if the behavior does not decrease (or gets worse) with NCR?*

This may happen, although it is less likely with this program than with others. When the target behavior is no longer effective in obtaining the desired reinforcer, it may occur more frequently (called an extinction burst). If it occurs during NCR, it is possible the schedule of delivery is not dense enough. Try shortening the time between reinforcer delivery. If there is still no effect it is very likely that your functional assessment was incorrect and that there is a different reinforcer maintaining the unwanted behavior. It would be best to return to taking A-B-C data and repeat the functional assessment. You may also try making a wider variety of potentially reinforcing items available while you repeat the functional assessment.

*What if I cannot ignore some of the target behaviors?*

In cases where the target behavior is very serious or life threatening, it is best to start with much shorter schedules. A general guideline would be to set the initial schedule to 20% of the interbehavior interval. With very serious behaviors you should consider starting with a continuous presentation of the reinforcer until replacement behaviors can be developed. Of course, it is imperative that you also have an emergency plan to ensure the safety of all the people involved in the intervention.

## Forms: Noncontingent Reinforcement With Extinction

5.10 Partial Interval Data, 30-Minute Intervals

5.11 Partial Interval Data, 2-Minute Intervals

5.12 Noncontingent Reinforcement with Extinction: Simple Plan

5.13 Formulas for Calculating Percentage of Intervals of Targeted Behavior and Interbehavior Interval

5.14 Formulas for Determining Increases or Decreases in Frequency of Noncontingent Reinforcement

*FORM 5.10* ■ **PARTIAL INTERVAL DATA, 30-MINUTE INTERVALS**

■ Condition: Baseline or Treatment

Recording Method: Partial interval

■ CLIENT: _____

CHART STARTED: _____

Day/Month/Year

■ BEHAVIOR: _____

■ Interval Length: 30 minutes          Total Observation Time: __          Session length: __

☐ Behavior did **NOT** occur                    ☒ Behavior **DID** occur

Day of the month/Start time

| Interval # | Interval end time | 1 : | 2 : | 3 : | 4 : | 5 : | 6 : | 7 : | 8 : | 9 : | 10 : | 11 : | 12 : | 13 : | 14 : | 15 : |
|---|---|---|---|---|---|---|---|---|---|---|---|---|---|---|---|---|
| 1 | 6:30 A.M. | | | | | | | | | | | | | | | |
| 2 | 7:00 A.M. | | | | | | | | | | | | | | | |
| 3 | 7:30 A.M. | | | | | | | | | | | | | | | |
| 4 | 8:00 A.M. | | | | | | | | | | | | | | | |
| 5 | 8:30 A.M. | | | | | | | | | | | | | | | |
| 6 | 9:00 A.M. | | | | | | | | | | | | | | | |
| 7 | 9:30 A.M. | | | | | | | | | | | | | | | |
| 8 | 10:00 A.M. | | | | | | | | | | | | | | | |
| 9 | 10:30 A.M. | | | | | | | | | | | | | | | |
| 10 | 11:00 A.M. | | | | | | | | | | | | | | | |
| 11 | 11:30 A.M. | | | | | | | | | | | | | | | |
| 12 | 12:00 P.M. | | | | | | | | | | | | | | | |
| 13 | 12:30 P.M. | | | | | | | | | | | | | | | |
| 14 | 1:00 P.M. | | | | | | | | | | | | | | | |
| 15 | 1:30 P.M. | | | | | | | | | | | | | | | |
| 16 | 2:00 P.M. | | | | | | | | | | | | | | | |
| 17 | 2:30 P.M. | | | | | | | | | | | | | | | |
| 18 | 3:00 P.M. | | | | | | | | | | | | | | | |
| 19 | 3:30 P.M. | | | | | | | | | | | | | | | |
| 20 | 4:00 P.M. | | | | | | | | | | | | | | | |
| 21 | 4:30 P.M. | | | | | | | | | | | | | | | |
| 22 | 5:00 P.M. | | | | | | | | | | | | | | | |
| 23 | 5:30 P.M. | | | | | | | | | | | | | | | |
| 24 | 6:00 P.M. | | | | | | | | | | | | | | | |
| 25 | 6:30 P.M. | | | | | | | | | | | | | | | |
| 26 | 7:00 P.M. | | | | | | | | | | | | | | | |
| 27 | 7:30 P.M. | | | | | | | | | | | | | | | |
| 28 | 8:00 P.M. | | | | | | | | | | | | | | | |
| 29 | 8:30 P.M. | | | | | | | | | | | | | | | |
| 30 | 9:00 P.M. | | | | | | | | | | | | | | | |
| 31 | 9:30 P.M. | | | | | | | | | | | | | | | |
| 32 | 10:00 P.M. | | | | | | | | | | | | | | | |

## *FORM 5.11* ■ PARTIAL INTERVAL DATA, 2-MINUTE INTERVALS

■ Condition: Baseline or Treatment  Recording Method: Partial interval

■ CLIENT: _____  CHART STARTED: _____

**Day/Month/Year**

■ BEHAVIOR: _____

■ Interval Length: 2 minutes  Total Observation Time: ___  Session length: ___

☐ Behavior did **NOT** occur  ☒ Behavior **DID** occur

**Day of the month/Start time**

| Interval # | Interval Length | 1 : | 2 : | 3 : | 4 : | 5 : | 6 : | 7 : | 8 : | 9 : | 10 : | 11 : | 12 : | 13 : | 14 : | 15 : |
|---|---|---|---|---|---|---|---|---|---|---|---|---|---|---|---|---|
| 1 | 2 | | | | | | | | | | | | | | | |
| 2 | 4 | | | | | | | | | | | | | | | |
| 3 | 6 | | | | | | | | | | | | | | | |
| 4 | 8 | | | | | | | | | | | | | | | |
| 5 | 10 | | | | | | | | | | | | | | | |
| 6 | 12 | | | | | | | | | | | | | | | |
| 7 | 14 | | | | | | | | | | | | | | | |
| 8 | 16 | | | | | | | | | | | | | | | |
| 9 | 20 | | | | | | | | | | | | | | | |
| 10 | 22 | | | | | | | | | | | | | | | |
| 11 | 24 | | | | | | | | | | | | | | | |
| 12 | 26 | | | | | | | | | | | | | | | |
| 13 | 28 | | | | | | | | | | | | | | | |
| 14 | 30 | | | | | | | | | | | | | | | |
| 15 | 32 | | | | | | | | | | | | | | | |
| 16 | 34 | | | | | | | | | | | | | | | |
| 17 | 36 | | | | | | | | | | | | | | | |
| 18 | 38 | | | | | | | | | | | | | | | |
| 19 | 40 | | | | | | | | | | | | | | | |
| 20 | 42 | | | | | | | | | | | | | | | |
| 21 | 44 | | | | | | | | | | | | | | | |
| 22 | 46 | | | | | | | | | | | | | | | |
| 23 | 48 | | | | | | | | | | | | | | | |
| 24 | 50 | | | | | | | | | | | | | | | |
| 25 | 52 | | | | | | | | | | | | | | | |
| 26 | 54 | | | | | | | | | | | | | | | |
| 27 | 56 | | | | | | | | | | | | | | | |
| 28 | 58 | | | | | | | | | | | | | | | |
| 29 | 60 | | | | | | | | | | | | | | | |
| 30 | 62 | | | | | | | | | | | | | | | |
| 31 | 64 | | | | | | | | | | | | | | | |
| 32 | Total | | | | | | | | | | | | | | | |

*FORM 5.12* ◼ **NONCONTINGENT REINFORCEMENT WITH EXTINCTION: SIMPLE PLAN**

◼ Person served: _____

◼ Target Behavior: _____

◼ Behavioral diagnostic category: _____

◼ Target Rate: _____

◼ Designated time period(s): _____

◼ Baseline data across five times/sessions:

    1. _____

    2. _____

    3. _____

    4. _____

    5. _____

◼ % of intervals in which target behavior occurred:    Baseline _____    Target _____

◼ % of intervals in which reinforcement occurred:    Baseline _____    Target _____

◼ Interbehavior interval:    Baseline _____    Target _____

◼ Initial schedule of noncontingent reinforcement:

    ◼ ____ Fixed time schedule every ____ minutes/hours/days

        OR

    ◼ ____ Variable time schedule on average every ____ minutes/hours/days

◼ Reinforcer(s) to be used:

    1. _____

    2. _____

    3. _____

    4. _____

    5. _____

    ◼ Special instructions for delivery of reinforcer(s):

    _____

    _____

    _____

◼ Criterion for increasing the amount of time between reinforcers: _____

◼ Criterion for decreasing the amount of time between reinforcers: _____

◼ Criterion for withholding the scheduled reinforcer delivery: _____

---

*FORM 5.13* ◼ **FORMULAS FOR CALCULATING PERCENTAGE OF INTERVALS OF TARGETED BEHAVIOR AND INTERBEHAVIOR INTERVAL**

◼ *Percent of occurrence:* This formula will help you determine how often a behavior is occurring. Use this information to assess treatment effects.

    ◼ **(Total intervals target behavior occurred ÷ Total Intervals Observed) × 100 = % of intervals of target behavior.**

◼ *Rate:* This formula will help you determine on average how much time passes between the occurrence of targeted behaviors (interbehavior interval). Use this information to help set the frequency of noncontingent reinforcement.

    ◼ **Total Minutes Observed ÷ Total intervals target behavior occurred = rate or average interbehavior interval.**

*FORM 5.14* ■ **FORMULAS FOR DETERMINING INCREASES OR DECREASES IN FREQUENCY OF NONCONTINGENT REINFORCEMENT**

■ *Formula for 10% increase in time between reinforcement.*

■ Current reinforcement interval $\times$ 1.10 = (10% increase in time)

■ *Formula for 5% increase in time between reinforcement.*

■ Current reinforcement interval $\times$ 1.05 = (5% increase in time)

■ *Formula for 10% decrease in time between reinforcement.*

■ Current reinforcement interval $\times$ 0.90 = (10% decrease in time)

■ *Formula for 5% decrease in time between reinforcement.*

■ Current reinforcement interval $\times$ 0.95 = (5% decrease in time)

## More Information

Buchanan, J. A., & Fisher, J. E. (2002). Functional assessment and non-contingent reinforcement in the treatment of disruptive vocalization in elderly dementia patients. *Journal of Applied Behavior Analysis, 35,* 99–103.

Carr, J. E., Bailey, J. S. Ecott, C.,L., Lucker, K. D., & Weil, T. M. (1998). On the effects of non-contingent delivery of differing magnitudes of reinforcement. *Journal of Applied Behavior Analysis, 31,* 313–321.

Fisher, W. W., O'Connor, J. T., Kurtz, P. F., DeLeon, I. G., & Gotjen, D. L. (2000). The effects of non-contingent delivery of high- and low-preference stimuli on attention-maintained destructive behavior. *Journal of Applied Behavior Analysis, 33,* 79–83.

Fischer, S. M., Iwata, B. A., & Mazaleski, J. L. (1997). Non-contingent delivery of arbitrary reinforcers as treatment for self-injurious behavior. *Journal of Applied Behavior Analysis, 30,* 239–249.

Goh, H., Iwata, B. A., & DeLeon, I. G. (2000). Competition between non-contingent and contingent reinforcement schedules during response acquisition. *Journal of Applied Behavior Analysis, 33,* 195–205.

Goh, H., Iwata, B. A., & Kahng, S. (1999). Multicomponent assessment and treatment of cigarette pica. *Journal of Applied Behavior Analysis, 32,* 297–316.

Hagopian, L. P., Crockett, J. L., van Stone, M., DeLeon, I. G., & Bowman, L. G. (2000). Effects of non-contingent reinforcement on problem behavior and stimulus engagement: The role of satiation, extinction, and alternative reinforcement. *Journal of Applied Behavior Analysis, 33,* 433–449.

Hagopian, L. P., Fisher, W. W., & Legacy, S. M. (1994). Schedule effects of non-contingent reinforcement on attention-maintained destructive behavior in identical quadruplets. *Journal of Applied Behavior Analysis, 27,* 317–325.

Hanley, G. P., Piazza, C. C., Fisher, W. W., Contrucci, S. A., & Maglieri, K. A. (1997). Evaluation of client preference for function-based treatment packages. *Journal of Applied Behavior Analysis, 30,* 459–473.

Kahng, S., Iwata, B. A., DeLeon, I. G., & Wallace, M. D. (2000). A comparison of procedures for programming non-contingent reinforcement schedules. *Journal of Applied Behavior Analysis, 33,* 223–231.

Kahng, S., Iwata, B. A., DeLeon, I. G., & Worsdell, A. S. (1997). Evaluation of the "control over reinforcement" component in functional communication training. *Journal of Applied Behavior Analysis, 30,* 267–277.

Kahng, S., Iwata, B. A., Thompson, R. H., & Hanley, G. P. (2000). A method for identifying satiation versus extinction effects under non-contingent reinforcement schedules. *Journal of Applied Behavior Analysis, 33,* 419–432.

Lalli, J. S., Casey, S. D., & Kates, K. (1997). Non-contingent reinforcement as treatment for severe problem behavior: Some procedural variations. *Journal of Applied Behavior Analysis, 30,* 127–137.

Lindberg, J. S., Iwata, B. A., Roscoe, E. M., Worsdell, A. S., & Hanley, G. P. (2003). Treatment efficacy of non-contingent reinforcement during brief and extended application. *Journal of Applied Behavior Analysis, 36,* 1–19.

Marcus, B. A., & Vollmer, T. R. (1996). Combining non-contingent reinforcement and differential reinforcement schedules as treatment for aberrant behavior. *Journal of Applied Behavior Analysis, 29,* 43–51.

Poling, A., & Normand, M. (1999). Non-contingent reinforcement: An inappropriate description of time-based schedules that reduce behavior. *Journal of Applied Behavior Analysis, 32,* 237–238.

Reed, G. K., Piazza, C. C., Patel, M. R., Layer, S. A., Bachmeyer, M. H., Bethke, S. D., et al. (2004). On the relative contributions of non-contingent reinforcement and escape extinction in the treatment of food refusal. *Journal of Applied Behavior Analysis, 37,* 27–41.

Roscoe, E. M., Iwata, B. A., & Goh, H. (1998). A comparison of non-contingent reinforcement and sensory extinction as treatments for self-injurious behavior. *Journal of Applied Behavior Analysis, 31,* 635–646.

Roscoe, E. M., Iwata, B. A., & Rand, M. S. (2003). Effects of reinforcer consumption and magnitude on response rates during non-contingent reinforcement. *Journal of Applied Behavior Analysis, 36,* 525–539.

Thompson, R. H., Iwata, B. A., Hanley, G. P., Dozier, C. L., & Samaha, A. L. (2003). The effects of extinction, non-contingent reinforcement, and differential reinforcement of other behavior as control procedures. *Journal of Applied Behavior Analysis, 36,* 221–238.

Van Camp, C. M., Lerman, D. C., Kelley, M. E., Contrucci, S. A., & Vorndran, C. M. (2000). Variable-time reinforcement schedules in the treatment of socially maintained problem behavior. *Journal of Applied Behavior Analysis, 33,* 545–557.

Vollmer, T. R. (1999). Non-contingent reinforcement: Some additional comments. *Journal of Applied Behavior Analysis, 32,* 239–240.

Vollmer, T. R., Ringdahl, J. E., Roane, H. S., & Marcus, B. A. (1997). Negative side effects of non-contingent reinforcement. *Journal of Applied Behavior Analysis, 30,* 161–164.

Vollmer, T. R., Iwata, B. A., Zarcone, J. R., Smith, R. G., & Mazaleski, J. L. (1993). The role of attention in the treatment of attention-maintained self-injurious behavior: Non-contingent reinforcement and differential reinforcement of other behavior. *Journal of Applied Behavior Analysis, 26,* 9–21.

## 2.0 SMA FUNCTIONS: PREMACK CONTINGENCY OPTION

### Brief Description

In a Premack contingency, the desired reinforcer is produced following the client's successful compliance with a designated regimen of tasks or demands. This has also sometimes been referred to as Grandma's rule, that is, you don't get your dessert until you eat your vegetables. The more technical definition of the Premack principle is making access to a high probability behavior contingent on performing a low probability behavior (Premack & Bahwell, 1959).

To implement a Premack contingency as a replacement behavior option, one first determines the maintaining reinforcer for the target behavior. You then determine a set of tasks that have to be performed before access to the reinforcer is delivered. The reinforcing item or activity is withheld until the client performs the specified task.

The advantage of using a Premack contingency as a replacement behavior option is that it uses the specific reinforcer that was previously maintaining the client's target behavior. This contingency introduces a requirement to perform a set of tasks that will delay but not eliminate access to the reinforcing item or event. This replacement behavior option reduces some of the difficulties associated with extinction. It also usually reduces the overall rate of access to the preferred item or event. The Premack contingency option can be used with any SMA subcategory, with the possible exception of SMA 2.2: Peer attention.

### Apparatus

Data sheets—See Form 5.15 "Simple Frequency Data With Formulas"

Reinforcing items or events—If tangible items or activities have been identified as the maintaining reinforcers, and will be delivered on a Premack contingency, a sufficient supply must be available.

### Baseline Measurement

1. Identify the target behavior's function.
2. Operationally define or pinpoint the target behavior, with specific criteria for onset and offset of behavior (if not readily evident).
3. Determine the observation period, possibly by reviewing scatter plot or A-B-C data to identify periods of time when behavior is highly likely.
4. Construct the data sheet to reflect the length of the observation period, trying to keep the length reasonably similar during all baseline sessions.
5. During observation, record either the occurrence of the target behavior, the duration of the target behavior, or the intensity of the behavior (which measure will depend on the target behavior).
6. Repeat step 5 until the observation period ends.
7. Conduct at least five more baseline sessions.
8. Graph or display the data across all baseline sessions.

## Procedures for Premack Contingency

1. Either at certain times of the day or under certain antecedent conditions that occasion the target access behavior, require the client to engage in a simple designated task, determined by an analysis of client's level of ability.
2. When the client completes the requirement of the task, provide the reinforcer.
3. Repeat steps 1 and 2 with each request.
4. As a function of success in ameliorating the target behavior, progressively increase the duration or quantity of the task required.
5. Ensure that the target behavior does not produce the desired reinforcer. (extinction)

### Procedures for Premack Contingency When Used as a Supplement for an SMA Requesting (Mand) Program

1. Contingent upon a request by the client for the reinforcer, direct the client to engage in a simple designated task, determined by an analysis of client's level of ability. (Note: initially the only task required will be the request itself.)
2. When the client completes the requirement of the task, provide reinforcer.
3. Repeat steps 1 and 2 with each request.
4. As a function of success in ameliorating the target behavior, progressively increase the duration or quantity of the task required.
5. Ensure that the target behavior does not produce the desired reinforcer (extinction).

### Thinning the Schedule of Delivery of Maintaining Reinforcer

Once the target behavior is reduced the behavior analyst can increase the response effort or time delay to obtain the desired event or item. This can be done in two ways:

1. Increase the duration or complexity of each task.
2. Increase the number of tasks required to earn the reinforcer.

Progressively altering either or both of these factors will increase the length of time the client will have to wait before getting the reinforcer following a request.

*If utilizing this behavior option for* Direct Access behaviors (1.0 DA): *Utilize the same baseline and treatment procedures as above, except that chain interruption would occur instead of extinction when the target behavior is displayed.*

## How It Works

It is often the case that the social environment has made it too easy for the person to get certain events or reinforcers. Therefore, access to such events occurs at unreasonable levels. To want someone's attention is not a sin! But it is tough to accommodate such a desire when it is demanded every few minutes. While this may be an acceptable state of affairs for infants, as children get older they have to be "weaned off" of such frequent and lengthy attention from their parent. Some children do not undergo such conditioning and learn to engage in disruptive and disastrous behaviors to continually access attention or preferred items or activities. The same problem can occur once the person is taught to request reinforcers. Requesting may occur too often once developed, with access to the tangible or social reinforcer provided beyond a reasonable level. Hence, this Premack contingency program also is used to supplement the requesting program described earlier.

A Premack contingency is well suited to reduce the client's constant desire for a given reinforcer. Requiring the performance of a less preferred task as a condition for access to reinforcement is a strategy that will eventually "wean them off" of frequent access. Clinical applications of the Premack contingency typically result in the client not requesting the desired event as often, given the requirement to perform tasks to access the reinforcer. In these cases there was also no increase in target behavior.

*TABLE 5.12* ■ **SUMMARY OF A-B-C OBSERVATIONS ACCESSING CHIPS**

| Antecedent Conditions | Target Behavior | What Happened? | What Was Natural Result of Behavior? |
|---|---|---|---|
| During break after having eaten her snack, asks for a bag of chips. Staff said no. | Threw plate on the floor, refused to pick it up, yelling, asked to go to a quiet area because the voices were bothering her. | Went to quiet area for 5 minutes. Received bag of chips after remaining calm. | Irrelevant. |
| Doing an art project, eating some chips and drinking a soda, getting close to lunch. Asked for additional chips from staff, staff said no. | Shredded the project she had just completed. Threw paints on the floor and said she had demons in her. | Stopped doing the art project and went to quiet area until lunch break. Received chips with lunch. | Irrelevant. |

### Hypothetical Example

#### Lays Potato Chips: Bet You Can't Have Just One

Mary, a client diagnosed with schizophrenia, was referred for behavior analysis services due to engaging in property destruction while at her day program.

The initial referral to the behavior analyst, Ms. Chance, stated that the staff needed help with Mary's property destruction. Ms. Chance went to the day program and interviewed several staff. She then constructed Table 5.12 from the information provided.

Ms. Chance observed Mary on several occasions and noticed that there was a pattern of escalating behavior. It often started with a simple request by Mary to get more chips. When such a request was ignored, Mary engaged in behavior that resulted in her going to the break room. When Mary was sent to the break room someone usually gave her another bag of chips. On some occasions several bags were obtained, depending on which staff person was escorting her to the break room. Given that the behavior was frequently followed by the addition of staff interaction and chips, it seemed likely that the behavior served an access function. Ms. Chance considered an escape function, however Mary had demonstrated several behaviors that were effective in escaping and avoiding demands in the day program, so she concluded that escape was unlikely to be the function. Additionally, the target behavior rarely occurred under task demand conditions. This information seemed to rule out socially mediated escape diagnoses.

Ms. Chance observed that the target behavior only happened when other people were around and never when Mary was alone. She considered a 2.1 SMA: staff attention diagnosis but ruled it out because she observed Mary using skills that were very effective in both initiating and maintaining conversations with staff members. She considered a 2.2 SMA: peer attention diagnosis but ruled it out because the rate of Mary's target behavior did not change based on the presence or absence of peers.

This left the most likely diagnosis to be 2.3 SMA: tangible reinforcer, food item, specifically an extra bag of chips (see Table 5.13).

*TABLE 5.13* ■ **DIAGNOSTIC TABLE**

| Diagnosis | 2.3 SMA: tangible reinforcer, food item |
|---|---|
| Target behavior(s): | Property destruction |
| Function: | Access food item potato chips |
| Target behavior likely under following contexts: | Anytime Mary sees a bag of chips or is informed that chips are in the facility |
| Target behavior unlikely under following contexts: | After she has consumed several bags of chips |
| Rule out: | 2.1 SMA: staff attention<br>2.2 SMA: peer attention |

Ms. Chance presented her hypothesis to the treatment team. The team expressed some concern and disagreement with Ms Chance's analysis. They believed that the property destruction was a direct result of the client's auditory hallucinations and should be treated with increased dosages of antipsychotic medication. The basis for their belief was that Mary reported hearing voices during these property destructive incidents.

As a point of compromise, Ms. Chance offered to test her hypothesis over the next 5 days. The test was a simple one. About every 60 minutes Mary would be given two bags of chips. If hallucinations were a driving factor for the property destructive behavior, the addition of the chips should have no effect. However, if chips were enabling the function of the target behavior, the rate should decrease. The team agreed, and the test was implemented. During these 5 days, there were no reports of auditory hallucinations, no requests to go to the break room, and no incidents of property destruction.

This new information was presented to the team. The team would not give up their belief about Mary's hallucinations being key to property destruction, even with the new evidence. They indicated that the change in these behaviors was probably due to a progress with Mary's condition and that the chips being given to her were irrelevant. To test this hypothesis, they all agreed to simply withhold chips entirely for several days to see what happened. They removed all bags of chips from the day program area to ensure that none would be inadvertently provided. During the next 5 days Mary reported auditory hallucinations each day, went to the break room one to three times per day, and engaged in property destruction on four occasions (see Example Form 5.15). The following week they returned to providing two bags of chips about every 60 minutes, and again there were no reports of auditory hallucinations, no requests to go to the break room, and no events of property destruction.

---

### EXAMPLE FORM 5.15 ■ FREQUENCY COUNT DATA SHEET

■ Client: _____ Mary _____                     CHART STARTED: _____

                                                            **Day/Month/Year**

■ BEHAVIOR: <u>Hallucinations and property destruction</u>
■ Total Observation Time: <u>1800</u> MIN (<u>1</u>, <u>360</u>-minute session/day)
■ Session length: <u>360 min</u>
■ Number of Days: <u>5</u>
■ Place an X on the appropriate day box each time the target behavior occurs

|  | 1 | 2 | 3 | 4 | 5 | Totals |
|---|---|---|---|---|---|---|
| Reports of hallucinations | X | XXX | XX | XXX | XX | |
| Daily Rate | 1 | 3 | 2 | 3 | 2 | 11 |

A. Total Minutes Observed: <u>1800</u>
B. Total occurrences observed: <u>11</u> Rate/minute = B/A <u>**11/1800**</u> = <u>**.006**</u>
C. Range (low) <u>1</u> to (high) <u>3</u>, Avg = <u>2.2</u> Rate/hour = (B/A)60 (<u>**11/1800**</u>)60 = **0.37**

|  | 1 | 2 | 3 | 4 | 5 | Totals |
|---|---|---|---|---|---|---|
| Property destruction | | X | X | X | X | 4 |
| Daily Rate | | | | | | |

A. Total Minutes Observed: <u>1800</u>
B. Total occurrences observed: <u>4</u> Rate/minute = B/A <u>**4/1800**</u> = <u>**.002**</u>
C. Range (low) <u>0</u> to (high) <u>1</u>, Avg = <u>0.8</u> Rate/hour = (B/A)60 (<u>**4/1800**</u>)60 = <u>**0.13**</u>

Finally, the team agreed that the unwanted behaviors seemed to be functioning to produce the desired bags of chips.

Ms. Chance could have continued providing two bags of chips every 60 minutes, however, that would pose a problem. The consumption of that amount of potato chips daily would pose a significant health risk. Simply reinforcing requesting behavior was also not a practical plan for Mary for the same reason.

Ms. Chance decided that a Premack contingency might work in this case to enable a new set of behaviors as functional in accessing chips. The Premack contingency would also allow a gradual reduction in the desire for such chips over time, as the work requirement increased.

Ms. Chance developed a list of activities based on observing things that Mary would occasionally complete. *(Note: These are not functionally equivalent replacement behaviors, they are arbitrarily selected tasks.)*

## PREMACK TASK LIST

Person served: _____ **Mary** _____
List of activities to be required prior to **accessing chips**

| | Description of activities including any idiosyncrasies, such as time of day or who delivers the reinforcer. |
|---|---|
| 1 | Go for a walk |
| 2 | Painting |
| 3 | Reading |
| 4 | Talking with friends |
| 5 | Working on assembly tasks |
| 6 | Setting up the break room for snacks/lunch |
| 7 | Systematic relaxation |
| 8 | Cleaning up after break/lunch |
| 9 | Self report recording of symptoms and side effects |
| 10 | Brush teeth |
| 11 | Comb hair |

Ms. Chance then set up a Premack contingency (see Example Form 5.16). Any time Mary made a request for chips the following contingencies were introduced. Mary could earn a bag of chips after she combed her hair. To earn a second bag before the next break she would be required to brush her teeth and record her self report of symptoms and side effects of medication. To earn a third bag, she would need to complete an assembly task, do systematic relaxation, and either set up or clean up the break room. In this way, her requests could always be fulfilled but with increasing effort on her part and a concomitant time delay in accessing the chips.

The plan was implemented, and Ms. Chance graphed property destruction as well as hair brushing (see Figure 5.4). The intervention had a clear effect on the rate of property destruction and increased the rate of hair brushing.

## *EXAMPLE FORM 5.16* ■ PREMACK CONTINGENCY: SIMPLE PLAN

- ■ Person served: **Mary**
- ■ Target Behavior **Property destruction**
- ■ Behavioral diagnostic category: **2.3 SMA: tangible reinforcer, food item, Chips**
- ■ Designated time Period(s): **During day program**
- ■ Baseline data across five times/sessions:

  1. __2__
  2. __3__
  3. __1__
  4. __3__
  5. __2__

- ■ Rate of Low probability behavior:  Baseline **0/day**  Target **2/day**
- ■ Rate of high probability behavior:  Baseline **2.2/day**  Target **0**
- ■ Initial Standard for Low Probability behavior: **Upon making a request for chips Mary will be asked to complete the following: Combing her hair for 2 minutes.**
- ■ Description of how high probability behavior will be provided (how much, how often, etc.): **Will be given one bag of chips to consume; if she wants a second bag before the next break time, see special instructions.**
- ■ Criterion for increasing the duration/complexity of the low probability behavior: **When Mary has gone 5 consecutive days with no property destruction, increase the low probability behavior required by adding one additional task from the table prior to her having access to the bag of chips.**
- ■ Criterion for decreasing the duration/complexity of the low probability behavior: **If Mary engages in property destruction for two consecutive days, change the required response to setting up or cleaning up the break room.**
- ■ Procedure for withholding/preventing the high probability behavior if not earned: **Bags of chips will be maintained in a locked cabinet and given only at break times or if Mary meets the contingency.**
- ■ Special instructions for delivery of reinforcer(s):
- ■ **If Mary has already earned one bag of chips during the time period before a break/lunch and wants to earn another bag she may do so by completing two times the number of tasks specified in the low probability behavior description.**

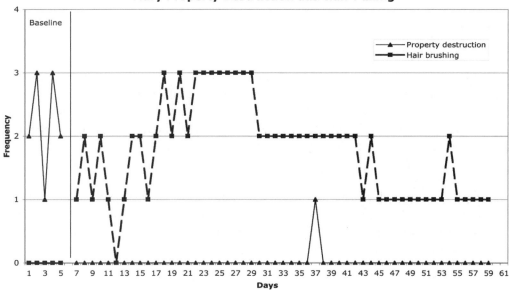

*Figure 5.4* ■ Property destruction and hair pulling.

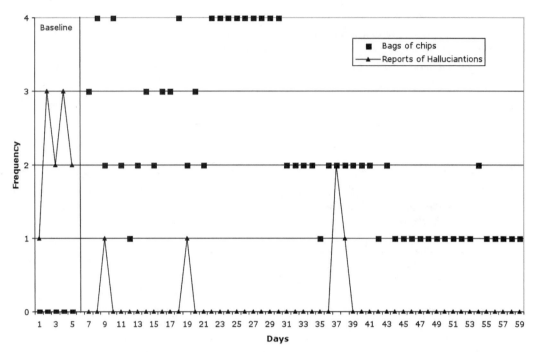

**Figure 5.5** ■ Hallucination and chip consumption.

There was some concern that Mary was now eating chips nonstop. Ms. Chance graphed the number of bags of chips Mary was earning per day and included Mary's report of hallucinations as there had been some concern that this intervention would be too stressful and increase her symptoms. As can be seen in Figure 5.5, the Premack contingency had an immediate effect on Mary's report of hallucinations. This reduction continued across the intervention. Mary did increase her chip intake for a period of time, but as the Premack contingency was systematically increased, her chip intake reduced to one bag per day.

### What If?

*What if the person refuses to do the required behavior?*

If your analysis is correct, the person should, after some short period of time, engage in the low probability behavior because it allows access to some preferred event. If this does not occur, assess to make sure they can actually perform the low probability behavior, that is, they do not have a skills deficit. You may reduce the difficulty of the low probability behavior to make it more likely they will contact the reinforcer.

*What if I cannot prevent the person from engaging in the behavior to be used as a reinforcer?*

In order to use the Premack contingency you must have an effective chain interruption procedure if the behavior is a 1.0 DA diagnosis. If you cannot do this it is best to use one of the other intervention programs initially, such as noncontingent reinforcement, prior to attempting a Premack contingency.

*Forms: Premack Contingency*

5.15 Simple Frequency Data With Formulas
5.16 Premack Contingency: Simple Plan

---

*FORM 5.15* ■ **SIMPLE FREQUENCY DATA WITH FORMULAS**

■ Client: _____      **CHART STARTED:** _____

                                                                                      Day/Month/Year

■ Behavior: _____

■ Total Observation Time: __MIN__ (__, ___-minute session/day)      Session length: __min__

■ Number of Days: __

■ Place an X on the appropriate day box each time the target behavior occurs

| | 1 : | 2 : | 3 : | 4 : | 5 : | 6 : | 7 : | Totals |
|---|---|---|---|---|---|---|---|---|
| Target Behavior | | | | | | | | |
| Daily Rate | | | | | | | | |

A. Total Minutes Observed: __

B. Total occurrences observed: __ Rate/minute = B/A __/__ = ____

C. Range (low) __ to (high) __, Avg = __ Rate/hour = (B/A)60 (__/__)60 = ____

| | 8 : | 9 : | 10 : | 11 : | 12 : | 13 : | 14 : | Totals |
|---|---|---|---|---|---|---|---|---|
| Target Behavior | | | | | | | | |
| Daily Rate | | | | | | | | |

A. Total Minutes Observed: __

B. Total occurrences observed: __ Rate/minute = B/A __/__ = ____

C. Range (low) __ to (high) __, Avg = __ Rate/hour = (B/A)60 (__/__)60 = ____

---

*FORM 5.16* ■ **PREMACK CONTINGENCY: SIMPLE PLAN**

■ Person served: _____

■ Target Behavior: _____

■ Behavioral diagnostic category: _____

■ Designated time Period(s): _____

■ Baseline data across five times/sessions:

    1. _____
    2. _____
    3. _____
    4. _____
    5. _____

■ Rate of low probability behavior:    Baseline _____  Target _____

■ Rate of high probability behavior:    Baseline _____  Target _____

■ Initial standard for low probability behavior _____

■ Description of how high probability behavior will be provided (how much, how often, etc.): ____

■ Criterion for increasing the duration/complexity of the low probability behavior: _____

■ Criterion for decreasing the duration/complexity of the low probability behavior: _____

■ Procedure for withholding/preventing the high probability behavior if not earned: _____

    ■ Special instructions for delivery of reinforcer(s):

---

## More Information

Allison, J. (1976). Contrast, induction, facilitation, suppression and conservation. *Journal of the Experimental Analysis of Behavior, 25,* 185–198.

Amari, A., Grace, N. C., & Fisher, W. W. (1995). Achieving and maintaining compliance with the ketogenic diet. *Journal of Applied Behavior Analysis, 28,* 341–342.

Hanley, G. P., Iwata, B. A., Roscoe, E. M., Thompson, R. H., & Lindberg, J. S. (2003). Response-restriction analysis: II. Alteration of activity preferences. *Journal of Applied Behavior Analysis, 36,* 59–76.

Hanley, G. P., Iwata, B. A., Thompson, R. H., & Lindberg, J. S. (2000). A component analysis of "stereotypy as reinforcement" for alternative behavior. *Journal of Applied Behavior Analysis, 33,* 285–297.

Homme, L. E., de Baca, P. C., Devine, J. V., Steinhorst, R., & Rickert, E. J. (1963). Use of the premack principle in controlling the behavior of nursery school children. *Journal of the Experimental Analysis of Behavior, 6,* 544.

Konarski, E. A., Jr., Johnson, M. R., Crowell, C. R., & Whitman, T. L. (1980). Response deprivation and reinforcement in applied settings: A preliminary analysis. *Journal of Applied Behavior Analysis, 13,* 595–609.

Mitchell, W. S., & Stoffelmayr, B. E. (1973). Application of the Premack principle to the behavioral control of extremely inactive schizophrenics. *Journal of Applied Behavior Analysis, 6,* 419–423.

Mithaug, D. E., & Mar, D. K. (1980). The relation between choosing and working prevocational tasks in two severely retarded young adults. *Journal of Applied Behavior Analysis, 13,* 177–182.

Premack, D. (1963). Rate differential reinforcement in monkey manipulation. *Journal of the Experimental Analysis of Behavior, 6,* 81–89.

Premack, D. (1970). A functional analysis of language. *Journal of the Experimental Analysis of Behavior, 14,* 107–125.

Premack, D., & Bahwell, R. (1959). Operant-level lever pressing by a monkey as a function of interest interval. *Journal of the Experimental Analysis of Behavior, 2,* 127–131.

Premack, D., & Premack, A. J. (1963). Increased eating in rats deprived of running. *Journal of the Experimental Analysis of Behavior, 6,* 209–212.

Premack, D., & Schaeffer, R. W. (1962). Distributional properties of operant-level locomotion in the rat. *Journal of the Experimental Analysis of Behavior, 5,* 89–95.

Premack, D., & Schaeffer, R. W. (1963). Some parameters affecting the distributional properties of operant-level running in rats. *Journal of the Experimental Analysis of Behavior, 6,* 473–475.

Premack, D., Schaeffer, R. W., & Hundt, A. (1964). Reinforcement of drinking by running: Effect of fixed ratio and reinforcement time. *Journal of the Experimental Analysis of Behavior, 7,* 91–96.

## 2.0 SMA FUNCTIONS: ACCESS MAND (REQUEST) OPTION

### Brief Description

In this replacement behavior option, the desired reinforcer, whether it be social attention or access to tangible reinforcer, is accessed upon an appropriate request (mand) from the client. Concurrently, the target behavior no longer functions to efficiently access the desired reinforcer, that is, programmed extinction.

To implement a requesting behavior program for a target behavior that is diagnosed with an SMA function, you should first determine what specific form the request should take. Next, when the new requesting behavior occurs, it is reinforced each time with the specific items or event that was requested. If the target behavior occurs, the reinforcer is not provided until the person engages in the specified requesting behavior. By providing reinforcement in this way, we ensure that engaging in the replacement requesting behavior results in a differentially higher rate of reinforcement than the target behavior (differential reinforcement of an alternate behavior, DRA).

The advantage of using this procedure is that it develops or teaches a specific behavior that will result in access to a specific reinforcer when the person is most motivated to obtain that particular reinforcer. This makes the acquisition of the skill relatively rapid and generally results in a robust response that can be shaped and generalized to overcome other target behaviors. A disadvantage of this option involves an initial interruption in routine due to immediately complying with the person's request by delivering the specific item or event. This option is a bit more labor intensive than the DRO option and requires a higher level of expertise and interaction on the part of those implementing the intervention.

### Terms

*Mand:* A verbal operant behavior under the control of a specific motivating operation that produces a socially mediated specific reinforcer. In the case of a positive reinforcer, a request for access to a specific reinforcer. The form may be vocal, sign language, gestural, written, or any combination that has a specific desired effect on the audience of this request.

### Apparatus

Data sheets—See Form 5.17 "Simple Frequency Data on Target and Replacement Behaviors"

Reinforcing items or events—If tangible items or activities have been identified as the maintaining reinforcers and will be delivered, a sufficient supply must be available.

### Baseline Measurement

It is important to first determine the form of the requesting behavior that will be developed or increased prior to baseline data collection. Next, collect baseline data on both the target behavior and the replacement behavior using Form 5.17.

If the frequency of the requesting behavior is low, you might consider contriving an antecedent condition that deprives or withholds the maintaining reinforcer, and observe what behavior occurs (target or replacement behavior). See trigger analysis in chapter 2 for greater detail on conducting this assessment. Realize that the conditions of deprivation have to be extant in order for either behavior to be realized. Try to make sure that no one provides the reinforcer prior to your assessment.

A simple frequency data sheet such as Form 5.17 should provide sufficient baseline data to decide how to proceed with your assessment and intervention.

## Procedures

1. Identify the reinforcer (e.g., food, toys, drink, physical contact).
2. Identify the time and setting when the reinforcer is not readily available, and ensure that the client is slightly deprived of it (i.e., wants it). *It is essential that the client be motivated to access the desired item or event.* The judgment of when he wants the item can generally be along the same conditions and times under which the 2.0 SMA target behavior occurred. Using the same level of deprivation that existed as a motivating condition for the problem behavior, you now use the following procedures to develop the replacement behavior.
3. Determine the initial request response to be targeted for reinforcement (with access to specific reinforcer), for example, vocal response, manual signed response, pointing to a communication board, and so forth.
4. Present the general instruction "What do you want?" with the item, object, or activity within sight.
5. Use a prompt that is as intrusive as necessary to evoke the request.
6. Contingent upon the occurrence of the specified requesting behavior, present the reinforcer in small quantities (e.g., a piece of food) or short duration (e.g., 2 minutes of toy play), and record the occurrence of the behavior on the data sheet.
7. If the target behavior occurs, remove the reinforcer for a short period of time and start again at step 4. (extinction)
8. Repeat steps 3–6 for as long as the person is motivated to request the reinforcer. When the person's enthusiasm wanes, end access to the reinforcer until motivation can be re-established.
9. As the client becomes more competent, provide less of a prompt, and time delay the prompt, allowing him or her the opportunity to respond ahead of the prompt.
10. Provide opportunities for requesting in real life by occasionally depriving the client of some reinforcer for a brief period of time, then reinforcing (and if necessary prompting) the request.

*If utilizing this behavior option for* Direct Access behaviors (1.0 DA): *Utilize the same baseline and treatment procedures as above, except that chain interruption would occur instead of extinction when the target behavior is displayed.*

## How It Works

Teaching a requesting behavior (mand) works by establishing an alternate form of behavior that will allow the person to more effectively and efficiently access the same maintaining reinforcer as the target behavior. Once the person has a behavior in their repertoire that can function as a request, you enable its function by making sure that it is more effective and efficient than the target behavior in accessing reinforcement. Once the mand is functional, the fading or thinning process allows for the natural contingencies in the environment to control the requesting behavior so that it will maintain over time.

*TABLE 5.14* ■ **SUMMARY OF FALLING TO THE FLOOR A-B-C DATA**

| Antecedent Conditions | Target Behavior | What Happened? | What Was Natural Result of Behavior? |
|---|---|---|---|
| 1. In resource room, completed math task; asked to read from workbook. | Fell to floor. | Teacher requested that she get up (x4), teacher rubbed her shoulders (x2), teacher got favorite book and presented it at the table. Student got up and looked at book with teacher. | Possible sensation \|produced when laying on the floor. |
| 2. Finished reading from workbook, class preparing for lunch. | Fell to floor. | Teacher requested that she get up (x2), teacher rubbed her shoulders and requested (x2), teacher offered to sit with her at lunch and read her book. Student got up, picked up her book, and went to lunch with teacher. | Possible sensation produced when laying on the floor. |
| 3. Working on math task. Completed task. Sitting at desk quietly; no interaction for 5 minutes. | Fell to floor and brief loud vocalization. | Teacher requested that she get up (x1), teacher rubbed her shoulders (x4), teacher got favorite book and presented it at the table. Student got up and looked at book with teacher. | Possible sensation produced when laying on the floor. |

## Hypothetical Example

As an example, let's examine a case of a child who drops to the floor regularly. Mr. Smith, a school psychologist, was asked to assess the female student. He began by reviewing available records and interviewing the teaching staff. Mr. Smith was informed by the teaching staff that several interventions had been tried with little success. The classroom staff tried pleading with the student to get up, but to no avail. They had tried ongoing counseling as well as crisis counseling when she was laying on the floor. One of the teacher's aides did mention that the only thing that would get her to cooperate in the classroom was looking at her favorite picture book. Given this information and the fact that the staff at this point were somewhat frustrated with the lack of success, Mr. Smith decided to perform a descriptive functional assessment (A-B-C analysis) from his direct observations. Table 5.14 summarizes his findings.

Mr. Smith noticed that falling to the floor occurred if the student was required to work on a task but that it also occurred when she had no academic demands placed on her. He concluded that the falling behavior was probably not functioning to escape an instructional task or demand. He also noticed that the interaction with the teacher and her favorite book were more likely to be given to her immediately after falling behavior occurred. He then turned to identifying if the reinforcer was directly accessed or socially mediated. He interviewed several staff and family members who indicated that she had never been known to fall on the floor if she was alone. He concluded that the falling behavior was most likely functioning to access socially mediated reinforcement (2.0 SMA category).

Mr. Smith set about determining the specific 2.0 SMA diagnosis. He reviewed the available data and found that the falling on the floor behavior occurred even while the teaching staff were interacting with the student, regardless of which staff person was involved with her. This ruled out 2.1 SMA: adult attention. He also ruled out 2.2 SMA: peer attention because falling behavior happened when peers were present and when they were not.

Mr. Smith noticed that in each event of falling behavior the student only got up off the floor when her favorite book was offered to her. It did not seem to matter who offered the book. He was convinced that 2.3 SMA: tangible reinforcer (favorite picture book) was the most likely diagnosis (see Table 5.15).

### TABLE 5.15 ■ DIAGNOSTIC TABLE FALLING TO THE FLOOR

| Diagnosis | 2.3 SMA: tangible reinforcer (favorite picture book). |
| --- | --- |
| Target behavior(s): | Falling on the floor during class. |
| Function: | Access to favorite picture book. |
| Target behavior likely under following contexts: | If it has been longer than 1 hour since the student had looked at the picture book. |
| Target behavior unlikely under following contexts: | While looking at the picture book or immediately following looking at the book. |
| Rule out: | 2.1 SMA: adult attention<br>1.1 DA: immediate sensory stimulation |

Mr. Smith tested his hypothesis by making sure that the student did not have access to the picture book for several hours. He then waited for her to fall on the floor. He had instructed the staff to do nothing when the student fell to the floor. When the target behavior occurred Mr. Smith picked up her favorite picture book, making sure that the student saw the book in his hands, placed the book on her desk, and walked away. The student immediately got up off the floor and began to look at the book. Mr. Smith was now sure of his diagnosis.

Because this student was currently not capable of significant vocal speech, a nonvocal request needed to be considered. Mr. Smith decided to develop a plan that calls for the student to use a nonvocal request, such as raising her hand, as the behavior that will be socially mediated and will result in the delivery of her favorite book. Falling on the floor will be disabled through the use of programmed extinction. This dual contingency is specified in Table 5.16.

Note that in Table 5.16, the request (raises her hand) for the teacher to bring the book to read is designated as the replacement mand behavior. Such a request will now result in an adult providing her with the book. Prior to writing the plan, Mr. Smith requested that the teacher record some data on the frequency of falling to the floor behavior and the frequency of raising one's hand across 55-minute observation sessions over 6 days. The data was recorded on Example Form 5.17.

With this frequency data in hand, and an understanding of the function of the falling behavior, Mr. Smith designed an intervention plan. He determined that the falling behavior occurred about every 55 minutes. He also knew that falling only occurred if the student had been deprived of access to her picture book. Additionally, his data indicated that the student very rarely exhibited the replacement behavior of raising her hand.

While there were many replacement behavior options that could be used to stop the falling behavior, Mr. Smith decided that a requesting behavior would not only address the current problem, but would be a skill that the student would need in various situations in the future. Mr. Smith decided that the requesting behavior he would try to establish first was having the student raise her hand. This is the general behavior used in most classroom settings if you want to request something. He further decided that for the behavior to be effective the student would have to do it while seated at her desk. Mr. Smith knew that the targeted behavior of falling to the ground was more likely around 11 A.M. each day,

### TABLE 5.16 ■ EXAMPLE OF REPLACEMENT BEHAVIOR—REQUESTING BEHAVIOR

| Reinforcer | Undesired Form (target behavior) | Replacement Behavior |
| --- | --- | --- |
| Adult reads/shows student favored book. | Falls to the floor. | Request (raises hand) for adult to bring book. |

**EXAMPLE FORM 5.17 ■ FREQUENCY COUNT DATA SHEET**

■ Client: **Student A**

CHART STARTED: _____
Day/Month/Year

■ Behavior: **Falling to Floor**
■ Total Observation Time: **330 MIN** (**2**, **55**-minute session/day)          Session length: **55 min**
■ Number of Days: **6**
■ Place an X on the appropriate day box each time the behavior occurs

|  | Day 1 | Day 2 | Day 3 | Day 4 | Day 5 | Day 6 | Totals |
|---|---|---|---|---|---|---|---|
| Falling to floor | X | XXX | XX |  |  |  | 6 |
| Raising hand |  |  | X |  |  |  | 1 |

A. Total Minutes Observed: **330**
B. Total Target behavior occurrences observed: **6**
C. Total Replacement behavior occurrences observed: **1**

when the student was at her desk. He decided the best way to capture a high level of motivation for the picture book was to set up training for about 11 A.M. in the classroom at the student's desk. Mr. Smith made sure that at all other times the picture book would be placed in the teacher's desk so that there would be no chance of inadvertently reducing the motivation for the book by allowing free access.

Mr. Smith set the initial reinforcement schedule for every incident of hand raising to produce 1 minute of time with the picture book. In this way, Mr. Smith would ensure a high rate of reinforcement for the preferred requesting behavior of the student raising her hand. To increase the speed of this process Mr. Smith also specified an extinction contingency. If the student engaged in falling on the floor, the picture book would be unavailable to her for 3 minutes. After 3 minutes, prompting of the replacement mand behavior would resume.

Mr. Smith specified that the following prompt sequence should be used, during times when falling to the floor was more likely. The first prompt would be delivered vocally and progress to more helpful or intrusive prompts if hand raising did not occur. The instructions to the staff were as follows:

1. Provide the prompt "What do you want?"
2. If no response, provide the prompt again with the book in view.
3. If no response, provide the prompt with the addition of a gestural prompt.
4. If no response, provide the prompt with the addition of modeling the response.
5. If no response, provide the prompt with the addition of a physical prompt.
6. If no response, provide increasing physical prompt using least to most prompting.
7. Once the request occurs, provide the requested reinforcer.
8. Repeat for as long as the student is motivated to request the reinforcer. When enthusiasm wanes, end access to the book.

Mr. Smith also wanted to make sure that the student would eventually raise her hand when she wanted the picture book without anyone prompting her to do so. In order to accomplish this he developed a plan for slowly decreasing the prompts that were provided. He determined that once the student could raise her hand with prompts for 3 consecutive days, the response was learned to a level that allowed him to reduce or fade the prompts.

### *EXAMPLE FORM 5.18* ■ **TEACHING REQUESTING BEHAVIOR PLAN**

■ Person Served: **Student A**

■ Target Behavior: **Falling on floor**

■ Behavioral diagnostic category: **SMA 2.3: tangible reinforcer, favorite book**

■ Requesting Behavior: **Requesting book**

    A. Form of request: vocal request; manual signed request; requesting by pointing to a communication board; use augmentative device to request; other: **Gesture**

    B. Description of Initial request to be reinforced: **Rising of her hand while seated**

■ Reinforcer(s) to be used:

| | Type | Amount of time |
|---|---|---|
| | 1. **Picture book** | 1. **1 min** |
| | 2. _____ | 2. ____ |

■ Target Rate: **Greater than once per hour**

■ Instructions to assure motivation:

    Train at Time and place that target behaivor is most likely which is:

        **Training at 11:00am in the classroom at her desk**

    Assure limited access to reinforcing item at other times by: **The book will be kept in the teachers desk drawer at all other times**

■ Rate of target behavior:        Baseline **1/hr**    Target **0/day**

■ Rate of Requesting Behavior:    Baseline **1/day**    Target **1/hr**

■ Initial schedule of Differential reinforcement:

    A. Provide contrived reinforcer after every **1** (number of ) requests and with no more than a **5** Sec delay

■ Targeted final schedule of Differential Reinforcement:

    A. Assure reinforcer delivery after every **2** (number of) requests with no more than a **15** Sec/Min delay

■ Replacement behavior is reinforced:

■ If the requesting behavior occurs independently provide reinforcer requested.

■ If the requesting behavior does not occur under the targeted conditions

■ Provide the following prompts: (using **Vocal** ~~Sign Gesture Visual~~)

1. Provide the prompt "What do you want?"

2. If no response provide the prompt again with the item item/object/activity within sight

3. If no response provide the above prompt with the addition of a gestural prompt

4. If no response provide the above with the addition of modeling the response

5. If no response provide the above with the addition of a physical prompt

6. If no response provide increasing physical prompt using least to most prompting

7. Once the request occurs provide the requested reinforcer.

8. Repeat for as long as the child/client is motivated to request the reinforcer.

9. When the client's "enthusiasm" wanes, you can end access to the reinforcer for that time period

■ **If target behavior occurs:**

■ Extinction, (no access to the requested reinforcer) for **3** minutes, then begin prompt sequence for replacement behavior listed above.

■ If replacement Mand behavior occurs after this time period provide the requested reinforcer.

    ■ Special instructions for delivery of small amount of reinforcer(s):

    _____

    _____

■ Criterion for Fading prompts: **When target rate for replacement behavior is reached on 3 consecutive days reduce the level of helpfulness of the prompt first by waiting for 5 seconds before providing the prompt and then by reducing the prompt from vocal to simple hand gestures and eventually to the level of prompts that would usually be in place in the classroom.**

**Frequency Falling and Hand Raising Student A**

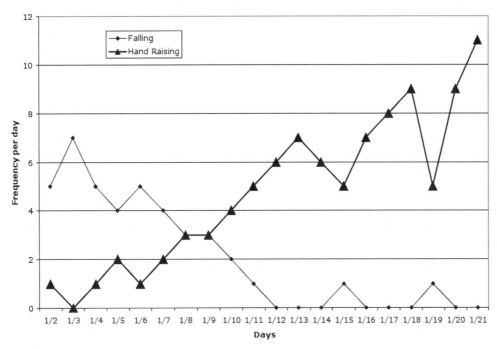

***Figure 5.6*** ■ Falling data.

He decided to do this in two ways. First, Mr. Smith set up a brief delay in the delivery of the prompts. That is, when the book was taken out of the desk for a training session, rather than give the student a vocal prompt, he would wait 5 seconds to allow her to raise her hand independently. Second, he reduced the vocal prompt to simply "what?" with a plan to further stop the vocal prompt entirely. As the student continued to demonstrate hand raising as a way to request the book, Mr. Smith would occasionally delay doing the formal training procedure and wait for the student to independently raise her hand, at which time the picture book would be taken out of the desk and provided to her (see Example Form 5.18).

The plan was implemented and produced the data displayed in Figure 5.6. As Mr. Smith expected, this plan was successful in reducing the occurrence of falling behavior and increasing the rate of hand raising. By 1/14 the requesting behavior had met the criteria for fading prompts. The prompts were successfully faded, and the student was requesting her book independently. Falling behavior occurred on two occasions after hand raising was established.

After reviewing the two falling incidents, Mr. Smith determined that he needed to generalize the requesting behavior to items other than the picture book. Based on the success of this program it was determined that the student could probably learn American sign language quickly, so a specific program to help her develop signed requests (mands) was developed.

## What If?

*What if the behavior does not decrease (or gets worse) with DRA?*

When using DRA with extinction we often see an initial worsening of the target behavior. The technical term for this is an *extinction burst*. Just like it's name implies, it is a brief and often intense increase in the target behavior that happens when the behavior no longer produces the reinforcer. You should see a dramatic decrease in the behavior within 3 sessions or days. If the behavior continues at a high rate for longer than that you will need to confirm that the behavior you have set up as the alternative behavior is actually producing the identified reinforcer. You should also ensure that extinction is indeed occurring for the target behavior. If the alternative behavior has never been observed to occur, consider specifically training the manding behavior in a more structured format prior to using DRA.

*What if I cannot ignore some of the target behaviors?*

If the target behavior has life-threatening consequences or cannot be ignored, you can program a DRA without extinction. In this case all the elements of the DRA would be the same with the exception that when the target behavior occurs we will continue to respond to it as we have in the past. This will make the behavior change process somewhat slower because the difference in level of reinforcement will not be as great. This can be countered to some extent by interrupting the target behavior and using positive practice of the alternative behavior.

*What If the person has never been observed to have exhibited a requesting behavior?*

In this case you will have to first teach a behavior that can be used effectively to request some tangible reinforcer. This generally involves a task analysis and some specific teaching procedures to ensure that the skill is well established in the client's repertoire. Discrete Trial Training and Precision Teaching are procedures that have been used to successfully teach these skills.

### Forms: Differential Reinforcement of Other Behaviors With Extinction

5.17 Simple Frequency Data on Target and Replacement Behaviors
5.18 Teaching Requesting Behavior: Simple Plan

## FORM 5.17 ■ SIMPLE FREQUENCY DATA ON TARGET AND REPLACEMENT BEHAVIORS

■ Client: _____    CHART STARTED: _____

Day/Month/Year

■ Behavior: _____

■ Total Observation Time: __MIN__ (__, ___-minute session/day)    Session length: __min__

■ Number of Days: __

■ Place an X on the appropriate day box each time the behavior occurs

| | 1 : | 2 : | 3 : | 4 : | 5 : | 6 : | 7 : | Totals |
|---|---|---|---|---|---|---|---|---|
| Target Behavior | | | | | | | | |
| Replacement Behavior | | | | | | | | |

| | 8 : | 9 : | 10 : | 11 : | 12 : | 13 : | 14 : | Totals |
|---|---|---|---|---|---|---|---|---|
| Target Behavior | | | | | | | | |
| Replacement Behavior | | | | | | | | |

| | 15 : | 16 : | 17 : | 18 : | 19 : | 20 : | 21 : | Totals |
|---|---|---|---|---|---|---|---|---|
| Target Behavior | | | | | | | | |
| Replacement Behavior | | | | | | | | |

| | 22 : | 23 : | 24 : | 25 : | 26 : | 27 : | 28 : | Totals |
|---|---|---|---|---|---|---|---|---|
| Target Behavior | | | | | | | | |
| Replacement Behavior | | | | | | | | |

A. Total Minutes Observed: __

B. Total Target behavior occurrences observed: __

C. Total Replacement behavior occurrences observed: __

## FORM 5.18 ■ TEACHING REQUESTING BEHAVIOR: SIMPLE PLAN

■ Person served: _____

■ Target Behavior: _____

■ Behavioral diagnostic category: _____

■ Requesting Behavior:

    A. Form of request: vocal request; manual signed request; requesting by pointing to a communication board; use augmentative device to request; other _____

    B. Description of initial request to be reinforced: _____

    _____

■ Reinforcer(s) to be used:

| | Type | Amount |
|---|---|---|
| | 1. _____ | 1. _____ |
| | 2. _____ | 2. _____ |
| | 3. _____ | 3. _____ |
| | 4. _____ | 4. _____ |
| | 5. _____ | 5. _____ |

■ Target Rate: _____

■ Instructions to ensure motivation:

■ Train at time and place that target behavior is most likely, which is: _____

    _____

■ Ensure limited access to reinforcing item at other times by: _____

    _____

■ Designated time period(s) to implement: _____

■ Rate of target behavior:             Baseline _____    Target _____

■ Rate of Requesting Behavior      Baseline _____    Target _____

■ Initial schedule of Differential reinforcement:

    A. Provide contrived reinforcer after every _____ number of requests and with no more than a _____ Sec/Min delay

■ Targeted final schedule of differential reinforcement:

    A. Ensure reinforcer delivery after every _____ number of requests with no more than a _____ Sec/Min delay

■ Replacement behavior is reinforced:

■ If the requesting behavior occurs independently, provide reinforcer requested

■ If the requesting behavior does not occur under the targeted conditions, provide the following prompts: (using Vocal Sign Gesture Visual).

1. Provide the prompt, "What do you want?"

2. If no response, provide the prompt again with the item item/object/activity within sight.

3. If no response, provide the prompt with the addition of a gestural prompt.

4. If no response, provide the prompt with the addition of modeling the response.

5. If no response, provide the prompt with the addition of a physical prompt.

6. If no response, provide increasing physical prompt using least to most prompting.

7. Once the request occurs, provide the requested reinforcer.

8. Repeat for as long as the child/client is motivated to request the reinforcer.

9. When the client's "enthusiasm" wanes, end access to the reinforcer for that time period.

■ If target behavior occurs:

■ Extinction (no access to the requested reinforcer) for _____ minutes then begin prompt sequence for replacement behavior listed above.

■ If replacement requesting behavior occurs during this time period, provide the requested reinforcer

    ■ Special instructions for delivery of small amount of reinforcer(s):

    _____

    _____

■ Criterion for fading prompts: _____

■ Criterion for increasing the amount of delay in the delivery of reinforcer: _____

## More Information

### Teaching Requesting Skills

Arntzen, E., & Almås, I. K. (2002). Effects of mand-tact versus tact-only training on the acquisition of tacts. *Journal of Applied Behavior Analysis, 35,* 419–422.

Bosch, S., & Fuqua, R. W. (2001). Behavioral cusps: A model for selecting target behaviors. *Journal of Applied Behavior Analysis, 34,* 123–125.

Bowman, L. G., Fisher, W. W., Thompson, R. H., & Piazza, C. C. (1997). On the relation of mands and the function of destructive behavior. *Journal of Applied Behavior Analysis, 30,* 251–265.

Brown, K. A., Wacker, D. P., Derby, K. M., Peck, S. M., Richman, D. M., Sasso, et al. (2000). Evaluating the effects of functional communication training in the presence and absence of establishing operations. *Journal of Applied Behavior Analysis, 33,* 53–71.

DeLeon, I. G., Fisher, W. W., Herman, K. M., & Crosland, K. C. (2000). Assessment of a response bias for aggression over functionally equivalent appropriate behavior. *Journal of Applied Behavior Analysis, 33,* 73–77.

Derby, K. M., Wacker, D. P., Berg, W., DeRaad, A., Ulrich, S., Asmus, J., et al. (1997). The long-term effects of functional communication training in home settings. *Journal of Applied Behavior Analysis, 30,* 507–531.

Drasgow, E., Halle, J. W., & Ostrosky, M. M. (1998). Effects of differential reinforcement on the generalization of a replacement mand in three children with severe language delays. *Journal of Applied Behavior Analysis, 31,* 357–374.

Goh, H., Iwata, B. A., & DeLeon, I. G. (2000). Competition between noncontingent and contingent reinforcement schedules during response acquisition. *Journal of Applied Behavior Analysis, 33,* 195–205.

Henry, L. M., & Horne, P. J. (2000). Partial remediation of speaker and listener behaviors in people with severe dementia. *Journal of Applied Behavior Analysis, 33,* 631–634.

Kahng, S., Hendrickson, D. J., & Vu, C. P. (2000). Comparison of single and multiple functional communication training responses for the treatment of problem behavior. *Journal of Applied Behavior Analysis, 33,* 321–324.

Lalli, J. S., Mauro, B. C., & Mace, F. C. (2000). Preference for unreliable reinforcement in children with mental retardation: The role of conditioned reinforcement. *Journal of Applied Behavior Analysis, 33,* 533–544.

Marcus, B. A., & Vollmer, T. R. (1996). Combining noncontingent reinforcement and differential reinforcement schedules as treatment for aberrant behavior. *Journal of Applied Behavior Analysis, 29,* 43–51.

Northup, J., Wacker, D., Sasso, G., Steege, M., Cigrand, K., Cook, J., et al. (1991). A brief functional analysis of aggressive and alternative behavior in an outclinic setting. *Journal of Applied Behavior Analysis, 24,* 509–522.

Partington, J. W., Sundberg, M. L., Newhouse, L., & Spengler, S. M. (1994). Overcoming an autistic child's failure to acquire a tact repertoire. *Journal of Applied Behavior Analysis, 27,* 733–734.

Peck, S. M., Wacker, D. P., Berg, W. K., Cooper, L. J., Brown, K. A., Richman, D., et al. (1996)Choice-making treatment of young children's severe behavior problems. *Journal of Applied Behavior Analysis, 29,* 263–290.

Rehfeldt, R. A., & Root, S. L. (2005). Establishing derived requesting skills in adults with severe developmental disabilities. *Journal of Applied Behavior Analysis, 38,* 101–105.

Richman, D. M., Wacker, D. P., & Winborn, L. (2001). Response efficiency during functional communication training: Effects of effort on response allocation. *Journal of Applied Behavior Analysis, 34,* 73–76.

Sprague, J. R., & Horner, R. H. (1992). Covariation within functional response classes: Implications for treatment of severe problem behavior. *Journal of Applied Behavior Analysis, 25,* 735–745.

Tiger, J. H., & Hanley, G. P. (2004). Developing stimulus control of preschooler mands: An analysis of schedule-correlated and contingency-specifying stimuli. *Journal of Applied Behavior Analysis, 37,* 517–521.

Vollmer, T. R. Borrero, J. C. Lalli, J. S., & Daniel, D. (1999). Evaluating self-control and impulsivity in children with severe behavior disorders. *Journal of Applied Behavior Analysis, 32,* 451–466.

Wallace, M. D., Iwata, B. A., & Hanley, G. P. (2006) Establishment of mands following tact training as a function of reinforcer strength. *Journal of Applied Behavior Analysis, 39,* 17–24.

Winborn, L., Wacker, D. P., Richman, D. M., Asmus, J., & Geier, D. (2002). Assessment of mand selection for functional communication training packages. *Journal of Applied Behavior Analysis, 35,* 295–298.

Yamamoto, J., & Mochizuki, A. (1988). Acquisition and functional analysis of manding with autistic students. *Journal of Applied Behavior Analysis, 21,* 57–64.

### Differential Reinforcement of Alternative Behavior

Goh, H., Iwata, B. A., & DeLeon, I. G. (2000). Competition between noncontingent and contingent reinforcement schedules during response acquisition. *Journal of Applied Behavior Analysis, 33,* 195–205.

Lee, R., McComas, J. J., & Jawor, J. (2002). The effects of differential and lag reinforcement schedules on varied verbal responding by individuals with autism. *Journal of Applied Behavior Analysis, 35,* 391–402.

McCord, B. E., Thomson, R. J., & Iwata, B. A. (2001). Functional analysis and treatment of self-injury associated with transitions. *Journal of Applied Behavior Analysis, 34,* 195–210.

Piazza, C. C., Moes, D. R., & Fisher, W. W. (1996). Differential reinforcement of alternative behavior and demand fading in the treatment of escape-maintained destructive behavior. *Journal of Applied Behavior Analysis, 29,* 569–572.

Ringdahl, J. E., Kitsukawa, K., Andelman, M. S., Call, N., Winborn, L., Barretto, A., et al. (2002). Differential reinforcement with and without instructional fading. *Journal of Applied Behavior Analysis, 35,* 291–294.

Roane, H. S., Fisher, W. W., Sgro, G. M., Falcomata, T. S., & Pabico, R. R. (2004). An alternative method of thinning reinforcer delivery during differential reinforcement. *Journal of Applied Behavior Analysis, 37,* 213–218.

Vollmer, T. R., Roane, H. S., Ringdahl, J. E., & Marcus, B. A. (1999). Evaluating treatment challenges with differential reinforcement of alternative behavior. *Journal of Applied Behavior Analysis, 32,* 9–23.

## 4.0 SME FUNCTIONS: PREMACK CONTINGENCY OPTION

### Brief Description

In a Premack contingency, the desired reinforcer is produced following the client's successful compliance with a designated regimen of tasks or demands. This has also been referred to as Grandma's rule, that is, you don't get your dessert until you eat your vegetables. The more technical definition of the Premack principle is making access to a high probability behavior contingent on performing a low probability behavior (Premack & Bahwell, 1959).

To implement a Premack contingency for SME functions, the staff, parent, or teacher determines what negative reinforcer the target behavior is removing (what task, event, or person the unwanted behavior is escaping or avoiding). You would then determine a set of tasks that have to be performed before escape or avoidance is allowed. The reinforcing event (removal of the negative reinforcer) is withheld until the client performs the specified task.

The advantage of using a Premack contingency is that it still allows for escape of the aversive event to be used as a negative reinforcer. The requirement to perform a set of tasks will build in a delay of the removal of the negative reinforcer. The client subsequently learns to tolerate the aversive event or activity for longer periods of time. This replacement behavior option reduces some of the difficulties associated with extinction. It also usually reduces the overall rate of terminating or avoiding the negative reinforcer (similar to that produced in tolerance training). The Premack contingency can be used with any SME subcategory.

### Apparatus

Data sheets—See Form 5.19 "Simple Frequency Data With Formulas"

### Baseline Measurement

1. Identify the target behavior to be observed.
2. Operationally define or pinpoint the target behavior, with specific criteria for onset and offset of behavior (if not readily evident).
3. Determine the observation period, possibly reviewing scatter plot or A-B-C data to identify periods of time when behavior is highly likely.
4. Construct the data sheet to reflect the length of the observation period, trying to keep the length reasonably similar during all baseline sessions.
5. During observation, record either the occurrence of the target behavior, the duration of the target behavior, or the intensity of the behavior (which measure you select will depend on the target behavior).
6. Repeat step 5 until the observation period ends.
7. Conduct at least four more baseline sessions.
8. Graph or display the data across all baseline sessions.

### Procedures for Premack Contingency

1. Either at specified times of the day or under antecedent conditions that occasion the target escape behavior, require the client to engage in a simple designated task determined by an analysis of client's level of ability.

2. When the client completes the designated task, remove the aversive event allowing him to escape the negative reinforcer.
3. Repeat steps 1 and 2 with each occurrence of the conditions that have in the past preceded escape behaviors.
4. As a function of success in ameliorating the target behavior, progressively increase the duration or quantity of the task required.
5. Ensure that the target behavior does not produce negative reinforcement. (escape extinction)

### Procedures for Premack Contingency When Used as a Supplement for Requesting Program

1. Contingent upon a request by the client to terminate an activity or event or have an item removed from the area, require the client to engage in a simple designated task, determined by an analysis of client's level of ability.
2. When the client completes the designated task, remove the aversive event, allowing him to escape the negative reinforcer.
3. Repeat steps 1 and 2 with each request.
4. As a function of success in ameliorating the target behavior, progressively increase the duration or quantity of the task required.
5. Ensure that the target behavior does not produce the desired reinforcer. (escape extinction)

### Thinning the Schedule of Delivery of Maintaining Reinforcer

Once the target behavior is reduced the behavior analyst can increase the response effort or time to remove the undesired event or item. This can be done in two ways:

1. Increase the duration or complexity of each task.
2. Increase the number of tasks required to earn the reinforcer.

Progressively altering either or both of these factors will increase the length of time the client will have to tolerate the aversive condition (whether it be a task demand or social situation) before a request to remove the event is honored.

*If utilizing this behavior option for* Direct Escape behaviors (3.0 DE): *Utilize the same baseline and treatment procedures as above, except that chain interruption would occur instead of extinction when the target behavior is displayed.*

## How It Works

It is often the case that the social environment has made it too easy for the person to escape or avoid certain events. Therefore, escape or avoidance of such events occurs at unreasonable levels. To want to get out of an unpleasant event is not a sin! But it surely is tough to accommodate such a desire when it prevents learning of important life skills or endangers the person's health. If a child cannot tolerate sitting in a group activity in early elementary school for longer than 30 seconds, such an inability will result in fewer learning opportunities and perhaps removal from the classroom.

A problem may also appear once a mand (request) for escape is taught and acquired. Requesting "out" may occur too often once developed, resulting in the person staying in the relatively aversive situation far too short a time compared to her peers. Hence, this Premack contingency program also is used as a supplement to the escape mand (requesting) program.

A Premack contingency is well suited to reduce the client's desire to avoid a given event, Requiring the performance of a task as a condition for removal of a negative reinforcer is a strategy that will eventually wean them off of frequent avoidance and increase the ability to tolerate a nonpreferred condition for longer periods of time.

**TABLE 5.17** ■ **SUMMARY OF TOY PLAY A-B-C DATA**

| Antecedent Conditions | Target Behavior | What Happened? | What Was Natural Result of Behavior? |
|---|---|---|---|
| Given a reading assignment. Starts to read for a few minutes while the staff is watching him. | Gets out some toy cars he brought from home, quits reading, starts to whine and tantrum as soon as the teacher looks at him. | Teacher had to send him out to calm down. He comes back in time to start math. | None noted. |
| Given a reading assignment. Starts to read for a few minutes while the staff is watching him. | Quits reading and plays with his toys as soon as the aide turns away from him. | Teacher redirects him, he tantrums and gets sent out of class to calm down. | None noted. |

## Hypothetical Example

### I Need a Break, My Brain Is Swelling

John was a mainstreamed fourth grade student. The initial referral to the behavior analyst, Ms. White, stated that the staff needed help with John's tantrum behavior. Ms. White went to the classroom and interviewed the teacher and teacher's aide. She constructed Table 5.17 from the information they provided.

Ms. White observed John on several occasions and noticed that the target behavior only occurred during reading. John would read for about 5 to 10 minutes, as long as one of the special education personnel were looking at him. As soon as she turned away he would put down his book and very quietly take out one of his toys and start to play. When one of the aides looked at him, he would attempt to hide the toys by picking up his reading book. When the aide looked away, he would go back to playing with his toys. If the aide caught him and came over and attempted to direct him back to reading he would begin to complain, yell, throw items off the desk, stomp his feet, and so forth. Following each outburst the aide directed him to the quiet area in the classroom to allow him time to engage in his "self-calming" skills. He would then return to the class when "calm." Ms. White noticed that with each self-calming session, the time it took him to calm usually lasted until the assignment changed from reading to math. In other words, as a result of the "self-calming" procedure, he missed the remainder of the reading period.

Ms. White considered the function of such behaviors to possibly be 2.1 SMA: staff attention. However, she ruled this out as John was observed at other times to have very effective skills to start conversations and evoke attention from staff members during other times of the day. The critical piece of information was the timing of the end of the tantrum and self-calming behaviors. It was perfectly correlated with the end of the reading assignment. This left the most likely diagnosis to be 4.2 SME: lengthy tasks, specifically the reading task (see Table 5.18). It appeared that John could read the material, however, he just ran out of steam at some point in the lengthy reading period.

Ms. White presented her hypothesis to the teacher. The teacher expressed some concern and disagreement with Ms White's analysis. She believed that the tantrum was just an

**TABLE 5.18** ■ **DIAGNOSTIC TABLE FOR TANTRUMS AND TOY PLAY**

| Diagnosis | 4.2 SME: lengthy tasks, reading |
|---|---|
| Target behavior(s): | Tantrums and playing with toys during reading periods |
| Function: | Escapes the reading task |
| Target behavior likely under following contexts: | During reading periods that last longer than 5 minutes |
| Target behavior unlikely under following contexts: | During any other class time or activity including short duration reading tasks |
| Rule out: | 2.1 SMA: adult attention |

effort to get her attention. Ms. White offered to test her hypothesis over the next 6 days. The test was a simple one.

A. Three days with a 1-hour period of coloring pictures; no reading during this time with no attention provided at this time.
B. Three days with a 1-hour period of reading with frequent attention.

For 1 hour each day John would be alternately asked to either engage in a coloring activity or the usual reading assignments. The time period for these two activities would be the same each of the 6 days. During the coloring activity, he would receive no attention from any of the adults. If he displayed tantrums during this time, it would provide some evidence that the tantrums were functioning to access attention. During the reading period, he would receive frequent attention. If he had more tantrums during this typical reading activity, when compared to the coloring activity, escape motivated tantrum behavior seemed plausible.

The teacher agreed, and Ms. White implemented the procedure. It produced the data presented in Example Form 5.19.

From this data it was very clear that the tantrums were functioning to escape the reading assignments. Ms. White also found that John would engage in the reading assignment for an average of 5 minutes. Any attempts to direct him back to reading after 5 minutes would result in tantrum behaviors. This occurred in all of the reading periods. Ms. White reviewed the IEP and found there was no indication that John had visual impairments of any kind.

---

### EXAMPLE FORM 5.19 ■ FREQUENCY COUNT DATA SHEET

■ **Client:** John                                                      CHART STARTED: _____

                                                                                                    **Day/Month/Year**

■ **Behavior: Tantrums**
■ **Total Observation Time:** <u>360 MIN</u> (<u>1</u>, <u>60</u>-minute session/day)
■ **Session length <u>60 min</u>**
■ **Number of Days: <u>6</u>**
■ Place an X on the appropriate day box each time the target behavior occurs

| Reading | 1 | 2 | 3 | 4 | 5 | 6 | Totals |
|---|---|---|---|---|---|---|---|
| Tantrums | XX | XX | XX | XX | XX | | |
| Total | 2 | 2 | 2 | 2 | 2 | 0 | 10 |

A. Total Minutes Observed: <u>180</u>
B. Total occurrences observed: <u>10</u>
C. Range (low) <u>2</u> to (high) <u>2</u>, Avg = <u>2</u>

| Coloring activity | 1 | 2 | 3 | 4 | 5 | 6 | Totals |
|---|---|---|---|---|---|---|---|
| Tantrums | | | | | | | 0 |
| Total | 0 | 0 | 0 | 0 | 0 | 0 | 0 |

A. Total Minutes Observed: <u>180</u>
B. Total occurrences observed: <u>0</u>
C. Range(low) <u>0</u> to (high) <u>0</u>, Avg = <u>0</u>

Ms. White could have simply set up a program that allowed a requesting behavior to escape reading (by asking to color instead). This clearly would have ended the tantrum behaviors. However, it would not be conducive to his continued learning and development. She decided that a Premack contingency would be better suited as it would reduce the level of tantrums while slightly increasing the amount of reading time during the beginning phase of intervention. The Premack contingency would also gradually alter John's desire to escape reading activities over time, as the work requirement (to get out of reading and into coloring) increased. Ms. White had noticed during her observations that John would also play with Sudoku math puzzles during his free time.

Ms. White set up the following Premack contingency. John would be given access to Sudoku math puzzles or coloring activities following completion of a specified amount of reading. In the initial contingency he could end the reading task and access 5 minutes of Sudoku or coloring by completing one page of reading (see Example Form 5.20).

The plan was implemented, and Ms. White graphed tantrums as well as pages read. The intervention had a clear effect on the rate of tantrums and increased the rate of reading. Ms. White also graphed the number of times John was earning access to Sudoku or coloring. As can be seen in Figure 5.7, the Premack contingency had an immediate effect on John's tantrum behavior as well as his reading. John quickly progressed to an acceptable reading standard. During periods 22 thorough 30 he was exceeding the Premack requirement such that he was accessing Sudoku or coloring for a total of 15 minutes per reading period. His reading output remained relatively high, and as the reading requirement was increased, his total time doing math puzzles decreased. There were two occurrences of tantrum behavior during this intervention. One occurred during the first

---

*EXAMPLE FORM 5.20* ■ **PREMACK CONTINGENCY: PLAN**

- Person served: **John**
- Target Behavior **Tantrums**
- Behavioral diagnostic category: **SME 4.2: lengthy tasks, reading task.**
- Designated time Period(s): **Reading period**
- Baseline data across five times/sessions:
  1. __1__
  2. __1__
  3. __1__
  4. __1__
  5. __1__
- Rate of Low probability behavior: Baseline __0 pgs/period__  Target __10 pgs/period__
- Rate of high probability behavior: Baseline __1/period__  Target __0__
- Initial Standard for Low Probability behavior: **Upon request by the teacher to begin reading, John will be required to complete 1 page of reading.**
- Description of how High Probability behavior will be provided: (how much, how often etc.) **Will be provided 5 minutes to play Sudoku or color in a book following each page of reading.**
- Criterion for Increasing the duration/complexity of the low probability behavior: **When John has gone 5 consecutive days with no tantrum behaviors increase the low probability behavior required by adding one additional paragraph to the reading requirement.**
- Criterion for Decreasing the duration/complexity of the low probability behavior: **If John engages in tantrums for 3 consecutive reading periods change the required response to 3 paragraphs.**
- Procedure for withholding/preventing the high probability behavior if not earned: **All toys will be removed from John and Sudoku puzzles/coloring will only be available from the teacher.**
- Special instructions for delivery of reinforcer(s):
- **If John completes multiples of the reading task at one time he can be given multiples of the reinforcer. That is if he reads two pages in a row he can earn 10 minutes of Sudoku, etc.**

**John Reading**

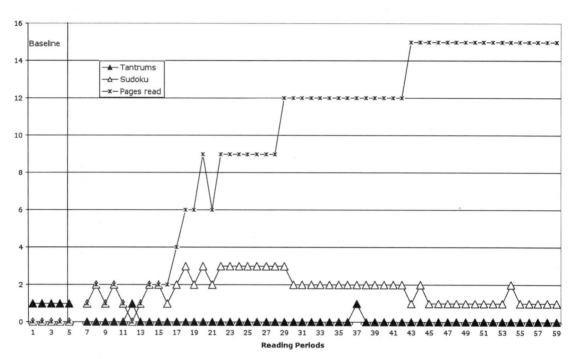

*Figure 5.7* ■ Reading and tantrums.

increase in the response requirement. The second occurred during a stable point in the intervention.

## What If?

*What if the person refuses to do the required behavior?*

You must impose conditions that do not allow escape of the task via any behaviors except those you have specified in the plan, that is, completing tasks. If your analysis is correct, the person should after some short period of time engage in the low probability behavior because it is the only way to escape or avoid the less preferred event.

You must be sure that the client can actually perform the low probability behavior, that is, they do not have a skills deficit (see Appendix A for inept repertoire diagnosis). You may want to reduce the difficulty of the low probability behavior to make it more likely they will contact the reinforcer.

## Forms: Premack Contingency

5.19 Simple Frequency Data With Formulas
5.20 Premack Contingency: Simple Plan

## FORM 5.19 ■ SIMPLE FREQUENCY DATA WITH FORMULAS

■ Client: _____     CHART STARTED: _____

**Day/Month/Year**

■ Behavior: _____
■ Total Observation Time: ___MIN (__, ___-minute session/day)     Session length: ___min
■ Number of Days: __
■ Place an X on the appropriate day box each time the target behavior occurs

|  | 1 : | 2 : | 3 : | 4 : | 5 : | 6 : | 7 : | Totals |
|---|---|---|---|---|---|---|---|---|
| Target Behavior |  |  |  |  |  |  |  |  |
| Daily Rate |  |  |  |  |  |  |  |  |

|  | 8 : | 9 : | 10 : | 11 : | 12 : | 13 : | 14 : | Totals |
|---|---|---|---|---|---|---|---|---|
| Target Behavior |  |  |  |  |  |  |  |  |
| Daily Rate |  |  |  |  |  |  |  |  |

A. Total Minutes Observed: __
B. Total occurrences observed: __
C. Range (low) __ to (high) __, Avg = __

## FORM 5.20 ■ PREMACK CONTINGENCY: SIMPLE PLAN

■ Person served: _____
■ Target Behavior: _____
■ Behavioral diagnostic category: _____
■ Target Rate: _____
■ Designated time Period(s): _____
■ Baseline data across five times/sessions:     1. _____
                                                2. _____
                                                3. _____
                                                4. _____
                                                5. _____
■ Rate of Low probability behavior:     Baseline _____ Target _____
■ Rate of high probability behavior:    Baseline _____ Target _____
■ Initial Standard for Low Probability behavior _____
_____
■ Description of how high probability behavior will be provided: (how much, how often etc.) _____
■ Criterion for Increasing the duration/complexity of the low probability behavior: _____
■ Criterion for Decreasing the duration/complexity of the low probability behavior: _____
■ Procedure for withholding/preventing the high probability behavior if not earned: _____
_____

   ■ Special instructions for delivery of reinforcer(s):
   _____
   _____
   _____

*More Information*

Allison, J. (1976). Contrast, induction, facilitation, suppression and conservation. *Journal of the Experimental Analysis of Behavior, 25,* 185–198.

Amari, A., Grace, N. C., & Fisher, W. W. (1995). Achieving and maintaining compliance with the ketogenic diet. *Journal of Applied Behavior Analysis, 28,* 341–342.

Hanley, G. P., Iwata, B. A., Roscoe, E. M., Thompson, R. H., & Lindberg, J. S. (2003). Response-restriction analysis: II. Alteration of activity preferences. *Journal of Applied Behavior Analysis, 36,* 59–76.

Hanley, G. P., Iwata, B. A., Thompson, R. H., & Lindberg, J. S. (2000). A component analysis of "stereotypy as reinforcement" for alternative behavior. *Journal of Applied Behavior Analysis, 33,* 285–297.

Homme, L. E., de Baca, P. C., Devine, J. V., Steinhorst, R., & Rickert, E. J. (1963). Use of the premack principle in controlling the behavior of nursery school children. *Journal of the Experimental Analysis of Behavior, 6,* 544.

Konarski, E. A., Jr., Johnson, M. R., Crowell, C. R., & Whitman, T. L. (1980). Response deprivation and reinforcement in applied settings: A preliminary analysis. *Journal of Applied Behavior Analysis, 13,* 595–609.

Mitchell, W. S., & Stoffelmayr, B. E. (1973). Application of the Premack principle to the behavioral control of extremely inactive schizophrenics. *Journal of Applied Behavior Analysis, 6,* 419–423.

Mithaug, D. E., & Mar, D. K. (1980). The relation between choosing and working prevocational tasks in two severely retarded young adults. *Journal of Applied Behavior Analysis, 13,* 177–182.

Premack, D. (1963). Rate differential reinforcement in monkey manipulation. *Journal of the Experimental Analysis of Behavior, 6,* 81–89.

Premack, D. (1970). A functional analysis of language. *Journal of the Experimental Analysis of Behavior, 14,* 107–125.

Premack, D., & Bahwell, R. (1959). Operant-level lever pressing by a monkey as a function of intertest interval. *Journal of the Experimental Analysis of Behavior, 2,* 127–131.

Premack, D., & Premack, A. J. (1963). Increased eating in rats deprived of running. *Journal of the Experimental Analysis of Behavior, 6,* 209–212.

Premack, D., & Schaeffer, R. W. (1962). Distributional properties of operant-level locomotion in the rat. *Journal of the Experimental Analysis of Behavior, 5,* 89–95.

Premack, D., & Schaeffer, R. W. (1963). Some parameters affecting the distributional properties of operant-level running in rats. *Journal of the Experimental Analysis of Behavior, 6,* 473–475.

Premack, D., Schaeffer, R. W., & Hundt, A. (1964). Reinforcement of drinking by running: Effect of fixed ratio and reinforcement time. *Journal of the Experimental Analysis of Behavior, 7,* 91–96.

## 4.0 SME FUNCTIONS: TOLERANCE TRAINING OPTION (OR DIFFERENTIAL NEGATIVE REINFORCEMENT OF ALL OTHER BEHAVIORS)

### Brief Description

In tolerance training or differential negative reinforcement of other behavior( DNRO), the specific maintaining reinforcer is contingent on the absence of the target behavior in a given period of time. In this case the maintaining reinforcer is the avoidance or termination of an event, item, or person that is aversive to the client. DNRO is one of the simplest of all behavior reduction procedures. One could also view a DNRO as a reinforcement system that allows the person to escape or avoid a specific negative reinforcer by engaging in a variety of behaviors, as long as the targeted behavior does not occur.

To implement a DNRO program, the staff, parent, or teacher determines if the target behavior occurred during a specified interval of time. If it occurred, escape or avoidance is prevented, and the interval is reset for the full DNRO period. If the target behavior did not occur, reinforcement in the form of termination of an unpleasant event or task is provided at the end of the designated interval. By providing reinforcement in this way, engaging in any behavior other than the targeted behavior pays off better. Concurrently, the target behaviors functional relation to escape or avoidance of an aversive event is disabled.

The advantage of using a DNRO procedure is that it is easy to implement, and it specifically focuses on the reduction of the unwanted behavior. It is not designed to teach any new behavior or to target any specific behavior for an increase. Differential reinforcement has been one of the most widely used procedures for dealing with the reduction of unwanted behaviors.

### Terms

*Interbehavior interval:* The length of time that passes between the end of one targeted behavior and the beginning of the next occurrence of the targeted behavior.

*DNRO interval:* The length of time the person must abstain from engaging in the target behavior in order to escape or avoid the aversive event.

*Thinning the schedule of delivery of maintaining reinforcer:* The process of gradually increasing the time that elapses before the negative reinforcer is removed.

*Escape:* Engaging in behavior that terminates the presence of an aversive task or event.

*Avoidance:* Engaging in behavior that prevents one from coming in contact with an aversive task or event.

*Aversive stimulus:* A task, event, or person that when presented evokes a response that avoids or escapes the stimulus.

## Apparatus

Timing device—This can be a kitchen timer, alarm clock, computer with alarm feature, etc. A tape recorder with beeps at designated intervals, or a calendar, depending on the length of the schedule of noncontingent reinforcement. It's purpose is to prompt the staff person, teacher, or parent to remove the aversive event.

Data sheets—See Form 5.21 "Simple Frequency Data With Formulas"

## Baseline Measurement

1. Identify the target behavior to be observed.
2. Operationally define or pinpoint the behavior being observed, with specific criteria for onset and offset of behavior (if not readily evident).
3. Determine the observation period, possibly reviewing scatter plot or A-B-C data to identify periods of time when behavior is highly likely.
4. Construct the data sheet to reflect the length of the observation period, trying to keep the length reasonably similar in multiple baseline sessions.
5. During observation, record the occurrence of the target behavior.
6. Repeat step 5 until the observation period ends.
7. Sum the total number of occurrences of the target behavior, and enter that number on the data sheet.
8. Divide the session length by the total frequency of target behavior (see following examples) to arrive at the interbehavior interval for that session.
9. Complete at least four more baseline sessions.
10. Graph or display the interbehavior interval across all baseline sessions, noting the range and mean.

### Calculating the Interbehavior Interval

Suppose we had the data in Table 5.19 and wanted to determine the interbehavior interval.

To calculate the interbehavior interval for the entire 5 days of observation, simply take the total number of minutes for observations, and divide the number by the total number of occurrences of the target behavior. In this case:

**TABLE 5.19 ■ INTERBEHAVIOR INTERVAL DATA**

Behavior: __Hitting__

Total Observation Time: __600 MIN__ (1, 120-minute session/day)  Session length: __120 min__

Number of Days: __5.__

|  | 1 | 2 | 3 | 4 | 5 | Totals |
|---|---|---|---|---|---|---|
| Hitting | xx | xxx | xxxxx | xx | xxxxxx | |
| | | | | | | 18 |
| Interbehavior interval | 60 min | 40 min | 24 min | 60 min | 20 min | 33.33 min |

600 total minutes ÷ 18 total occurrences of behavior = an interbehavior interval of 33.33 minutes.

If we were to calculate the interbehavior interval for day 1 it would be:

120 minutes ÷ 2 occurrences of behavior = an interbehavior interval of 60 minutes.

If we were to calculate the interbehavior interval for day 5 it would be:

120 minutes ÷ 6 occurrences of behavior = an interbehavior interval of 20 minutes.

## DNRO With Extinction Procedures

1. From baseline data, calculate the interbehavior interval.
2. Determine the schedule for the removal of the negative reinforcer. The initial schedule should be set so that removal of the negative reinforcer occurs at or more frequently than the average interbehavior interval, for example, initial interval set at 20% below the average interbehavior interval. (An average interbehavioral interval 33 minutes times 80% would equal 26.4 minutes.) This becomes the DNRO interval length.
3. Set the timing device to the initial removal schedule.
4. When the timer goes off, terminate the negative reinforcer if the person has not engaged in the target behavior for the entire time period, and then reset the timer.
5. As soon as the client engages in the target behavior during the interval, do not allow escape or avoidance of the aversive event, use extinction procedures as needed, and reset the timer for the full DNRO interval.
6. Thin the schedule of the negative reinforcement.

### Thinning the Schedule of Removal of the Negative Reinforcer

When the target behavior goal is achieved, increase the length of the DNRO interval and set a new target behavior goal. The steps for thinning the schedule follow.

1. When the target behavior goal is achieved increase the DNRO interval by 5%–10%. For example, if the DNRO interval was 5 minutes, and the target behavior goal was met, then the new schedule for removal might be set at 5 minutes, 30 seconds.
2. With each week of success in achieving the target behavior goal, the schedule of removal is thinned by progressively increasing the DNRO interval by 10%.
3. If the target behavior occurs at a rate consistently higher than the established goal over a given week, consider returning to the previous DNRO interval.
4. If you have made several attempts at thinning the schedule but are unable to get past a particular DNRO interval, it may be best to keep the schedule at that level while incorporating another functional treatment program.

*If utilizing this behavior option for* Direct Escape behaviors (3.0 DE): *Utilize the same baseline and treatment procedures as above, except that chain interruption would occur instead of extinction when the target behavior is displayed.*

## How It Works

As with all differential reinforcement, DNRO works by altering the contingencies such that engaging in the target behavior reduces the frequency and magnitude of reinforcement. Prior to the DNRO contingency, the exhibition of the target behavior was functional. The social environment *enabled* such a behavior by frequently removing the negative reinforcer contingent upon its occurrence. The DNRO schedule *disables* this function by further postponing the removal of the aversive event contingent on an occurrence of the target behavior, that is, the DNRO interval is reset. Therefore, doing anything other than the target behavior is a more efficient path to escape or avoid the aversive event.

*TABLE 5.20* ■ **SUMMARY OF DESK HITTING A-B-C DATA**

| Antecedent Conditions | Target Behavior | What Happened? | What Was Natural Result of Behavior? |
|---|---|---|---|
| 1. Seated in desk, working on math. | Hit desk with open hand with enough force for it to be audible outside the classroom. | Teacher goes to desk and talks with Fred regarding disrupting class. | Sensation produced when striking desk and sound produced. |
| 2. Seated in desk, working on reading. | Hit desk with open hand with enough force for it to be audible outside the classroom. | Teacher goes to desk and talks with Fred regarding disrupting class. | Sensation produced when striking desk and sound produced. |
| 3. Seated in desk taking math test. | Completed math test. Sat quietly while others finished taking test. | Praise from teacher for doing well. | Inconsequential. |
| 4. Seated in desk free period. | Did various tasks. No one longer than 5 minutes. | Praise from the teacher for doing well. | Inconsequential. |
| 5. Sitting in desk, prompted to begin reading. | Took out book and began to read. | Teacher ended reading period after 10 minutes due to an assembly. | Inconsequential. |

## Hypothetical Example

### The 20-Minute Child

Fred was an elementary school student in a regular education classroom. Mr. Delgadillo received a referral to develop a plan to reduce the disruptive desk hitting of Fred. Mr. Delgadillo was not sure what was maintaining the desk hitting behavior, so he decided to set up an A-B-C chart, and he collected data for a 2-week period. A sample of the data collected is presented in Table 5.20.

After examining the previous A-B-C descriptive data, Mr. Delgadillo set about answering the question, "What are the common elements in the events involving desk hitting?" and "How do they differ from the events that did not produce desk hitting?" Mr. Delgadillo discovered Fred did not engage in desk hitting when he was working on tasks of his choice, even if no one interacted with him for periods as long as 45 minutes, which ruled out 2.1 SMA: adult attention and 2.2 SMA: peer attention as the likely maintaining function. Desk hitting was never followed by the presentation of a tangible item eliminating a hypothesis of 2.3 SMA: tangible reinforcer as a maintaining function. Mr. Delgadillo noticed that desk hitting only happened if Fred worked on a task, not of his choosing, for greater than 15 minutes without a break. After an event of desk hitting was interrupted by the teacher, Fred would typically stop work on the undesired task for an average of 5 minutes while the teacher corrected his behavior. Fred would then sometimes be offered a different, more preferred task to work on.

Mr. Delgadillo determined the most likely hypothesis is that desk hitting is being maintained by 4.2 SME: relatively lengthy tasks (see Table 5.21). Having formulated a hypothesis, Mr. Delgadillo collected data during a 4-hour session (240 minutes) each day for 5 days. The data indicated that Fred was hitting the desk at a rate of about three times per hour (see Example Form 5.21).

The interbehavior interval was calculated by determining

Total Minutes Observed (1200 minutes) ÷ Total Frequency target behavior occurred (58 occurrences) = average interbehavior interval (20.7 minutes).

With this data in hand, and an understanding of the function of the desk hitting behavior, Mr. Delgadillo formulated an intervention plan (see Example Form 5.22). Because the problem was not a skills deficit and really just required changing the contingencies to increase the length of time Fred was reading, Mr. Delgadillo settled on differential reinforcement. Because the target behavior was maintained by an escape function,

*EXAMPLE OF FROM 5.21* ■ **FREQUENCY COUNT DATA SHEET**

■ **Client:** Fred

CHART STARTED: _____**6-21**_____
**Day/Month/Year**

■ **Behavior: Desk Hitting**
■ Total Observation Time: **1200 MIN (1, 240**-minute session/day)
■ Number of Days: **5.**

Session length: **240** min

| | 1 | 2 | 3 | 4 | 5 | Totals |
|---|---|---|---|---|---|---|
| Desk Hitting | xxxxxxx | xxxxxxxxxxx | xxxxxxxxxxxxx | xxxxxxxxxxxxxx | xxxxxxxxxxx | 58 |
| Daily Rate | 1.75/hr | 2.75/hr | 3.25/hr | 4/hr | 2.75/hr | 2.9/hr |
| Interbehavior interval | 34.29min | 21.82min | 18.46min | 15min | 21.82min | 20.69min |

A.  Total Minutes Observed: **1200** Interbehavior interval = *A/B* **1200/58** = **20.69 min** Rate/hour = (B/A)60 **(58/1200)60 = 2.9/hr**

Mr. Delgadillo decided to use tolerance training (DNRO). Having determined that the desk hitting behavior occurred about every 20 minutes, he set the initial DNRO interval to 15 minutes to ensure that Fred was very likely to obtain reinforcement more often under this plan.

Prior to implementing the program Mr. Delgadillo informed the staff that an extinction burst would probably occur and that they should be prepared for this event. He also made sure to be in the classroom during the implementation of the program so that he could support the teaching staff and assure them that the program was implemented correctly. The program was implemented, and the following data was collected and is presented in Figure 5.8.

As Mr. Delgadillo expected and as can be seen in the graph, the DNRO was successful in reducing the occurrence of desk hitting behavior. It is interesting to note that as Mr. Delgadillo predicted, on 6/25, the desk hitting behavior worsened. This is a familiar and expected pattern when using extinction, called an *extinction burst*. Following this burst (increase in rate from prior level), the desk hitting behavior steadily and quickly declined. Because Mr. Delgadillo had let the teaching staff know what to expect, they were prepared for this and stuck with the plan. By 7/14 the behavior had met the criteria for thinning the DNRO schedule, so Mr. Delgadillo increased the interbehavior interval by 10% such that reinforcement was now delivered every 17 minutes. Mr. Delgadillo continued this thinning process until the desk hitting behavior was no longer occurring.

**TABLE 5.21** ■ **DIAGNOSTIC TABLE FOR DESK HITTING**

| Diagnosis | 4.2 SME: relatively lengthy tasks |
|---|---|
| Target behavior(s): | Desk hitting |
| Function: | Escape a reading task after greater than 15 minutes of continuous reading |
| Target behavior likely under following contexts: | Reading for time periods exceeding 15 minutes |
| Target behavior unlikely under following contexts: | Free time or working on tasks other than reading |
| Rule out: | 2.1 SMA: adult attention<br>2.2 SMA: peer attention<br>2.3 SMA: tangible reinforcer |

*EXAMPLE FORM 5.22* ■ **TOLERANCE TRAINING OR DIFFERENTIAL NEGATIVE REINFORCEMENT WITH EXTINCTION: PLAN**

- ■ Person Served: **Fred**
- ■ Target Behavior: **Desk hitting**
- ■ Behavioral diagnostic category: **SME 4.2: task duration**
- ■ Target Rate: **0 events per week**
- ■ Designated time Period(s): **All class periods**
- ■ Baseline data across five times/sessions:    1.    **7**
- ■ Intervals with no occurrence of desk hitting    2.    **11**
  
                                    3.    **13**
  
                                    4.    **16**
  
                                    5.    **11**
- ■ Rate of target behavior:                Baseline **2.9/hour**       Target **0**
- ■ Inter-behavior interval:                  Baseline **20.7 min**     Target **24hours**
- ■ Initial schedule of Differential Negative Reinforcement:
  - ■ **_X_** Fixed time schedule every **_15_** minutes/hours/days

                                     OR
  - ■ **___** Variable time schedule on average every **___** minutes/hours/days
- ■ Reset Timer: End of each interval
  - ■ **_X_** End of each interval AND if target behavior occurs
- ■ Reinforcer(s) to be used:          1. **Stop current task and give a short break (5 min)**
  
                                    2. _____
  
                                    3. _____
  
                                    4. _____
  
                                    5. _____
- ■ Special instructions for delivery of reinforcer(s):
1. **If desk hitting occurs, immediately reset the timer to 15 minutes and record data.**
2. **Reset timer to 15 min at the end of the earned 5-minute break.**
- ■ Criterion for increasing amount of time between reinforcers: **When desk hitting behavior occurs in <1% of intervals observed for 3 consecutive days, increase time between delivery of reinforcement by 10%.**
- ■ Criterion for decreasing amount of time between reinforcers: **If desk hitting behavior occurs in more than 5% of observed intervals for 3 consecutive days, decrease time between delivery of reinforcement by 1 minute.**
- ■ Criterion for withholding the scheduled reinforcer delivery: **Occurrence of desk hitting.**

## What If?

*What if the behavior does not decrease (or gets worse) with DNRO?*

When using DNRO with extinction we often see an initial worsening of the target behavior. The technical term for this is an *extinction burst*. Just like it's name implies, it is a brief and often intense increase in the target behavior that happens when the behavior no longer produces the reinforcer. You should see a dramatic decrease in the behavior within 3 sessions or days. If the behavior continues at a high rate for longer than that you will need to confirm that the item or event you are removing contingently is actually reinforcing for the person. The other possibility is that the DNRO interval is simply too long for the person to contact the reinforcer at a high enough rate to reinforce other behaviors. In this case, shortening the DNRO interval is an option you should consider. If this is still ineffective you should consider a more focused reinforcement strategy perhaps starting with noncontingent reinforcement (see NCR program).

**Frequency of Desk Hitting Per Day**

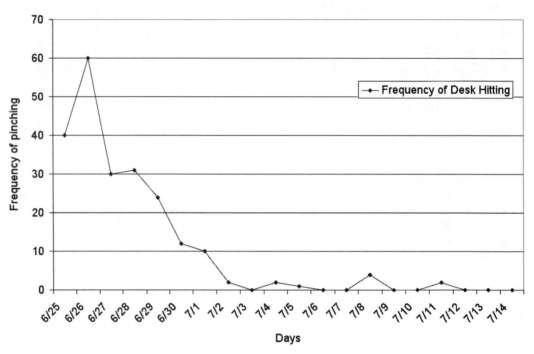

*Figure 5.8* ■ Frequency of desk hitting.

*What if I cannot ignore some of the target behaviors?*

If the target behavior has life-threatening consequences or cannot be ignored, you can program a DNRO without extinction. In this case all the elements of the DNRO would be the same with the exception that when the target behavior occurs we will continue to respond to it as we have in the past. This will make the behavior change process somewhat slower because the difference in level of reinforcement will not be as great. This can be countered to some extent by shortening the DNRO interval thus increasing the density of reinforcement for all other behaviors.

### Forms: Differential Negative Reinforcement of Other Behaviors

5.21 Simple Frequency Data With Formulas

5.22 Differential Negative Reinforcement of Other Behavior With Extinction: Simple Plan

5.23 Formulas for Calculating Percentage of Intervals of Targeted Behavior and Interbehavior Intervals

5.24 Formulas for Determining Increases or Decreases in Frequency of Differential Negative Reinforcement

## FORM 5.21 ■ SIMPLE FREQUENCY DATA WITH FORMULAS

■ Client: _____     CHART STARTED: _____
                                                              **Day/Month/Year**

■ Behavior: _____

■ Total Observation Time: __MIN__ (__, __-minute session/day)     Session length: __min__

■ Number of Days: __

■ Place an X on the appropriate day box each time the target behavior occurs

|  | 1 : | 2 : | 3 : | 4 : | 5 : | 6 : | 7 : | Totals |
|---|---|---|---|---|---|---|---|---|
| Target Behavior |  |  |  |  |  |  |  |  |
| Daily Rate |  |  |  |  |  |  |  |  |
| Inter-behavior interval |  |  |  |  |  |  |  |  |

A.  Total Minutes Observed: __ Interbehavior interval = *A/B* __/__ = ____

■ Rate/hour = (B/A)60   (__/__)60 = ____

|  | 8 : | 9 : | 10 : | 11 : | 12 : | 13 : | 14 : | Totals |
|---|---|---|---|---|---|---|---|---|
| Target Behavior |  |  |  |  |  |  |  |  |
| Daily Rate |  |  |  |  |  |  |  |  |
| Inter-behavior interval |  |  |  |  |  |  |  |  |

A.  Total Minutes Observed: __ Interbehavior interval = *A/B* __/__ = ____

B.  Total occurrences observed: __

C.  Range (low) __ to (high) __, Avg = __Rate/hour = (B/A)60   (__/__)60 = ____

*FORM 5.22* ■ **DIFFERENTIAL NEGATIVE REINFORCEMENT OF OTHER BEHAVIOR WITH EXTINCTION: SIMPLE PLAN**

■ Person served: _____

■ Target Behavior: _____

■ Behavioral diagnostic category: _____

■ Target Rate: _____

■ Designated time Period(s): _____

■ Baseline data across five times/sessions:

      1. _____

      2. _____

      3. _____

      4. _____

      5. _____

■ Rate of target behavior:      Baseline _____    Target _____

■ Interbehavior interval:      Baseline _____    Target_____

■ Initial schedule of Differential Negative reinforcement:

    ■ ___ Fixed time schedule every ___ minutes/hours/days

               OR

    ■ ___ Variable time schedule on average every ___ minutes/hours/days

■ Reset Timer:

    ■ ___ End of each interval

    ■ ___ End of each interval AND if target behavior occurs

■ Reinforcer(s) to be used:      1. _____

(item or event to be      2. _____

removed or avoided)      3. _____

      4. _____

      5. _____

    ■ Special instructions for delivery of reinforcer(s):

    _____

    _____

    _____

■ Criterion for increasing amount of time between reinforcers: _____

_____

■ Criterion for decreasing amount of time between reinforcers: _____

_____

■ Criterion for withholding the scheduled reinforcer delivery: _____

_____

### *FORM 5.23* ■ FORMULAS FOR CALCULATING PERCENTAGE OF INTERVALS OF TARGETED BEHAVIOR AND INTERBEHAVIOR INTERVAL

■ *Interbehavior Interval:* This formula will help you determine on average how much time passes between the occurrence of targeted behaviors (interbehavior interval). Use this information to help set the frequency of differential negative reinforcement.

■ **Total Minutes Observed ÷ Total Behavior Occurrences Observed = Average inter-behavior interval**

■ *Rate:* This formula will help you to determine how often the behavior occurs in a given amount of time. Use this formula if you have different lengths of observation periods to allow for ongoing comparison of data.

■ **Number of occurrences of behavior ÷ Length of observation In minutes = rate of behavior per minute**

■ **Rate per hour = (rate per minute)60**

■ **Rate per day = (rate per minute)1440**

### *FORM 5.24* ■ FORMULAS FOR DETERMINING INCREASES OR DECREASES IN FREQUENCY OF DIFFERENTIAL NEGATIVE REINFORCEMENT

■ *Formula for 10% increase in DNRO interval (time between negative reinforcement).*

■ Current reinforcement interval $\times$ 1.10 = (10% increase in time).

■ *Formula for 5% increase in DNRO interval.*

■ Current reinforcement interval $\times$ 1.05 = (5% increase in time).

■ *Formula for 10% decrease in DNRO interval.*

■ Current reinforcement interval $\times$ 0.90 = (10% decrease in time).

■ *Formula for 5% decrease in DNRO interval.*

■ Current reinforcement interval $\times$ 0.95 = (5% decrease in time).

## More Information

Barton, L. E., Brulle, A. R., & Repp, A. C. (1986). Maintenance of therapeutic change by momentary DRO. *Journal of Applied Behavior Analysis, 19,* 277–282.

Conyers, C., Miltenberger, R., Maki, A., Barenz, R., Jurgens, M., Sailer, A., et al. (2004). A comparison of response cost and differential reinforcement of other behavior to reduce disruptive behavior in a preschool classroom. *Journal of Applied Behavior Analysis, 37,* 411–415.

Cowdery, G. E., Iwata, B. A., & Pace, G. M. (1990). Effects and side effects of DRO as treatment for self-injurious behavior. *Journal of Applied Behavior Analysis, 23,* 497–506.

Goetz, E. M., Holmberg, M. C., & LeBlanc, J. M. (1975). Differential reinforcement of other behavior and non-contingent reinforcement as control procedures during the modification of a preschooler's compliance. *Journal of Applied Behavior Analysis, 8,* 77–82.

Haring, T. G., & Kennedy, C. H. (1990). Contextual control of problem behavior in students with severe disabilities. *Journal of Applied Behavior Analysis, 23,* 235–243.

Harris, S. L., & Wolchik, S. A. (1979). Suppression of self-stimulation: Three alternative strategies. *Journal of Applied Behavior Analysis, 12,* 185–198.

Heard, K., & Watson, T. S. (1999). Reducing wandering by persons with dementia using differential reinforcement. *Journal of Applied Behavior Analysis, 32,* 381–384.

Lindberg, J. S., Iwata, B. A., Kahng, S., & DeLeon, I. G. (1999). DRO contingencies: An analysis of variable-momentary schedules. *Journal of Applied Behavior Analysis, 32,* 123–136.

Luce, S. C., Delquadri, J., & Hall, R. V. (1980). Contingent exercise: A mild but powerful procedure for suppressing inappropriate verbal and aggressive behavior. *Journal of Applied Behavior Analysis, 13,* 583–594.

Marcus, B. A., & Vollmer, T. R. (1996). Combining noncontingent reinforcement and differential reinforcement schedules as treatment for aberrant behavior. *Journal of Applied Behavior Analysis, 29,* 43–51.

Martinez, S. S. (1977). Comparison of extinction, DRO 0-sec, and DRO 6-sec in the elimination of imitative responding under discrete-trial paradigms. *Journal of Applied Behavior Analysis, 10,* 315.

Mazaleski, J. L., Iwata, B. A., Vollmer, T. R., Zarcone, J. R., & Smith, R. G. (1993). Analysis of the reinforcement and extinction components in DRO contingencies with self-injury. *Journal of Applied Behavior Analysis, 26,* 143–156.

McCord, B. E., Iwata, B. A., Galensky, T. L., Ellingson, S. A., & Thomson, R. J. (2001). Functional analysis and treatment of problem behavior evoked by noise. *Journal of Applied Behavior Analysis, 34,* 447–462.

Piazza, C. C., Fisher, W. W., Hanley, G. P., Hilker, K., & Derby, K. M. (1996). A preliminary procedure for predicting the positive and negative effects of reinforcement-based procedures. *Journal of Applied Behavior Analysis, 29,* 137–152.

Repp, A. C., Barton, L. E., & Brulle, A. R. (1983). A comparison of two procedures for programming the differential reinforcement of other behaviors. *Journal of Applied Behavior Analysis, 16,* 435–445.

Repp, A. C., & Deitz, S. M. (1974). Reducing aggressive and self-injurious behavior of institutionalized retarded children through reinforcement of other behaviors. *Journal of Applied Behavior Analysis, 7,* 313–325.

Rolider, A., & Van Houten, R. (1985). Movement suppression time-out for undesirable behavior in psychotic and severely developmentally delayed children. *Journal of Applied Behavior Analysis, 18,* 275–288.

Thompson, R. H., Iwata, B. A., Hanley, G. P., Dozier, C. L., & Samaha, A. L. (2003). The effects of extinction, noncontingent reinforcement, and differential reinforcement of other behavior as control procedures. *Journal of Applied Behavior Analysis, 36,* 221–238.

Vollmer, T. R. (1999). Noncontingent reinforcement: Some additional comments. *Journal of Applied Behavior Analysis, 32,* 239–240.

Vollmer, T. R., Iwata, B. A., Zarcone, J. R., Smith, R. G., & Mazaleski, J. L. (1993). The role of attention in the treatment of attention-maintained self-injurious behavior: Noncontingent reinforcement and differential reinforcement of other behavior. *Journal of Applied Behavior Analysis, 26,* 9–21.

Woods, D. W., & Himle, M. B. (2004). Creating tic suppression: Comparing the effects of verbal instruction to differential reinforcement. *Journal of Applied Behavior Analysis, 37,* 417–420.

## 4.0 SME FUNCTIONS: ESCAPE MAND (PROTEST OR NEGOTIATING BEHAVIOR) OPTION

### Brief Description

In this replacement behavior option, the removal of the negative reinforcer, whether it be aversive tasks, events, or people, occurs upon an appropriate mand (request) from the client. Concurrently, the target behavior no longer functions to efficiently escape the aversive event, that is, programmed extinction. This is an application of differential reinforcement, specifically differential negative reinforcement of an alternative behavior (DNRA). In this option the alternative behavior is a request (mand) to terminate, or protest of the, conditions that are aversive to the client.

To implement an escape mand replacement behavior program for a problem behavior that is diagnosed with an 4.0 SME function, you determine what specific form the request or protest should take. Such a form will result in the contingent removal of a negative reinforcer (escape or avoidance). In the beginning part of this program, each time the new request or protest behavior occurs it must result in removing the negative reinforcer. If the target behavior occurs it should result in the loss of opportunity to escape or avoid the aversive event (extinction) until the protesting behavior is utilized. By removing the negative reinforcer only if the person uses the specified protesting behavior, the specified replacement behavior "pays off" better than the target behavior. The underlying process here is called differential reinforcement of an alternative behavior (DRA)

The advantage of using this procedure is that it teaches a specific behavior that will result in the removal of a negative reinforcer when the person is most motivated to escape or avoid that particular negative reinforcer. This makes the acquisition of the skill relatively rapid and generally results in a robust response that can be shaped and generalized to overcome other target behaviors. A disadvantage of this option involves an initial interruption in the client's routine due to a parent or staff person immediately complying with the persons request to escape or avoid the aversive stimulus. This option is a bit more labor intensive than DNRO and requires a higher level of expertise and interaction on the part of the people implementing the intervention.

### Terms

*Mand:* A verbal operant behavior under the control of a specific motivating operation that produces a socially mediated specific reinforcer (in the case of a negative reinforcer, a request to escape or avoid).

*Escape:* Engaging in behavior that terminates the presence of an aversive task or event.

*Avoidance:* Engaging in behavior that prevents one from coming in contact with an aversive task or event.

*Aversive stimulus:* A task, event, or person to which the person will make a response that avoids or terminates the stimulus.

## Apparatus

Data sheets—See Form 5.25 "Simple Frequency Data on Target and Replacement Behavior"

## Baseline Measurement

It is important to first determine the form of the protesting behavior that will be developed or increased prior to baseline data collection. Next, you can collect baseline data on both the target behavior and the replacement behavior using Form 5.25.

If the frequency of the target behavior is low, you might consider using a trigger analysis, that is, contriving an antecedent condition that causes the person to encounter the aversive task, event, or person, and observe what behavior occurs (target or replacement behavior). See trigger analysis in chapter 2 for greater detail on conducting this assessment. Realize that the conditions of aversive stimulation have to be present in order for either behavior to occur. Try to make sure that no one, in any way, removes or reduces the aversive conditions prior to the end of your assessment.

## Procedures

1. Present the person with a nonpreferred task, object, or activity (e.g., a wash cloth, least preferred math task, or food item they dislike) with instruction (e.g., "Here, have this." Or "Do this.").
2. After a short time delay (0–2 seconds), provide a general prompt, "What's wrong?"
3. Reinforce a desired protest response (either handing back object or saying or signaling "No!").
4. If the identified form of the replacement response is vocal and a vocal protest response does not occur to the general prompt, or if the target behavior occurs, model vocal protest (e.g., "stop," "no," "I do not want to do that," or "I don't want that").
5. If the identified form of the replacement response is nonvocal and a nonvocal protest response does not occur to general prompt, or if the target behavior occurs, physically guide the protest response, either handing back the object or manually signing "no" or "stop."
6. Reinforce any approximation of the desired form of protest (vocal or nonvocal) by removing the nonpreferred object or stopping the activity and initiating a more preferred activity. Do not allow the target behavior to result in the removal of the nonpreferred item or activity. (escape extinction)
7. During subsequent protest opportunities, provide less guidance (or modeling) of the protest response until it occurs independently and immediately to the presentation of the nonpreferred task, object, person, or activity.
8. Utilize many different nonpreferred activities and objects during structured training sessions to teach a generalized skill of protesting.
9. Consider developing a Requesting Behavior Option Plan in conjunction with this skill.
10. Provide opportunities for protesting behaviors in real life by occasionally handing the client a nonpreferred item or engaging him in a nonpreferred activity. Reinforce protest with removal of nonpreferred item or activity.

*Capturing Motivation—It is essential that the person being assessed is motivated to escape or avoid the task, event, or person. The judgment of when he wants to avoid or escape the task, event, or person can generally be along the same conditions under which the 4.0 SME target behavior occurred. Using this same level of aversive stimulation that existed as a motivating condition for the problem behavior, you now use the above procedures to develop the replacement behavior.*

### Modification for Use with Direct Escape Behaviors

1. Utilize the same baseline measurement procedures.
2. When the target behavior occurs, use chain interruption procedures and follow the Escape Mand Replacement Behavior Option instructions starting with step 4 as listed previously.

## How It Works

Teaching a protesting behavior (mand) works by establishing an alternate form of behavior that will allow the person to more effectively and efficiently escape or avoid the same maintaining negative reinforcer as the target behavior. By ensuring that the alternate behavior "pays off" better for the person, the function of alternative behavior is enabled and the function of the target behavior is disabled. Once the person has an alternative behavior in their repertoire that can function as a protest, you enable its function by making it more effective and efficient than the target behavior in removing the negative reinforcer. Once the mand is functional, the fading or thinning process allows for the natural contingencies in the environment to control the protesting behavior so that it will maintain over time.

### Hypothetical Example

#### "I'm Bored"

As an example, let's look at how the Escape Mand Replacement Behavior Option might be applied to the case of the child that learned how to get a 5-minute break by throwing things in class.

Mr. Jones, a behavior analysis consultant, was told by the teaching staff that once or twice a day, for no apparent reason, Susan would get out of her seat, grab an item off of her desk or someone else's desk, and throw it as hard as she could against the wall. Staff contended that the problem behaviors were occurring "for no good reason" and just came "out of the blue." The staff commented that it was probably due to some mental illness. Given the variability and lack of specific information in staff reports, Mr. Jones needed to find a way to obtain reliable information. He decided to perform a descriptive functional assessment (A-B-C analysis) from his direct observations. Table 5.22 summarizes his findings.

Mr. Jones reviewed his observations. He noted that the behavior only occurred after Susan had been working on a task for over 20 minutes. Although Susan's throwing behavior produced attention from the teacher, she engaged in other behaviors that were equally successful in getting teacher attention. Mr. Jones noted that throwing objects also resulted in Susan's removal from the assignment for a period of time. This finding ruled out 2.1 SMA: staff attention as the maintaining contingency for the throwing behavior. The sensory result of throwing items did not appear to be the purpose of the behavior, given the relative infrequency of such behavior and that it was more likely to occur when working on an assignment for relatively long periods of time. Further, Susan appeared happy or excited by the prospect of being sent to time out. Mr. Jones also noticed that Susan was compliant with demands to complete short duration tasks.

Mr. Jones concluded that the most likely maintaining contingency was 4.2 SME: relatively lengthy school assignments (see Table 5.23). Currently, Susan's throwing of

*TABLE 5.22* ■ **SUMMARY OF THROWING ITEMS A-B-C DATA**

| Antecedent Conditions | Target Behavior | What Happened? | What Was Natural Result of Behavior? |
|---|---|---|---|
| 1. Independent seat work, math problems. | Throwing things. | Teacher prompted Susan to step into the hallway and counseled her about her behavior. Susan was apologetic and talkative. Returned to seat work after discussion. | Material landing on the floor; visual/auditory effect |
| 2. Independent seat work, vocabulary words. | Throwing things. | Teacher prompted Susan to take a break in the hallway. Susan complied. The teacher prompted her to return in about 5 minutes. Susan went back to her seat work. | Material landing on the floor; visual/auditory effect. |
| 3. Standardized assessment testing. | Throwing things. | Susan was sent to time out for 5 minutes. She went willingly and appeared happy to go. After time out she returned to the testing. | Material landing on the floor; visual/auditory effect. |

items is frequently followed by being removed form the school work task for at least 5 minutes.

The 4.2 SME diagnosis made perfect sense in regards to why the behavior appeared to occur randomly and only once or twice per day. Susan was willing to engage in school work, but if it continued for too long, she found a way to get a break.

Mr. Jones considered using tolerance training (DNRO), however, this student could already stay on task for an acceptable length of time, and during his observations he had never observed Susan making a request of the teacher. Mr. Jones decided to train a requesting behavior using DNRA. This would not only result in a reduction of throwing things but would develop a skill that could be used to effectively escape many aversive situations in the school setting.

Prior to writing the plan, Mr. Jones requested that the teacher record baseline data on the frequency of throwing things and the frequency of requesting a break across 55-minute-long observation sessions over 6 days. The data was recorded on Example Form 5.25.

With this frequency data in hand and an understanding of the function of the throwing behavior, Mr. Jones formulated an intervention plan (see Example Form 5.26). He determined that throwing things occurred under the conditions of having been working continuously on a seat work task for over 20 minutes. His data also indicated that the student very rarely exhibited the replacement behavior of requesting a break, and when the request was made it did not result in getting a break.

Mr. Jones knew that the targeted behavior of throwing things was more likely around 11 A.M. each day, when the student was at her desk and had been doing school work for over 20 minutes. He decided the best way to capture a high level of motivation for the

*TABLE 5.23* ■ **DIAGNOSTIC TABLE FOR THROWING OBJECTS**

| Diagnosis | 4.2 SME: relatively lengthy school assignments. |
|---|---|
| Target behavior(s): | Throwing objects. |
| Function: | Terminates her engagement with the task for assignments that last longer than 20 minutes. |
| Target behavior likely under following contexts: | Task duration exceeding 20 minutes. |
| Target behavior unlikely under following contexts: | Short duration tasks with breaks interspersed. |
| Rule out: | 2.1 SMA: staff attention<br>4.1 SME: unpleasant social situations |

taking a break was to set up training for about 11 A.M. in the classroom at the student's desk after she had been continuously working for at least 20 minutes.

Mr. Jones decided that the protesting behavior he would try to establish was having the student simply pull out a laminated break card, show it to the teacher, and wait for the teacher to acknowledge or approve the request. Susan would then set a timer for 5 minutes of break time. Subsequently, after the break, she would return to work.

Mr. Jones set the initial reinforcement schedule such that every presentation of a break card produced 5 minutes of break time. In order to limit the amount of break time used, Mr. Jones set an additional contingency that if in any period (morning or afternoon) Susan did not go over her allotted number of break cards, she earned five points toward a video of her choice at her parent's home. She had to earn 30 points by Friday afternoon in order to earn the video (i.e., no more than two periods in the week where she took more than two breaks).

To increase the speed of this process Mr. Jones also specified another contingency. Specifically, if the student engaged in throwing things, any break cards left were immediately removed for the remainder of the morning or afternoon session. If she continued throwing materials, she would be removed from the area for the protection of other students and placed in time out until she "calmed down." Following time out, she would be told that she had extra work to do during recess at the principal's office area (reverse Premack). Further, she would not earn five points and would have to return to the assignment during the class period.

Mr. Jones specified that the following prompt sequence should be used in teaching Susan to request a break. The first prompt would be delivered vocally and progress to more helpful or intrusive prompts if the prompt card was not presented. The instructions to the staff were as follows:

1. After at least 20 minutes of seat work, provide the prompt, "Do you want a break?"
2. If no response, provide the same prompt with the addition of a gestural prompt of pointing to the break card.
3. Once the request via the break card occurs, allow Susan to take a break for 5 minutes.

Mr. Jones also wanted to make sure that Susan would eventually present a break card when she wanted a break from school work without anyone prompting her to do so. In

**EXAMPLE FORM 5.25 ■ FREQUENCY COUNT DATA SHEET**

■ Client: Susan                                             CHART STARTED: _____

                                                                          **Day/Month/Year**

■ Behavior: **Throwing things**
■ Total Observation Time: **330 MIN** (**2**, **55**-minute session/day)        Session length **55 min**
■ Number of Days: **6**
■ Place an X on the appropriate day box each time the behavior occurs

|                  | Day 1 | Day 2 | Day 3 | Day 4 | Day 5 | Day 6 | Totals |
|------------------|-------|-------|-------|-------|-------|-------|--------|
| Throwing things  | X     | X     | XX    | X     |       | X     | 6      |
| Requesting a break |     |       | X     |       |       |       | 1      |

A. Total Minutes Observed: <u>330</u>
B. Total Target behavior occurrences observed: <u>6</u>
C. Total Replacement behavior occurrences observed: <u>1</u>

### EXAMPLE FORM 5.26 ■ TEACHING REQUESTING BEHAVIOR: SIMPLE PLAN

■ Person served: **Susan**

■ Target Behavior: **Throwing items**

■ Behavioral diagnostic category: **4.2 SME: Socially mediated escape, lengthy school assignments**

■ Protesting/Negotiating Behavior: **Requesting a break**

   A. Form of protest: vocal request; manual signed request; requesting by pointing to a communication board; use augmentative device to request; other:

   **Holding up of break card**

   B. Description of initial protest to be reinforced: **Show one of her break cards to the teacher; wait for acknowledgment, and set the timer for five minutes**

■ Reinforcer(s) to be used:

| | Type | Amount |
|---|---|---|
| 1. | **End task/recess** | 1. **5 min** |
| 2. | _____ | 2. _____ |

■ Target Rate: **No more than 4 times per day.**

■ Instructions to assure motivation:

■ Train at Time and place that target behaivor is most likely which is:

■ **Training in the classroom at her desk after at least 20 minutes of continuous seat work task.**

■ Ensure limited escape from the negatively reinforcing item at other times by: **Redirecting back to task after throwing behaviors**

■ Rate of target behavior:  Baseline **1/hr**  Target **0/day**

■ Rate of Protesting Behavior  Baseline **1/day**  Target **2/day**

■ Initial schedule of Differential Negative reinforcement:

   A. Remove/terminate the unwanted event/item after every **1** (number of ) protests and with no more than a **5** Sec delay

■ Targeted final schedule of Differential Negative Reinforcement:

   A. No more than **2** (number of) protests in a **Half day** (time period)

■ Replacement behavior is reinforced:

■ If the protesting behavior occurs independently, terminate the negative reinforcer.

■ If the protesting behavior does not occur under the targeted conditions, provide the following prompts: (using **Vocal** Sign Gesture Visual)

1. **Provide the prompt "Do you want a break?"**

2. **If no response, provide the prompt again with the item break card and timer within sight.**

3. **If no response, provide the prompt with the addition of a gestural prompt.**

4. **If no response, provide the prompt with the addition of modeling the response.**

5. **Once the protest occurs, set the timer and provide a 5-minute break.**

6. **Repeat up to 4 times per day (2 in the A.M. and 2 in the P.M.)**

■ **If target behavior occurs:**

■ **Specifically if Susan engaged in throwing things, any break cards left are immediately removed for the remainder of the morning or afternoon session. If she cannot be stopped from continuing throwing materials, she will be removed from the area for the protection of other students and placed in time out until she "calms down." Following time out, she will be told that she has extra work to do during recess at the principal's office area (Reverse Premack). Further, she does not earn five points and has to return to the assignment during the class period.**

   ■ Special instructions for delivery of small amount of reinforcer(s):

   **Breaks are to last no longer than 5 minutes and a maximum of four times per day.**

■ Criterion for Fading prompts: **When target rate for replacement behavior is reached on 3 consecutive days, reduce the level of helpfulness of the prompt first by waiting for 5 seconds before providing the prompt, and then by reducing the prompt from vocal to simple hand gestures, and eventually to the level of prompts that would usually be in place in the classroom.**

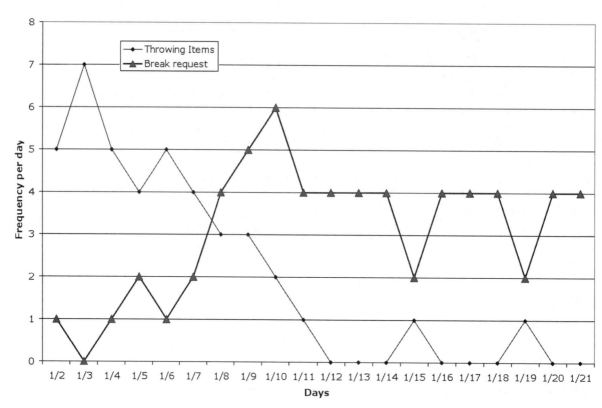

***Figure 5.9*** ■ Breaks and throwing items.

order to accomplish this he developed a plan for slowly decreasing the prompts that were provided. He determined that once Susan could present a break card with prompts for 3 consecutive days, the staff would be taught to reduce or fade the prompts.

The program was implemented and produced the data displayed in Figure 5.9. As Mr. Jones expected, this plan was successful in reducing the occurrence of throwing behavior and increasing the rate of protesting behavior (mand for a break). By 1/14 the protesting behavior had met the criteria for fading prompts. The prompts were gradually faded until Susan was requesting her break independently.

### What If?

*What if the behavior does not decrease or gets worse?*

When using this option, which is DNRA with extinction, we often see an initial worsening of the target behavior. The technical term for this is an *extinction burst*. Just like its name implies, it is a brief and often intense increase in the target behavior that happens when the behavior no longer produces termination of the negative reinforcer. You should see a dramatic decrease in the behavior within 3 sessions or days. If the behavior continues at a high rate for longer than that, you will need to confirm that the behavior you have set up as the protesting behavior is actually resulting in termination of the negative reinforcer. You should also ensure that extinction is indeed occurring for the target behavior.

*What if the person is asking to escape all the time?*

If the protesting behavior becomes too frequent you can set up some limits and incentives as described in the example. That is, you can decrease the number of requests that will be honored over time. To do this you will need to set up an additional contingency to differentially reinforce lower rates of requesting behavior. This is the same basic differential reinforcement process, but you provide reinforcement contingent on the target behavior occurring below a specific standard. You then progressively set the standard at a lower rate.

*What If the person has never been observed to have exhibited a request or protest behavior?*

In this case you will have to first teach a behavior that can be used effectively to protest the presentation of some negative reinforcer. This generally involves a task analysis and some specific teaching procedures to ensure that the skill is well established in the client's repertoire. Discrete Trial Training and Precision Teaching are specific teaching procedures that have been used effectively for this purpose.

### Forms: Differential Negative Reinforcement of Other Behaviors

5.25 Simple Frequency Data on Target and Replacement Behavior
5.26 Teaching Requesting Behavior: Simple Plan

*FORM 5.25* ■ **SIMPLE FREQUENCY DATA ON TARGET AND REPLACEMENT BEHAVIORS**

■ Client: _____    CHART STARTED: _____

Day/Month/Year

■ Behavior: _____

■ Total Observation Time: __MIN (__, __-minute session/day)    Session length: __min

■ Number of Days: __

■ Place an X on the appropriate day box each time the behavior occurs

| | 1 : | 2 : | 3 : | 4 : | 5 : | 6 : | 7 : | Totals |
|---|---|---|---|---|---|---|---|---|
| Target Behavior | | | | | | | | |
| Replacement Behavior | | | | | | | | |

| | 8 : | 9 : | 10 : | 11 : | 12 : | 13 : | 14 : | Totals |
|---|---|---|---|---|---|---|---|---|
| Target Behavior | | | | | | | | |
| Replacement Behavior | | | | | | | | |

| | 15 : | 16 : | 17 : | 18 : | 19 : | 20 : | 21 : | Totals |
|---|---|---|---|---|---|---|---|---|
| Target Behavior | | | | | | | | |
| Replacement Behavior | | | | | | | | |

| | 22 : | 23 : | 24 : | 25 : | 26 : | 27 : | 28 : | Totals |
|---|---|---|---|---|---|---|---|---|
| Target Behavior | | | | | | | | |
| Replacement Behavior | | | | | | | | |

| | 29 : | 30 : | 31 : | 1 : | 2 : | 3 : | 4 : | Totals |
|---|---|---|---|---|---|---|---|---|
| Target Behavior | | | | | | | | |
| Replacement Behavior | | | | | | | | |

A. Total Minutes Observed: __

B. Total Target behavior occurrences observed: __

C. Total Replacement behavior occurrences observed: __

## FORM 5.26 ■ TEACHING REQUESTING BEHAVIOR: SIMPLE PLAN

■ Person served: _____

■ Target Behavior: _____

■ Behavioral diagnostic category: _____

■ Protesting/negotiating behavior: _____

      A.  Form of protest: vocal request; manual signed request; requesting by pointing to a communication board; use augmentative device to request; other: _____.

      B.  Description of Initial protest to be reinforced: _____

      _____

■ Reinforcer(s) to be used:

| | Type | Amount |
|---|---|---|
| | 1. _____ | 1. _____ |
| | 2. _____ | 2. _____ |
| | 3. _____ | 3. _____ |
| | 4. _____ | 4. _____ |
| | 5. _____ | 5. _____ |

■ Target Rate: _____

■ Instructions to ensure motivation:

    ■  Train at time and place that target behaivor is most likely, which is: _____

    _____

    ■  Ensure limited escape from the negatively reinforcing item at other times by: _____

    _____

■ Designated time period(s) to implement: _____

■ Rate of target behavior:               Baseline _____    Target _____

■ Rate of protesting behavior          Baseline _____    Target _____

■ Initial schedule of differential negative reinforcement:

■ Targeted final schedule of differential negative reinforcement:

■ No more than ____ (number of) protests in a ____ (time period)

■ Replacement behavior is reinforced:

■ If the requesting behavior occurs independently terminate the negative reinforcer.

■ If the protesting behavior does not occur under the targeted conditions Provide the following prompts: (using Vocal Sign Gesture Visual)

1.  Provide the prompt, "What do you want?"

2.  If no response, provide the prompt with the addition of a gestural prompt.

3.  If no response, provide the prompt with the addition of modeling the response.

4.  If no response, provide the prompt with the addition of a physical prompt.

5.  If no response, provide increasing physical prompt using least to most prompting.

6.  Once the protest occurs, terminate the negative reinforcer.

7.  Repeat for as long as the person is motivated to escape the negative reinforcer.

■ **If target behavior occurs:**

■ Extinction (no escape from the negative reinforcer) for ____ minutes then begin prompt sequence for replacement behavior listed above.

■ If replacement, protesting behavior occurs during this time period provide escape from the negative reinforcer.

    ■  Special instructions for delivery of small amount of reinforcer(s):

    _____

    _____

■ Criterion for fading prompts: _____

_____

■ Criterion for increasing the amount of delay in the delivery of reinforcer: _____

_____

*More Information*

*Teaching Requesting Skills*

Arntzen, E., & Almås, I. K. (2002). Effects of mand-tact versus tact-only training on the acquisition of tacts. *Journal of Applied Behavior Analysis, 35,* 419–422.

Bowman, L. G., Fisher, W. W., Thompson, R. H., & Piazza, C. C. (1997). On the relation of mands and the function of destructive behavior. *Journal of Applied Behavior Analysis, 30,* 251–265.

Brown, K. A., Wacker, D. P., Derby, K. M., Peck, S. M., Richman, D. M., Sasso, G. M., et al. (2000). Evaluating the effects of functional communication training in the presence and absence of establishing operations. *Journal of Applied Behavior Analysis, 33,* 53–71.

DeLeon, I. G., Fisher, W. W., Herman, K. M., & Crosland, K. C. (2000). Assessment of a response bias for aggression over functionally equivalent appropriate behavior. *Journal of Applied Behavior Analysis, 33,* 73–77.

Derby, K. M., Wacker, D. P., Berg, W., DeRaad, A., Ulrich, S., Asmus, J., et al. (1997)The long-term effects of functional communication training in home settings. *Journal of Applied Behavior Analysis, 30,* 507–531.

Drasgow, E., Halle, J. W., & Ostrosky, M. M. (1998). Effects of differential reinforcement on the generalization of a replacement mand in three children with severe language delays. *Journal of Applied Behavior Analysis, 31,* 357–374.

Henry, L. M., & Horne, P. J. (2000). Partial remediation of speaker and listener behaviors in people with severe dementia. *Journal of Applied Behavior Analysis,. 33,* 631–634.

Kahng, S., Hendrickson, D. J., & Vu, C. P. (2000). Comparison of single and multiple functional communication training responses for the treatment of problem behavior. *Journal of Applied Behavior Analysis, 33,* 321–324.

Lalli, J. S., Mauro, B. C., & Mace, F. C. (2000). Preference for unreliable reinforcement in children with mental retardation: The role of conditioned reinforcement. *Journal of Applied Behavior Analysis, 33,* 533–544.

Northup, J., Wacker, D., Sasso, G., Steege, M., Cigrand, K., Cook, J., et al. (1991). A brief functional analysis of aggressive and alternative behavior in an outclinic setting. *Journal of Applied Behavior Analysis, 24,* 509–522.

Partington, J. W., Sundberg, M. L., Newhouse, L., & Spengler, S. M. (1994). Overcoming an autistic child's failure to acquire a tact repertoire. *Journal of Applied Behavior Analysis, 27,* 733–734.

Peck, S. M., Wacker, D. P., Berg, W. K., Cooper, L. J., Brown, K. A., Richman, D., et al. (1996). Choice-making treatment of young children's severe behavior problems. *Journal of Applied Behavior Analysis, 29,* 263–290.

Richman, D. M., Wacker, D. P., & Winborn, L. (2001). Response efficiency during functional communication training: Effects of effort on response allocation. *Journal of Applied Behavior Analysis, 34,* 73–76.

Sprague, J. R., & Horner, R. H. (1992). Covariation within functional response classes: Implications for treatment of severe problem behavior. *Journal of Applied Behavior Analysis, 25,* 735–745.

Vollmer, T. R., Borrero, J. C., Lalli, J. S., & Daniel, D. (1999). Evaluating self-control and impulsivity in children with severe behavior disorders. *Journal of Applied Behavior Analysis, 32,* 451–466.

Wallace, M. D., Iwata, B. A., & Hanley, G. P. (2006). Establishment of mands following tact training as a function of reinforcer strength. *Journal of Applied Behavior Analysis, 39,* 17–24.

Winborn, L., Wacker, D. P., Richman, D. M., Asmus, J., & Geier, D. (2002). Assessment of mand selection for functional communication training packages. *Journal of Applied Behavior Analysis, 35,* 295–298.

Yamamoto, J., & Mochizuki, A. (1988). Acquisition and functional analysis of manding with autistic students. *Journal of Applied Behavior Analysis, 21,* 57–64.

*Differential Reinforcement of Alternative Behavior*

Goh, H., Iwata, B. A., & DeLeon, I. G. (2000). Competition between noncontingent and contingent reinforcement schedules during response acquisition. *Journal of Applied Behavior Analysis, 33,* 195–205.

Lee, R., McComas, J. J., & Jawor, J. (2002). The effects of differential and lag reinforcement schedules on varied verbal responding by individuals with autism. *Journal of Applied Behavior Analysis, 35,* 391–402.

McCord, B. E., Thomson, R. J., & Iwata, B. A. (2001). Functional analysis and treatment of self-injury associated with transitions. *Journal of Applied Behavior Analysis, 34,* 195–210.

Piazza, C. C., Moes, D. R., & Fisher, W. W. (1996). Differential reinforcement of alternative behavior and demand fading in the treatment of escape-maintained destructive behavior. *Journal of Applied Behavior Analysis, 29,* 569–572.

Ringdahl, J. E., Kitsukawa, K., Andelman, M. S., Call, N., Winborn, L., Barretto, A., et al. (2002). Differential reinforcement with and without instructional fading. *Journal of Applied Behavior Analysis, 35,* 291–294.

Vollmer, T. R., Roane, H. S., Ringdahl, J. E., & Marcus, B. A. (1999). Evaluating treatment challenges with differential reinforcement of alternative behavior. *Journal of Applied Behavior Analysis, 32,* 9–23.

## 4.0 SME FUNCTIONS: ALTERNATE DIRECT ESCAPE FORM

### Brief Description

In this replacement behavior option, the negative reinforcer is removed by the client engaging in a chain of behaviors that directly terminates or avoids the aversive item or event, independent of anyone else's intervention.

To implement a direct escape program, you must determine what chain of behaviors can directly remove the aversive items or event. If the person can fluently perform the requisite chain of behaviors, a simple rearrangement of contingencies is all that is usually required. Performance of the chain of behaviors is allowed to remove the negative reinforcer. Concurrently, extinction of the target behavior (i.e., socially mediated) is programmed.

If the person does not currently possess the direct escape behavior, their behavior must be shaped to produce an effective response (see inept repertoire diagnosis in Appendix A). In some cases, the entire chain of behaviors may have to be taught. In other cases, a few components of the chain may be lacking.

If the client can perform the chain of behaviors, but not fluently (i.e., with acceptable speed and accuracy), fluency training is required. Once the client has acquired fluent performance of the chain of behaviors, differential negative reinforcement as delineated in this program is implemented.

The advantage of this replacement behavior option is that it allows the client to independently escape or avoid aversive items or events without reliance on other people or having to use communication or social skills. The direct escape option develops a specific chain of behaviors that will continue to be functional for the client over time. Once these behaviors are acquired they can be utilized in other situations through the process of shaping and generalization.

## Terms

*Trigger analysis:* Setting up all the conditions hypothesized to occasion the target behavior, and documenting the occurrence (or lack thereof) of the target behavior and direct escape replacement behavior.

## Apparatus

Data sheets—See Form 5.27 "Simple Frequency Data With Formulas"

## Baseline Measurement

There are two different types of information you need to obtain. First, you need to determine how often the target behavior is occurring under relevant conditions. Additionally, you need the frequency of occurrence of the proposed alternate form of direct escape behavior under relevant conditions.

The frequency measure is simply a count of each time the person engages in the target behavior and a count of each time they perform the alternate form direct escape behavior under the same conditions. This type of data is best collected via a trigger analysis. When considering this option baseline rates for the direct access behavior are typically at or near zero.

## Trigger Analysis (see Form 5.28)

1. Contrive or capture a situation in which escape or avoidance of the item or event is highly likely. To accomplish this, set up motivational conditions, usually through temporary exposure to the negatively reinforcing items or events.
2. Observe the person's behavior relative to the chain of alternate form direct escape behaviors.
3. Record the time the person takes to initiate the response and terminate the negative reinforcer.
4. Record which steps were completed and any prompts required to facilitate the performance of the steps.
5. Record if the negative reinforcer was terminated.

6. Repeat steps 1–5 at least two more times.
7. Graph or display the data across all baseline sessions.

If the baseline trigger analysis data indicates that the person does not appear to have the designated alternate form of direct escape behaviors in their repertoire, you will first need to teach the specific chain of behaviors to fluent performance.

If the baseline data indicates that the person is not performing the direct escape behavior, start by teaching the behavior using discrete trials. If the baseline data indicates that they are able to perform the behavior, then skip to incidental teaching.

### Discrete Trials

1. Present the aversive item or event to the person.
2. Prompt him to perform the first step in the alternate direct escape behavior.
3. Provide reinforcement contingent on completing the behavior or chain of behaviors.
4. If he does not complete the chain of behaviors, provide an additional prompt to help him complete the next step.
5. Provide reinforcement, preferably in the form of escape or avoidance of the aversive item or event you want him to directly escape with this behavior.
6. If he engages in the target behavior extinction in the form of blocking escape or avoidance should occur until the target behavior has been absent for some short period of time. Then resume prompts to engage in the identified alternate form of the direct escape behavior.
7. Record data.
8. On each successive trial, shape more independent responding by reducing the level of prompt provided.
9. Once he is performing the task without the need for additional prompts, change to incidental teaching method.

### Incidental Teaching

1. Observe for conditions under which he would usually engage in the target behavior.
2. If he directly escapes or avoids an item or event without engaging in a target behavior, allow him to do so.
3. If he does not escape or avoid the item or event, provide a prompt to engage in the direct escape behavior.
4. If he does not complete the task, provide an additional prompt to help him complete the next step.
5. On each successive trial, shape more independent responding by reducing the level of prompt provided.
6. If he engages in the target behavior extinction in the form of blocking escape or avoidance should occur until the target behavior has been absent for some short period of time. Then resume prompts to engage in the identified alternate form of the direct escape behavior.
7. Record data.

*If utilizing this behavior option for* Direct Escape behaviors (3.0 DE): *Utilize the same baseline and treatment procedures as above, except that chain interruption would occur instead of extinction when the target behavior is displayed.*

### Ensure Escape or Avoidance of the Negative Reinforcer!

It is critical that during the time that the person is learning to perform the alternate form direct escape chain of behaviors that the negative reinforcer be terminated every time the alternate form direct escape behavior occurs. If the rate of the alternate form direct escape replacement behaviors becomes too high with ad lib escape, you may consider setting up a DNRO or Premack contingency as an additional replacement behavior option to gradually reduce the rate of escape.

## How It Works

When the person is motivated to escape a particular item or event and he can do so directly, it will become functional very quickly. The alternate direct escape form behavior will probably remove the negative reinforcer at a higher rate and more reliably than the target behavior which required other people to be involved. There is no reliance on ancillary skills such as initiating a social interaction or making a request.

### Hypothetical Example

#### I Want to Change, Please

John is a person diagnosed with schizophrenia living in a locked psychiatric facility who was referred for services due to "stripping off his clothes." Mr. Clay was assigned the case and began the assessment process by reviewing the data the facility was keeping. He then proceeded to interview the staff of the facility to understand the definitions of the targeted behaviors and gain information about the conditions under which the behavior occurs.

The data Mr. Clay obtained from the records for the previous week is presented in Example Form 5.27A.

Mr. Clay asked the staff to describe what the behavior looked like the last time it happened and if there was much variation across occurrences. The staff reported that it was typically the same each time. John would walk up to the nurses station and remain there briefly. He would then walk around the facility and begin to slowly unbutton his clothing. He would often be in a moderate state of undress. He would then return to the nurses' station and tell the staff that "animals don't wear clothes." The staff indicated that if they talked with him he would briefly stop disrobing. However, after a short period of time he would resume saying animals don't wear clothes and proceed to remove his clothing one piece at a time. The staff told Mr. Clay they believed his behavior was the result of some traumatic experience he had while wearing a wool sweater. Mr. Clay was interested in their rationale for such and inference and asked why they hypothesized this? One staff member said, "He seems to make more delusional statements and strip more often when he is wearing a wool sweater."

---

**EXAMPLE FORM 5.27A ■ SIMPLE FREQUENCY DATA**

■ CLIENT: _____John_____     CHART STARTED: _____

  Day/Month/Year

■ BEHAVIOR: __stripping_____
■ Total Observation Time: __MIN__ (__, __-minute session/day)     Session length __min__
■ Number of Days: **7**
■ Place an X on the appropriate day box each time the behavior occurs

| | 1 | 2 | 3 | 4 | 5 | 6 | 7 | Totals |
|---|---|---|---|---|---|---|---|---|
| Target Behavior | xxxx | xxxxx | xxx | xxxxx | xxxx | xxxxx | xxxxxx | |
| Daily Rate | 4 | 5 | 3 | 5 | 4 | 5 | 6 | 32 |

Mr. Clay suspected that the odd repetitive statements and the wool sweater might have something to do with the function of the behavior. He asked the staff a series of questions:

*Mr. Clay:* Does he strip if he is not wearing a wool sweater?

*Staff:* Oh yes, it also happens when most of his clothing is in the laundry and he has only the clothes he doesn't like left to choose from.

*Mr. Clay:* Do you ever find John in his room with no clothes on and no one else around?

*Staff:* No, he usually only strips when we are around.

*Mr. Clay:* Has John ever failed to dress after showering?

*Staff:* No, he generally doesn't like the other clients to see him naked.

*Mr. Clay:* So, given a choice of his preferred clothing items and being naked, which would he choose?

*Staff:* Oh, he would definitely be in sweat pants and a t-shirt.

Because John was not likely to strip if no one else was there to see it, Mr. Clay was fairly certain that the behavior did not function to access sensory stimulation secondary to being naked. Further questioning revealed that the behavior only happened when John had on clothing he did not pick out himself and that the "stripping" behaviors stopped as soon as he changed into more preferred clothing. With this information Mr. Clay was reasonably sure that the behavioral served an escape function and that the diagnosis would be 4.4 SME: aversive physical stimuli or event (see Table 5.24).

Mr. Clay wondered why John would make delusional statements and strip as a way to get a change of clothes. Why would he not just go to his room and change? He asked the staff if they had ever seen John change into preferred clothing independent of staff. The staff replied "No, if we let him change once, he would keep changing all day, and if we let him choose his own clothes he will wear the same dirty clothes day after day. Clothes changing is just a part of his delusional system around being an animal. His delusions are so bad that we had to put all his clothes in a locked closet to stop him form changing all the time."

Now the delusional statements made sense to Mr. Clay, as did the stripping behavior. The only way to get out of wearing uncomfortable clothing was through staff mediation. Staff would only provide the change of clothes if John stripped off his other clothing. The delusional statements were an attempt to tell the staff what he wanted.

Mr. Clay could have simply instructed the staff to follow the current procedure of blocking access to clothing and added an extinction component by instructing staff to

**TABLE 5.24 ■ DIAGNOSTIC TABLE FOR STRIPPING BEHAVIOR**

| Diagnosis | 4.4 SME: aversive physical stimuli/event |
|---|---|
| Target behavior(s): | Stripping off clothing |
| Function: | Escape uncomfortable clothing items |
| Target behavior likely under following contexts: | Wearing less preferred clothing, most notably wool sweaters, and not allowed direct access to alternative clothing items under this condition. |
| Target behavior unlikely under following contexts: | Free access to preferred clothing |
| Rule out: | 2.1 SMA: adult attention<br>1.1 DA: immediate sensory stimuli |

have John put on the same clothes each time he stripped. However, John would probably have developed a new set of behaviors that made the clothing unwearable. He decided that staff will simply teach John to change into preferred clothing when he was uncomfortable. Mr. Clay found out from the staff that John's favorite outfit was light weight sweat pants and a loose fitting cotton t-shirt. The staff objected to this plan saying that they had tried that before, and he would just wear the same clothes every day. When they took away the clothes he wore everyday, he would change clothing constantly all day long.

In order to test the staff members' hypothesis, Mr. Clay set up a simple analysis to find out what John might do given free access to choose and change his own clothes. Mr. Clay asked the staff to dress John in clothing that they reported he was very likely to strip off. Mr. Clay asked that they also provide him with the key to John's room and clothing closet (recall that access to his clothes had been prevented by placing them in a locked closet, which he could only access with staff assistance). Mr. Clay then waited at the nurses' station for John to stop by and make the statement that animals don't wear clothes. When this occurred, Mr. Clay provided a simple prompt of "would you like to change into some different clothes?" The instructions for this trigger analysis and the data are presented on Example Form 5.28.

Mr. Clay also observed that John wore the clothing items for the rest of the day. John did not engage in multiple changes of clothing, indicating that it was indeed most likely the aversive stimulation from particular clothes that was establishing the value of stripping behavior.

---

### EXAMPLE FORM 5.27B ■ SIMPLE FREQUENCY DATA

■ **Client:** John

CHART STARTED: _____

Day/Month/Year

■ Target Behavior: **Stripping**
■ Direct Escape Behavior: **Changing clothes in discrete area**
■ **Total Observation Time:** __MIN__ (__, ___-minute session/day)     Session length: __min__
■ Number of Days: **7**
■ Place an X on the appropriate day box each time the behavior occurs

| Target | 1 | 2 | 3 | 4 | 5 | 6 | 7 | Totals |
|---|---|---|---|---|---|---|---|---|
| Stripping | xx | x | | | | | | |
| Daily Rate | 2 | 1 | 0 | 0 | 0 | 0 | 0 | 3 |

A. Total Minutes Observed: __
B. Total occurrences observed: **3**
C. Range (low) **0** to (high) **2**, Avg = **0.43**

| Replacement | 8 | 9 | 10 | 11 | 12 | 13 | 14 | Totals |
|---|---|---|---|---|---|---|---|---|
| Changing clothes in discrete area | xxx | xx | xxx | xx | xx | xx | xx | |
| Daily Rate | 3 | 2 | 3 | 2 | 2 | 2 | 2 | 16 |

A. Total Minutes Observed: __
B. Total occurrences observed: **16**
C. Range (low) **2** to (high) **3**, Avg = **2**

*EXAMPLE FORM 5.28* ■ **TRIGGER ANALYSIS INSTRUCTION AND DATA**

TRIGGER ANALYSIS TRIAL INSTRUCTION

■ Client name: _____ **John** _____

■ Antecedent set up:

■ Motivation for the reinforcing item will be assured by: **Dressing him in clothing items that have previously occasioned stripping behavior**

■ Availability of the reinforcing item will be indicated by: **A verbal prompt and alternative clothing items available in his room**

■ Type and sequence of prompts to be used: **Verbal then gestural**

■ Preferred response: *Chooses and puts on preferred clothing items.* **No more than one clothing change in an 8 hour period of time.**

■ Conditions regarding access to the reinforcing item:

    ■ How much: **1 clothing change**

    ■ How long: **N/A**

| Step 1 | Initiation |
|--------|------------|
| Step 2 | Go to room |
| Step 3 | Open Closet |
| Step 4 | Pick out shirt |
| Step 5 | Pick out pants |
| Step 6 | Disrobe in private area |
| Step 7 | Put on new clothing |

■ I = Independent  P = prompted  N = did not complete

| | Date | Time Start | Time End | Step | | | | | | | % Task Comp. |
|---|------|-----------|----------|---|---|---|---|---|---|---|-------------|
| **Trial** | | | | 1 | 2 | 3 | 4 | 5 | 6 | 7 | |
| 1 | 1/1 | 11:30 | 12:00 | P | I | I | I | I | I | I | 86% |
| 2 | 1/1 | 4:30 | 4:50 | P | I | I | I | I | I | I | 86% |
| 3 | 1/2 | 4:30 | 4:45 | P | I | I | I | I | I | I | 86% |
| 4 | 1/3 | 11:30 | 11:40 | P | I | I | I | I | I | I | 86% |
| 5 | 1/4 | 11:30 | 11:40 | P | I | I | I | I | I | I | 86% |
| 6 | 1/5 | 11:30 | 11:40 | P | I | I | I | I | I | I | 86% |

■ Independent completion rate: Whole task: **0/6**

■ Prompted completion rate: Whole task: **6/6**

■ Time to complete task:

    ■ Longest **30 min**

    ■ Shortest **10 min**

    ■ Average **15.83 min**

Mr. Clay now could develop a simple contingency plan that he knew would eliminate the "stripping." If John had not been able to complete the task Mr. Clay would have completed a Task Analysis and developed a plan to teach him the skill using a combination of Discrete Trial Training, Incidental Teaching, Chaining, and behavioral fluency.

Mr. Clay developed the a simple direct escape plan (see Example Form 5.29). If John "strips," he will be required to dress in the clothes he had just removed until the target behaviors had been absent for 10 minutes. If John goes to his room and changes into preferred clothing, he is free to wear them. John is to have free access to preferred clothing at all times. Staff will continue taking data on "stripping" and also record number of times John changes her clothing per shift.

The plan was implemented and produced the data presented on Example Form 5.27B.

As can be seen in the data, the program was very successful in disabling the function of the stripping behavior and enabling the function of choosing and discretely changing into more comfortable clothing. It is also interesting to note that clothes changing did not occur at an excessive rate. One further note of interest is that there were no more delusional statements regarding animals not wearing clothes.

The next phase in the training process would be to teach John to independently identify the general fabrics and styles of clothing he prefers so that he can pick them out when he is shopping for new clothing.

### What If?

*What if the person refuses or is unable to complete the direct escape behavior?*

This would require teaching the person the skill first. If they were unable to acquire the skill then some environmental set up would be needed to allow them a way to escape the negative reinforcer directly. If that were still not possible an alternative might be to use noncontingent negative reinforcement.

---

*EXAMPLE FORM 5.29* ■ **DIRECT ESCAPE: PLAN**

- ■ Person served: **John**
- ■ Target Behavior: **Stripping**
- ■ Behavioral diagnostic category: **4.4 SME- aversive physical stimuli/event**
- ■ Direct access behavior: **Changing into preferred clothing**
- ■ Designated time Period(s): **Any**
- ■ Rate of Target behavior:              Baseline **4.6 per day**     Target **0**
- ■ Rate of Direct access behavior:        Baseline **0**            Target **2 per day**
- ■ Initial form or task analysis of direct access behavior: **Choose preferred clothing items and dress himself in a discrete location (bedroom/bathroom), changing clothes no more than once per 8-hour time period.**
- ■ Reinforcing item/event to be directly escaped: **Nonpreferred clothing.**
- ■ When and how will it be made available: **Initially preferred clothing items will simply be available in his now unlocked closet.**
- ■ How to respond to the target behavior: **Have John get redressed in the clothing he just stripped off. After 10 minutes of no stripping behavior, prompt him to go to his room to choose and change clothes to more preferred clothing items.**
- ■ Types of prompts to be used:
  - ☐ Visual   ☒ Vocal   ☒ Gestural   ☐ written   ☐ Touch   ☐ Graduated Guidance
- ■ When to use prompts: **Vocal prompt to change into preferred clothing items should be made when John stops by the nurses' station and makes the statement that "animals do not wear clothes."**

*What if the direct escape behavior results in the person escaping the negative reinforcer at too high a rate?*

If this occurs the simplest solution would be to implement a DNRO or Premack contingency option such that the person could still directly escape the negative reinforcer but the complexity or duration of the behavior required prior to escape could be increased and thereby reduce the frequency of escape.

*What if the person can do the direct escape behavior but they are too slow?*

If the person is simply taking too long to complete the task you should consider fluency training or DRH (differential reinforcement of higher rates of behavior). In fluency training the focus is on breaking down each component step of the overall task to be completed and increasing the speed of movement of each component rather than focusing on accurate performance of the entire task. Accuracy of the entire task develops as each component can be performed fluently. DRH focuses on differentially reinforcing the person performing the behavior faster. So the faster they do the behavior, the greater the pay off. Both methods are effective at speeding up slow performances.

## Forms: Direct Escape

5.27 Simple Frequency Data With Formulas
5.28 Direct Escape Trigger Analysis Trial Data Sheet
5.29 Direct Escape: Simple Plan

---

### FORM 5.27 ■ SIMPLE FREQUENCY DATA WITH FORMULAS

■ Client: _____          CHART STARTED: _____

                                                         **Day/Month/Year**

■ Behavior: _____

■ Total Observation Time: __MIN__ (__, __-minute session/day)          Session length __min__

■ Number of Days: __

■ Place an X on the appropriate day box each time the behavior occurs

| | 1 : | 2 : | 3 : | 4 : | 5 : | 6 : | 7 : | Totals |
|---|---|---|---|---|---|---|---|---|
| Target Behavior | | | | | | | | |
| Daily Rate | | | | | | | | |

A. Total Minutes Observed: __

B. Total occurrences observed: __

C. Range (low) __ to (high) __, Avg = __

| | 8 : | 9 : | 10 : | 11 : | 12 : | 13 : | 14 : | Totals |
|---|---|---|---|---|---|---|---|---|
| Direct Escape Behavior | | | | | | | | |
| Daily Rate | | | | | | | | |

A. Total Minutes Observed: __

B. Total occurrences observed: __

C. Range (low) __ to (high) __, Avg = __

## FORM 5.28 ■ DIRECT ESCAPE TRIGGER ANALYSIS TRIAL DATA SHEET

■ Client Name: _____

■ Antecedent set up: _____

■ Motivation for the escape from the negatively reinforcing item will be ensured by: _____

_____

■ Availability of escape from the negative reinforcer will be indicated by: _____

_____

■ Type and sequence of prompts to be used: _____

_____

■ Preferred response: _____

_____

■ Conditions regarding escape from the negatively reinforcing item:
  ■ How much: _____
  ■ How long: _____

| Step 1 | |
|--------|--|
| Step 2 | |
| Step 3 | |
| Step 4 | |
| Step 5 | |
| Step 6 | |
| Step 7 | |

■ I = Independent    P = prompted    N = did not complete

| | Date | Time Start | Time End | Step | | | | | | | % Task Comp. |
|---|---|---|---|---|---|---|---|---|---|---|---|
| Trials | | | | 1 | 2 | 3 | 4 | 5 | 6 | 7 | |
| 1 | | | | | | | | | | | |
| 2 | | | | | | | | | | | |
| 3 | | | | | | | | | | | |
| 4 | | | | | | | | | | | |
| 5 | | | | | | | | | | | |
| 6 | | | | | | | | | | | |
| 7 | | | | | | | | | | | |
| 8 | | | | | | | | | | | |
| 9 | | | | | | | | | | | |
| 10 | | | | | | | | | | | |

■ Independent completion rate: Whole task: _____

■ Prompted completion rate: Whole task: _____

■ Time to complete task: Longest: _____ Shortest: _____ Average: _____

*FORM 5.29* ■ **DIRECT ESCAPE: SIMPLE PLAN**

■ Person served: _____

■ Target Behavior: _____

■ Behavioral diagnostic category: _____

■ Designated time Period(s): _____

■ Rate of Target behavior:            Baseline _____ Target _____

■ Rate of Direct Escape behavior:      Baseline _____ Target _____

■ Initial form or task analysis of direct escape behavior: _____

_____

■ Negatively reinforcing item/event to be directly escaped: _____

_____

■ When and how will escape be made possible: _____

_____

■ How to respond to the target behavior: _____

_____

■ Types of prompts to be used:

    ☐ Visual      ☐ Vocal      ☐ Written      ☐ Touch      ☐ Graduated Guidance

■ When to use prompts: _____

_____

## More Information

Bosch, S., & Fuqua, R. W. (2001). Behavioral cusps: A model for selecting target behaviors. *Journal of Applied Behavior Analysis, 34,* 123–125.

Dattilo, J., & Camarata, S. (1991). Facilitating conversation through self-initiated augmentative communication treatment. *Journal of Applied Behavior Analysis, 24,* 369–378.

Mithaug, D. K., & Mithaug, D. E. (2003). Effects of teacher-directed versus student-directed instruction on self-management of young children with disabilities. *Journal of Applied Behavior Analysis, 36,* 133–136.

Thompson, R. H., & Iwata, B. A. (2000). Response acquisition under direct and indirect contingencies of reinforcement. *Journal of Applied Behavior Analysis, 33,* 1–11.

Vaughn, B. J., & Horner, R. H. (1997). Identifying instructional tasks that occasion problem behaviors and assessing the effects of student versus teacher choice among these tasks. *Journal of Applied Behavior Analysis, 30,* 299–312.

## 4.0 SME FUNCTIONS: NONCONTINGENT ESCAPE (NCE) OPTION

### Brief Description

In noncontingent escape, or NCE, the specific maintaining negative reinforcer is removed following a given period of time. The negative reinforcer is removed even if the target behavior has or is occurring. One could view an NCE as a reinforcement system that reduces the rate of behavior by removing the motivation to engage in the target behavior or that operates by disrupting the contingent relationship between the behavior and the removal of the negative reinforcer.

To implement this option you would determine how frequently to remove the negative reinforcer. You would then remove the negatively reinforcing item based on that schedule.

The advantage of using an NCE procedure is that it is easy to implement and generally will rapidly reduce the occurrence of target behaviors. NCE procedures generally do not teach or strengthen any new replacement behaviors. They alter the rate of the target behavior initially by removing the motivation underlying the targeted behavior. Generally, NCE will be used in conjunction with other replacement behavior options that are designed to strengthen specific replacement behaviors (DNRA) or tolerance (DNRO). NCE may not be useful in situations where frequent escape from the maintaining reinforcer is impractical, not feasible, or dangerous.

## Terms

*Schedule of reinforcement:* The interval schedule of noncontingent removal of the maintaining negative reinforcer.

*Interbehavior interval:* The length of time that passes between the end of one targeted behavior and the beginning of the next occurrence of the targeted behavior.

*Thinning schedule of removal of the maintaining negative reinforcer:* The process of gradually increasing the amount of elapsed time between removal of the negative reinforcer.

## Apparatus

Timing device—This can be a kitchen timer, alarm clock, computer with alarm feature, tape recorder with beeps at designated intervals, or a calendar, depending on the length of the schedule of noncontingent reinforcement. It's purpose is to prompt the staff person, teacher, or parent to provide the reinforcer.

Data sheets—See Form 5.30 "Partial Interval Data, 30-Minute Intervals"

## Baseline Measurement

Baseline measurement consists of determining the interbehavior interval for the target behavior. To accomplish this, a partial interval method is used for recording the occurrence of the target behavior. Partial interval methods of recording are useful when dealing with behaviors that may be difficult to keep track of or when staff persons have many other duties besides collecting data.

### Steps to Collect Baseline Data Using Partial Interval Recording

1. Identify the target behavior to be observed.
2. Operationally define or pinpoint the behavior being observed.
3. Determine the observation period, possibly reviewing scatter plot or A-B-C data to identify periods of time when behavior is highly likely.
4. Determine the length of the observation period, and divide the observation period into equal interval blocks (keeping these the same across baseline sessions).
5. Construct the data sheet.
6. During observation, enter date and time of day on data sheet and set timing device for interval length.
7. At the end of each interval, if the target behavior occurred at all, place an X in the corresponding interval on the data sheet.
8. Repeat step 7 until the observation period ends.
9. Sum the total number of intervals in which a target behavior occurred, and enter that number on the data sheet.
10. Continue observing client and target behavior for at least four more baseline sessions.

For example, the staff person records partial interval data on the rate of occurrence of the targeted behavior on the following data sheet. Observations are made five times per day, for 10 minutes. If the behavior occurs within a given 2-minute interval, an X is placed on that respective interval. Therefore, the data sheet in Table 5.25 for 1 day of observation reveals a grid, involving five intervals per observation across five observation sessions.

### *TABLE 5.25* ■ BASELINE INTERBEHAVIOR INTERVAL

Condition: <u>**Baseline**</u> or ~~Treatment~~

Recording Method: Partial interval

Interval Length: 2 minutes

CLIENT: _____**Arthur**_____               CHART STARTED: _____**2-1-08**_____

                                                                                                                   Day/Month/Year

BEHAVIOR: _____**XXX**_____

**Total Observation Time:** 50 MIN (1, 10-minute session/day)          Session length: <u>10 min</u>

Number of Days: <u>5.</u>

               ☐ Behavior did **NOT** occur                                   ☒ Behavior **DID** occur

**Day of the month/Start time**

| Interval # | Day 1 10:30 | Day 2 12:10 | Day 3 1:10 | Day 4 2:15 | Day 5 2:45 |
|---|---|---|---|---|---|
| 1 | | X | X | X | X |
| 2 | X | X | | X | X |
| 3 | | X | X | | |
| 4 | X | | | X | |
| 5 | | X | X | X | X |
| total | 2 | 4 | 3 | 4 | 3 |

**Grand total = 16 intervals with target behavior over a possible 25 intervals**

**Inter-behavior interval = 50 min./16 intervals with behavior = 3.125 minutes**

As you can see, in the first observation period (column marked day 1), the client engaged in the target behavior only during the second and fourth interval during the entire 10-minute observation. During the next observation period, he engaged in the target behavior in intervals 1, 2, 3, and 5. The totals at the bottom of each column are out of a possible of 5 intervals that the behavior can be recorded. Summing across the row labeled "total" yields 16 intervals in which the target behavior was recorded as having occurred (against a total of 25 intervals for 5 days of observation). With this ratio 16/25, one can compute the percentage of occurrence, in this case 64% of intervals.

The interbehavior interval can also be calculated by dividing the number of minutes of observation for the week (50) by the number of intervals that the target behavior occurred (16), which yields an average interbehavior interval of 3.125 minutes. In other words, the target behavior occurs about every 3 minutes. In this example it is important to note that the rate of target behavior is relatively stable across the five observation periods. If it were more variable, one should examine what factors were different at each observation to account for the variability in rate of occurrence.

## NCE Procedures

1. From baseline data, calculate the interbehavior interval.
2. Determine your schedule of escape from the maintaining negative reinforcer. (The initial schedule should be set so that reinforcement occurs at or more frequently than the shortest interbehavior interval, e.g., initial interval set at 80% of the average interbehavior interval.)
3. Identify conditions under which the client will be exposed to the negative reinforcer.
4. During the identified time periods set the timing device to the initial escape schedule.

5. When the timer goes off, remove the negative reinforcer for a prespecified period of time. The duration of escape will depend on the specific negative reinforcer. If possible, do not let the target behavior produce escape.
6. Reset the timer.
7. Record data on data sheet.

### Thinning the Schedule of Delivery of Maintaining Reinforcer

The schedule is thinned when the target behavior goal is achieved. When the goal is achieved, increase the length of time between the removal of the negative reinforcer, and set a new target behavior goal. The steps for thinning the schedule follow.

1. When the target behavior goal is achieved with the program, increase the length of the interval between NCE by 5%–10%. For example, if the length of time between noncontingent escape was 5 minutes and the target behavior goal was met, the new schedule for escape might be set at 5 minutes, 30 seconds.
2. With each week of success in achieving the target behavior goal, the schedule of delivery is increased progressively by 10%.
3. If the target behavior occurs at a rate higher than the target behavior goal consistently over a given week, consider returning to the previous schedule of reinforcement.
4. If you have made several attempts at thinning the schedule but are unable to get past a particular rate of escape, it may be best to keep the schedule at that level while incorporating another functional treatment option.

## How It Works

1. By eliminating the client's motivation for escape from a particular negatively reinforcing item or event. When there is no motivation to escape the item or event, there is no reason for the person to engage any behaviors that previously removed that negative reinforcer.
2. By disrupting the learned contingency between the client's target behavior and the removal of the negatively reinforcing event. That is, the negative reinforcing event is removed on some time schedule regardless of occurrence of the target behavior, so the person may learn that the unwanted behavior is no longer correlated with the removal of the negative reinforcer. (extinction by unpairing)

### Hypothetical Example

#### Enough Is Enough
Kalena, a third grade student in a special education classroom, hits herself in the head and face when she is pressed to continue a task (4.2 SME: lengthy task, chore, or assignment). In the past, when she engaged in this behavior, she was moved to another activity, whereupon such self-injury ceased. Dr. Stengel was asked to asses this child and find a way to reduce the self-injury. After obtaining a general description of the behavior, Dr. Stengel observed Kalena in her classroom over the course of 5 days. Using partial interval data collection, Dr. Stengel obtained the data presented in Example Form 5.31A.

In graphing the data recorded on Form 5.31, it appeared that there was an increasing trend in the occurrence of the target behavior (2, 3, 4, and 5 intervals on consecutive days). (See Figure 5.10.)

Dr. Stengel could have calculated the interbehavior interval on the cumulated data, and it would have looked like this:

100 minutes ÷ 18 intervals with aggression = 5.56 Minutes

*EXAMPLE FORM 5.31A* ■ **PARTIAL INTERVAL DATA**

■ Condition: <u>Baseline</u> or ~~Treatment~~
■ CLIENT: Kalena

Recording Method: Partial interval
CHART STARTED: _____ **7/5** _____
**Day/Month/Year**

■ BEHAVIOR: Self-injury
■ Interval Length: **2 minutes** Total Observation Time: <u>100 MIN</u>
☐ Behavior did **NOT** occur

Session length: <u>20 min</u>
☒ Behavior **DID** occur

**Day of the month**

| Interval # | Interval end time | 7/5 | 7/6 | 7/7 | 7/8 | 7/9 |
|---|---|---|---|---|---|---|
| 1 | 2 | | x | x | | |
| 2 | 4 | x | | | | x |
| 3 | 6 | | | x | x | |
| 4 | 8 | | x | | | x |
| 5 | 10 | | | | x | |
| 6 | 12 | | | x | x | x |
| 7 | 14 | | | | | |
| 8 | 16 | x | x | | | x |
| 9 | 18 | | | x | x | x |
| 10 | 20 | | | | | |
| | Total | 2 | 3 | 4 | 4 | 5 |

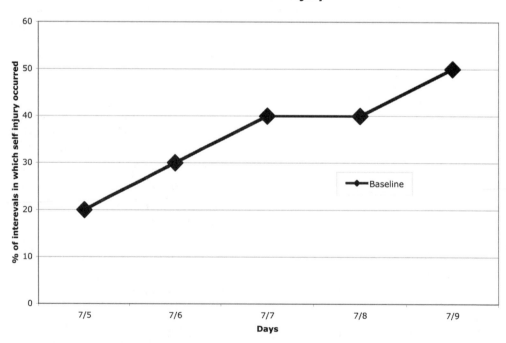

**Kalena Self Injury**

*Figure 5.10* ■ Baseline self-injury data.

In order to increase the likelihood of getting a positive effect quickly, Dr. Stengel calculated the interbehavior interval based on the session with the most occurrences, thus ensuring that the rate of noncontingent escape was higher than the rate of escape she was currently receiving for self-injurious behaviors (SIB).

Dr. Stengel counted the total number of minutes of the observation (20) and divided it by the total number of intervals in which SIB occurred (5). This gave her an average interbehavior interval of 4 minutes.

20 minutes ÷ 5 intervals with self injury = 4 Minutes

Dr. Stengel now knew the rate of the target behavior but did not yet know the function. She determined that the behavior was probably socially mediated as it never occurred when Kalena was alone and had only been observed when adults and students were in close proximity. From her observations, Dr. Stengel had noticed that the SIB seemed to only occur when Kalena was working on math assignments and stopped when the math assignment was removed. This information made it less likely that the SIB functioned to access attention. If SIB was maintained by attention it should happen at times other than when math work is given to Kalena. The target behavior stopped after math was removed, indicating the behavior likely functioned to produce escape. Kalena would, however, start to work on math for a period of time prior to engaging in SIB. Dr. Stengel hypothesized that SIB probably served to terminate relatively lengthy math tasks (4.2 SME: relatively lengthy tasks; see Table 5.26).

To test this hypothesis, Dr. Stengel set up the following conditions. For 8 days during math class she would present math work to Kalena. On 4 days she would present assignments that lasted an entire 15 minutes (full = F), that is, student keeps working until 15 minutes is up. On the other 4 days she would present short assignments that last only 3–5 minutes (short = S). Once the assignment was finished the session would end, and Kalena could go to an entertaining activity for 30 seconds. After the 30-second break, Kalena was asked to do another math assignment of 3–5 minutes. This cycle was repeated three times so that the total time on task was equivalent to the 15-minute full condition. The only difference in instructions for the short condition was that Dr. Stengel provided the prompt, "let's do just this one task before we take a break." Each time SIB occurred in either short or full sessions Dr. Stengel gave Kalena a 1–2 minute break from the assignment. The assessment produced the data listed in Table 5.27.

Dr. Stengel now was fairly certain that her hypothesis was correct and that she could probably reduce the rate of SIB using a simple NCE contingency.

**TABLE 5.26 ■ DIAGNOSTIC TABLE FOR SELF-INJURY**

| Diagnosis | 4.2 SME: relatively lengthy tasks |
| --- | --- |
| Target behavior(s): | Self-injury |
| Function: | Escape a math task after greater than 5 minutes of continuous math |
| Target behavior likely under following contexts: | Math for time periods exceeding 5 minutes |
| Target behavior unlikely under following contexts: | Free time or working on tasks other than math |
| Rule out: | 2.1 SMA: adult attention<br>2.2 SMA: peer attention<br>4.1 SME: unpleasant social situations<br>4.3 SME: Relatively difficult tasks/chores<br>4.4 SME: aversive physical stimuli/event |

*TABLE 5.27* ■ **SIB HYPOTHESIS TEST**

| Session | 1 | 2 | 3 | 4 | 5 | 6 | 7 | 8 |
|---|---|---|---|---|---|---|---|---|
| Type (F or S) | F | F | S | F | S | S | F | S |
| Number of behaviors | 8 | 7 | 1 | 12 | 4 | 1 | 6 | 0 |
| On-task rate % | 40 | 30 | 70 | 25 | 60 | 75 | 45 | 65 |

Dr. Stengel decided to start with an NCE schedule that required the aide to remove the task from Kalena every 4 minutes. She provided the staff with a simple plan to deliver NCE (see Example Form 5.32).

She started the intervention on the 12th. The staff were very excited by the results of their intervention. The data are presented on Example Form 5.31B.

We can present the same data in graphical format to more easily see the trends (see Figure 5.11).

Based on the data that no aggression had occurred for 3 consecutive days, Dr. Stengel changed the schedule of escape to every 3.5 minutes.

3 Minutes (Current schedule) × 1.10 (10 percent increase) = 3.3 minutes

(Note: Because the time frames were relatively short, and Dr. Stengel knew that her timing device would make it difficult to track anything smaller than half a minute, she rounded up to 3.5 minutes.)

There was one event of self-injury on the first day of the new schedule but no further occurrences for 3 days after that. Dr. Stengel continued this process until the schedule had been thinned to every 10 minutes. After consultation with the teacher and teacher's aide as to the feasibility, Dr. Stengel decided to keep the NCE schedule at this level while they taught Kalena some new behaviors that she could use to request a break. Kalena continued to have no events of self-injury. During the acquisition, a simple request for a break, in this case signing "break," it was noted that Kalena could make the request quite well during training but was not using it during seat work in class. Dr. Stengel surmised that the noncontingent escape that was keeping the self-injury from occurring did so by eliminating the motivation to do any behavior that functioned to produce adult attention. She therefore began thinning the schedule of noncontingent escape. Upon reducing the noncontingent escape, Kalena began to use the requesting behavior she had learned. Dr. Stengel continued to collect data and thin the schedule of noncontingent escape until reaching the targeted interbehavior interval of 15 minutes. Dr. Stengel then discontinued the noncontingent escape but continued to take data for 1 month to ensure that the replacement behavior would continue to be effective in escaping lengthy seat work tasks.

### EXAMPLE FORM 5.31B ■ PARTIAL INTERVAL DATA

- Condition: ~~Baseline~~ or **Treatment**
- Interval Length: 2 minutes
- CLIENT: Kalena

- BEHAVIOR: Self-injury
- Total Observation Time: <u>100 MIN</u>

Recording Method: Partial interval

CHART STARTED: _____7/12_____
**Day/Month/Year**

Session length <u>20 min</u>

☐ Behavior did **NOT** occur          ⊠ Behavior **DID** occur

#### Day of the month

| Interval # | Interval end time | 7/12 | 7/13 | 7/14 | 7/15 | 7/16 | 7/17 | 7/18 | 7/19 | 7/20 | 7/21 | 7/22 | 7/23 | 7/24 |
|---|---|---|---|---|---|---|---|---|---|---|---|---|---|---|
| 1 | 2 | | | | | | | | | | | | | |
| 2 | 4 | x | | | | | | | | | | | | |
| 3 | 6 | x | | | | x | | | | | | | | |
| 4 | 8 | | | | | | | | | | | | | |
| 5 | 10 | x | | | | | | | | | | | | |
| 6 | 12 | | | | | | | | | | | | | |
| 7 | 14 | | | | | | | | | | | | | |
| 8 | 16 | | | | | | | | | | | | | |
| 9 | 18 | | | | | | | | | | | | | |
| 10 | 20 | | | | | | | | | | | | | |
| | **Total** | 3 | 0 | 0 | 0 | 1 | 0 | 0 | 0 | 0 | 0 | 0 | 0 | 0 |

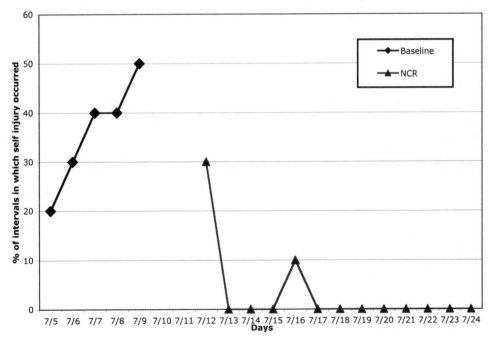

*Figure 5.11* ■ Self-injury data.

---

**EXAMPLE FORM 5.32**

- Person Served: **Kalena**
- Target Behavior: **Self injury**
- Target Behavior Goal: **self injury in less than 1% of observed intervals**
- Designated time Period(s): **Math time 25 minutes per day**
- Baseline data across five times/sessions:

  1. __2__
  2. __3__
  3. __4__
  4. __4__
  5. __5__

- % of intervals in which target behavior occurred: Baseline **40%**  Target **<1%**
- % of intervals in which negative reinforcement occurred: Baseline ___  Target ___
- Inter-behavior interval: Baseline **4 min**  Target **15 min**
- Initial schedule of non-contingent reinforcement:

  - **X** Fixed time schedule every **3** minutes

    OR

  - ___ Variable time schedule on average every ___ minutes/hours/days

- Reinforcer(s) to be used:

  1. **Remove schoolwork for 30 seconds**
  2. _____
  3. _____
  4. _____
  5. _____

- Special instructions for removal of negative reinforcer(s):

  **Remove all school work and allow Kalena to engage in any desk activity of her choosing during the 30 seconds. Following the 30 seconds place the work in front of her and direct her to begin working**

- Criterion for Increasing amount of time between reinforcers: **When self injurious behavior occurs in <1% of intervals observed for 3 consecutive days. Increase time between noncontingent escape by 10**

- Criterion for Decreasing the amount of time between reinforcers: **If self injurious behavior occurs in more than 5% of observed intervals for 3 consecutive days decrease time between non-contingent escape by 1 minute.**

---

## What If?

*What if the behavior does not decrease (or gets worse) with NCE?*

This may happen, although it is less likely with this program than with others. When the target behavior is no longer effective in escaping the negative reinforcer, it may occur more frequently (called an *extinction burst*). If it occurs during NCE, it is possible the schedule of delivery is not dense enough. Try shortening the time between allowing escape. If there is still no effect, it is very likely that your functional assessment was incorrect and that there is a different reinforcer maintaining the target behavior. It would be best to return to taking A-B-C data and repeat the functional assessment.

## Forms: Noncontingent Escape

5.30 Partial Interval Data, 30-Minute Intervals

5.31 Partial Interval Data, 2-Minute Intervals

5.32 Noncontingent Escape: Simple Plan

5.33 Formulas for Calculating Percentage of Intervals of Targeted Behavior and interbehavior Interval

5.34 Formulas for Determining Increases or Decreases in Frequency of Noncontingent Escape

## FORM 5.30 ■ PARTIAL INTERVAL DATA, 30-MINUTE INTERVALS

■ Condition: Baseline or Treatment  Recording Method: Partial interval

■ CLIENT: _____  CHART STARTED: _____

**Day/Month/Year**

■ BEHAVIOR: _____

■ Interval Length: 30 minutes  Total Observation Time: —  Session length: __

☐ Behavior did **NOT** occur  ☒ Behavior **DID** occur

**Day of the month/Start time**

| Interval # | Interval end time | 1 : | 2 : | 3 : | 4 : | 5 : | 6 : | 7 : | 8 : | 9 : | 10 : | 11 : | 12 : | 13 : | 14 : | 15 : |
|---|---|---|---|---|---|---|---|---|---|---|---|---|---|---|---|---|
| 1 | 6:30 A.M. | | | | | | | | | | | | | | | |
| 2 | 7:00 A.M. | | | | | | | | | | | | | | | |
| 3 | 7:30 A.M. | | | | | | | | | | | | | | | |
| 4 | 8:00 A.M. | | | | | | | | | | | | | | | |
| 5 | 8:30 A.M. | | | | | | | | | | | | | | | |
| 6 | 9:00 A.M. | | | | | | | | | | | | | | | |
| 7 | 9:30 A.M. | | | | | | | | | | | | | | | |
| 8 | 10:00 A.M. | | | | | | | | | | | | | | | |
| 9 | 10:30 A.M. | | | | | | | | | | | | | | | |
| 10 | 11:00 A.M. | | | | | | | | | | | | | | | |
| 11 | 11:30 A.M. | | | | | | | | | | | | | | | |
| 12 | 12:00 P.M. | | | | | | | | | | | | | | | |
| 13 | 12:30 P.M. | | | | | | | | | | | | | | | |
| 14 | 1:00 P.M. | | | | | | | | | | | | | | | |
| 15 | 1:30 P.M. | | | | | | | | | | | | | | | |
| 16 | 2:00 P.M. | | | | | | | | | | | | | | | |
| 17 | 2:30 P.M. | | | | | | | | | | | | | | | |
| 18 | 3:00 P.M. | | | | | | | | | | | | | | | |
| 19 | 3:30 P.M. | | | | | | | | | | | | | | | |
| 20 | 4:00 P.M. | | | | | | | | | | | | | | | |
| 21 | 4:30 P.M. | | | | | | | | | | | | | | | |
| 22 | 5:00 P.M. | | | | | | | | | | | | | | | |
| 23 | 5:30 P.M. | | | | | | | | | | | | | | | |
| 24 | 6:00 P.M. | | | | | | | | | | | | | | | |
| 25 | 6:30 P.M. | | | | | | | | | | | | | | | |
| 26 | 7:00 P.M. | | | | | | | | | | | | | | | |
| 27 | 7:30 P.M. | | | | | | | | | | | | | | | |
| 28 | 8:00 P.M. | | | | | | | | | | | | | | | |
| 29 | 8:30 P.M. | | | | | | | | | | | | | | | |
| 30 | 9:00 P.M. | | | | | | | | | | | | | | | |
| 31 | 9:30 P.M. | | | | | | | | | | | | | | | |
| 32 | 10:00 P.M. | | | | | | | | | | | | | | | |

*FORM 5.31* ■ **PARTIAL INTERVAL DATA, 2-MINUTE INTERVALS**

■ Condition: Baseline or Treatment
■ CLIENT: _____

Recording Method: Partial interval
CHART STARTED: _____

**Day/Month/Year**

■ BEHAVIOR: _____

■ Interval Length: 2 minutes          Total Observation Time: —          Session length: __

☐ Behavior did **NOT** occur                    ☒ Behavior **DID** occur

**Day of the month/Start time**

| Interval # | Interval Length | 1 : | 2 : | 3 : | 4 : | 5 : | 6 : | 7 : | 8 : | 9 : | 10 : | 11 : | 12 : | 13 : | 14 : | 15 : |
|---|---|---|---|---|---|---|---|---|---|---|---|---|---|---|---|---|
| 1 | 2 | | | | | | | | | | | | | | | |
| 2 | 4 | | | | | | | | | | | | | | | |
| 3 | 6 | | | | | | | | | | | | | | | |
| 4 | 8 | | | | | | | | | | | | | | | |
| 5 | 10 | | | | | | | | | | | | | | | |
| 6 | 12 | | | | | | | | | | | | | | | |
| 7 | 14 | | | | | | | | | | | | | | | |
| 8 | 16 | | | | | | | | | | | | | | | |
| 9 | 20 | | | | | | | | | | | | | | | |
| 10 | 22 | | | | | | | | | | | | | | | |
| 11 | 24 | | | | | | | | | | | | | | | |
| 12 | 26 | | | | | | | | | | | | | | | |
| 13 | 28 | | | | | | | | | | | | | | | |
| 14 | 30 | | | | | | | | | | | | | | | |
| 15 | 32 | | | | | | | | | | | | | | | |
| 16 | 34 | | | | | | | | | | | | | | | |
| 17 | 36 | | | | | | | | | | | | | | | |
| 18 | 38 | | | | | | | | | | | | | | | |
| 19 | 40 | | | | | | | | | | | | | | | |
| 20 | 42 | | | | | | | | | | | | | | | |
| 21 | 44 | | | | | | | | | | | | | | | |
| 22 | 46 | | | | | | | | | | | | | | | |
| 23 | 48 | | | | | | | | | | | | | | | |
| 24 | 50 | | | | | | | | | | | | | | | |
| 25 | 52 | | | | | | | | | | | | | | | |
| 26 | 54 | | | | | | | | | | | | | | | |
| 27 | 56 | | | | | | | | | | | | | | | |
| 28 | 58 | | | | | | | | | | | | | | | |
| 29 | 60 | | | | | | | | | | | | | | | |
| 30 | 62 | | | | | | | | | | | | | | | |
| 31 | 64 | | | | | | | | | | | | | | | |
| 32 | Total | | | | | | | | | | | | | | | |

## *FORM 5.32* ■ NONCONTINGENT ESCAPE: SIMPLE PLAN

- ■ Person served: _____
- ■ Target Behavior: _____
- ■ Behavioral diagnostic category: _____
- ■ Target Rate: _____
- ■ Designated time period(s): _____
- ■ Baseline data across five times/sessions:

  1. _____
  2. _____
  3. _____
  4. _____
  5. _____

- ■ % of intervals in which target behavior
  occurred:                         Baseline _____    Target _____
- ■ % of intervals in which negative reinforcement
  occurred:                         Baseline _____    Target _____
- ■ Interbehavior interval:          Baseline _____    Target _____
- ■ Initial schedule of noncontingent escape:

  - ■ ____ Fixed time schedule every ____ minutes/hours/days

    OR

  - ■ ____ Variable time schedule on average every ____ minutes/hours/days

- ■ Reinforcer(s) to be used:

  1. _____
  2. _____
  3. _____
  4. _____
  5. _____

  - ■ Special instructions for removal of negative reinforcer(s):

    _____
    _____
    _____

- ■ Criterion for increasing amount of time between removal of negative reinforcers: _____

  _____

- ■ Criterion for decreasing the amount of time between removal of negative reinforcers: _____

  _____

## *FORM 5.33* ■ FORMULAS FOR CALCULATING PERCENTAGE OF INTERVALS OF TARGETED BEHAVIOR AND INTERBEHAVIOR INTERVAL

- ■ *% of occurrence:* This formula will help you determine how often a behavior is occurring. Use this information to assess treatment effects.
  - ■ **(Total intervals target behavior occurred ÷ Total Intervals Observed) ✕ 100 = % of intervals of target behavior**
- ■ *Rate:* This formula will help you determine on average how much time passes between the occurrence of targeted behaviors (interbehavior interval). Use this information to help set the frequency of noncontingent escape.
  - ■ **Total Minutes Observed ÷ Total intervals target behavior occurred = rate or average interbehavior interval**

> ### *FORM 5.34* ■ **FORMULAS FOR DETERMINING INCREASES OR DECREASES IN FREQUENCY OF NONCONTINGENT ESCAPE**
>
> ■ *Formula for 10% increase in time between negative reinforcement*
> ■ Current reinforcement interval × 1.10 = (10% increase in time)
> ■ *Formula for 5% increase in time between negative reinforcement*
> ■ Current reinforcement interval × 1.05 = (5% increase in time)
> ■ *Formula for 10% decrease in time between negative reinforcement*
> ■ Current reinforcement interval × 0.90 = (10% decrease in time)
> ■ *Formula for 5% decrease in time between negative reinforcement*
> ■ Current reinforcement interval × 0.95 = (5% decrease in time)

## More Information

Coleman, C. L., & Holmes, P. A. (1998). The use of non-contingent escape to reduce disruptive behaviors in children with speech delays. *Journal of Applied Behavior Analysis, 310,* 687–690.

Kodak, T., Miltenberger, R. G., & Romaniuk, C. (2003). The effects of differential negative reinforcement of other behavior and non-contingent escape on compliance. *Journal of Applied Behavior Analysis, 36,* 379–382.

O'Callaghan, P. M., Allen, K. D., Poewll, S., & Salama, F. (2006). The efficacy of non-contingent escape for decreasing children's disruptive behavior during restorative dental treatment. *Journal of Applied Behavior Analysis, 39,* 161–171.

Vollmer, T. R., Marcus, B. A., & Ringdahl, J. E. (1995). Non-contingent escape as treatment for self-injurious behavior maintained by negative reinforcement. *Journal of Applied Behavior Analysis, 28,* 15–26.

# Appendix A: Diagnostic Classification System for the Replacement Behavior (DCS-RB)

Too often, assumptions are made about the strength or presence of the alternate replacement behavior. Evidence demonstrating the strength of the alternate behavior during the assessment process is rarely considered or collected. With assumptions about the current strength of the replacement behavior, mistakes in the plan can happen. How many times have you heard a teacher or parent say, "She can do that. She is just being lazy. I know she knows that stuff. She just does not finish her work because she is lazy [implying motivation is the sole issue]. That is why I take away recess everyday for the *last 30 school days*. Someday I will get to her. I will teach her that she needs to be a responsible student."

This hypothetical teacher strongly believes that the student's motivation is the sole factor in whether the daily assignment will be completed or not. As a result of this assumption, the teacher determines that removal of reinforcement should occur for problem behaviors that arise during this student's engagement with the task. Although this strategy might make "sense" if the child is capable of performing the task competently, it is doomed to failure if the child needs active instruction in order to learn the task. If the child is incapable of performing the specific requirements of the assignment, all the reinforcement in the world, or removal thereof, will be of little utility.

Diagnosing the strength of the replacement behavior is just as necessary as the prior assessment and diagnostic activities for the problem behavior. In some circumstances, to increase the designated replacement behavior, you just need to alter the contingencies for problem and replacement behaviors. However, in other cases, such a strategy would prove ineffective in increasing the alternate behavior. If the replacement behavior is nonexistent in the client's repertoire, merely strengthening the rate of reinforcement for the replacement behavior would not have the desired effect. In these cases, it is necessary to utilize techniques that shape and build a new behavior. It is critical to understand the nature of the replacement behavior in the client's current repertoire. The focus is on determining the reasons for the low (or nonexistent) occurrence of alternate acceptable behavior.

Perhaps an example from the animal laboratory would be informative and entertaining. Let us say Ms. Jones, an undergraduate student in an animal learning class, was given an assignment. She has to teach her slightly food-deprived rat to press the bar in the operant chamber to get food. She accomplished that in a reasonable period of time. She notices that her rat, when not pressing the bar, enjoys the following activities while in the chamber: sniffing one of the corners, grooming its underbelly, and standing up on its hind legs. These behaviors occur with some regularity once the rat has received some food for his bar-pressing responses.

Ms. Jones's lab instructor now gives the class a second assignment. They are to place bar pressing on extinction, while selecting an alternate replacement response that will now result in food. If Ms. Jones wants to complete this second assignment as quickly as possible, what replacement behavior should she pick? If she selects a behavior she has not seen before, will simple differential reinforcement be effective in developing such a behavior?

**TABLE A.1 ■ DIAGNOSTIC CATEGORY AND REQUIRED INTERVENTION**

| Diagnostic Category | Intervention Required for Strengthening Replacement behavior |
|---|---|
| Misdirected Contingency Problems | Differential reinforcement, simply rearranging contingencies in favor of replacement behavior |
| Inept Repertoire Problems | Shaping, prompting, and direct teaching of replacement behavior, as well as differential reinforcement, rearranging contingencies in favor of replacement behavior |
| Faulty Discrimination Problems | Generalization strategies, as well as differential reinforcement, rearranging contingencies in favor of replacement behavior |

Would Ms. Jones need to shape and develop the alternate replacement behavior of standing up on hind legs? Alternatively, would simple differential reinforcement produce the change in rates of behavior? Would simply punishing the bar pressing behavior result in an increase in standing behavior?

As this example illustrates, selecting an alternate behavior that is already in the repertoire merely requires a simple rearrangement of reinforcement contingencies. However, selecting an alternate behavior that is not currently in the repertoire of the animal requires more than differential reinforcement of the target and replacement behavior. It requires shaping and differential reinforcement. In the latter case, the selected behavior has to be developed. In the former case, the selected behavior just has to be strengthened. Just as Ms. Jones diagnosed the strength of potential replacement behaviors, so, too, must the applied behavior analyst.

The three diagnostic categories in Table A.1 are offered to classify the current status of the low occurrence or nonexistence of the replacement behaviors in the client's repertoire (adapted from Bailey & Bostow, 1976; Cipani & Trotter, 1990).

The same methods of data collection presented in Chapter 2 are applicable here for collecting enough information to diagnose the replacement behavior. Assessment methods will not be covered in great detail here to avoid duplication.

## MISDIRECTED CONTINGENCIES DIAGNOSIS

In this diagnostic category, alternate replacement behaviors do not occur as frequently as needed because they produce a rate of reinforcement that is far less (or nonexistent) than the schedule for problem behavior. For example, while in the grocery store, a child nicely asks her mother for a box of cookies.

| | |
|---|---|
| Child: | Mommy, can I have a box of cookies? |
| Mother: | *(not wanting to fulfill that request, she ignores it)* |
| Child: | I asked if I can have the cookies, please? |
| Mom: | No cookies today! |
| Child: | But I really want the cookies. *(begins crying)* |
| Mom: | I don't want you to eat too many cookies. Don't you think that you should stop eating as many cookies as you do? |
| Child: | I don't eat that many. *(continuing to cry)* |
| Mom: | *(begins moving away from cookies)* |
| Child: | *(Cries and falls on the floor)* |

*Mom:*    Get up. You are making a spectacle of yourself. If you will be good, I will get one box after I get the chicken for dinner.

Child:    *(gets up and gradually stops sobbing while holding onto the shopping cart)*

What just happened? The child asks nicely but is told that she is not getting cookies. Then the child begins crying and screaming for the cookies. The mother continues to explain why she cannot get cookies for her daughter today. After several minutes of the child's tirade with the mother's retorts, the mother gives the child the cookies (to terminate the tantrum when she falls to the floor of the grocery store). We can all see that the tantrum serves a socially mediated access function (2.3 SMA: tangible reinforcer). However, what is important to note in this hypothetical scenario is that an acceptable behavior did occur, yet, it was not as effective (from the child's viewpoint) in getting cookies as the tantrums. We would expect tantrums to become more probable and requesting nicely less probable (and profitable), given these *misdirected* contingencies. The current social environment selects tantrums as the means to getting cookies, not requesting. Yet, this parent will be adamant about not giving cookies, saying her child should learn how to not beg for things. She will often forget that cookies are given on occasion, and unfortunately, it is the undesirable behavior that wins out.

What is needed is a change in the rate of reinforcement for the replacement behavior. The child is capable of requesting. To solve this problem, requesting (or some other replacement behavior such as omission training) just needs to have a stronger density of reinforcement relative to tantrum behavior during shopping outings. Perhaps the child can earn a desired item if she goes for a period of time without asking or throwing a tantrum during the shopping trip.

Similarly, a client may demonstrate a high rate of tantrum behavior to escape or avoid certain staff requests. When this client is requested to perform some cleaning activity in his room, such as dusting or vacuuming, he throws a tantrum. He will often verbally protest such a task vociferously, and then he slams doors, kicks furniture and walls, and walks outside. When the client does occasionally comply, such compliance to one request is typically followed by the presentation of additional tasks. If he dusts the table in his room and completes the task, the staff praise him for his work and then tell him to vacuum the rug! Compliance only seems to bring on more work. However, severe tantrums result in the staff terminating current and future task demands until a later time. They claim that the client is too upset to perform chores, and they decide to try asking him when he is feeling better.

What is the contingency analysis in this example? Terminating task demands occurs when the client throws a tantrum. In contrast, completing an assigned chore or task results in staff issuing additional requests (while we have him on a roll!). It is not that the replacement behavior is nonexistent, but rather that when it does occur, it is followed by more low probability events (i.e., another chore). However, tantrum behavior seems to be more capable of getting the desired results: temporary termination of the task or chore. The following questions in Table A.2 help you determine if a misdirected contingencies diagnosis fits the nature of the replacement behavior problem. Also included is the data set needed to address such a question.

The basic nature of this classification is the misdirected reinforcement contingencies for both the problem and replacement behaviors. Problems in this diagnostic category can be simply addressed by rearranging contingencies in favor of replacement behavior. Shifting the schedule of reinforcement (either positive or negative) to be more dense for the replacement behavior, while eliminating (or drastically reducing) the rate of reinforcement for the problem behavior should produce the desired effect. With behaviors functioning to access a positive reinforcer, the occurrence of the replacement behavior is scheduled to

*TABLE A.2* ■ **QUESTIONS FOR MISDIRECTED CONTINGENCY DIAGNOSIS**

1.  Does an appropriate replacement behavior occur at all, under the same or similar conditions as the problem behavior? Record both the occurrence of the target problem behavior as well as any occurrence of an alternate replacement behavior when the motivational and antecedent context situations occur. If possible, conduct a trigger analysis test (see Chapter 2; Rolider, 2003), and prompt the replacement behavior to determine if client can perform such behavior.

2.  If the client performed the appropriate behavior recently, was it reinforced with access to the positive reinforcer or escape from the negative reinforcer? Or was reinforcement withheld until the problem behavior occurred? Collecting this data can be achieved through an A-B-C descriptive analysis in the client's natural environment. Record the occurrence of the antecedent conditions as well as the consequent conditions when any appropriate behavior occurs to determine if such behavior is successfully mediated by staff or parents.

3.  Does the problem behavior appear to be maintained because the reinforcement contingencies are more dense for the problem behavior relative to the replacement behavior? Collecting this data can be achieved through an A-B-C descriptive analysis in the client's natural environment for both target and appropriate behaviors.

4.  If the problem behavior was eliminated, would the alternate replacement behavior exist in the client's repertoire? Would it increase in frequency if reinforced? (Similar to Question 1.)

5.  Does the rate of the replacement behavior vary across time, ranging from low levels on some days or time periods to some days in which there is an adequate level of the behavior? Record the rate of occurrence of an alternate replacement behavior across a sufficient period of time in the baseline condition.

produce a higher rate of the specific reinforcer than the problem behavior. If one has accurately identified the maintaining reinforcer, this strategy will be successful in altering the rates of problem and replacement behaviors in the desired directions.

In the case of negative reinforcement, removal of the aversive event is contingent upon the occurrence of the replacement behavior. Concurrently, the problem behavior's relationship to escape is eliminated or markedly impaired. If at all possible, the problem behavior should never produce escape. Simple contingency management techniques involving differential reinforcement, token economies, or behavioral contracts can be utilized. Procedures such as differential reinforcement of other behavior, differential reinforcement of alternate behavior, differential reinforcement of low-rate behavior, or differential reinforcement of high-rate behavior are contingencies that can be used with this diagnostic category.

To make the problem behavior less probable, its occurrence can function as a mand to the adult to present a less preferred activity. In this contingency, a higher probability behavior (i.e., target behavior) is followed by a lower probability behavior, resulting in a punishing effect on the target behavior. This unique punishment contingency is the opposite of the common use of the Premack principle, and we have coined the term *Reverse Premack* to define such an operation (see Chapter 4). Contingent upon the occurrence of the target behavior, the client or child is directed to engage in a less preferred activity (i.e., lower probability behavior; see Table A.3). In this manner, the function of the target behavior is further weakened, making the display of the alternate behavior more attractive to the client or child.

*TABLE A.3* ■ **REINFORCEMENT CONTINGENCIES**

|  | Replacement Behavior | Problem Behavior |
|---|---|---|
| Density of reinforcement | Greater | Less or nonexistent |
| Effort to perform behavior required for reinforcement | Less effort needed | Greater time or effort required |
| Timeliness | Immediate | Reverse Premack instituted, produces considerable delay or postponement of reinforcer |

## INEPT REPERTOIRE DIAGNOSIS

Not all cases involve merely increasing an already existing operant behavior as the replacement behavior. Many children and adult clients, particularly individuals with severe disabilities, often engage in the problem behavior because of the lack of alternate appropriate behaviors in their repertoire. Communication deficits often translate into a person's inability to produce an appropriate response to allow care agents to meet the individual's needs. Aberrant behaviors such as self-abuse, tantrums, and aggression often fill the void and eventually result in the delivery of the desired reinforcer. Such problem behaviors are often strengthened through reinforcement because of the substantial lack of a competing response.

This diagnostic category involves the client not having the capability to perform an alternate replacement behavior that recruits reinforcement. An *inept repertoire* can exist because the client cannot perform the target replacement behavior. As an example, a child with autism may throw a tantrum when he wants cookies. If one assumes the child is capable of requesting the cookie, an adult would wait until such occurs before giving the cookies to him. However, if the child is either nonverbal or not capable of asking nicely, then one will have to wait a long time. Many times, personnel working with individuals with severe disabilities misdiagnose the absence of replacement behaviors as representing the former diagnosis. A common decry is, "He can do it if he wants to, he's just being Johnny!" Given that analysis, staff become entrenched in their belief that such behavior is in the repertoire of the client and simply wait for its occurrence to provide reinforcement. However, if the behavior never occurs, reinforcement will not be delivered. What happens then? Staff eventually succumb to reinforcing the target problem behavior, ensuring that it has become more intense as a result of inadvertently thinning the schedule of reinforcement.

Although this example deals with access behaviors, misdiagnosing inept repertoire problems can have disastrous results with escape functions as well. A client aggresses against teaching personnel under conditions of excessive demands or requests. This client may not be capable of communicating to the staff person that he does not understand the task, or that he feels the number of demands are excessive, or some other such concern. The staff understand that aggression should not function to escape demands, but they are not aware that more acceptable forms of protest, negotiating, or requests for help need to be taught to the client. Staff may assume he "knows" how to communicate his needs. As a result of this misdiagnosis, they attribute his aggressive behavior to being "spoiled." The following real-life case illustrates this misdiagnosis and how contingencies are ineffective with an inept repertoire.

### I Still Will Not Do My Work!

I (E.C.) consulted on a case in the mid 1990s involving a student who was placed in a mainstream third grade class but also served part time in a special day class for students with mild disabilities. My involvement occurred as a result of county mental health's involvement in the family situation. The involvement of mental health and CPS was the result of a family problem, whereupon he was removed from the home and placed in foster care. Prior to his removal from his biological parents, he was expelled from school. His expulsion from school was a result of attacking two teachers and the principal in two separate incidents. When he returned back home, he was placed on home instruction, 1 hour a day.

Unfortunately, his home instruction was not going well. Every day the resource teacher would show up after school hours. On a regular basis, she would leave within 20–25 minutes when he refused to do his assignments and work that she brought for him. Of course, her contingent leaving upon his initial verbal refusal and subsequent failure to engage in the assignment was not a wise behavioral intervention. Such a plan would make verbal opposition very viable in terms of its ability to avoid performing the assignment. I felt that what was primarily needed was a powerful contrived reinforcer to compete with the power of the avoidance contingency inherent in the home instruction setting.

As a result of some interviews of school staff and his resource teacher, I discovered an interesting phenomenon regarding this student. Prior to his expulsion, he would go into his former teacher's first grade class and help her with the first grade students every so often. This teacher indicated that she did not have any problems with him and that she did not have problems with him when he was in first grade. Here was the powerful unique reinforcer needed, and it was something that he currently had no access to. The contingency I designated was the following: every day you complete your work during the home instruction period, you earn a star. When you have four stars, you can go on campus and help the first grade teacher.[1] This had all the makings of a successful intervention on paper.

However, the first week results were discouraging to say the least, with the student having earned only one star. This result was confusing to me. I wondered why he would not want to engage in his assigned work; given it was only about 45 minutes of work at most. I innocently asked the resource teacher how the assignments were prepared. Her answer was the shining light: the third grade teacher prepared them. Of note is the following: this is a student who functions competently at a first grade level in reading and math. This student was inept when it came to third grade level content in math and reading. The third grade material created an *instructional mismatch*. Even a strong contingency would not override his aversion to workbook material that he was incapable of performing. Once that instructional mismatch was fixed, the contingency worked just fine, with him reliably earning four stars in about four days. He did so well the resource teacher advanced the idea to bring him back to the school.

An inept repertoire can still exist even if the target behavior can be performed. In some cases, a client may be able to perform the replacement behavior but not fluently. In this circumstance, an inept repertoire is still relevant. The inept repertoire consists of an appropriate behavior that may occur, but takes too long to occur. A child who uses his fingers to add, subtract, multiply, and divide may be able to come up with a correct answer, but he will need more time to complete an assignment. Hence, simply placing a reinforcement contingency on completion may do little good. One can only go so fast on your fingers! Teaching this child to memorize the facts would prove beneficial. Typing on a keyboard with one finger is obviously less fluent than proficient keyboarding skills. If typing takes too long with the one-finger approach, the individual will probably prefer handwriting. In contrast, the person who has great keyboarding skills probably prefers to type an essay out on the computer rather than write it by hand.

Table A.4 presents questions to pose when considering an acquisition diagnosis as well as the data sets needed to answer these questions.

There are inconsiderable treatment implications for a diagnosis of an inept repertoire. Unlike misdirected contingencies, merely manipulating reinforcement contingencies for the replacement behavior is insufficient. The practitioner needs to design shaping components into the behavioral intervention, both in terms of developing the response, or chain of responses, in addition to increasing the frequency of behavior. Of course, differential reinforcement is required, but steps must be taken to build the behavior. Strategies that teach the client how to perform the appropriate behavior are necessary.

For replacement behaviors that will directly produce the reinforcer, shaping and prompting programs utilizing a task analysis are indicated. The chain of behaviors that result in the reinforcer being produced must be taught, using chaining techniques, prompting,

---

*TABLE A.4* ■ **QUESTIONS FOR AN INEPT REPERTOIRE DIAGNOSIS**

1. Does the appropriate replacement behavior occur at a zero or nonexistent level across time and stimulus conditions? Collect this data by recording both the occurrence of problem and replacement behaviors across a baseline. If possible conduct a trigger analysis test (see Chapter 2; Rolider, 2003), and prompt the replacement behavior to determine if client can perform such behavior.

2. Does the replacement behavior occur, but not at a fluent level? Collect this data by observing the occurrence of the behavior to determine if the length of time it takes the client to perform the skill is inordinately long.

3. Under the best circumstances does the client appear not able to perform the alternate replacement behavior either in topography, level, or fluency? Collecting this data can be achieved through an A-B-C descriptive analysis in the client's natural environment as well as an analogue test providing specific reinforcement for the replacement behavior in some sessions versus the same maintaining reinforcer for the problem behavior in other sessions.

---

and fading. Specifics on these techniques can be found in basic textbooks on behavior modification.

In the case of replacement behaviors that involve communicative skills, prompting, fading, and differential reinforcement are needed. These communicative skills, such as requesting specific reinforcers, requesting help, making choices, negotiating tasks, and protesting tasks, events, or activities, will need to be developed. For nonvocal persons, augmentative or alternative communication systems are available (see text by Cipani, 1992, for further details).

## DETERMINING DIAGNOSES VIA EXPERIMENTAL MANIPULATION

If the rate of the replacement behavior is low, can one automatically assume that the diagnosis for the replacement behavior would be an inept repertoire? Determining the nature of the target replacement behavior has value, particularly in clinical situations where treatment failure has preceded the current effort. An experimental test may be needed to discern which of the first two diagnostic categories is operable in a given case. An experimental manipulation of differential reinforcement contingencies would provide telling data.[2]

An experimental test regarding the function of the replacement behavior would have the following experimental design and test conditions (see Table A.5). A dense reinforcement schedule for replacement behavior is contrived in one condition. This is preceded by a control condition where a dense schedule of reinforcement for target problem behavior

---

*TABLE A.5* ■ **BASIC ELEMENTS OF AN EXPERIMENTAL TEST FOR REPLACEMENT BEHAVIOR**

■ Two test conditions; implement after analogue assessment for target behavior; preferably a sequential design, AB, or reversal design.

■ Target problem behavior's function has been demonstrated to be accurate (i.e., hypothesis/diagnosis).

■ Functional Replacement Behavior has been identified.

■ Sessions can be brief and interceded with short breaks.

■ Motivational variables must be maximized!

■ Data needs to be collected on both the replacement and target behaviors.

■ In the control condition: the functional reinforcer is contingent on target behavior occurrence (control condition).

■ Other test condition: functional reinforcer is contingent upon replacement behavior (experimental condition).

■ Use of AB or reversal designs.

---

occurrence is instituted. A sequential AB experimental design should allow for the intervention to *build up* the effect by implementing the condition for a period of time, without incurring carryover effects as might be the case in a multi-element design. If necessary, a brief reversal to the baseline control condition could establish the experimental control of the independent variable.

What will the data show? First, your hypothesis about the function of the target behavior needs to be accurate. Given sufficient motivating conditions, providing the identified functional reinforcer contingently will increase whatever behavior produces it in a given test condition. Therefore, changing the behavior that produces it, in two test conditions, will demonstrate a change in the level of those behaviors upon the contingency. If the replacement behavior is in the repertoire of the client, than one would observe an increase in its frequency when its function is made to produce the reinforcer in Phase B, while the target behavior decreases in frequency due to extinction (see Table A.6).

Let us say you have a 4-year-old child who engages in high rates of self-injury during the school day. The results of an analogue assessment on the target behavior revealed that self-injury serves an attention function. Therefore, you select the following target objectives for this child: (1) decrease self-injury under motivational conditions of relative deprivation of adult attention and (2) increase an alternate attention-getting behavior, such as "look at me," under those same antecedent conditions.

Let us say that you designate the alternate replacement behavior as the child saying, "Come here." Does a structured training program need to systematically teach this behavior? Before designing a treatment regimen, you conduct an experimental analysis of the replacement behavior. In phase A, the target behavior results in attention, whereas in Phase B, the replacement behavior does. To signal the switch in contingencies, a different therapist is used for this condition, and the replacement behavior "Come here" is prompted and modeled by another child with the delivery of the reinforcer.

If misdirected contingencies is a correct diagnosis of the replacement behavior strength, the response "Come here" would be at low rates during phase A where self-injury is made to produce adult attention on a continuous schedule. However, in Phase B, the mand "Come here" should show a quick increase in frequency. Concurrently, the rate of self-injury results shows a dramatic and quick drop in Phase B. This experimental test demonstrates that both behaviors are in the repertoire of this child and can be easily brought under control of the schedule of reinforcement. If you are filling out a form that asks how you plan to teach the replacement behavior, you can respond, "I do not need to teach it. It just requires a manipulation of misdirected contingencies."

What if the replacement behavior is not in the repertoire of the client? In that case, the effect of the change in differential reinforcement procedures in Phase B would be telling (see Table A.7). One would not observe an increase in the frequency of the replacement behavior when the functional reinforcer is provided for it in Phase B. Phase B would also see possibly some residual level of target behavior, in spite of extinction procedures. Additionally, other behaviors may occur as the client attempts to engage in behaviors that will

*TABLE A.6* ■ **QUESTIONS FOR AN INEPT REPERTOIRE DIAGNOSIS**

|  | Phase A:<br>Reinforce target behavior | Phase B:<br>Reinforce replacement behavior |
| --- | --- | --- |
| Target behavior frequency | high | low |
| Replacement behavior frequency | low | high |

*TABLE A.7* ■ **DATA REVEALING AN INEPT REPERTOIRE DIAGNOSIS**

| | Phase A:<br>Reinforce target behavior | Phase B:<br>Reinforce replacement behavior |
|---|---|---|
| Target behavior frequency | high | More frequent than replacement behavior |
| Replacement behavior frequency | Very low or nonexistent | Very low or nonexistent |

abate the MO. This would be due to the failure of any response to produce reinforcement in this analogue test (i.e., extinction burst).

If the case of the child who engaged in self-injury was more suited for an inept repertoire, the replacement behavior would not show an increase in Phase B. This analysis reveals that the alternate behavior cannot be increased simply by switching contingencies. Rather, the behavior needs to be taught directly, possibly using a discrete trials format with incidental teaching procedures. Teaching staff may need to do more than just wait for the alternate behavior to occur so they can reinforce that behavior.

Another area where these experimental tests on the replacement behavior may be useful is in traditional diagnosis using the *DSM* classification system. Many disorders are characterized by the absence of some skill or behavior. Traditional assessment of such may involve direct observation or reports from significant others on the client's inability to exhibit such a skill. An experimental analysis of the nonexistent skill can possibly shed light on the reason for its nonoccurrence.

For disorders that primarily involve the lack of a behavior or skill as a symptom, simple static measures of the presence or absence of such behavior in a given individual may reflect one of two factors: (1) behavior is not presently in the repertoire of the individual, or (2) the motivative condition is habitually not sufficient to make the behavior occur. By manipulating the functional reinforcer (or some powerful contrived reinforcer) for the hypothesized deficit skill, one can determine if the failure to perform the skill under usual contexts is the result of a weakened MO. If the behavior appears when reinforcement contingencies are strengthened for its occurrence, such evidence would support the conjecture that the client does not have a given "symptom" of a particular mental disorder. Being able to turn the replacement behavior on and off by switching contingencies within several sessions in temporal succession would be strong evidence to rule out such a symptom as having durable quality. If a client's level of attention to an instructional presentation can be rapidly changed by altering the contingencies for attending, or some other antecedent environmental variable, can such a person be said to have symptoms indicative of inattention? It is not the purview of the current material to highlight and exemplify how such tests can be constructed to provide evidence that a child or adult may not have a hypothesized specific mental disorder, such as, ADHD, Asperger's, or Prader-Willi syndrome? However, demonstrating that behavior is situational certainly belies a view that such a symptom is not an inherent skill deficit.[3] This dynamic form of assessment is certainly more valuable in discerning the role of the current environment than the current reliance on static measures.

## FAULTY DISCRIMINATION

This diagnosis presents frequency data for the replacement behavior that can mimic the first diagnostic category, misdirected contingencies. However, through an A-B-C descriptive analysis for the replacement behavior, one would see that the occurrence of the replacement behavior is under restricted conditions. In other words, the appropriate replacement behavior has failed to generalize to all the relevant conditions. The replacement behavior is occurring, but it is restricted to a few antecedent conditions. A good example of a stimulus control problem is when a child performs some desirable response, such as an appropriate request for a reinforcer with one teacher. However, with another teacher or her parents, she does not request but instead whines and throws tantrums. Of course, one would suggest differential reinforcement contingencies as the probable reason for such a discrimination.

Let's use the previous example to illustrate a stimulus control problem. The child may be able to request cookies when she wants them, but this behavior only occurs when the mother is at home in front of the cookie jar. Under these conditions, requesting occurs regularly when the child wants cookies. However, if the mother is not present (e.g., the father is the only one in the room), requesting does not occur. Rather, the child throws tantrums and whines when the father is present, which the father reinforces. Additionally, the tantrum also occurs if the mother and child are in a different area of the house or outside. This describes a scenario that illustrates a stimulus control problem with the replacement behavior.

Faulty discrimination as a diagnosis is different from the inept repertoire diagnosis in that the behavior is in the current repertoire of the client, but its occurrence is limited to certain conditions. Stimulus control problems differ from the change of rate problems in that the occurrence of the replacement behavior has failed to generalize to all relevant stimuli or settings. With faulty discrimination problems, the replacement behavior would occur (with regularity) to one setting or one person, but does not occur to other, different settings (or persons) at an acceptable level. Table A.8 presents two questions to consider in evaluating the possibility that a replacement behavior should be diagnosed as a stimulus control problem.

These problems are treated with generalization strategies, whereby the behavior is transferred to new settings, people, or time. If the replacement behavior occurs in one to a few settings and the treatment goal is to generalize the behavior to settings and antecedent conditions where it is not currently occurring, then a systematic approach to programming for generalization needs to occur. Reinforcement of the behavior when it does occur in the new target settings or conditions will certainly be a part of the program. However, the design of the behavioral intervention for the replacement behavior will involve methods to generalize the behavior from its current antecedent conditions to new conditions.

With stimulus control problems, you need intervention programs that transfer the behavior from the current conditions or settings occasioning it to the target relevant additional conditions and settings. Strategies involving discrimination and generalization training and errorless transfer of stimulus control are appropriate (LaVigna, Willis, & Donnellan, 1989; Touchette, MacDonald, & Langer, 1985). Again, differential reinforcement of the replacement behaviors occurring in new settings will also be involved. However, in order to initially occasion the replacement behavior in the novel target setting, stimulus control techniques need to be utilized.

**TABLE A.8 ■ QUESTIONS FOR FAULTY DISCRIMINATION DIAGNOSIS**

1. Does the replacement behavior occur to one or just a few antecedent conditions? Collecting this data can be achieved through an A-B-C descriptive analysis in the client's natural environment.

2. Does it not occur under other relevant antecedent conditions? Collecting this data can be achieved through an A-B-C descriptive analysis in the client's natural environment.

## Notes

1. It took some talking to the principal on my part about the child's return to campus. She required the presence of a psychiatric technician everywhere he went, funded by mental health before relenting to this request by mental health.
2. This material adapted from: Cipani, E. (2008). Analogue assessment for replacement behaviors. *International Journal of Behavioral Consultation and Therapy, 4,* 374–379. Used with permission.
3. Of course, demonstrating that the skill does not occur with reinforcement should not be used as a sole measure for evidence of the existence of a particular *DSM* disorder.

# Appendix B: Why Artie Can't Learn[1]

A teacher presents the following lesson in a hypothetical preschool classroom in everyday Americana:

*Teacher:* Today we are going to learn about prepositions. I have a large box in the middle of the room. Does everyone see the box? We will use that box. Listen carefully. When I call your name, stand up and see if you can follow my direction. I want Sarah to stand up. (Sarah stands up.) Good, Sarah, I want you to stand in front of the box. Show us where "in front of" the box is.

*Sarah: Demonstrates correct behavior by getting in front of the box; Artie is looking at a discolored spot on the drop ceiling.*

*Teacher:* Good Sarah. You stood in front of the box. You did not stand behind the box. Class did Sarah stand on the box?

*Most of class:* No.

*Teacher:* Where did Sarah stand?

*Kid raising hand:* She stood in front of the box.

*Teacher:* Let's try another one. Bobby stand up. *(Bobby complies and stands up.)* Good, Bobby, I want you to stand behind the box. Show us where to stand so that you are "behind" the box *(vocal emphasis on behind is made).*

*Bobby: Walks to the box and stands behind it.*

*Teacher:* Very good Bobby. You stood behind the box. You did not stand in front of the box. Class did Bobby stand inside the box?

*Most of class:* No.

*Teacher:* Where did Bobby stand?

*Kid raising hand:* He stood behind the box.

*Teacher: Stops lesson seeing Artie is still looking at the ceiling, and has not paid attention during this entire time.* Artie, you need to pay attention. How can you learn where "in front of" is if you don't watch!" *(Artie still does not attend)*

*Teacher: Moves closer to Artie.* OK. Artie, get behind the box.

*Artie: He gets up and piles inside the box.*

*Teacher:* Now see Artie, if you were listening, you would have gotten behind the box, instead of inside the box. Now pay attention so you can learn the difference between "inside," "in front of," and "behind."

In reviewing this scenario, ask yourself which students profited from this lesson.

■ Did Sarah learn?
■ Did Bobby learn?
■ Did Artie learn?
■ Why did Artie not learn?

Perhaps you have seen children like Artie in preschool classes, that is, children who do not attend while a lesson is being presented. Attending skills in the early grade levels is critical to academic success. Listening to the teacher as well as observing the teacher and other students demonstrate a skill, such as placing an object in a box versus outside the box, is critical to skill acquisition in preschool. One-to-one direct teaching, prompting, and requiring child attention is not usually provided. Rather, instruction is geared toward the entire group via the oral presentation of a lesson. In the previous scenario, children who watched their classmates get up and place themselves in a position relative to the box will hopefully learn the relational concept involved in prepositions. The ability to acquire skills by observing others has been termed *observational learning*. Much of what young children learn is through observation. If a child does not attend in the first place, it is hard to learn observationally.

Artie's ability to profit from this form of instruction is very unlikely. He does not attend to the verbal presentation by the teacher. He does not observe his classmates performing the requested behavior. Subsequently, he will probably be unable to imitate those actions when asked. If his ability to observe and imitate the behavior performed by another child or the teacher does not improve, will he be any further along in his acquisition of prepositional relations?

*Looks Good, but Smells Bad!* While traditional forms of teaching/instruction for preschool children may look great, the efficacy for young children with autism is minimal at best. Given the previous scenario, is it wise to deploy an instructional approach whose requisite for success is the attending skills of the child? Does that make sense for children like Artie, when their attending skills are minimal to nil? Here is a hypothetical example of looking good, but smelling bad.

*The Itsy-Bitsy Spider.* It is the start of the class time, and all the children arrive in their special education preschool classroom. The five students in the class have autism, with severe adaptive and cognitive deficits. Only one of them says words, but not in any useful or functional sense (she repeats mama every so often). The class is heavily staffed, with a credentialed teacher and two instructional aides.

It is the beginning of the day, and that means "the morning circle," a staple in everyday preschool programs for language capable children. Such a format in a regular preschool class with language capable children conjures up an image of children learning though doing and saying. But this is a special education class with language deficient children. The teacher walks over to the CD player and pushes the play button, while all five children are seated in a semicircle around the teacher's chair at the front of the carpet area. The instructional aides, whose job is to help keep the children in their seat (no small feat), are seated behind the children. The music comes on:

"The itsy bitsy spider, went up the water spout . . ."

Any observer to this class sees the following. Of the five students in the class, four of them at any one time are engaged in some other distracting activity, such as hand weaving, turning around, tantrum behavior, or getting out of their seat. All the children seem oblivious to the concept that this is a learning activity and continue to not attend as the music plays on. One student makes eye contact with the teacher for awhile. But within a second he gets up and starts jumping around, upon which time he is directed to sit back down by the nearest adult.

The aides are in rhythm and sing their hearts out with the lead of the teacher. But what also is apparent is the lack of vocal responding from the five students. Of course, one might expect that, given four of them have no capability to produce intelligible words. Even the child who does speak upon occasion does not join in, but rather seems interested in the knot in her shoelaces. Are the children supposed to be singing? One could make a convincing argument that the production of words via sing-song is a great way to enhance a young child's sophistication in language. But there is a caveat: you have to be able to produce words and actively engage in the activity to learn.

A naïve conception of many personnel who work with children with severe disabilities is that repeated practice using this group approach will eventually work. They believe that children like Artie just take longer to learn. Hence, they do these group activities month after month, year after year. When asked, these people proclaim, "he will get it eventually, it just takes more time and patience." Four years later, Artie (now age 8) still does not sing the first five words of the "itsy bitsy spider." What did they mean by getting it *eventually*?

*Why Is Group Daily Practice Not the Answer for Artie?* An interesting series of experiments sheds light on this learning enigma with children with autism. Lovaas and his colleagues (addressed why children with autism often took a long time to acquire a target skill, even when being directly taught by an experienced behavior therapist (Lovaas, Koegel, & Screibman, 1979). These researchers conducted a number of experiments that included two phases. In the first study, the following two phases were implemented (Lovaas, Schreibmamn, Koegel, & Rehm, 1971). In the first phase, each child was taught to press a bar when one target stimulus (called a *discriminative stimulus*) was presented and not to press the bar in its absence. The discriminative stimulus comprised three elements (called a *compound stimulus*): (1) a moderately bright visual light (red floodlight), (2) an auditory stimulus (white noise sound), and (3) a tactile event (pressure cuff on child's leg). Here is what this phase of the study looked like. Imagine that the child is in the experimental room with the therapist. When all three of these elements are presented simultaneously, the child was taught to press a bar. The occurrence of the child pressing the bar when all three elements are presented would result in food reinforcement. No food reinforcement was presented for bar pressing in the absence of this presentation. The research study encompassed training on this simple discrimination to three groups of children: (1) "normal" children, (2) children with mental retardation, and (3) children with autism.

Children in all three of the groups acquired this discrimination. All children pressed the bar when all three elements were presented simultaneously and didn't press the bar in their absence. A reasonable person would assume that all these children have come to equate any of the elements as the basis for responding. In other words, the child attended to all three elements (light, white noise, and pressure on leg) equally, and his or her response was under control of any and all of these elements.

The second phase of the study tested that notion. In this phase, each element was presented in isolation to see whether its presence would evoke the bar press (this was called single cue testing). The single cue test involved 70 presentations of one of the elements (probably divided equally) to each child. The experimenter noted for each presentation whether the child pressed the bar when a given element was presented. For example, in this phase, the white noise would come on and then end. Sometime later, the light would come on and then be terminated. The numbers of times the child pressed the bar in the presence of each element (light, white noise, and pressure cuff on the leg) was tabulated.

The results were astounding. The nonhandicapped children (called "normal" in the study) responded to each of the elements equally. In other words, whether the light, white noise, or pressure to the leg was presented singly, the child pressed the bar. In contrast, the children with autism primarily pressed the bar to just one of the elements; three of these children responded to the auditory stimulus, while two would press the bar only when presented with the red floodlight. None of the children with autism responded to the pressure cuff. This "restricted focus" characterized these children when compared to nonhandicapped same-aged peers.[2] Had the autistic children only attended to one of the elements to the exclusion of the other two during phase I training? It seemed so! But what does it mean?

*What Are the Implications for Teaching Children with Autism?* In one word: profound! First, to get the attention of a child with autism requires instructional procedures that make that a requisite of their attention for task presentation. Hence, even small group teaching strategies do not ensure that attention because it is hard to get initial and sustained attention when working with several children at once. If the children are not attending to your instructional presentation, bet dollars to dimes that they are not going to learn the task, irrespective of how much practice they are given every day. However, even if you get attention to an instructional command in one-to-one training, the child may still not learn the skill. If he attends to an irrelevant piece of the instruction, even repeated practice will be futile in his acquisition of the skill. An example will best illustrate this.

Let us say you are trying to teach a child with autism to discriminate a request for a coat versus a request to get shoes. You will attempt to teach the child to respond differentially to these two different commands, "Pick up the coat" and "Pick up the shoes," as they both are lying on the bed. Although we see this as a fairly simple skill to acquire, you should now see that these commands comprise multiple elements. In addition to nonverbal actions that may or may not accompany these commands, there are also four words for each command.

Given these two commands, what element (or feature) tells you what behavior is being requested? In other words, what is the most critical element to focus on in order to get this right? The answer: the last word of each command, that is, coat vs. shoes. Remember that while you may believe the child is attending to all the elements of these commands, if they are autistic, they are probably attending to one element within the compound stimulus. If they focus on the last word uttered and discern the different syllables involved in each (coat vs. shoes), they will learn this task.

But suppose they focus on the word "Pick." Unfortunate for this child, the word "pick" is inherent in both commands. Therefore, unless she attends to a different element, she will only be able to guess which article of clothing to pick up. Correcting their mistake will prove fruitless. She will continue to not learn the task, despite practice day after day on that skill. Her attending to only one element in this compound stimulus will keep her from mastering this simple discrimination. In my (E.C.) clinical work with children with autism, it is often the case that they ignore all the different unique phonemes of the English language that comprise words.

This results in the *illusion* of learning when they respond correctly to a designated task. Let me illustrate with the previous teaching example. Suppose the tone or voice volume with which the trainer or parent says the first command, "pick up the shoes," is markedly louder than the command "pick up the pants." The child may look like she has learned the difference between the two commands, but again it is just an illusion. When she hears a loud voice volume, she picks up the shoes. When she hears the teacher present a command in a softer voice, she picks up the coat. She makes her decision on what to pick up by listening intently to the voice volume, not the syllables of the last word.

It is now obvious what is wrong with this manner of learning. When other people do not use the same differential voice volume for each of these two commands, the child appears to have not learned at all. Again, what she actually learned is the louder voice volume means pick up the shoes, softer volume means pick up the coat.

Let's look at another everyday teaching example and examine the ramifications of restricted focus. Here are two white cards that a teacher might use to teach a child to learn to read the printed numbers 1 vs. 2 (see below).

How does any child learn the difference? By the teacher saying "one" when presented with the card that has number 1 on it and "two" for the other card? By attending to the difference between the form of the number 1 vs. the number 2, right? He might learn that with a vertical line, he says "1" when asked what number this is. In contrast, the number with the curve is the element he uses to respond differently, that is, he says "2." Attending to those single elements with the numbers 1 and 2 will be fine as long as the lesson does not proceed to other numbers. When the instructional program proceeds to other numbers that share a similarity of those elements, e.g., "4" with the number 1 and "3" with the number 2, life will become more difficult. What might he say when asked what the number "3" is? You guessed it. He might say "2." If he is to acquire more sophistication with reading numbers, he will have to make his selection on the basis of critical differences in the other elements of these two numbers.

Let's complicate this example even further. Suppose this child does not attend to the form of the numbers. He ignores those elements. Rather, he just sees two rectangle shaped cards with something printed on each. Looking at the shape of the cards that have the printed number will be no help in responding correctly. Over time, he demonstrates differential responding to these two numbers. Can we assume that he has learned these two numbers? Such responding may just be an illusion of skill acquisition. Suppose, as the school year wears on, the card with the number "1" gets ripped at the corner (whereas the card with the number 2 is not ripped at the corner). He begins to use that difference as a basis for answering "1" when presented that card, and "2," when he is presented the nonripped card. Of course, a new set of cards with these two numbers makes his skill "go away." You can see that his "restricted focus" to a single, unfortunately irrelevant element in this task will be to his detriment in acquiring the skill of reading numbers.

What do these examples demonstrate? As long as the child with autism continues to focus on one (possibly irrelevant or redundant) element within any given compound stimulus, the concept you are trying to teach will never be learned. You could give weeks, months, or years of teaching to develop a target skill and get nowhere. *With children with autism, it matters how you teach, not just that you teach. All teaching strategies are not created equal!*

## Notes

1. Taken in whole from: Cipani, E. (2008). *Triumphs in early autism treatment.* New York: Springer Publishing, pp. 175–183. Used with permission.
2. Termed *stimulus overselectivity* in the research study.

# Appendix C: Errorless Learning

When problem behavior is a function of difficult tasks, assignments, or instructions, an approach termed *errorless learning* has been shown to be effective in developing discrimination learning. The basic research has been extensive and was the result of a landmark study published in 1962 by Dr. H. S. Terrace of Columbia University.

## THE TERRACE STUDY

In the 1960s, the prevailing view on the development of discriminated operant behavior was that differential reinforcement and extinction were not only necessary, but sufficient (Keller & Schoenfeld, 1950). Organisms (human and nonhuman) acquired discrimination behavior by the alternate presentation of the discriminative stimulus and nondiscriminative stimulus with differential reinforcement contingencies applied. Responding under the presence of the discriminative stimulus (termed the S+) was reinforced, while responding in the presence of the nondiscriminative stimulus (termed the S−) was not reinforced. As a result, the behavior occurring to the S+ became strengthened. Concurrently, that same behavior occurring to the S− underwent extinction, a weakening effect. It was considered necessary for the organism to initially respond to the S−; with the subsequent extinction process the factor needed for the organism to acquire discriminated responding. This popular theory was called the *extinction hypothesis* (Keller & Schoenfeld, 1950), and it contended that the generation of errors was a necessary condition for acquiring selected task discriminations.

This approach can be illustrated in the following instructional hypothetical example. Suppose a teacher is interested in teaching kindergarten students how to read two words that are similar, such as "rat" and "ran," as the instructional lesson for the day. This teacher has written these two words on the white board in front of the classroom. She touches one word and looks at the students and makes the following request, "this word is ___." The students respond. She would then alternate between pointing to the word "rat" and "ran," with the students orally responding each time. Some, or possibly many, students would initially make errors in reading the word *rat* when the printed word pointed to is *ran* (and vice versa). Of course, mistakes are corrected by the teacher, in which she will read the word correctly when she hears a student or several answer incorrectly. It is taken for granted that the correction of errors will eventually lead to the mastery of this discrimination by most, if not all, of the students.

There are many educators who believe that acquiring skills must be a significantly challenging experience, hence, the production of errors is an inevitable result of teaching a new skill. Learning through trial and error is often lauded as the "real way" to skill acquisition. Great learning occurs when the student deals with obstacles and frustration (errors) on the path to discovery of concepts. Therefore, in some situations, extreme perseverance (in the face of lengthy nonreinforcement) is stipulated as a necessary requirement on the part of the learner.

Is it possible that the generation of errors in instructional presentations hampers more than helps the learner acquire (and retain) relevant skills? For some children, the production of errors early in the learning process does not recover, and they fail to acquire the skill to mastery.[1] It is unfortunate that when these children fail to acquire skills, the explanation of the phenomena does not usually involve any fault or flaw of the training program design. Rather, the fault is seen as some internal mechanism that did not allow the student to acquire the task (e.g., dyslexia). *An understanding of the role of prolific errors in the initial skill acquisition and skill maintenance could be a possible explanation for lifelong patterns of skill deficit in some children.*

Are high error rates beneficial for initial acquisition and retention of discriminated behavior? Terrace (1963a) assessed the role of different instructional conditions in generating low or high error rates. He used a simple color discrimination task (red versus green) with 32 male white pigeons. In the operant chamber, when the key was illuminated red, the discriminative condition (S+) for food reinforcement was in effect for pecking the key. When the key was illuminated green, the S− condition was in effect. The S− condition involved the absence of food reinforcement for pecks occurring to the green key.

All the pigeons were initially given training and reinforcement for pecking the red illuminated key in the chamber on a variable interval 1-minute schedule. The S− was not presented during this initial training. The four specific experimental conditions followed the establishment of a stable key peck response rate for each pigeon.

The four experimental conditions comprised two levels of two variables: (a) when discrimination training is initiated and (b) how discrimination training proceeds. The "when" variable tested the following proposition: to be effective, discrimination training should proceed only after waiting a sufficient period of time. Therefore, this variable involved two levels: early versus late discrimination training. For half the birds, discrimination training was initiated 30 seconds after pecking to the red key reached criterion. This constituted the definition of the early discrimination training condition. The late condition involved presenting discrimination training 21 sessions after pecking to the red key had been established.

The second variable, that is, how discrimination training is conducted, tested directly the extinction hypothesis. There were two levels of this variable: constant versus progressive. In the constant training condition, the S+ and the S− were alternated every 3 minutes. When the S+ was presented for a given 3-minute interval, pecking to that key was reinforced with food. When the S+ key was turned off and the key was illuminated to make a green key, pecking resulted in no food; hence an extinction condition was imposed. This arrangement reflects simple differential reinforcement contingencies. It is often called *trial and error* learning in the non-ABA literature.

The progressive training condition presented the S+ in the same manner as that in the constant condition. The major difference in how discrimination training was conducted was in the manipulation of the S− presentation, which was altered in form and duration. The alteration of this stimulus condition occurred in three phases. In the first phase, the green key was not illuminated, thereby rendering the chamber completely dark. This condition occurred for only 5 seconds, followed by the presentation of the S+ key for 3 minutes. To reiterate, for 3 minutes, pecking the red key was reinforced with food. This was followed by 5 seconds of a dark chamber, and pecking the key would produce no food during this time. These two conditions were alternated during phase one. In a progressive manner, the duration of the dark chamber (the S−) was gradually increased from 5 seconds to 30 seconds in small increments of time during this first phase. Therefore, at the end of phase 1, the S− condition involved 30 seconds of a dark chamber, followed by 3 minutes of the S+ presentation. To reiterate, extinction in the S− condition was still in effect.

In phase two, the S− condition involved the key getting progressively brighter by altering the voltage going into the key from 0 volts (dark chamber) to 80 V (key illuminated at maximum intensity producing green) for 5 seconds. Phase two terminated with the S− condition being a green key fully illuminated for 5 seconds. Phase three then involved progressive alterations of the duration of the green key presentation from 5 seconds to 3 minutes.

Therefore, the experimental design utilized was a 2 × 2 factorial, with an equal number of birds assigned to each condition. The four experimental conditions were the following: the EP, or early-progressive group (discrimination training given 5 seconds after pecking behavior was established with progressive introduction of the S−); the EC, or early-constant group (early discrimination training with alteration of the S+ and S− at criterion level); the LP, or late-progressive group; and the LC, or late-constant group. To determine the effectiveness of these four conditions, Terrace measured the error rate across the training for all four groups (1963a). An error was recorded any time the pigeon pecked the green key during the S− presentation. In addition, 2 weeks after the pigeon had acquired the color discrimination, a retention test was provided. Again, error rates (responses to the S− condition) were measured for all subjects.

The results were illuminating. The birds in the EP condition made significantly fewer errors than any of the other three experimental groups during the initial acquisition. The range of errors for the eight birds in this group was 0–8 errors. Terrace noted the imposition of the dark chamber developed a superstitious behavior. The bird would jerk away from the key, which was incompatible with pecking the key. Therefore, pecking the key became unlikely under the conditions of the dark chamber. This was contrasted with the LC group, which made the most errors, that is, pecks to the S− key. In the LC group, the range of errors was 1,922 to 4,153. These pigeons evidenced pecking to the green key from sessions one through later sessions, with frequent bursts of responding to the S− across later sessions of discrimination training. Further, the birds making large number of errors demonstrated several side effects of the instructional condition. Terrace (1963a) noted that the extinction condition seem to have acquired aversive properties for these birds. These bids showed emotional behaviors indicative of a "fright" response during the S− presentation.

What would be the effect of such training and error patterns on the retention of the color discrimination task? Would the birds who had few errors continue to respond correctly to the red and green keys? The performance of the four groups during retention testing showed the same results. The birds who made many errors continued to respond to the green key even though they had demonstrated mastery of this task 2 weeks prior. In lay terms, they *forgot* to not peck on the green key when it was illuminated. In contrast, the pigeons in the EP group *remembered* that the green key would not result in the delivery of food. The number of errors during acquisition correlated with retention of this discrimination skill subsequent to initial mastery.

This study was further validated by a follow-up study that demonstrated the same results with pigeons being trained on a vertical (S+) versus horizontal (S−) line discrimination (Terrace, 1963b). The pigeons used in this experiment were all participants of the earlier study (Terrace, 1963a). The experimental group was taught this task by initially superimposing the red color on the vertical line (S+) while the green color was superimposed on the horizontal line (S−). These superimposed elements were then faded progressively. The birds in the errorless condition again demonstrated efficient acquisition of the vertical-horizontal line discrimination task. In contrast, birds who received no superimposed element, but rather simply received a constant training procedure, demonstrated many errors.

Terrace's landmark research answered several questions. First, the extinction hypothesis was not verified when examining the results of the EP group. A progressive alteration of the S−, error rates produced acquisition with errors, and thus minimal experience with unreinforced trials, that is, extinction. Therefore, acquisition of discrimination behavior need not be accompanied by high rates of errors. Second, the generation of error rates appears to have undesirable side effects. These side effects were lowered rates of retention of the discrimination following acquisition, frequent bursts of responses in the extinction condition throughout training, and the exhibition of emotional responses in the extinction condition.

The effect that high error rates had on the generation of emotional behaviors has human parallels. Anecdotally, children who have difficulty performing at the level of the curriculum in school settings often demonstrate problem behaviors. Could this study have implications for human learning environments? One can see many examples of children and young adults who exhibit a variety of behavioral responses to learning situations where failure has pervaded.

The relationship between high error rates and undesirable behaviors in human participants was subsequently demonstrated in a landmark research study conducted at San Francisco State University (Weeks & Gaylord-Ross, 1981). In the first experiment, two children with severe disabilities were used as participants. The rate of correct responses in a discrimination task consisting of different figures on a paper was the dependent variable. In the first part of the research study, these researchers demonstrated that aberrant behavior could be altered in rate via the presentation of easy versus difficult discrimination tasks. The pointing behavior of the participant was to be occasioned by the instructor's verbal command, "point to the correct card." A correct response was pointing to the S+ card. In the easy condition, instructional tasks that the participant demonstrated competent performance in a pretest were delivered. The difficult condition involved a complex visual discrimination involving the figures.

The data obtained portrayed the following. As errors increased under the difficult condition, a concurrent increase in self-injury occurred for both students. Concurrently, presenting the easy discrimination task resulted in low rates of errors and low rates of self-injury. This part of the experiment demonstrated that individual error rates and aberrant behavior co-varied. The ability to turn aberrant behavior on and off as a result of the level of difficulty of the instruction was an important finding at that time (and still today). These authors found that engaging in high rates of self-injury was in large part a result of the instructional environment. Further, such human behavior seemed to parallel the anecdotal results obtained by the birds in the S− condition of the EC group.

While these results demonstrate that aberrant behavior can be ameliorated via the imposition of easy tasks, teachers are often left with the problem of targeting new skills. These more difficult instructional tasks may engender higher rates of aberrant behavior, concurrent with higher rates of errors in the initial acquisition. How does one get around that? In the second part of the experiment, these researchers demonstrated that presenting a difficult task can be done in a manner that does not lead to behavioral side effects and poor skill acquisition. They compared an errorless learning programmed approach with the mere presentation of the difficult task at criterion level on error rates and self-injury. The errorless method selected mimicked that of prior research, by presenting the S+ in full form while starting with the absence of all elements for the S−. To make a significant contrast between these two stimuli, a blank card was presented for the S− in the errorless condition. The elements of the S− were progressively introduced over 10 steps until the criterion level presentation of the S− was achieved. The manner in which the S− was altered to the next higher step was a function of consecutive correct responses. When the learner made five consecutive correct responses to the discrimination task, the S− at the next level was presented. If an error occurred, the next trial involved the presentation of the S− at the prior step.

Using this errorless approach, the high rate of correct responses dovetailed with this lower rate of self-injury. If the difficult discrimination task was taught using stimulus manipulations, the error rates were low to zero combined with a low rate of self-injury. In contrast, when the difficult discrimination task was taught with simple differential reinforcement and feedback, high error rates were obtained as well as higher rates of self-injury. These results parallel the Terrace (1963a, 1963b) results obtained with the EP group and the LC group.

This is an important study with tremendous implications for educational environments. Using errorless learning, new tasks that may inherently involve some increased difficulty to the individual student can be taught without generating extreme oppositional behavior. By manipulating the initial stimulus presentation, the rate of errors can be minimal while the student quickly acquires the initial discrimination. Again, remember that high error rates correlate with higher rates of aberrant behavior and vice versa. If new tasks have to be taught, using an instructional approach that generates correct responding quickly can be both efficient and pleasing to the student. With gradual progressive changes in the stimulus presentation over time, the student can eventually acquire the target criterion level discrimination skill with minimal errors and low rates of aberrant behavior.

## ADDITIONAL RESEARCH EVIDENCE

Following the demonstration of errorless learning by Terrace, other early operant researchers began to document the effects of stimulus manipulation on discrimination learning. For example, acquisition with few errors was obtained in teaching shape discrimination to six nursery school children between the ages of 3 and 6 years old (Moore & Goldiamond, 1964). In a delayed match-to-sample task, the rotation of the triangle was the relevant feature upon which a successful match to the sample would be made. The experimental procedure was the following. A Masonite board contained four windows. The match stimulus appeared at the top by itself. Below this window were three windows of sample triangles with different rotations, for example, one triangle pointed to the right, another triangle pointed up, and so forth. The match stimulus is presented first. After viewing this triangle and its rotation, the child was to match one of the three triangles in the three windows below with the match stimulus (no longer available for view).

To teach the children to match the triangles as a function of rotation, Moore and Goldiamond (1964) used a stimulus manipulation that involved a brightness feature superimposed on the S+ triangle that appeared in one of the three windows. In addition, the S− triangles were presented in dark windows (ala Terrace's alteration of the S− presentation). Over successive trial presentations, the S− triangles became progressively illuminated by increasing the voltage in small increments. This methodology allowed for the use of the superimposed element to effectively transfer stimulus control from the brightness feature to the critical distinction, that is, the triangle's rotation. All six children acquired this delayed matching discrimination to criterion.

In teaching a color discrimination involving red versus orange to children aged 3 to 5 years old, the discriminative stimuli varied along three dimensions (Powers, Cheney, & Agostino, 1970). The format for introducing the S− paralleled the methodology used in the Terrace (1963a) study. The three elements comprising the S− that differed from the S+ were: (a) color (critical feature), (b) presence of white noise (irrelevant feature), and (c) duration of S− presentation (irrelevant feature). Over six sessions, the nondiscriminative stimulus was gradually altered so that the length of time went from 5 seconds to 1 minute while the white noise progressively disappeared. At that point the only difference between the two stimulus conditions was the color presented. A control group was used to evaluate if presenting the S+ and the S− at criterion level would be just as effective as the experimental group with the stimulus manipulation of the S−. The results demonstrated the superiority of the experimental group in terms of lower rate of responses to the S− (i.e., errors) versus the control group.

A programmatic procedure that was originally termed *stimulus shaping* proved successful in teaching a circle versus ellipse discrimination to 19 male children with mental retardation (Sidman & Stoddard, 1967). Stimulus shaping referred to the manipulations of the S+ and/or S− where the initial visual form was shaped over successive changes to match the criterion level stimulus presentation. Stimulus shaping was seen as the analogy to behavioral shaping. In behavioral shaping, an existing operant behavior that constitutes an initial approximation to the criterion behavior is selected for reinforcement. This criterion for reinforcement is then altered, making the new behavioral criterion for reinforcement more frequent. The progressive alteration continues until the criterion form of the behavior desired is maintained by reinforcement. In the case of stimulus shaping, the behavior remains the same, but the stimuli are *shaped* to the criterion level presentation across instructional trials.

The criterion level stimulus discrimination involved the participant selecting the circle that appeared in one space on the board against eight other spaces that contained ellipses. The participant was reinforced if he selected the space that contained the circle. Reinforcement was withheld if he selected any of the eight spaces that contained an ellipse. The participants were divided into two groups: a stimulus shaping program group and a test-only group. All boys were tested initially to verify that they were unable to differentially respond to a circle versus an ellipse.

Participants in the stimulus shaping program group were provided initial discrimination training via a form versus no form task. On the panel with nine spaces, a circle appeared in one of the boxes. The remaining eight boxes were dark, that is, no form was visible. If the participant selected the space with the circle, reinforcement was delivered. Extinction was in effect for selecting any other space. Over a number of trials, progressive changes to the darkened boxes were made. The initial set of progressive changes involved changing the space in the panel from dark to light, but without any form appearing in the space. In the next phase of the stimulus shaping program, the ellipses in each of the eight boxes became more apparent although initially in a light form. Over four successive program changes the ellipse eventually matched the stimulus characteristics of the circle with the exception of the form.

The test-only group was simply provided the criterion level presentation (one circle and eight ellipses) from start to finish. The results were fairly dramatic. Only one of the nine children in the test-only group acquired the circle–ellipse discrimination. However, this participant made more errors than five of the children of the stimulus shaping program group. Seven of the 10 children in the stimulus shaping group acquired the circle–ellipse discrimination, although it was not error-free. Other research has verified stimulus shaping as an effective method for developing discriminative responding in non-handicapped children (Schillmoeller, Schillmoeller, Etzel, & LeBlanc, 1979) as well as for children with mild retardation (Mosk & Bucher, 1984).

Errorless learning applications have also been verified in research studies targeting the acquisition of vocational tasks with individuals with mental retardation (Gold, 1972, 1974; Irvin & Bellamy, 1977). In these studies, a superimposed cue or prompt (called *redundant cue* in these studies) was provided to allow the individual to quickly acquire a set of behaviors. This additional discriminative stimulus was progressively faded until the individual performed the task without a prompt. Another application of superimposed prompts involved teaching a 16-year-old male with mental retardation and diagnosed as organically blind to discriminate red versus yellow color (Stolz & Wolf, 1969). During the baseline assessment phase, the participant's incorrect responses to the red–yellow color discrimination task were 18 of 30 (40% correct). The additional discriminative stimulus was a different size of paper for the color red versus that used for yellow. This additional element generated rapid discriminative responding. Gradually the shape of the red paper was altered until the red and yellow papers were the same shape and size. This errorless program resulted in correct response rates about 70% when just the difference in color was present. This percentage represents a 30% increase over baseline and is above chance levels.

Superimposed prompts are popular in errorless learning formats for teaching visual discrimination skills. Superimposed prompts were also used in the study that involved teaching three adolescents with severe mental retardation a complex discrimination task (Touchette, 1971). The target criterion discrimination task involved different positioning of the alphabet letter, capital E. The S+ had the capital E upside down, and the S− presented the capital E facing up. Touchette's approach was to develop a color discrimination first (an easier skill to acquire). Once the participant was able to select the color red upon instructional command, it was used as an additional prompt on the inverted E (S+). When the participants reached criterion on this task with the superimposed prompt on the S+, the prompt was faded using a time-delay procedure. The time-delay procedure involved the delay in the prompt as a function of correct responses. When the subject was able to respond correctly with a given time delay (i.e., pointing to the inverted E), that time delay was increased 0.5 seconds over the next trial. An incorrect response generated a time delay that was 0.5 seconds faster. The final outcome of the study was that all three subjects with severe mental retardation acquired this rather sophisticated visual discrimination.

The Touchette (1971) study serves as an illustration of the effective use of prompting and time-delay fading procedures. The time-delay procedure used in the Touchette study started with a 0.0 second delay of the prompt from the criterion level presentation. It then proceeded to delay the prompt half a second contingent on a correct response. It is too often the case in the applied field that prompts are delayed in time before sufficient stimulus control is obtained to the prompt and discriminative stimulus. It is important to note that an error in the discrimination task required that the time delay be set back to half a second earlier than what existed when the error occurred. Again it is very important when using time delay as a fading method that reliable control of discriminated behavior is obtained prior to fading the prompt in time.

A time-delay fading procedure removes the prompt by progressively delaying the presentation of the prompt after the stimulus. This delay allows the person the opportunity to respond to the criterion level discriminative stimulus in the absence of the controlling prompt stimulus. Time delay has been extensively used in transferring stimulus control from the prompt to the target discriminative features in developing a variety of language skills (Halle, Marshall, & Spradlin, 1979; Streifel, Bryan, & Aikins, 1974). Prompts can also be removed by reducing progressively the amount of the prompt given, as in the case of the Stolz and Wolf (1969) study. These are often called *partial prompts* in clinical applications of prompting and fading.

## ERRORLESS TRANSFER OF STIMULUS CONTROL

It should be evident now that errorless learning refers more to the manner in which the discrimination task is presented than obtaining acquisition of discrimination behavior with no errors. While the error rate should be low, errorless learning instructional programs are not solely defined or characterized by the generation of zero rates of errors. Rather, it is a methodology that features a manner in which to develop initial discriminative behavior with minimal errors, by often altering (sometimes radically) the presentation of the S−. Discriminative responding should be obtained rapidly to the initial S+ and S− presentation.

The subsequent transfer of this discriminative capability across stimulus changes features progressive changes across one or several elements of the nondiscriminative stimulus. In other words, it is the *successful quick transfer of stimulus control* from one presentation to a slightly different presentation of the stimulus. Stimulus changes continue while maintaining correct discriminative responding until the criterion level stimulus presentation is achieved. Therefore, while some errors may occur, the transfer of stimulus control is the primary characteristic.

Errorless learning methods can involve either the manipulation of the S+ or S−. Many of the studies delineated previously selected only one of the stimuli to alter. It was often the case that the discriminative stimulus or S+ was presented at the criterion level from the beginning of the training program. In contrast, the initial presentation of the S− was significantly altered from its final form. A perfect example is the contrast between the presenting discriminative stimulus and the S− in the errorless program in the Weeks and Gaylord-Ross study (1981). While the S+ figure was presented at criterion form, the S− involved a blank space. Such a stark contrast develops discriminative behavior readily, even in learners who have great difficulty in differentiating basic visual forms. This was also the manner in which Sidman and Stoddard (1967) developed rapid discriminative responding: form versus no-form stimuli. Once discriminative responding is obtained to the initial set of stimuli, the critical elements are introduced progressively until discriminative behavior is occurring to this presentation. The remaining manipulations involved progressively introducing the irrelevant and redundant features of both stimuli. The initial discriminative task involving an S+ versus the absence of any elements of the S− is a common characteristic of errorless programs.

In a unique application of errorless learning, Taylor, Cipani, and Clardy (1991), demonstrated that undesired stimulus control may play a significant role in problems involving the development of toileting skills in children with disabilities. An elementary school–aged child with autism had failed to exhibit consistent elimination in the toilet, despite significant attempts on the part of his parents and teachers. To ensure the integrity of the data collection and treatment regimen without interruption, the study was conducted in the home environment. The rate of accidents during the baseline condition ranged from four to five during the observation session each day. Subsequent to the baseline, the Foxx-Azrin rapid method was utilized. Independent toileting did not occur during this condition, with the rate of accidents remaining at the same heightened level as during baseline. In fact the lead author, Steve Taylor, noted that the deployment of an intensive error correction procedure for accidents and contingent food reinforcement for successful eliminations with the Foxx-Azrin method had no effect on the child's "motivation" to eliminate in the toilet. Anecdotally, it was observed that the child would wait until he was off the toilet and the underwear was placed on him before he would eliminate. A return to baseline produced the same previous results involving high rates of accidents. Additionally, he continued to not eliminate in the toilet, except for one day (where two toilet eliminations occurred) during this condition.

Taylor and colleagues (1991) conceptualized the inability to eliminate in the toilet as one of inappropriate stimulus control. Up to this point in time, the presence of underwear on the body was the discriminative stimulus for elimination for this child. Concurrently, the absence of underwear was nondiscriminative for elimination. In order to switch stimulus control of the child's elimination, the child's underwear was removed during the training. The parallel to other errorless learning research is obvious. Removing the nondiscriminative stimulus during the initial training removes the opportunity to perform the elimination response and its presence. Hence, errors become very unlikely. It would be faded back in under conditions where the elimination response would be highly unlikely. A successful elimination in the toilet resulted in the placing of underwear on the child for

5 minutes. The probability of eliminating in his pants was low, given the recent behavior in the toilet. By putting the underwear on at this point in time, the discriminative stimulus for elimination was now being weakened, while the behavior to pants off was being strengthened. Each successful correct response resulted in the length of time the underwear was put on by a minute. Within a several week timeframe, the child was eliminating in the toilet, while his underwear was on for the full length of time. The nondiscriminative stimulus was faded in at full strength while maintaining the nonexistent rate of accidents to that condition. Follow-up data collection from the parents at 4 and 10 months from the initial errorless programming found no accidents occurring and multiple eliminations everyday in the toilet.

## THAT'S NOT NECESSARY, IT'S JUST EXTRA BAGGAGE!

In clinical applications of stimulus prompting, it is sometimes the case that additional stimuli are added to the S+ or S− that do not readily control discriminative responding. Unfortunately, in these applications, there is no errorless transfer of stimulus control because there was no feature that had stimulus control in the first place. Here is an example. Suppose a therapist was having difficulty teaching a child with severe disabilities to discriminate three different shapes, for example, a circle, a square, and a triangle. After hundreds of trials in which this therapist requests the child to point to the shape named, this child has not reached mastery on any of the shapes. The therapist reasons that the child loves colors and therefore decides to make the triangle red, the circle blue, and the square green as added "help." Subsequent to that manipulation, the child still continues to randomly select one of the three shapes presented. This additional prompt did not present an effective discriminative stimulus for this child. It would've been wise for this therapist to determine if the child could engage in discriminated behavior with the three colors to be used as prompts before adding this "extra baggage."

## GUIDELINES FOR APPLICATION

The empirical literature on errorless learning applies to discrimination learning tasks. In the basic research studies, the discrimination paradigm often involved reinforcing the behavior under the conditions of a compound stimulus being presented, and its absence being nondiscriminative for the same behavior. One can conceptualize this discrimination task as the presence of the behavior versus its absence under relevant discriminative conditions. Much of the applied empirical research on errorless learning has dealt with similar two-choice discrimination tasks that involve the presentation of two different compound stimuli, with the resulting responses being different for each stimulus presentation. One can conceive of teaching in a content area as a series of discriminations that are to be taught,[2] along with an analysis of features that should control a generalized response.

It is important to understand how to develop discriminated behavior in a two-choice discrimination task. It is true that most instructional tasks and objectives often involve multiple discriminations, both in terms of varied stimuli that result in the same generalized response as well as multiple discriminative stimuli that should occasion different responses. However, with students who fail to acquire such generalizations and discriminated behavior, I believe it is incumbent upon the therapist to determine if a single discrimination can be acquired by alternate presentation of two different compound stimuli. Performance on a two-choice task can be used to determine the possible source of stimulus control for errors with stimulus classes. Therefore, the following guidelines for application involve the selection of a discrimination task that presents just two discriminative stimuli that would result in two different responses.

In educational applications of errorless learning, particularly in regards to very sophisticated discriminations, it would be wise for the program designer to remove the redundant or irrelevant features in a discrimination task while presenting the S+. By presenting just the critical features of the S+, the contrast in critical features between the two stimuli can be made more prominent. Again, once discriminative responding has been obtained to the critical features, it is merely a matter of introducing the nondiscriminative features. This is progressively done until both stimuli are at criterion level presentation. Additionally, if the task involves not responding to the S−, the length of time the S− is presented should be markedly divergent from that of the S+ as conducted in the Terrace (1963a) study and the Taylor et al. (1991) study.

## ERRORLESS APPLICATION TO RECEPTIVE LANGUAGE INSTRUCTION (MAND COMPLIANCE)

It is evident that children have to acquire numerous auditory discriminations, especially in the area of language. In everyday structured training programs, the teaching of discriminated behavior to receptive commands can be a difficult task to acquire for some children with disabilities. In some cases, the child often fails to acquire the discrimination across a variety of vocal instructions. In a sense, they seem immune to learning the sound system of the English language (or other languages, as in the case of children living in other countries). But errorless paradigms can be applied successfully to develop an initial discriminative capability with respect to different auditory stimuli. The initial discriminated behaviors are then progressively made more sophisticated and complex in terms of the phonemes involved, until the child can "comprehend" verbal directions given in complete sentences. But how can this be achieved when the child appears to make no distinction between the various phonemes of the English language? The answer: voice volume (which usually has stimulus control over different behaviors, even in children with profound mental retardation).

In the mid-1980s, I taught a graduate class for future special education teachers. This class was unique[3] in that the curriculum interspersed supervised field work with didactic teaching in the same class. I conducted this graduate class in a developmental center for the handicapped to allow us to utilize this unique approach to teacher training. I often demonstrated the actual application of basic principles of prompting and fading for a group of graduate students by using a student from the center whom we had consent to work with. The graduate students would then "practice" these demonstrated skills with students they were assigned to (two graduate students to every child). In one particular case, the instructional task was the discrimination of "in front of" versus "on." The task required the child to respond differentially to the two commands ("on" versus "in front of") by placing a cube either in front of an object or on an object. Initial baseline responses to these two commands resulted in a large percentage of errors, even with corrective feedback given during each trial.

To develop rapid acquisition, I used voice intensity as a superimposed prompt to allow the student to discern more readily the two commands being presented. The command "in front of" was said in a loud voice and shortened to just "front." To facilitate teaching him where to put the cube, I used a small white piece of paper that served as a cue for its placement. The piece of paper was reduced in size until it was completely withdrawn within the first block of 20 trials. The initial instructional program provided training trials for just the command ("front"). I continued with the loud voice prompt "front" following the removal of the paper prompt.

I rapidly obtained correct responses to this altered command. At this point, I introduced the second command, "place the cube on the (object)." I whispered this command to contrast it with the loud voice for the other command. I also shortened this command to "on." The correct response to this whispered, shortened command rapidly ensued. A number of trials took place until he demonstrated mastery to this whispered command.

The discrimination-training program now commenced. I presented the two commands in an alternate fashion, while still maintaining the different voice prompts for each command. I immediately corrected errors so that the student performed the correct response on each trial. These alterations allowed this student to make the distinction between these two commands in their voice prompt form. With the correct response rate high for both commands, I gradually reduced the voice intensity of the "front" command, while I gradually increased the voice intensity of "on" to the point of a "normal" voice. If several consecutive incorrect responses occurred, I altered the intensity for the specific command to its prior level for the next few trials. Once discrimination behavior reached mastery level with these two commands at normal conversational voice (happened within one training session), I gradually reintroduced the additional words within each command. I lengthened the command "front" to "front of," then to "in front of," and so forth. The length of the commands was progressively altered until the entire command was presented, which was accomplished over the next several sessions.

This errorless format allows for immediate discriminative responding on the part of the child. The superimposed volume cue is readily discerned by most children, even those with profound intellectual disabilities. The fading of this superimposed prompt allows the child to eventually attend to the distinction between the two stimuli in terms of the different phonemes involved. This can be achieved with any set of auditory discrimination. The following table illustrates the methodology used and the training phases for teaching discriminated behavior with the following two commands: "Touch the spoon, touch the fork."

| | S+ | S− |
|---|---|---|
| Phase 1 | *Fork* (loudly) | Spoon (softly) |
| Phase 2 | *Fork* (less loud) | Spoon (less soft) |
| Phase 3–5 | *Fork* (less loud) | Spoon (less soft) |
| Phase 6 | *Fork* (conversation volume) | Spoon (conversation volume) |
| Phase 7 | *Touch the*[a] . . . . . fork | Touch thea . . . . . spoon |
| Phase 8 | *Touch the* . . . . . fork | Touch the . . . . . spoon |
| Phase 9 | Touch the fork | Touch the spoon |

[a]Said in soft voice and delayed for several seconds from critical feature.

Additional discriminations from the same stimulus classes (e.g., concept learning) can use the same superimposed prompt strategy to develop rapid discriminated behavior. For example, once the child is able to touch the fork and spoon given the appropriate command in conversational tone, the next item can be introduced with a different voice intensity. For example, the therapist would say "cup" in a loud voice, and such would be alternated with full commands to touch the other two items, which are available for selection as well as the cup. Once the child is responding successfully, the voice decibel level of the command "cup" is progressively altered until it is the same decibel level as the other two commands. The remaining parts of the command, "Touch the" are then brought in progressively as described in my earlier example.

This procedure can be replicated across succeeding new stimuli until the learner demonstrates that it is not needed by performing the correct selection to the command given at criterion level.

## WHAT IS WRONG WITH POINT PROMPTS?

In many applications of errorless learning, the use of a point prompt to indicate the correct selection to the child is often presented along with the instruction. A point prompt is an additional element of the stimulus that is intended to produce correct responding immediately, by inserting it prior to any possible error occurring. While point prompts achieve this, its use also has one significant drawback: it is often used for all stimuli presented in the discrimination task. Hence, it is redundant to all stimulus presentations. If it achieves stimulus control over the correct responding, it may "block" the attention to the critical features involved in the discrimination. Hence, the child becomes dependent upon that point prompt to respond correctly. In applied settings, it becomes quite evident when using a time-delay fading procedure—the children who are under control of the point prompt will often wait longer and longer periods of time to respond, as the length of time between stimulus presentation and point prompt occurs. In other words, they will sit motionless until the controlling stimulus is given and then respond.

In a classic study, Schreibman (1975) demonstrated how such an element (termed *extra-stimulus prompt*) obtaining stimulus control might have deleterious effects on the acquisition of a complex visual discrimination. The research involved four discriminations: two visual discriminations and two auditory discriminations. For example, in one of the visual discriminations, the S+ and S− were stick figures that differed only in regards to the positioning of the arms. The outstretched arms of the S+ formed a 45-degree angle, whereas the arms of the S− formed a downward angle (i.e., a 45-degree angle on both arms). This was the critical difference in the task, and therefore, these features were discriminative for reinforcement. The research study proceeded with an attempt to teach the discrimination by presenting the S+ and S− in full form (criterion level stimulus presentation) without any prompts to six children with autism. If the task was not acquired, a point prompt was used and systematically faded. The fading involved the presentation of the pointing finger to a position where it clearly demarcated the S+ to an eventual position where the pointing finger pointed to the space marking the middle of the S+ and S− . Unfortunately, all tasks taught through the point prompt were not learned. As the direction of point finger became indiscernible to the children, discriminative responding disappeared. Hence, the child's performance was under the control of some faded form of a point prompt.

While extra-stimulus prompts were unsuccessful in developing new visual discriminations, stimulus manipulations termed *within-stimulus prompting* were effective in obtaining discriminative responding. All the redundant features were removed, leaving just the critical discriminative features. In addition while the S+ presented the angle of the arms at its criterion level, the initial S− form was a blank card. This would allow for rapid discriminative responding, like the Terrace study. Over the next five steps of programmatic changes the S− is faded in, by initially presenting the angle of the arms in a dotted line and subsequently increasing the continuity and thickness of the line on the S−. At the end of the fifth step, the arms are in place only, but enlarged. The size of the arms is progressively altered in the next five steps, followed by the fading in of the redundant features to both the S+ and S− simultaneously. This procedure developed the desired performance, not by teaching attending to multiple features within a compound stimulus. Rather, the child was taught to attend to the critical feature that was discriminative for reinforcement.

The same process for the within-stimulus manipulation was followed by the auditory discriminations. Initially, the critical sound of the S+ was presented at normal voice intensity, while the S− presentation was silent. Once responding occurred to the S+, the S− critical feature was progressively voiced until it matched the S+ voice intensity. Finally, the redundant features of both stimuli were progressively faded into the presentation. The results for the auditory discrimination paralleled the success of the visual within-stimulus prompting method.

## Notes

1. How many children who are labeled dyslexic may actually be the result of educational experiences that propagated huge error rates?
2. ABA Math program is free electronically for users of this text, contact me (Ennio Cipani) at ennioc26@hotmail.com for a free electronic copy.
3. This course was originally developed by Dr. Hugh McBride.

# References

Alberto, P. A., & Troutman, A. C. (2006). *Applied behavior analysis for teachers* (7th ed.). Columbus, OH: Prentice Hall.

Ayllon, T., & Azrin, N. H. (1968). *The token economy: A motivational system for therapy and rehabilitation.* New York: Appleton-Century & Crofts.

Bailey, J. S., & Bostow, D. E. (1976). *Research methods in applied behavior analysis.* Tallahassee, FL: Copy Grafix.

Bailey J. S., Phillips, E. L., & Wolf, M. M. (1970). Home-based reinforcement and the modification of pre-delinquents' classroom behavior. *Journal of Applied Behavior Analysis, 3,* 223–233.

Bailey, J. S., & Pyles, D.A.M. (1989). Behavioral diagnostics. In E. Cipani (Ed.), *The treatment of severe behavior disorders: Behavior analysis approach* (pp. 85–107). Washington, DC: American Association on Mental Retardation.

Barlow, D. H., & Hayes, S. C. (1979). Alternating treatments design: One strategy for comparing the effects of two treatments in a single subject. *Journal of Applied Behavior Analysis, 12,* 199–210.

Barlow, D. H., & Hersen, M. (1984). *Single case experimental designs: Strategies for studying behavior change.* New York: Pergamon Press.

Barrish, H. H., Saunders, M., & Wolf, M. M. (1969). Good behavior game: Effects of individual contingencies for group consequences on disruptive behavior in a classroom. *Journal of Applied Behavior Analysis, 2,* 119–124.

Bijou, S. W., Peterson, R. F., & Ault, M. H. (1968). A method to integrate descriptive and experimental field studies at the level of data and empirical concepts. *Journal of Applied Behavior Analysis, 1,* 175–191.

Cantrell, R. P., Cantrell, M. L., Huddleston, C. M., & Woolridge, R. L. (1969). Contingency contracting with school problems. *Journal of Applied Behavior Analysis, 2,* 215–220.

Caudery, G. E., Iwata, B. A., & Pace, G. M. (1990). Effects and side effects of DRO as treatment for self-injurious behavior. *Journal of Applied Behavior Analysis, 23,* 497–506.

Cipani, E. (1990). The communicative function hypothesis: An operant behavior perspective. *The Journal of Behavior Therapy and Experimental Psychiatry, 21,* 239–247.

Cipani, E. (1994). Treating children's severe behavior disorders: A behavioral diagnostic system. *Journal of Behavior Therapy and Experimental Psychiatry, 25,* 293–300.

Cipani, E. (1995). Be aware of negative reinforcement. *Teaching Exceptional Children, 27,* 36–40.

Cipani, E. (1998). Three behavioral functions of classroom noncompliance: Diagnostic and treatment implication. *Focus on Autism and other Developmental Disabilities, 13,* 66–72.

Cipani, E. (2004). *Punishment on trial.* Reno, NV: Context Press.

Cipani, E. (2008a). *Classroom management for all teachers: Plans for evidence-based practice* (3rd ed.). Columbus, OH: Prentice Hall.

Cipani, E. (2008b). *Triumphs in early autism treatment.* New York: Springer Publishing.

Cipani, E., & Schock, K. (2007). *Functional behavioral assessment, diagnosis, and treatment: A complete system for education and mental health settings.* New York: Springer Publishing.

Cipani, E., & Spooner, F. (1997). Treating problem behaviors maintained by negative reinforcement. *Research and Intervention in Developmental Disabilities, 18,* 329–342.

Cipani, E., & Trotter, S. (1990). Basic methods of behavioral intervention. In E. Cipani & A. F. Rotatori (Eds.), *Behavior modification in special education* (pp. 137–201). Greenwich, CT: JAI Press.

Cooper, J. O., Heron, T. E., & Heward, W. L. (2007). *Applied behavior analysis* (2nd ed). Columbus, OH: Merrill/Prentice Hall.

Day, R. M., Rea, J. A., Schussler, N. G., Larsen, S. E., & Johnson, W. L. (1988). A functionally based approach to the treatment of self-injurious behavior. *Behavior Modification, 12,* 565–589.

DeLeon, I. G., & Iwata, B. A. (1996). Evaluation of multiple-stimulus presentation formats for assessing reinforcer preferences. *Journal of Applied Behavior Analysis, 29,* 519–533

DeLeon, I. G., Iwata, B. A., Connors, J., & Wallace, M. D. (1999). Examination of ambiguous stimulus preferences with duration-based measures. *Journal of Applied Behavior Analysis, 32,* 111–114.

Gold, M. (1972). The stimulus factors in skill training other retarded on a complex assembly task: Acquisition, transfer, and retention. *American Journal of Mental Deficiency, 76,* 517–526.

Gold, M. (1974). Redundant cue removal in skill training for the retarded. *Education and Training of the Mentally Retarded, 9,* 5–8.

Greenwood, C. R., Hops, H., Delquadri, J., & Guild, J. (1974). Group contingencies for group consequences in classroom management: A further analysis. *Journal of Applied Behavior Analysis, 7,* 413–425.

Hall, R. V., Lund, D., & Jackson, D. (1968). Effects of teacher attention on study behavior. *Journal of Applied Behavior Analysis, 1,* 1–12.

Halle, J. W., Marshall, G. M., & Spradlin, S. E. (1979). Time-delay: A technique to transfer language usage and facilitate generalization in retarded children. *Journal of Applied Behavior Analysis, 12,* 431–439.

Hart, B. M., Reynolds, N. J., Baer, D. M., Brawley, E. R., & Harris, F. R. (1968). Effect of contingent and non-contingent social reinforcement on the cooperative play of a preschool child. *Journal of Applied Behavior Analysis, 1,* 73–76.

Hesse, B. E. (1993). The establishing operation revisited. *The Behavior Analyst, 16,* 215–217.

Horner, R., & Day, H. (1991). The effects of response efficiency on functionally equivalent competing behaviors. *Journal of Applied Behavior Analysis, 24,* 719–732.

Inkster, A., & McLaughlin, T. F. (1993). Token reinforcement: Effects for reducing tardiness with a socially disadvantaged adolescent student. *B.C. Journal of Special Education, 17,* 176–182.

Irvin, C. K., & Bellamy, G. T. (1977). Manipulation of stimulus features in vocational skill training of the severe retarded: Relative efficacy. *American Journal of Mental Deficiency, 81,* 486–491.

Iwata, B. A. (1987). Negative reinforcement in applied behavior analysis: An emerging technology. *Journal of Applied Behavior Analysis, 20,* 361–378.

Iwata, B. A. (2006, May). *On extinction.* Paper presented at the meeting of the Association for Behavior Analysis, Atlanta, GA.

Iwata, B. A., Dorsey, M. F., Slifer, K. J., Bauman, K. E., & Richman, G. S. (1982). Toward a functional analysis of self-injury. *Analysis and Intervention in Developmental Disabilities, 2,* 3–20.

Iwata, B. A., Vollmer, T. R., & Zarcone, J. H. (1990). The experimental (functional) analysis of behavior disorders: Methodology, applications, and limitations. In A. C. Repp & N. N. Singh (Eds.), *Current perspectives in nonaversive and aversive interventions with developmentally disabled persons* (pp. 301–330). Sycamore, IL: Sycamore Publishing Co.

Kazdin, A. E. (1977). Assessing the clinical or applied importance of behavior change through social validation. *Behavior Modification, 1,* 127–452.

Kazdin, A. E. (1982). *Single-case research designs: Methods for clinical and applied settings.* New York: Oxford University Press.

Kazdin, A. E., & Matson, J. L. (1981). Social validation in mental retardation. *Applied Research in Mental Retardation, 2,* 34–51.

Keller, F. S., & Schoenfeld, W. N. (1950). *Principles of psychology.* New York: Appleton-Century-Crofts.

Lalli, J. S., Browder, D. M., Mace, F. C., & Brown, D. K. (1993). Teacher use of descriptive analysis data to improve interventions to decrease students' problem behaviors. *Journal of Applied Behavior Analysis, 26,* 227–238.

Laraway, S., Snycerski, S., Michael, J., & Poling, A. (2003). Motivating operations and terms to describe them: Some further refinements. *Journal of Applied Behavior Analysis, 36,* 407–414.

LaVigna, G. W., Willis, T. J., & Donnellan, A. M. (1989). The role of positive programming in behavioral treatment. In E. Cipani (Ed.), *The treatment of severe behavior disorders: Behavior analysis approaches* (pp. 55–84). Washington, DC: American Association on Mental Retardation.

Lennox, D. B., & Miltenberger, R. G. (1989). Conducting a functional assessment of problem behavior in applied settings. *The Journal of the Association for Persons with Severe Handicaps, 14,* 304–311.

Lerman, D. C., & Iwata, B. A. (1993). Descriptive and experimental analysis of variables maintaining self-injurious behavior. *Journal of Applied Behavior Analysis, 26,* 293–319.

Lovaas, O. I., Koegel, R., & Screibman, L. (1979). Stimulus overselecting in autism: A review of research. *Psychological Bulletin, 86,* 1236–1254.

Lovaas, O. I., Screibman, L., Koegel, R. L., & Rehm, R. (1971). Selective responding by autistic children to multiple sensory input. *Journal of Abnormal Psychology, 77,* 211–222.

Madsen, C. H., Jr., Becker, W. C., & Thomas, D. R. (1968). Rules, praise, and ignoring: Elements of elementary classroom control. *Journal of Applied Behavior Analysis, 1,* 139–150.

Martens, B. K., DiGennaro, F. D., Reed, D. D., Ezczech, F. M., & Rosenthal, B. D. (2008). Contingency space analysis: An alternative method for identifying contingent relations from observational data. *Journal of Applied Behavior Analysis, 41,* 69–81.

Martin, G. L., & Pear, J. (2007). *Behavior modification: What it is and how to do it* (8th ed.). Upper Saddle River; NJ: Pearson Education.

Mason, S. A., & Iwata, B. A. (1990). Artifactual effects of sensory-integrative therapy on self-injurious behaviors. *Journal of Applied Behavior Analysis, 23,* 361–370.

Matson, J. L., Esveldt-Dawson, K., & Kazdin A. E. (1983). Validation of methods for assessing social skills in children. *Journal of Clinical Psychology, 12,* 174–180.

Mazaleski, J. L., Iwata, B. A., Vollmer, T. R., Zarcone, J. R., & Smith, R. G. (1993). Analysis of the reinforcement and extinction component contingencies with self-injury. *Journal of Applied Behavior Analysis, 26,* 143–156.

Michael, J. (1988). Establishing operations and the Mand. *The Analysis of Verbal Behavior, 6,* 3–9.

Michael, J. (1993). Establishing operations. *The Behavior Analyst, 16,* 191–206.

Michael, J. L. (1982). Skinner's verbal operants: Some new categories. *The Analysis of Verbal Behavior, 1,* 1.

Michael, J. L. (2004). *Concepts and principles of behavior analysis* (rev. ed.). Kalamazoo, MI: Association for Behavior Analysis.

Michael, J. L. (2005, November). *Motivating operations.* Paper presented at the meeting of the Maryland Association for Behavior Analysis, Baltimore, MD.

Michael, J. L. (2007). Motivating operations. In J. O. Cooper, T. E. Heron, & W. L. Heward's (Eds.), *Applied behavior analysis* (2nd ed., pp. 374–391). Upper Saddle River, NJ: Pearson Education.

Miltenberger, R. (2004). *Behavior modification: Principles and procedures* (3rd ed.). Pacific Grove, CA: Wadsworth.

Moore, R., & Goldiamond, I. (1964). Errorless establishment of visual discrimination using fading procedures. *Journal of the Experimental Analysis of Behavior, 7,* 269–272.

Mosk, M. D., & Bucher, B. (1984). Prompting and stimulus shaping procedures for teaching visual-motor skills to retarded children. *Journal of Applied Behavior Analysis, 17,* 23–24.

O'Leary, K. D., Becker, W. C., Evans, M. B., & Saudargas, R. A. (1969). A token reinforcement program in a public school: A replication and systematic analysis. *Journal of Applied Behavior Analysis, 2,* 3–13.

Phillips, E. L. (1968). Achievement place: Token reinforcement procedures in a home-style rehabilitation setting for "pre-delinquent" boys. *Journal of Applied Behavior Analysis, 1,* 213–223.

Powers, R. B., Cheney, C. D., & Agostino, N. R. (1970). I wish training of a visual discrimination in preschool children. *The Psychological Record, 20,* 45–50.

Repp, A. C., Felce, D., & Barton, L. E. (1988). Basing the treatment of stereotypic and self-injurious behavior on hypotheses of their causes. *Journal of Applied Behavior Analysis, 21,* 281–289.

Rolider, A. (2003, September). *The use of antecedent analysis driven intervention to treat complex anti-social behavior among children in school settings.* Paper presented at the meeting of the Florida Association for Behavior Analysis, St. Petersburg Beach, FL.

Rolider, A., & Axelrod, S. (2000). *Teaching self-control to children through trigger analysis.* Austin, TX: Pro-Ed.

Rolider, N. U., Iwata, B. A., & Camp, E. M. (2006, September). *Functional analysis of low-rate problem behavior.* Paper presented at the 26th annual meeting of the Florida Association for Behavior Analysis, Daytona Beach, FL.

Sailor, W., Guess, D., Rutherford, G., & Baer, D. M. (1968). Control of tantrum behavior by operate techniques during experimental verbal training. *Journal of Applied Behavior Analysis, 1,* 237–243.

Schilmoeller, G. L., Schilmoeller, K. J., Etzerl, B. C., & LeBalnc, J. M. (1979). Conditional discrimination after errorless and trial-and-error training. *Journal of the Experimental Analysis of Behavior, 31,* 405–420.

Schmidt, G. W., & Ulrich, R. E. (1969). Effects of group contingent events on classroom noise. *Journal of Applied Behavior Analysis, 2,* 171–179.

Schock, K., Clay, C., & Cipani, E. (1998). Making sense of schizophrenic symptoms: Delusional statements may be functional in purpose. *Journal of Behavior Therapy and Experimental Psychiatry, 29,* 131–141.

Schreibman, L. (1975). Effects of within-stimulus and extra-stimulus prompting a discrimination learning in autistic children. *Journal of Applied Behavior Analysis, 8,* 92–112.

Schutte, R. C., & Hopkins, B. L. (1970). The effects of teacher attention on following instructions in a kindergarten class. *Journal of Applied Behavior Analysis, 3,* 117–122.

Sidman, M., & Stoddard, L. T. (1967). The effectiveness of fading in programming a simultaneous form discrimination for retarded children. *Journal of the Experimental Analysis of Behavior, 10,* 3–15.

Skinner, B. F. (1957). *Verbal behavior.* New York: Appleton-Century Crofts.

Solnick, J. V., Rincover, A., & Peterson, C. R. (1977). Some determinants of the reinforcing and punishing effects of time out. *Journal of Applied Behavior Analysis, 10,* 415–424.

Steege, M. W., Wacker, D. P., Berg, W. K., Cigrand, K. K., & Cooper, L. J. (1989). The use of behavioral assessment to prescribe and evaluate treatments for severely handicapped children. *Journal of Applied Behavior Analysis, 22,* 23–33.

Stolz, S. B., & Wolf, M. M. (1969). Visually discriminated behavior in a blind adolescent retardate. *Journal of Applied Behavior Analysis, 2,* 65–77.

Streifel, S., Bryan, K. S., & Aikins, D. A. (1974). Transfer of stimulus control from motor to verbal stimuli. *Journal of Applied Behavior Analysis, 7,* 123–135.

Sundberg, M. L. (1983). Language. In J. L. Matson & S. E. Bruening (Eds.), *Assessing the mentally retarded* (pp. 285–310). New York: Grune and Stratton.

Switzer, E. B., Deal, T. E., & Bailey, J. S. (1977). The reduction of stealing in second graders using a group contingency. *Journal of Applied Behavior Analysis, 10,* 267–272.

Taylor, S., Cipani, E., & Clardy, A. (1991). A stimulus control technique for improving the efficacy of an established toilet training program. *Journal of Behavior Therapy and Experimental Psychiatry, 25,* 155–160.

Terrace, H. S. (1963a). Discrimination learning with and without errors. *Journal of the Experimental Analysis of Behavior, 6,* 1–27.

Terrace, H. S. (1963b). Errorless transfer of a discrimination across two continua. *Journal of the Experimental Analysis of Behavior, 6,* 223–232.

Thomas, D. R., Becker, W. C., & Armstrong, M. (1968). Production and elimination of disruptive classroom behavior by systematically varying teacher's behavior. *Journal of Applied Behavior Analysis, 1,* 35–45.

Touchette, P. (1971). Transfer stimulus control: Measuring the moment the transfer. *Journal of the Experimental Analysis of Behavior, 15,* 347–354.

Touchette, P. E., MacDonald, R. F., & Langer, S. W. (1985). A scatter plot for identifying stimulus control of problem behavior. *Journal of Applied Behavior Analysis, 18,* 343–351.

Van Camp, C., Witherup, L., Vollmer, T., & Prestemon, A. (2006, September). *An evaluation of indirect verbal reports for identifying potential maintaining variables for low-rate problem behaviors.* Paper presented at the 26th annual meeting of the Florida Association for Behavior Analysis, Daytona Beach, FL.

Vargas, E. A. (1988). Event-governed and verbally-governed behavior. *The Analysis of Verbal Behavior, 6,* 11–22.

Vaughn, M. E., & Michael, J. (1982). Automatic reinforcement: An important but ignored concept. *Behaviorism, 10,* 217–227.

Vollmer, T. (2006, May). *On the utility of the concept of automatic reinforcement.* Paper presented at the annual conference of the Association for Behavior Analysis, Atlanta, GA.

Wahler, R. G. (1969). Setting generality: Some specific and general effects of child behavior therapy. *Journal of Applied Behavior Analysis, 2,* 239–246.

Walker, H. M., & Buckley, N. K. (1972). Programming generalization and maintenance of treatment effects across time and across settings. *Journal of Applied Behavior Analysis, 5,* 209–224.

Ward, M. H., & Baker, B. L. (1968). Reinforcement therapy in the classroom. *Journal of Applied Behavior Analysis, 1,* 323–328.

Weeks, M., & Gaylord-Ross, R. (1981). Task difficulty and aberrant behavior and severely handicapped students. *Journal of Applied Behavior Analysis, 14,* 449–463.

Zeilberger, J., Sampen, S. E., & Sloane, H. N. (1968). Modification of a child's problem behavior in the home with the mother as therapist. *Journal of Applied Behavior Analysis, 1,* 47–53.

Zimmerman, E. H., Zimmerman, J., & Russell, C. D. (1969). Differential effects of token reinforcement on instruction—following behavior in retarded students instructed as a group. *Journal of Applied Behavior Analysis, 2,* 101–112.

# Index